# Getting the Most Out of RootsMagic 11

ELEVENTH Edition

**Bruce Buzbee**

RootsMagic, Inc.
PO Box 1068
Salem, Utah 84653
USA

International Standard Book Number: 978-1-932932-19-5

*Trademarks*

## *About the Author*

Bruce Buzbee is the founder and president of RootsMagic, Inc., and the author of the RootsMagic genealogy software. He has been writing genealogy software for almost 40 years, having previously written the popular Family Origins software. Bruce is happily married with 5 children and 13 grandchildren.

## *Conventions*

| | |
|---|---|
| ☺ **Tip** | Advice on easier ways to accomplish a task. |
| **Warning** | Warns you about things you might not want to do. |
| **Note** | Additional information about the current topic. |
| Ctrl+Tab | A key sequence where the first key (in this case Ctrl) is held down while the next key (in this case Tab) is pressed and released. |

## TABLE OF CONTENTS

# INTRODUCTION

## WHAT IS ROOTSMAGIC?

RootsMagic is a genealogy database program, meaning that its main function is to provide a place to enter information about your family. But while RootsMagic is an easy program to learn to use, it is also one of the most powerful genealogy programs available.

Unfortunately, many people will barely touch the tip of the iceberg of RootsMagic's features. Hopefully this book will help you get the most out of your copy of RootsMagic.

## HOW THIS BOOK IS ORGANIZED

This book is not intended to be a software manual. I have tried to make it as informative as possible, while lacing it with insights about how to get the most out of the program.

In the first chapter we will create a sample database with a few individuals to get you up and running using RootsMagic. Subsequent chapters go into detail on various aspects of RootsMagic and your family history. An appendix at the end of the book provides a brief summary of fact types, hot keys, and the sentence template language..

And finally, while this book will cover RootsMagic from the ground up, it assumes that you have a working knowledge of computers, such as how to start a program, what a dialog box is, etc.

# GETTING STARTED

RootsMagic is a very easy program to learn, so we can just jump in and start entering your family. We will be skipping over some details, but don't worry, we will cover them all in later chapters.

## CREATING A DATABASE

Each time you run RootsMagic you will see the RootsMagic home page.

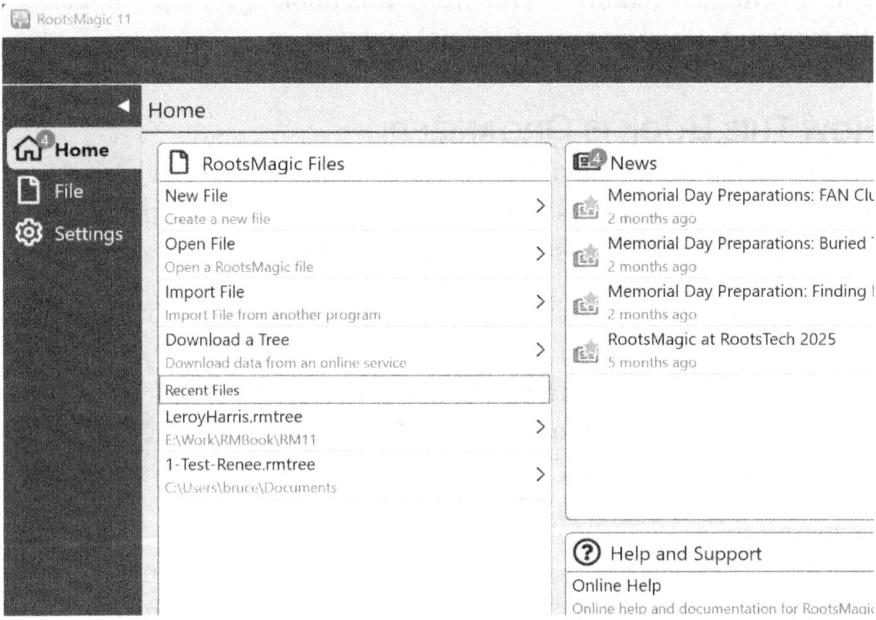


You can read the latest news and updates about RootsMagic, select a number of options for help and support for the program, and if there is an update available you will be able to update directly from this screen.

There are also several options for opening your data in the program. You can create, open, import or download information. If you have previously opened files in RootsMagic, those file names will also be selectable.

The first thing we will do is create a new database. There are several ways to do this; select New File from the Home page, or click the File menu on the left side of the screen and select Create a New RootsMagic File from the File page. RootsMagic will display the following screen.

You can create an empty file (to begin entering your family by hand), import data from another genealogy program, or download your family from a FamilySearch or Ancestry tree.

In this quick getting started we'll just create an empty file. When you click that option, RootsMagic will ask you to select the folder where you want to create the new file. You can select the default folder, select a recent folder, or click "Browse for Destination" at the bottom of the screen to use the system file manager to select a folder.

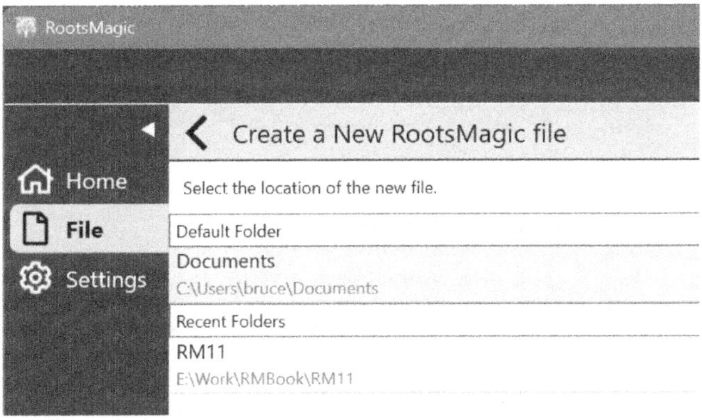


Once you have selected a folder, RootsMagic will open the system file manager where you can enter the name of your new database. It can be something simple like your last name, or longer like "The Smith Family Tree". You can then select several default options for your new database (which we'll cover a little later).

Don't worry if you aren't sure which settings you want to use. You can always change them later. After you have made your choices, simply click the OK button, and you have just created a new database to hold your information.

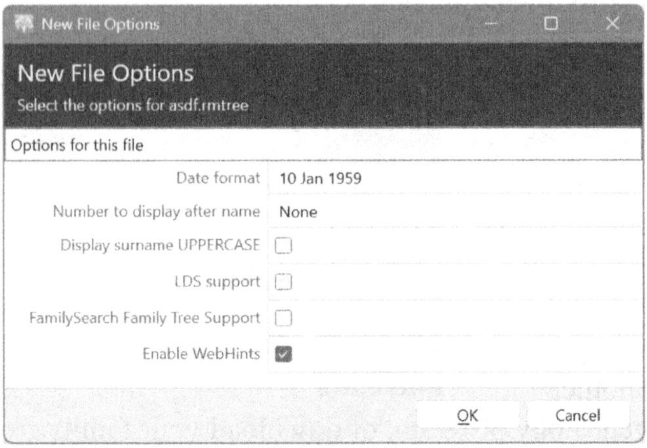


The main RootsMagic screen looks like a five-generation family tree. As you add people to your database, RootsMagic adds their names to the tree.

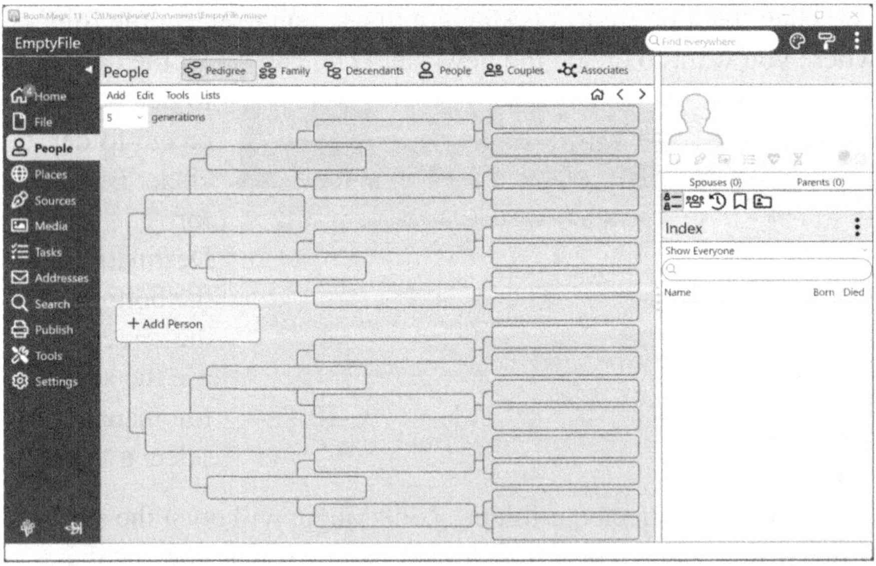


## ADDING YOURSELF

Let's start by adding your own information to the database that you just created. Click Add on the menu and then select Individual. Or you can just do it the easy way and click the starting position on the screen where it says +Add Person. This will bring up a screen where you can add your basic information.

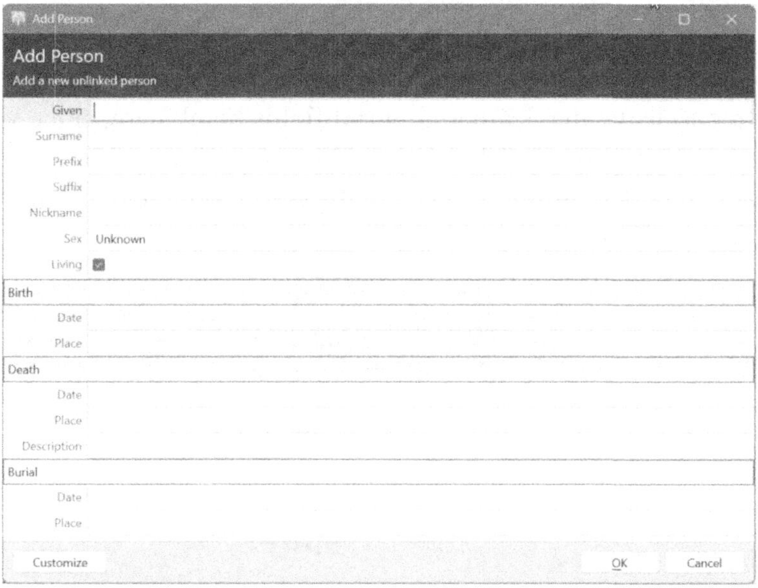


Simply fill in the blanks, using the Tab or Enter key to move on to the next field. If you don't know some of the information, just leave the field empty. If you make a mistake, you can move back to the previous field by pressing Shift+Tab or by clicking the mouse on the field you want to move to.

Enter your given names (first, middle, etc) in the Given field. Separate each name with a space, like: John Michael.

The Surname field is where you will enter your last name. If you are female, you should enter your maiden (birth) name here.

Enter your sex in the Sex field by typing M or F as appropriate. RootsMagic also supports Unknown as an option.

You can also enter any prefix that should come before your name (like Dr.), any suffix that would come after your name (like Jr.), and any nickname you are known by (we won't even go there).

You can also enter your birth date and birthplace. Enter the date in just about any format you want, and RootsMagic will convert it to the format you selected when you created the database. When you enter the birthplace, enter it from specific to general with a comma to separate each part of the place, like this:

Albuquerque, Bernalillo, New Mexico, United States

Feel free to leave the death and burial fields blank here, since you aren't dead (or buried). Click the OK button, and you should see the data entry screen for yourself, with your name, sex and birth information filled out.

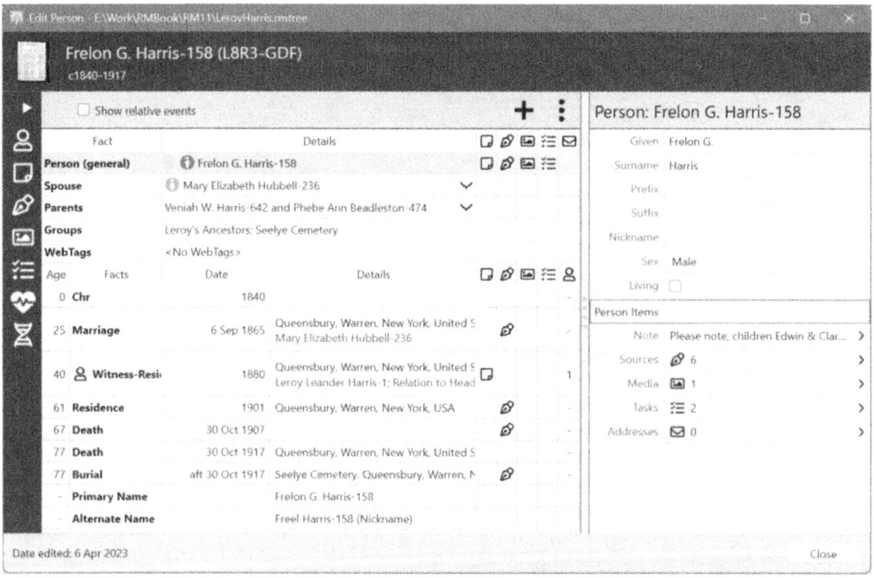

From this screen you can edit the information you just entered, or add other facts (like graduation, occupation, etc.), notes, sources (documentation), tasks, multimedia items, and your current address. Add as much information as you want, and if you forget anything you can always come back later to add or change the information. For now, just click Close to finish adding yourself.

## ADDING OTHER PEOPLE

One of the nice things about RootsMagic is that when you add a person to your database, it links the people together at the same time. Notice that when you press the arrow keys on the keyboard, or click on a person's name on the main pedigree view, the highlight bar moves to that person.

*To add your parents* to your database, make sure your name is highlighted on the main screen (by clicking your mouse on it), then select Add > Parents from the menu. On some screens you can just click on the parents slot where it says +Add father or +Add mother.

RootsMagic will open the same Add Person screen as when you added yourself, but it will have a side menu with 2 options: Add New Person and Select Existing Person.

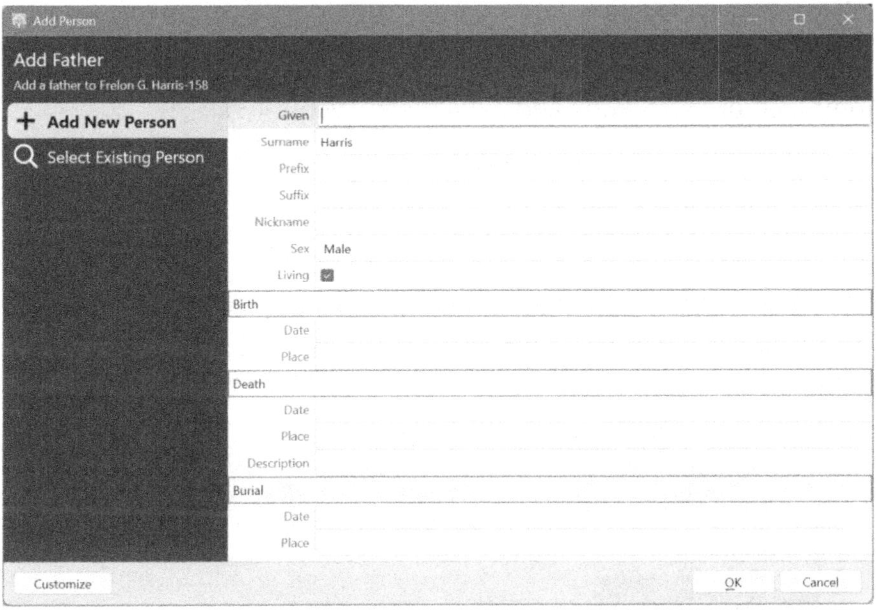


Since your father's information is not already in the database just add your father the same way you added yourself. After you have added your father, you will go through the exact same steps to add your mother.

Once you have entered your parents, RootsMagic will ask if you want to add a marriage event for them. If your parents were married, select Yes (even if you don't know the date, place, or anything else about the marriage). RootsMagic will never assume a couple is married unless you add a marriage event. If you don't add the marriage event here, you can always add it later.

*To add a spouse* to your database, highlight the person you want to add the spouse to (by clicking your mouse on the person's name in the tree), then select Add > Spouse from the menu. On some screens you can also click on the slot where it says "+Add spouse".

Adding a spouse is exactly the same as adding your parents. You will get to choose between adding a new person or linking to an existing person. You will also be asked if you want to add a marriage event for this couple.

If you want to add additional spouses to a person, just repeat these steps for each spouse.

*To enter an unmarried couple*, you will still use the Add Spouse command but just won't add a marriage event.

*To add children* to your database, highlight either the father or the mother, then select Add > Children from the menu. On the family screen you can click in the child list where it says +Add child.

Once again, you will get the option to add a new person, or link to an existing person. This time the dialog will look a little bit different.

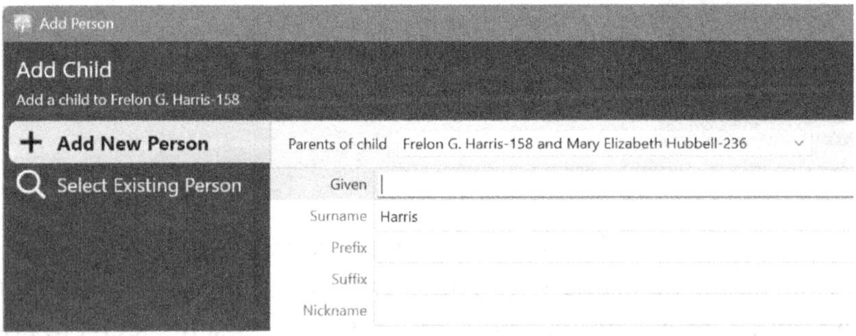


Since the parent may have more than one spouse, the add child dialog will also ask which family to add the child to, and will also provide an option to add the child to the person and a new spouse. Highlight the family you want to add the child to then choose whether to add a new child or select an existing child.

When you finish adding a child, RootsMagic will display the children in the family, and will ask you to arrange them in the proper birth order. Just use your mouse to drag and drop the children into the proper order, then click the OK button.

This child order is used when RootsMagic prints family group sheets, books, and other printouts where the children in a family are included.

That's all there is to it. Just highlight a person on the main screen and add a spouse, parents, or child to the person.

And now, on with the show…

# THE MAIN SCREEN

A genealogy program is usually thought of as a place to enter people and their relationships. But there are many other types of information you will want to keep track of as well, including sources, tasks, media, and more.

The main screen in RootsMagic consists of a side menu, pages for various types of information, a header bar, and menus that perform commands related to the current page.

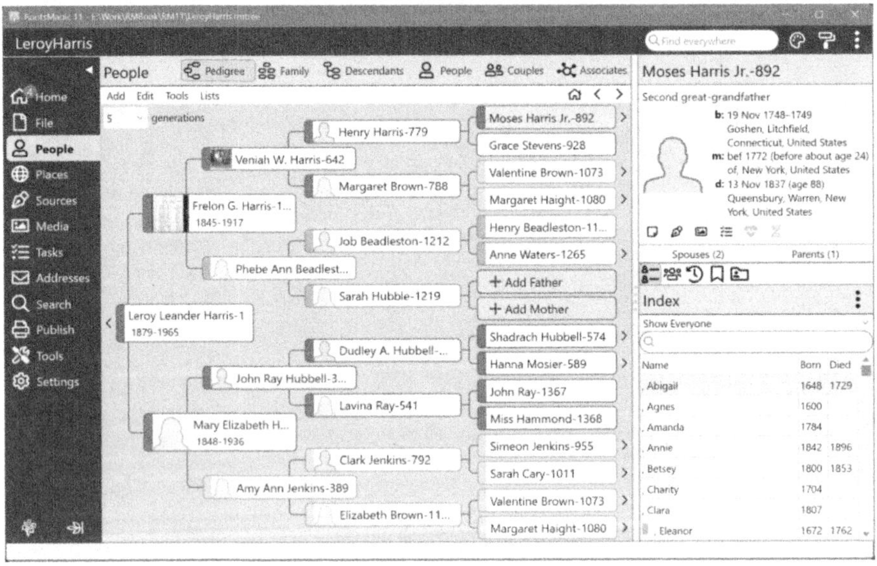


## SIDE MENU

One of the first things you may notice about RootsMagic is the main menu on the left side of the screen covering these different types of information. Selecting an item on the main menu displays the page for that particular type of data. For example, if you click Places in the menu, RootsMagic will change the right side of the screen to the Places page where you can work with the place list, mapping, and anything else related to places.

In addition to the Home and File pages mentioned in the previous chapter, there are pages for the different types of data that you can enter into RootsMagic: People, Places, Sources, Media, Tasks, and Addresses. There are also pages for Searching, Publishing, Tools, and Settings for the program.

At the bottom of the menu resides two icons; one for FamilySearch and another for Ancestry. You can click either of these icons to log into that service to access trees and WebHints.

As you become more familiar with the menu, you may decide you want it to take less room on the screen. You can simply click the left arrow at the top of the menu to collapse it to display just the icons for each menu item. At any time you can then click the arrow again to expand it back out.

## Pages

Each side menu item corresponds to a different page in RootsMagic.

- **Home:** This page displays general information about the current file, RootsMagic News, support links, and whether an update is available.
- **File:** This page provides commands to create and open databases, import and export data, as well as numerous tools to manipulate your database files.
- **People:** This page offers a number of views of people in your file, along with commands to add, edit, delete, and otherwise manipulate those people.
- **Places:** This page provides a list of all places in your file, as well as a map view and commands related to places.
- **Media:** This page displays all the media (pictures, video, etc.) your file is using, as well as tools to manipulate that media.
- **Tasks:** This page lets you create tasks that can be attached to people, places, sources, etc., and can be filtered to create custom research logs.

- **Addresses:** This page lets you keep track of addresses (for correspondence, other researchers, etc.), and for repositories (for research locations, source locations, etc.).
- **Search:** This page provides a number of ways to search for people, online, etc.
- **Publish:** This page offers a number of ways to publish your information: reports, websites, online family trees, shareable drives, and others.
- **Tools:** This page organizes a number of the tools in the program in a single, easy to use list.
- **Settings:** This page lets you change settings and preferences for the various RootsMagic features.

Each page is actually always there; the menu just switches between them. This means that if you are doing something on one page and then switch to another, when you come back to the original page it will be in the same state as it was when you left. For example, if you do a search in the Search page, then switch to the People page, when you switch back to the Search page the same search results will still be there to work with.

## HEADER

The header is the colored bar that spans across the top of the RootsMagic window. The header will be visible regardless of which page is currently in view. The name of the currently open database will be displayed on the left side of the header.

### Header Color

The color of the header will normally be based on whatever theme color you have set for RootsMagic, but it is also possible to set a "database color" in Settings, in which case the header will be displayed in that database color. This is useful if you have multiple databases and want an easy way to tell them apart when they are open.

## Search Box

You can enter anything in the header search box, and RootsMagic will do its "Find Everywhere" search, which is described in more detail in the chapter called "Search Page" (page 213). Basically, RootsMagic will search people, places, notes, sources, media, and many other records for the text you enter.

## Command Palette

The Command Palette is a powerful feature to help you easily find a command or feature when you aren't sure what page it might be on.

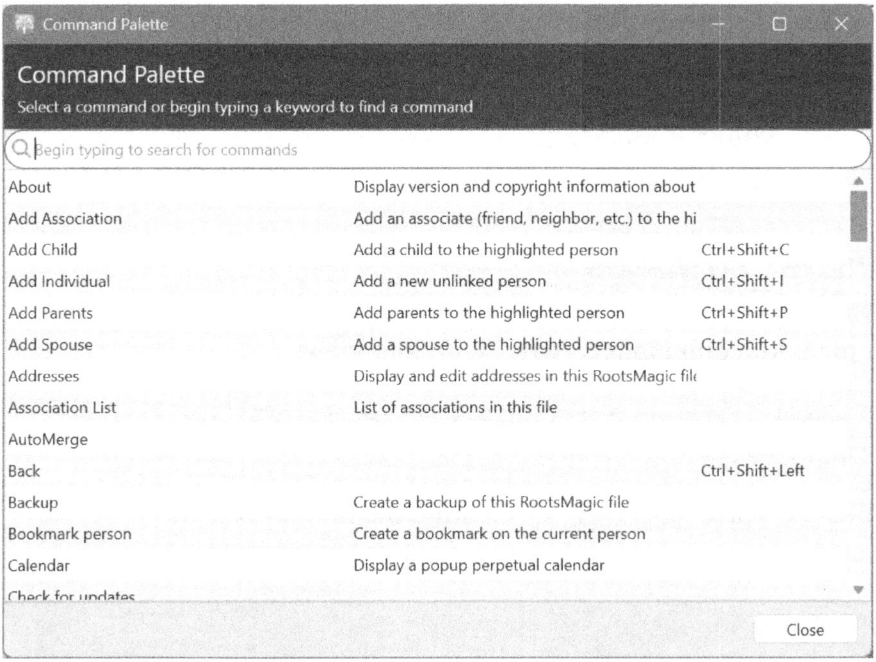


You can search for any command or feature, and then click on a result to be taken directly to that command within RootsMagic.

## Color Code Sets

The paint roller button lets you quickly switch between any of RootsMagic's 10 color code sets. If you hover your mouse pointer over the button a tool tip will display the currently selected color code set. Color coding is explained on page 91.

## System Menu

Clicking the 3-dot menu on the far right of the header will display a menu with the following options:

- **Help:** Opens your browser to the RootsMagic help system
- **Check for updates:** Checks to see if there are any updates to RootsMagic available
- **Learning Center:** Opens the learning center with links to various online help
- **Register RootsMagic:** Lets you register your copy of RootsMagic
- **Technical support:** Opens browser to technical support page at rootsmagic.com
- **Visit RootsMagic.com:** Opens browser to rootsmagic.com
- **About RootsMagic:** Displays the about box with version and other info.

## VIEWS AND MENUS

Most RootsMagic pages include more than one "view", as well as a menu of commands to work with that view.

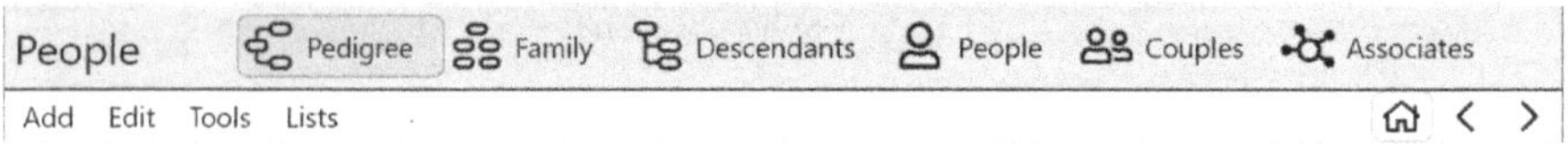


You can select any view by clicking the button for that view, and can select any command from a standard menu.

# HOME PAGE

The Home page is kind of a command center for RootsMagic. When you start RootsMagic, this page will be the default page that opens.

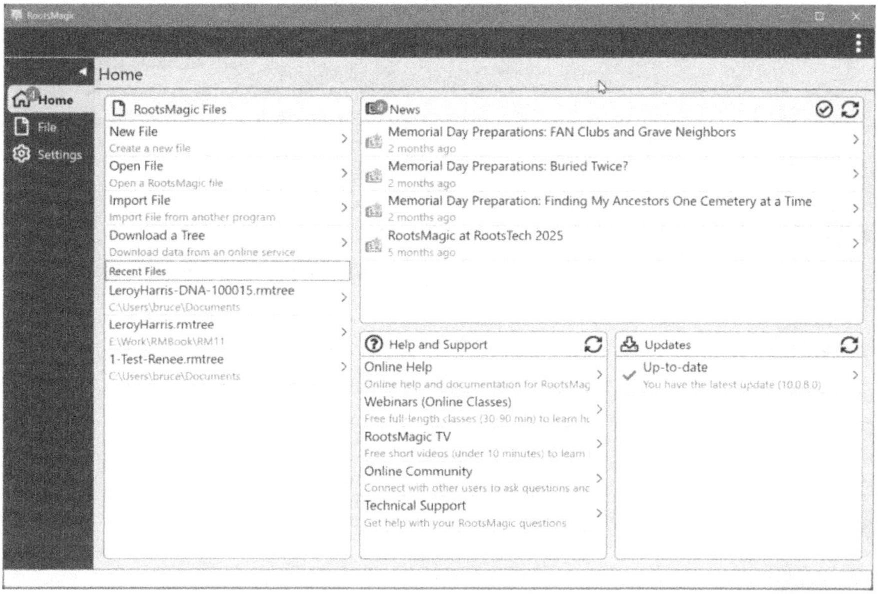


The left column of the Home page will provide some basic file options to create or open a RootsMagic file, or import or download data from an online tree like FamilySearch or Ancestry. It will also display a list of any recently used RootsMagic files that you can open by simply clicking on one.

The right side of the Home page contains 3 panels: News, Support, and Updates. The News panel displays a list of RootsMagic related news articles. When you click on and read an article, RootsMagic will mark it as read. You can also mark them all as read, or refresh the list with the buttons above the list.

The Support panel contains various ways to get help or information on using RootsMagic. The Updates panel will let you know if you are using the most recent version of RootsMagic, and if not will allow you to easily download and install the latest version.

The Home page will change just a little bit once you open a database. Instead of the file commands and recent file list, you will see a list of the properties of the current database, including the number of people, families, and other record types in the database. You can also click the Enhanced Properties button below the properties to open the enhanced properties tool.

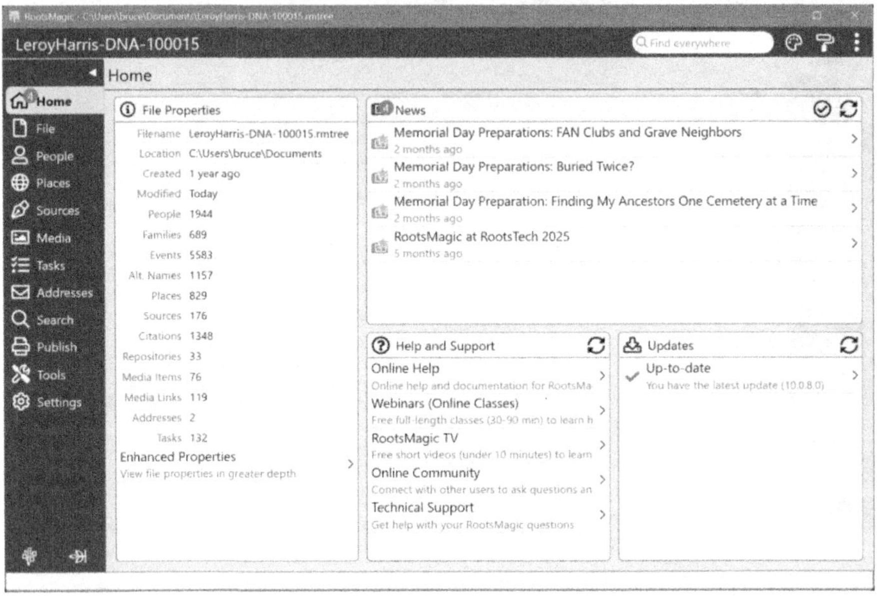

# FILE PAGE - USING DATABASES

The heart of any genealogy software is the database engine, and RootsMagic is no exception. A RootsMagic database can hold up to 2 billion individuals, so a single database can easily hold all the family members you can enter. If you *do* want to separate your information into different databases, RootsMagic will allow you to have as many databases as will fit on your hard disk.

The File page groups together the various functions for working with databases. Simply click File on the side menu and you will find commands for creating, opening, and otherwise manipulating database files.

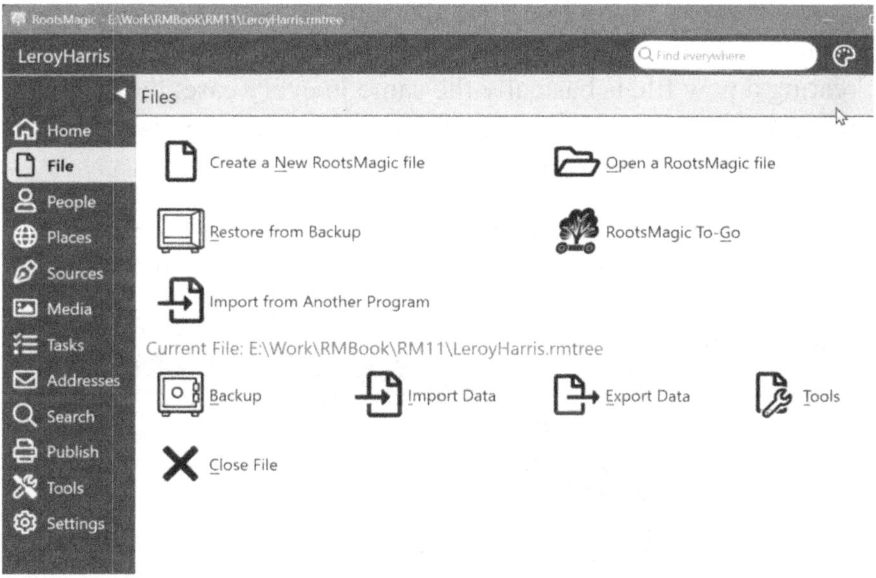


## CREATING A NEW DATABASE

Before you can do anything in RootsMagic, you must tell it to create a new database to store your information in.

*To create a new database* select the File page from the side menu, then select Create a New RootsMagic file. RootsMagic will display the following options for creating a new file.

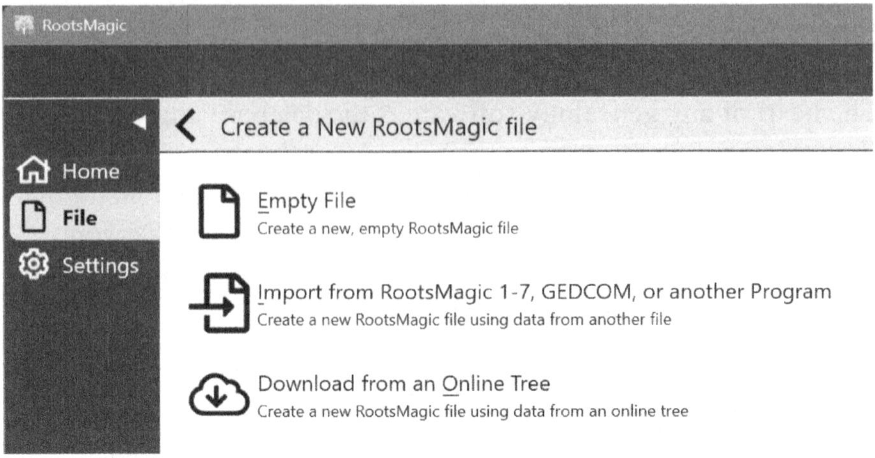


In addition to creating a new Empty file, there are also options to import information from another genealogy program, or to download information from either FamilySearch or Ancestry. Creating a new file is basically the same in every case; these other options just provide a quick way to populate your new database with pre-existing information.

When you choose to create a new file, RootsMagic will ask you to first select the folder you want to create your new file in. You can use the default folder (which can be set on the Settings page), or select from a list of recently used folders. If you prefer a different folder, click the Browse for Destination button at the bottom of the screen and use the file manager to select the folder you want.

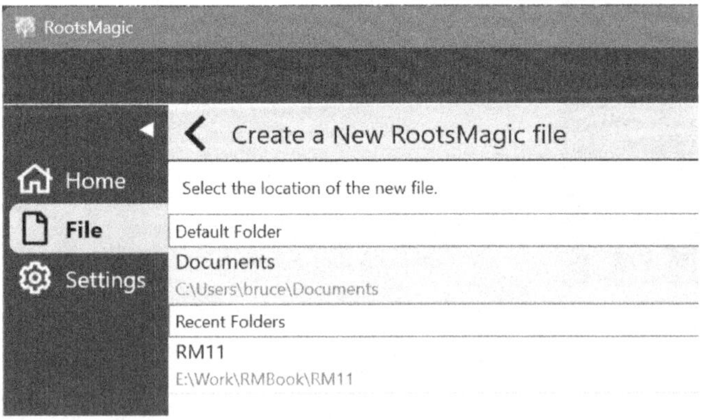

Once you have selected your folder, RootsMagic will display the file dialog where you can enter a file name for your new file. It can be something simple like your last name, or longer like "The Smith Family Tree".

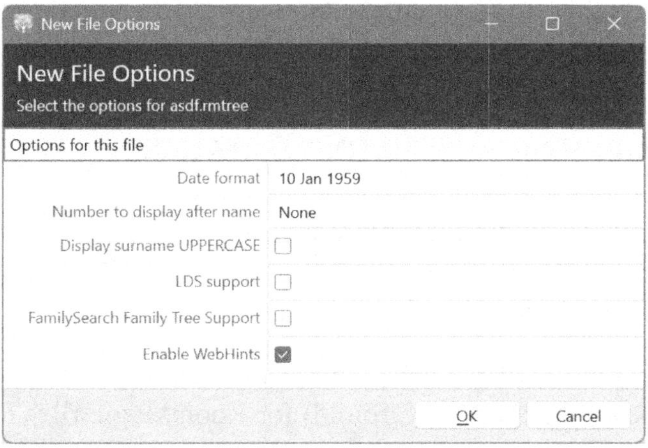


RootsMagic will then ask you to select a few options for your file.

*Date format* determines how RootsMagic will display dates you enter. You can actually enter dates in just about any format and RootsMagic will automatically convert them to the format you select here.

*Number to display after name* lets you choose whether RootsMagic displays the program assigned record number (RIN) after a person's name, a user entered reference number (REFN), the FamilySearch ID (FSID), or no number at all.

*Display surnames uppercase* lets you tell RootsMagic whether you want it to display and print surnames (last names) in all uppercase.

*LDS support* enables or disables the printing of LDS information on printouts and certain other LDS features.

*FamilySearch support* enables support for FamilySearch Family Tree.

*Enable WebHints* enables hints from FamilySearch, Ancestry, and other sites.

Simply select the options you want. Don't worry if you aren't sure which settings you want to use. You can always change them later. After you have made your choices, click the OK button, and you have just created a new database to hold your information.

## Opening an Existing Database

If you have created more than one database, you will need to be able to access the different databases. Selecting File from the side menu and then Open a RootsMagic file will let you select which database you want to use.

RootsMagic will display a list of recently used files, and will also search (in the background) for RootsMagic files in a few standard document folders. If you don't see the file you want, click the Browse for files button and RootsMagic will display the Open File dialog for you to find and open a file.

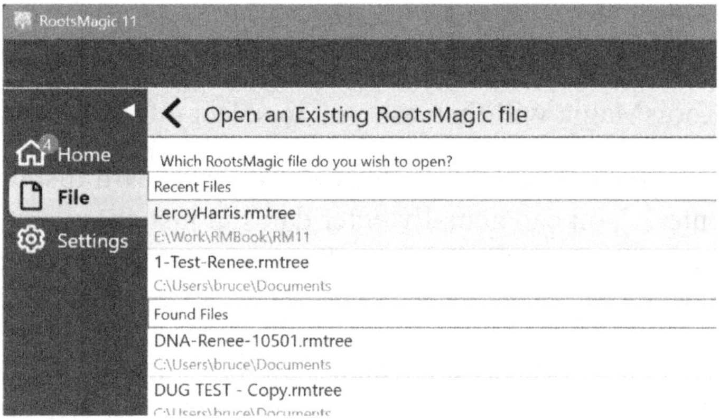


If you attempt to open a version 8-10 RootsMagic file, you will be asked if you want to convert the file to the current format. If you do so, the new file will no longer open in the older version.

*If you want to close a database*, just select Close file from the File page.

## Using Multiple Databases

RootsMagic allows you to have more than one database open on screen at the same time. Just open (or create) the additional databases exactly the same way you did the first, and RootsMagic will automatically display the two databases in separate windows on the screen.

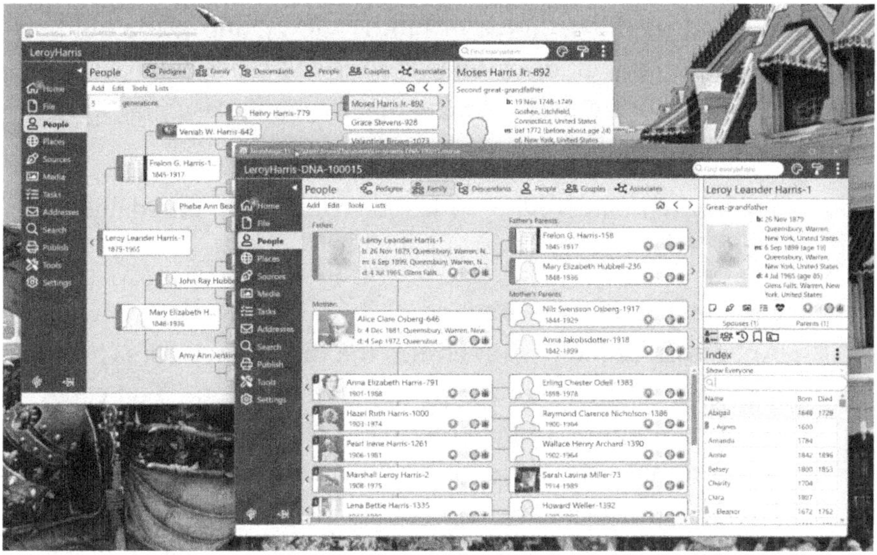


You may have up to 4 databases open at once, and the databases can be on separate monitors if you have more than one.

## DRAGGING AND DROPPING PEOPLE

If you have two different databases open at the same time, RootsMagic will let you drag and drop people from one database to the other.

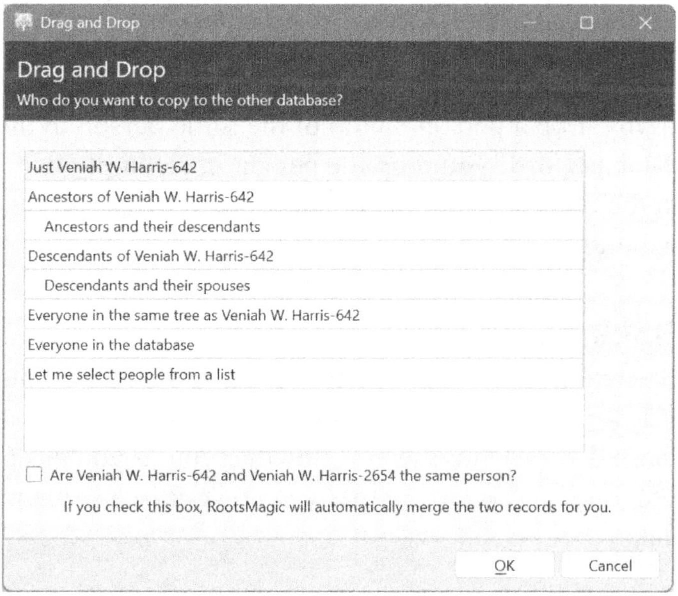


Dragging and dropping a person copies them to the new database, and does not remove them from the original database.

Simply click your mouse on a person in one

database (in either the pedigree or family view), and while holding the mouse button down, drag the person to the other database. RootsMagic will bring up the following screen in case you want to copy more than just that one person.

You can select which people you want to drag from one database to the other. Your options are:

- Just the person you dragged.
- Ancestors of the person copies the direct ancestors (parents, grandparents, etc.) of the person you dragged. You can enter the number of generations to copy. You can also select to have the children of the ancestors copied as well.
- Descendants of the person copies the direct descendants (children, grandchildren, etc.) of the person you dragged. You can enter the number of generations to copy. You can also select to have the spouses of descendants copied as well.
- Everyone in the same tree as the person copies everyone related to the person you dragged.
- Everyone in the database copies the entire database.
- Let me select people from a list brings up the selection screen (page 294) where you can select any group of people to copy.

If you drop a person on top of the same person in the other database, or if you drop the person in an empty parent or child slot in the other database, RootsMagic will offer you the chance to link the dragged person into the new database.

## Backing Up Your Database

If you only learn one thing from this book, this should be it. *Always keep a set of current backups of your data.* Nothing is more disheartening than losing everything you've entered into a program, and knowing that you don't have a backup copy of your data.

RootsMagic makes it easy to back up your data. It will even ask you if you want to back up your data whenever you close a database window. If you don't want RootsMagic to ask you to backup each time you exit, you can disable this option from the Settings page. To back up your data at any other time, select Backup from the File page.

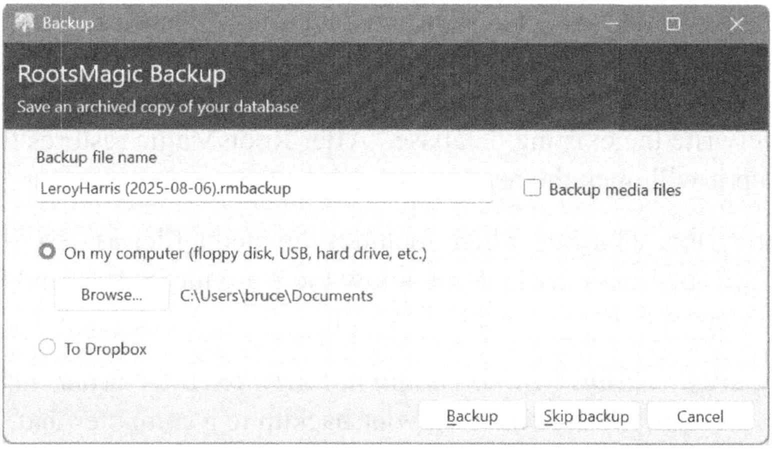


RootsMagic will display a default backup file name which includes the current day's date so you can easily keep multiple backups. The backup is a compressed version of your database and has a .rmbackup extension.

You can save your backup to a folder on your computer or to Dropbox. If you back up to a USB or the hard drive, you can click the Browse button to select the drive to save to.

If you backup to Dropbox, RootsMagic will prompt you to log into that service and then will upload your backup directly to the cloud.

> **Note**
>
> By default RootsMagic will back up links to multimedia items, but not the multimedia items themselves (photos, sound or video clips). If you click the checkbox "Backup media files", RootsMagic will also include those media items in the backup file. Keep in mind that this can greatly increase the size of your backup file.

*To restore a backed up database*, select Restore from backup from the File page. RootsMagic will search for and display a list of any backup files it finds on your computer. If you don't see the backup you want, click the Browse for file button to select the backup using the File Open dialog.

RootsMagic will then ask what folder you want to restore the backed up database in. You can choose between a default folder, a recently used folder, or you can click the Browse button to select any folder you desire. The restored database will have the same name as it had originally. If there is already a database with that name in the directory you choose, RootsMagic will ask if you want to overwrite the existing database. After RootsMagic restores the backup it will open the newly restored database.

If you restore a backup which includes the media files as described above, RootsMagic will let you know there are media files and will ask if you want to restore those as well.

*There are 2 reasons why you might not want to restore your media files.* First, if you are restoring your backup to a computer that already has your media files on the hard drive, restoring the media files will restore them all in a single subfolder under the folder containing your database and will adjust all the media links to point to those restored files (meaning you will end up with 2 copies of every media file on your hard drive). Secondly, it can take a while to restore hundreds or thousands of media items.

**☺ Tip**

While a single backup copy of each database is better than no backup, some backup techniques can provide even more protection.

When creating a backup, try not to always overwrite your previous backup. It is sometimes possible to have corruption in your database without knowing it and your backup could contain a corrupted database. By having multiple backups you can go back to earlier backups that may have been created before the corruption occurred.

## File and Database Tools

RootsMagic provides tools to manipulate not only your data file, but also the underlying database structure itself. File Tools include commands like renaming, copying, deleting, and comparing files, while Database Tools provide the ability to test and fix the underlying database itself.

To access the file and database tools, select Tools from the File page. The Tools option will only be available if you have a file open.

### Moving or Renaming Your Database

The Move/Rename command lets you rename or move your database. RootsMagic will ask you to select the folder where you want to move the current file. You can select any folder, including the one the file is already in. RootsMagic will then ask you for the name for the new file.

If you enter a new file name, but select the original folder then the file will simply be given the new name. If you change the folder on the rename screen, the file will be renamed *and* moved to the new folder.

### Copying Your Database

The Copy command lets you create an exact copy of your database. You can choose what folder and filename you want for the copy. This command can be useful if you want to make a copy of your database that you can make temporary changes to without affecting your main database.

### Deleting Your Database

Here is a command you should never use on your database, unless you are absolutely sure you don't need it anymore. The Delete command will completely remove the current database from your hard disk. You must mark the verification checkbox and then click the Delete this database button.

### Comparing Two RootsMagic Files

Have you ever had two copies of a database and wondered what the difference between the two was? The Compare Files command lets you compare the current file with another file you select and see the differences side by side, and then copy data back and forth between them. See page 339 for more information on comparing and syncing RootsMagic files.

### Database Tools

The database tools include 4 simple tools for cleaning up and testing the integrity of your database

1. **Test integrity:** tests the integrity of the underlying database structure. It looks for problems like database corruption, invalid indexes, etc.
2. **Rebuild indexes:** rebuilds the underlying indexes in the database. These are the low level links between the basic records in the file.
3. **Clean phantom records:** cleans up phantom records, which include things like blank children in families, etc.
4. **Compact:** removes unused records in the database. This can reduce the size of your .rmtree file.

## Importing Data

RootsMagic provides a number of ways to import information from other sources. Select Import Data from the File page and RootsMagic will display the following options.

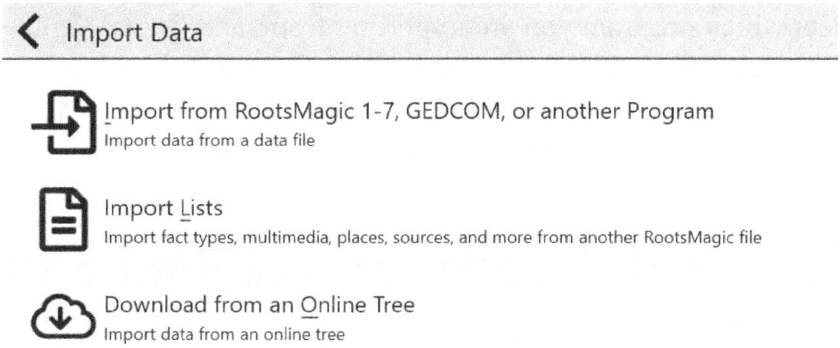


## Importing Data From Other Programs

RootsMagic can directly import data from Family Tree Maker (version 2006 and earlier), Personal Ancestral File (PAF) version 2 and later, Legacy Family Tree, The Master Genealogist (TMG), Family Origins version 4 and later, and all versions of RootsMagic version 7 and older. All information will be brought in to RootsMagic, including names, dates, places, links, notes, and image links.

> **☺ Tip**
>
> The Windows and Mac versions will have different imports enabled based on whether the original program was available on each platform.

*To import data from another program*, create a new database and select Import data, then Import from RootsMagic 1-7, GEDCOM, or another program on the File page.

Select which program you are importing from, and RootsMagic will search and display a list of any files of that type in your document folder. If you don't see the file you want to import, click the Browse button to display the File Open dialog to select the file you want.

> **☺ Tip**
>
> All imports except for GEDCOM import will only read a file into a new (empty) database. This isn't a problem unless you want to combine the data into an existing database. In this case, create a new database and import the file into that database. Then drag and drop the information into your existing database.

Importing a GEDCOM file into RootsMagic has a few extra steps beyond what the direct imports require.

GEDCOM is a file format. It is not a piece of software, although many software programs can read and write GEDCOM files. A GEDCOM filename ends with a .GED extension (like family.ged).

GEDCOM was developed by the Family History Department of The Church of Jesus Christ of Latter-day Saints (LDS Church) to provide a flexible, uniform format for exchanging computerized genealogical data

You will usually only import a GEDCOM into a new blank RootsMagic file. If you import a GEDCOM into an existing database, RootsMagic will mix all the names in the GEDCOM file with the names already in your database. If the GEDCOM contains names which are already in your database, you will end up with 2 copies of each of those people.

RootsMagic will then display the following dialog, which lets you add a source to each person or event in the GEDCOM file so you can tell where the record came from (only one source is added, and every person or event in the GEDCOM file will point to it).

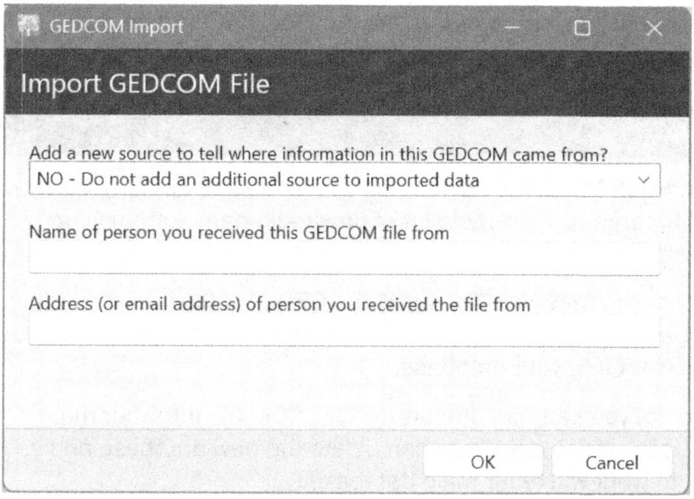


You can choose to add the source to every person, every fact, every person and fact, or to not add a source. If you choose to add a source, you need to enter the name and address of the person you received the GEDCOM from (in order to create the source).

*If a GEDCOM file is too large to fit on a single disk*, it may be broken into several smaller files. If you ever import one of these multi-disk GEDCOM files, RootsMagic will automatically ask you to insert the disk with the next part.

When you import a GEDCOM file, it is not linked in any way to the names you already had in your database. It is up to you to connect the new names from the GEDCOM with your existing family tree. If you have duplicate copies of individuals in your database, merging those records will link the trees together. Or you can use the Add Parents, Add Spouse and Add Child commands and choose the option to Select existing person to link the individuals together

If you import a GEDCOM file that contains data that RootsMagic does not know how to handle, it will be put into what is called a "listing file". The listing file has the same name as the GEDCOM file, except that the file extension is .LST instead of .GED. The listing file is a plain text file that you can look at with any text editor. It will list any lines from the GEDCOM file that it didn't understand..

> ☺ **Tip**
>
> While RootsMagic provides a "merge" feature (page 81) it is really hard to remove or merge a lot of unwanted names from your database if you combine in a GEDCOM file you didn't really want.
>
> Instead, you may want to import the GEDCOM file into a new (blank) database, so that you can view the new information to see if you really want it in your database.
>
> *If you do*, you can then import the GEDCOM file into your main database. *If you don't*, you can delete the new database and go back to work with your main database.
>
> *If you only want part of the GEDCOM file in your database*, just drag and drop the desired people from the new database into your main database.

## Importing Lists from Another File

There may come a time when you need to create a new database, but you have a bunch of custom fact types or sources that you don't want to have to retype into the new file. The Import Lists command will let you import various lists from another database into your current database. You will first select the file you want to import lists from, then you will select which lists to import.

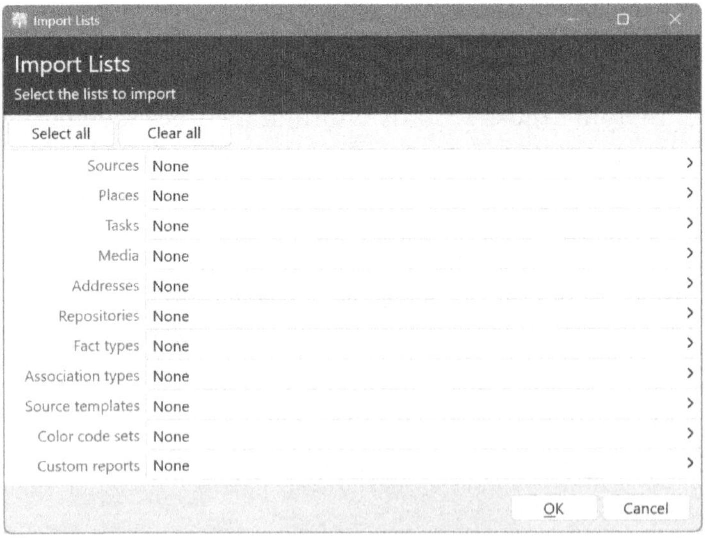

RootsMagic will display the types of lists you can import, and how many records from each of those list types will be imported. By default, no records are selected, but you can click Select all to select all the records in all the lists from the other file.

You can also click any individual list above, and RootsMagic will slide in all records of that type for you to choose from.

This screen lets you select just the specific records that you want to import. So, for example, if you have entered some places in another file, you can select that list and choose just the ones you want to import.

Although this command works best when importing lists into a new blank database, it will also import into an existing database. But be careful when importing into an existing database because it is possible to end up with duplicate entries in your lists that way.

### Importing from an Online Tree

In addition to importing files, RootsMagic also offers the option to download data from FamilySearch Family Tree, or from your own Ancestry Tree.

If your database already has information in it, the Ancestry download will be disabled since it is only possible to download the Ancestry tree into a new empty database.

### *Importing an Ancestry Tree*

When you select the Ancestry download, RootsMagic will first ask you to log in to Ancestry if you haven't already. Once you have logged in you will see a list of all your trees on Ancestry (there may be just one), along with any trees that have been shared with you.

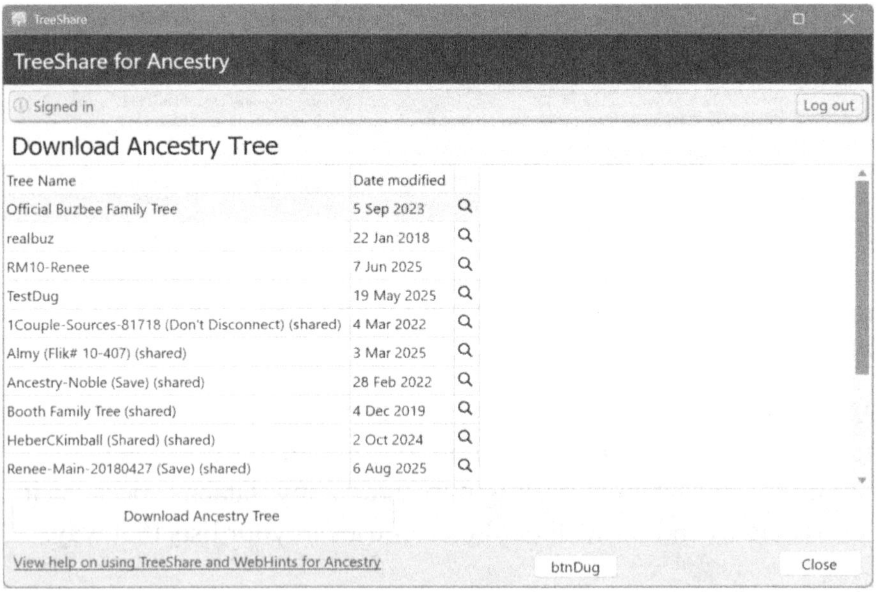


Simply highlight the tree you want to download and click the Download Ancestry Tree button. RootsMagic will download and import the full tree, including all names, families, sources, media and more.

Once the information has been downloaded, it will enable other Ancestry features such as Ancestry WebHints, all of which are described in the chapter titled "Ancestry TreeShare".

### *Importing from FamilySearch Family Tree*

Importing information from FamilySearch works somewhat differently than from Ancestry. While Ancestry trees are single smaller trees that are completely owned by the user, FamilySearch Family Tree is a huge global tree that is shared by everyone using FamilySearch.

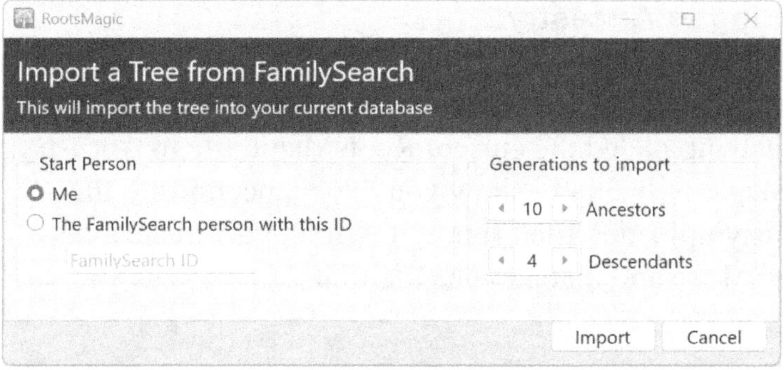


So instead of just downloading a complete named tree, you need to select a starting person and choose the number of generations of ancestors and descendants to download. The starting person can either be "Me", where RootsMagic will use the logged in user as the starting person, or you can enter the FamilySearch ID of the starting person.

## EXPORTING YOUR TREE

There may be times you want to share your information with the world (or at least a family member). RootsMagic lets you export your information in several ways: uploading to an Ancestry tree, creating a GEDCOM file, or saving to Dropbox to be used with the RootsMagic iOS app.

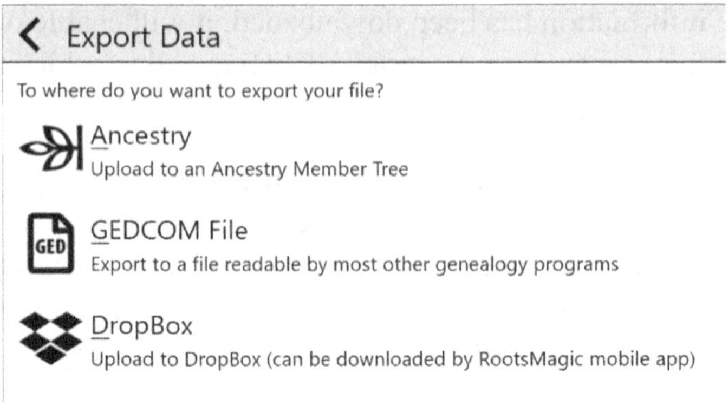


## Exporting to Ancestry

To upload your RootsMagic file to a new Ancestry tree, select Export Data, then Ancestry from the File page. If you have previously uploaded the current RootsMagic file to Ancestry, RootsMagic will simply show you the connections to the previously uploaded file. If not, it will let you create a new Ancestry Tree and upload your file to it.

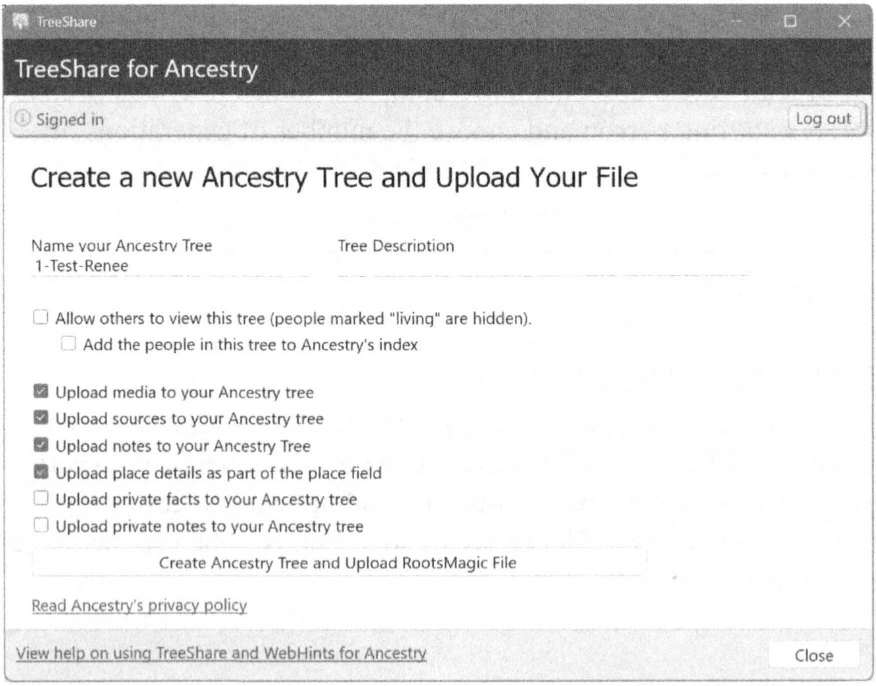

You can enter the name for your new Ancestry tree, plus an optional description. There are also a number of options to select from before RootsMagic will do the upload.

Allow others to view this tree - Leave this unchecked if you want your Ancestry tree to be private and hidden.

- **Add the people in this tree to Ancestry's index:** If you want people to be able to find your tree when they search for a name in it, then you can check this box.
- **Upload media:** This lets you choose whether to upload your media items.
- **Upload sources:** This lets you choose whether to upload your sources.
- **Upload notes:** This lets you choose whether to upload your notes.
- **Upload place details:** If you mark this checkbox, RootsMagic will prepend the place details to the place before uploading it to Ancestry.
- **Upload private facts:** This lets you choose whether to upload private facts.
- **Upload private notes:** This lets you choose whether to upload private notes.

Click the Create Ancestry Tree and Upload RootsMagic file button, and RootsMagic will upload the selected information to Ancestry. Each person in the newly uploaded tree will be connected to the corresponding person in RootsMagic, which lets you easily compare your RootsMagic data with your Ancestry data. More details on this is in the chapter titled “Ancestry TreeShare”.

## Creating a GEDCOM File

*To create a GEDCOM file* select Export Data, then GEDCOM file from the File page.

RootsMagic will ask you to select the folder where you want to create the new GEDCOM file. It will display a list of recent folders, but you can also click the “Browse” button to select any folder you want.

Once you have selected the folder, RootsMagic will open the File Save form to let you enter the name to give your GEDCOM file.

The GEDCOM options dialog will then appear for you to select the options you want.

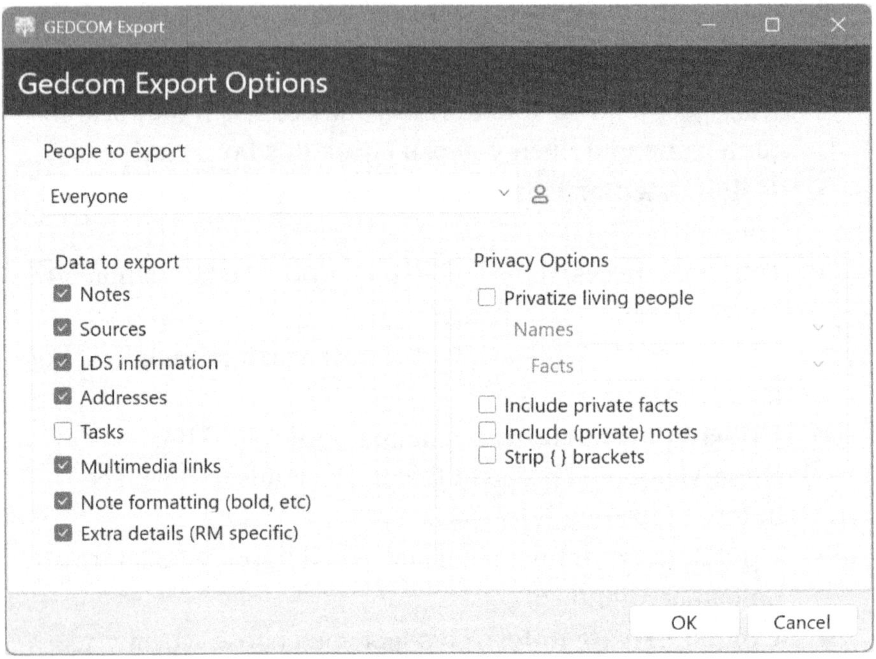


*People to export* lets you tell RootsMagic whether you want to export everyone in your database, or to select exactly which people you want to export. If you choose Select from a list RootsMagic will bring up a list of everybody in your database for you to select from. This selection list is the exact same screen described in the chapter titled "Custom Reports" (page 294). Simply select the individuals you want to include in the GEDCOM file.

*Privacy options* lets you filter the way information is exported for living people. If you don't check the "Privatize living people" box, people will be exported whether they are living or not. If you do check this box, RootsMagic will use the two drop lists to determine exactly how to do the filtering.

- **Names:** Lets you choose whether to export the full name of living people, or whether to export the word "Living".

- **Facts:** Lets you select whether to export the full date and place for each fact, or to not export the fact at all. You can also choose from several other filtering options, like date only, year only, place only, and year and place.

*Include private facts* lets you choose whether RootsMagic should include any facts (birth, marriage, death, etc.) that you have marked as "private".

*Include private notes* and *Strip brackets* let you choose whether RootsMagic should export any private notes you have entered. Private notes are described in more detail on page 138.

*Data to export* allows you to specify what types of data to export for each person.

- **Notes:** Check this box if you want notes included in the file.
- **Sources:** Check this box if you want sources and citations included in the file.
- **LDS information:** Check this box if you want to export LDS information like LDS baptisms, endowments, and sealings.
- **Addresses:** Check this box if you want current addresses included in the file. If you are sending the GEDCOM file to someone else, you probably don't want to include the addresses of all your relatives.
- **Tasks:** Check this box if you want your tasks to be exported.
- **Multimedia links:** Check this box if you want the links to your photos and other scrapbook items to be exported. This does **not** export the photos themselves, just the link information.
- **Note formatting:** Check this box if you want RootsMagic to export the bold, italic, and underlining in your notes. Most other genealogy programs can't handle the formatting codes, but this allows you to preserve the formatting when the GEDCOM file will be imported back into RootsMagic.
- **Extra details (RM specific):** RootsMagic normally includes data in the GEDCOM that is specific to RootsMagic. But sometimes you may need to turn those items off (like if you are

exporting the GEDCOM for a program or website that won't support those extra features).

After you select your options and click OK, RootsMagic will bring up the file save dialog where you can enter the name you want to give your GEDCOM file.

Also, while GEDCOM is a very flexible file format, most programs implement it a little differently. Most of this has to do with the types and amount of data each program is capable of storing. If you create a GEDCOM file from RootsMagic and import it into another program which isn't as powerful as RootsMagic, you may lose some of your information simply because the other program has no place to store the information.

> ☺ **Tip**
>
> RootsMagic allows you to specify whether any particular fact type should be exported when creating a GEDCOM file (they are all exported by default). For example, if you want to create a GEDCOM file but not include Occupation facts, you can select **"Fact type list"** from the Options menu on the Person page, highlight **"Occupation"** in the list, click the **"Edit"** button, then uncheck the GEDCOM Export checkbox. RootsMagic will then ignore the Occupation facts for everyone when creating a GEDCOM file (until you edit the fact type again and check the GEDCOM Export checkbox).

### Exporting to Dropbox

The Dropbox export lets you save your file in a format that can be used with the RootsMagic iOS app. You will be asked to sign in to Dropbox (or create a Dropbox account if you don't already have one), and then give permission for RootsMagic to access its folder in Dropbox. RootsMagic will then write the file to Dropbox to be accessed by the iOS app.

## RootsMagic To-Go

RootsMagic makes it easy to take your program and data along with you. RootsMagic To-Go lets you install the RootsMagic program on your flash-drive, and helps you move your

RootsMagic data back and forth between your main computer and the flash drive.

To run RootsMagic To-Go, select RootsMagic To-Go on the File page. The RootsMagic To-Go feature is a "wizard" that will step you through installing the RootsMagic program on a flash drive, and with transferring your RootsMagic data files back and forth between your computer and your flash drive.

It is actually possible to install both the Windows and Mac versions of RootsMagic on your flash drive so you can use that drive on either type of computer.

RootsMagic To-Go will display a list of drives that it detects, with removeable drives (like flash drives) listed first. It will also show you how much free space is available on each drive. Highlight the drive you want to use for your portable copy of RootsMagic and then click the Next button.

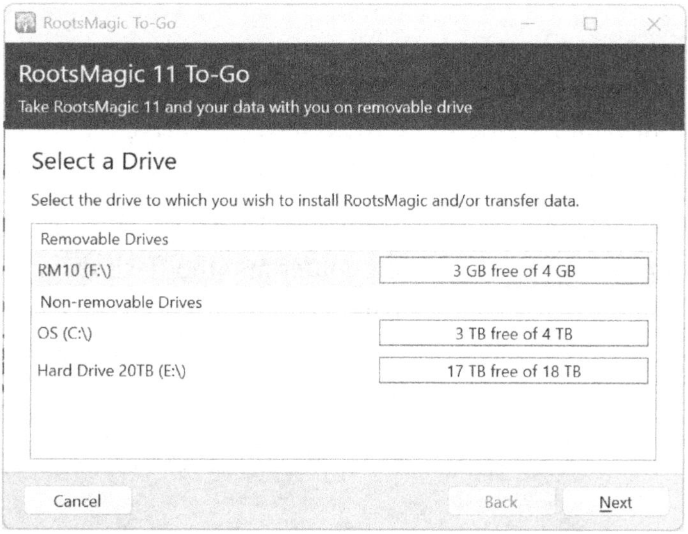


## Installing RootsMagic on Your Flash Drive

The next page of the wizard will let you know if the most recent version of RootsMagic is installed on the drive you selected.

If it is not installed, or if it is an older version, you can tell RootsMagic to install or update the program on the removable drive.

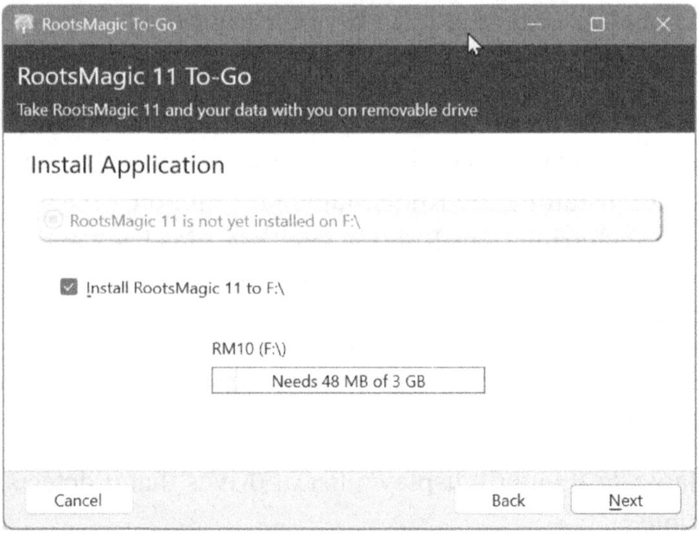


## Transferring Data

The final page of the RootsMagic To-Go wizard will help transfer your data files between the removable drive and to your home computer.

RootsMagic To-Go will display a list of files that are available to transfer between your computer and the flash drive. There may be files on your computer that need to be transferred to your flash drive, and there may be files on your flash drive that need to be transferred back to your computer.

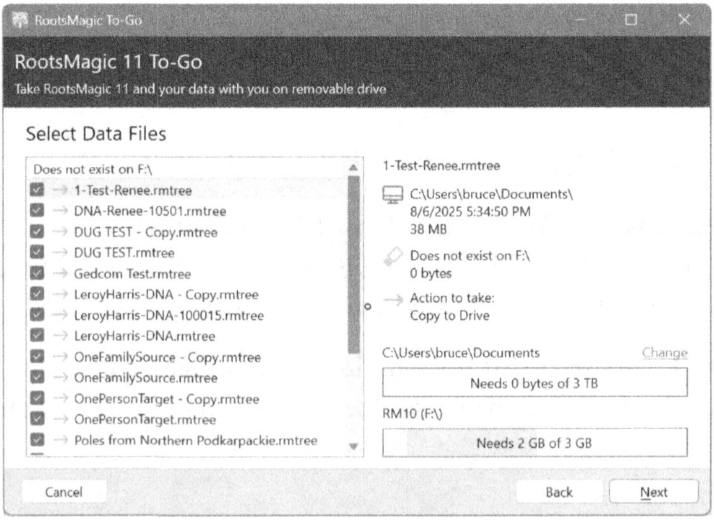

RootsMagic To-Go keeps track of which files have changed and tells you which way you need to copy each file. Highlighting any file in the list will tell you which direction the file needs to be copied. It will also tell you whether a file exists on both the computer and flash drive, or just on one of them.

> **Warning**
>
> When you transfer files, don't modify both the desktop copy and flash drive copy of the file without syncing your data in between. If you do happen to modify both copies of the data file, RootsMagic To-Go doesn't know which one to keep and tells you there is a conflict

Just mark the checkbox in front of any of the files you want to transfer, then click the Next button.

RootsMagic To-Go will show all the databases in whatever folder you've told RootsMagic to store your data files in. If you didn't specify a folder in RootsMagic, the Documents or My Documents folder will be used by default. If the folder is not the one you want to transfer from, click "Change" and you can set the sync folder for the computer.

> **Note**
>
> RootsMagic To-Go does not transfer your multimedia files to the removable drive. RootsMagic doesn't change the media pathnames in your file though, so when you transfer the file back to your desktop computer the media will remain linked.

# PEOPLE PAGE

One of the first things you may notice about the People page is that it offers six different views: Pedigree, Family, Descendants, People, Couples, and Associates. To switch between the views, simply click on the buttons above the views.

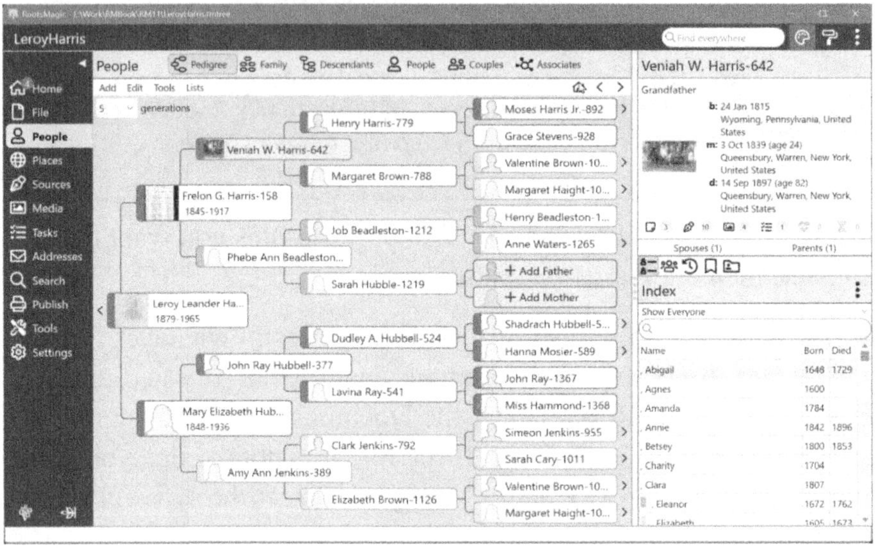


*To the right of the views is an information panel* where RootsMagic displays information about the currently highlighted person. When you highlight a new person in any view, RootsMagic will update this area with the person's picture, name, birth, marriage, and death information. If you prefer the information panel to be on the left side of the views, you can change this in the Display Settings.

## THE PEDIGREE VIEW

The Pedigree View displays a five-generation ancestor tree of your family.

As you add individuals to your database, RootsMagic fills out the tree for you. You can move from person to person using the arrow keys on your keyboard, or by clicking on a person's name with the mouse.

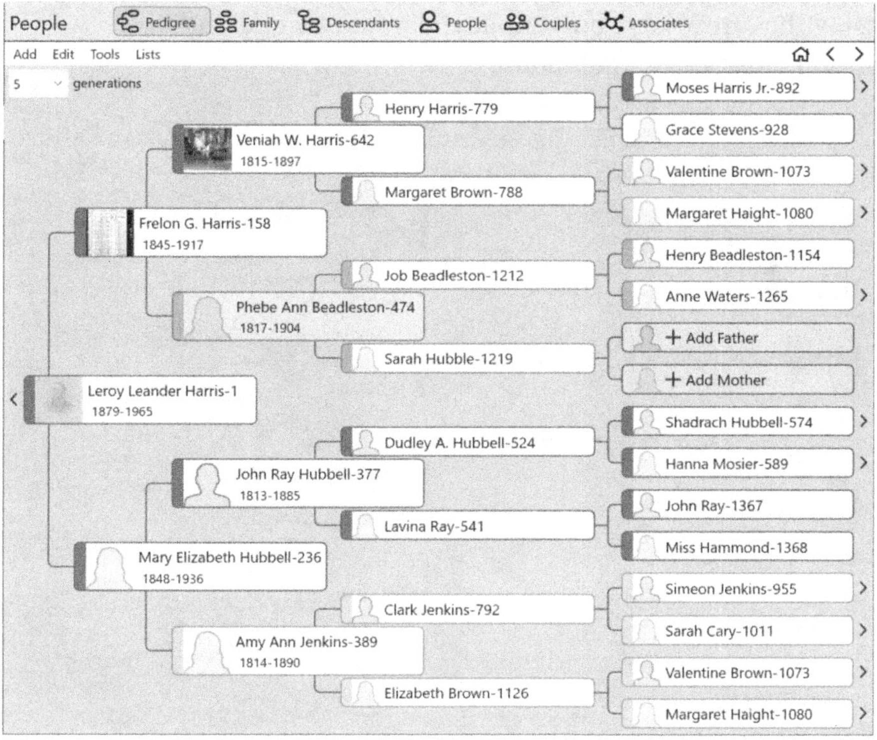


Once you have entered more generations than will fit on screen, RootsMagic will add small arrows next to names to show that there are more individuals you can move to. Just click your mouse on one of these arrows and RootsMagic will scroll the next generation onto the screen. You can also just press an arrow key in the appropriate direction to scroll to another generation.

In the upper left corner of the pedigree view you will see a drop list which you can click to switch between displaying 5 and 6 generations on the screen at once.

You can edit any person in the Pedigree View by double clicking your mouse on the person's name, or you can simply highlight a person and press the Enter key.

## The Family View

The Family View displays the father, mother, children and grandparents in a family. You can move from person to person using the arrow keys on your keyboard, or by clicking on a person's name with the mouse.

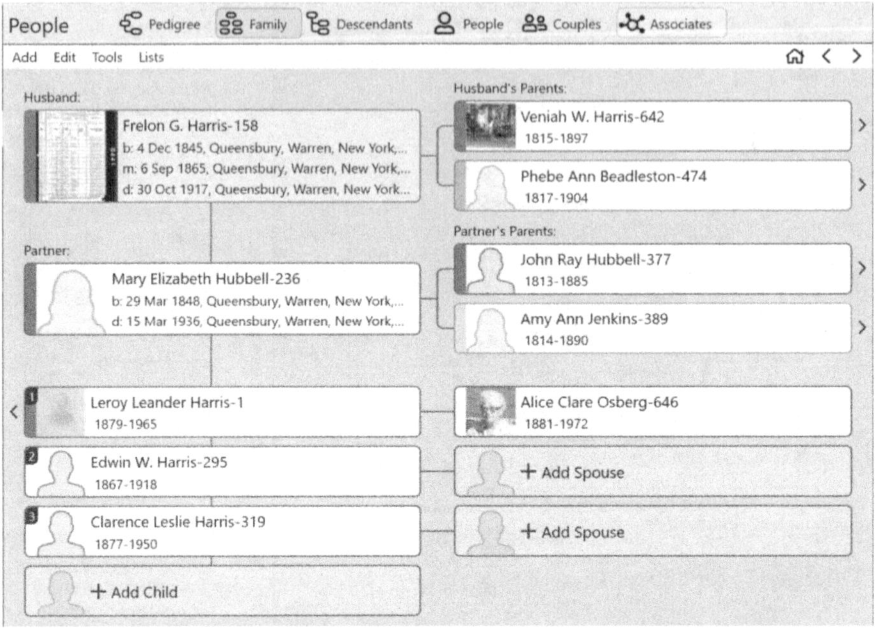


If grandparents are entered, a small arrow will appear to the right of the grandparent's name. Clicking your mouse on one of these arrows will move the grandparents into the parent position in the view.

RootsMagic will also add an arrow to the left of any child in the Family View who is married (or has a partner). Clicking your mouse on one of these arrows will change the view to the family where the child is an adult.

Like the Pedigree View, you can edit any person by double clicking your mouse on the person's name, or you can simply highlight a person and press the Enter key.

## The Descendants View

The Descendants View displays a five-generation indented descendant list of your family. The children of each person in the list are displayed under the parents, and are indented a small amount.

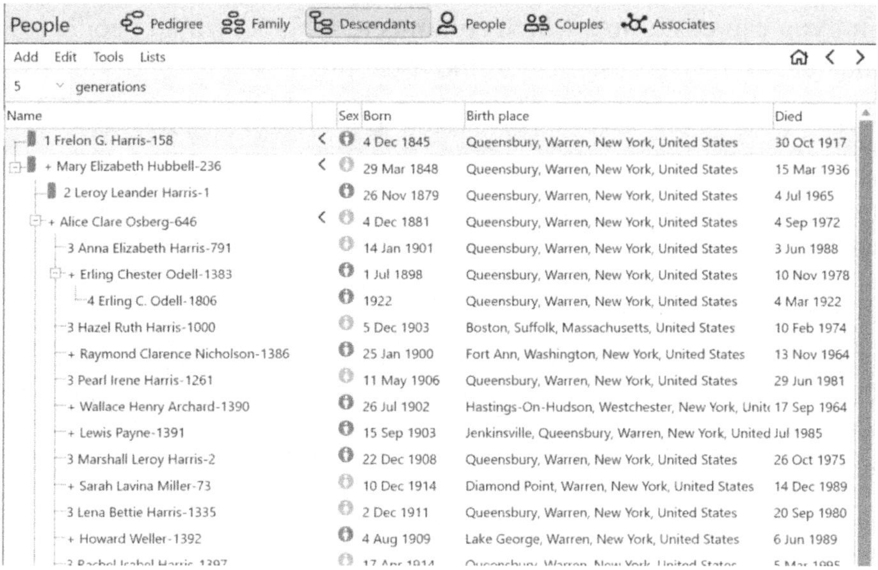

If the first person in the Descendants View has parents entered, a left arrow will appear to the right of their name. You can click on this arrow to move one generation back in time.

In addition, RootsMagic will put a left arrow to the right of any spouse who has parents entered as well, so that you can navigate to that part of the family. And before you ask why some people in the list *don't* have left arrows next to their names, it is because their parents are already displayed in the list.

If any person in the last generation displayed has children, a right arrow will be displayed to the right of their name. Clicking that arrow will scroll forward one generation in time to display that person's children.

In the upper left corner of the descendants view you will see a drop list where you can choose to display 2 through 7 generations on the screen at once.

## The People List View

The People List view is a list of people in your database. By default, it is an alphabetical list of the entire file with columns for sex, record number, birth date and place, and death date and place.

But you can customize which columns to include, which people to include, and what order to sort those people.

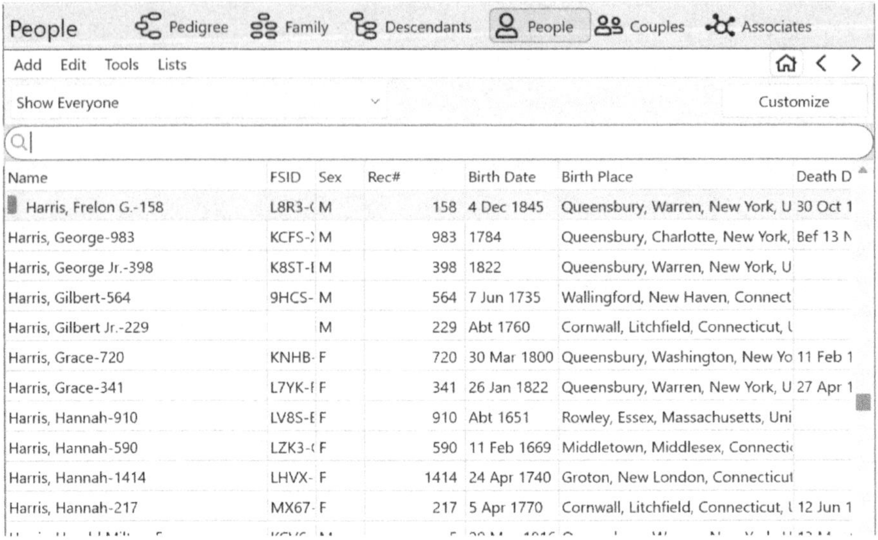


## Sorting the Columns

Even though the list is sorted by name, you can click the header on any column to sort by that column. So, for example, if you wanted to sort your file by birth date, just click the words Birth Date at the top of that column. If you click it a second time it will sort by that column in the other direction. You can do this for any column in the list.

You will usually have columns that go beyond the screen on the right. If you want to see those columns, use the scroll bar at the bottom of the list. RootsMagic will scroll the columns onto the screen, but will keep the name column on the screen so you don't lose track of which person the data belongs to.

## Choosing the People

The People list view will normally display everyone in your database, but you can filter the list to only include the people you want. Click the drop list that says Show Everyone above the list of people, and you can create or select a group of people to display. If the group is a "Rules" group, a button will appear to the right of the drop list to refresh the group based on the rules.

> ☺ **Tip**
>
> You can choose whether to show just the primary name for each person, or you can choose "Show alternate names" from the Tools menu to display people under any alternate names that have been entered for them. If a row is an alternate name RootsMagic will display a plus sign in front of the name.

## Choosing the Columns

But let's say you want different columns for each person. You can click the "Customize" button to choose which columns you really want to display. The customize form contains two lists of fields. The list on the left are fields that are available to display. The list on the right are the fields that are currently being displayed.

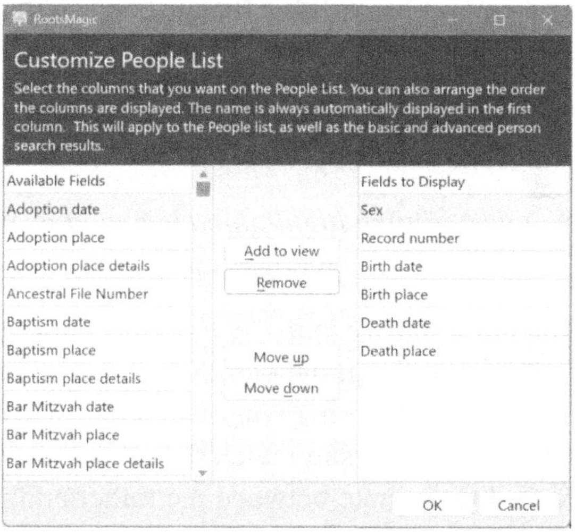


*To add a column to the People List view*, select from the "Available fields" and click "Add to view".

*To remove a column from the People List view*, select the column in "Fields to display" and click "Remove".

*To rearrange columns in the People List view*, select a column in "Fields to display" and click "Move up" or "Move down".

## The Couple List View

The Couple List view is a view of couples in the database. These can be either married or unmarried couples.

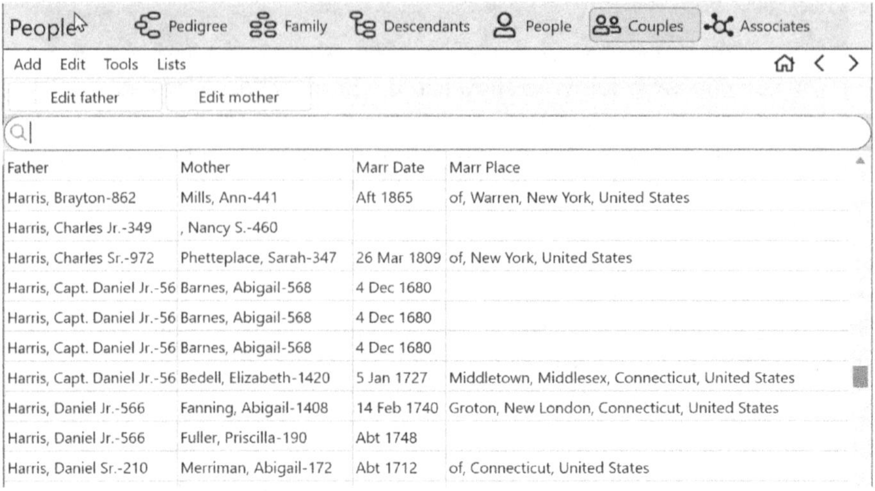


The couple list will list the husband, wife, and the marriage date and place.

*You can sort the couple list* by clicking the header of the column you want to sort by.

*You can edit the highlighted husband or wife* by clicking on the Edit father or Edit mother button.

*You can filter by individuals in the couple list* by typing who you are looking for in the search field in the format Surname, Given. You can enter a single name, and RootsMagic will display couples where either person match the name, or you can use the ampersand & to differentiate between the father and mother.

For example:

Smith, Pat will find anyone with Smith in the surname and Pat in the given name in either column.

,Pat will find anyone with Pat in the given name (regardless of surname)

Smith, Pat& will find anyone with Smith in the surname and Pat in the given name in the first column

&Smith, Pat will find anyone with Smith in the surname and Pat in the given name in the second column

Smith, Pat&Jones, Mary will find any couple where the father has Smith in the surname and Pat in the given names, and the mother has Jones in the surname and Mary in the given names

Smith&,Mary will find any couple where the father has Smith in the surname and the mother has Mary in the given name (note the comma in front of the mother's name)

## THE ASSOCIATION VIEW

The Association View is a list of associations in your database. An association is a relationship between two people that isn't necessarily a family relationship, for example friends, neighbors, teacher/student, or even slave holder/enslaved person.

| Relationship | Role 1 | Person 1 | Role 2 | Person 2 | Date | Place |
|---|---|---|---|---|---|---|
| Grave neighboı | Burial | Odell, Sylvia-383 | Burial | Harris, Asa Stowers-340 | | |
| Employment | Employer | Harris, Veniah W.-642 | Employee | Hennegan, Mary-941 | 1840 | St. Mε |
| Enslavement | Enslaver | Allen, Jonathan W.-1395 | Enslaved person | , Harriet M.-358 | 1830 | South |
| Friends | Friend | Harris, Veniah W.-642 | Friend | Hubbell, Betsey-1590 | From 1825 | |
| Godparent | Godparent | Harris, Veniah W.-642 | Godchild | Jenkins, Phebe Ann-932 | From 1820 | |
| Household | Household m | Hubbell, Betsey-1590 | Household mem | Storm, Sarah-1598 | | |
| Neighbors | Neighbor | Harris, Veniah W.-642 | Neighbor | Larrabee, Louisa-1381 | From 1835 to 185 | New ( |
| Neighbors | Neighbor | Hennegan, Mary-941 | Neighbor | Brown, Lucretia-1319 | From 1838 to 184 | |
| Neighbors | Neighbor | Hubbell, Dudley A.-524 | Neighbor | Jenkins, Elmer Stuart-1685 | From 1830 to 184 | Bosto |
| Education | Teacher | Odell, Sylvia-383 | Student | Brown, Lucretia-1319 | 1820 | |

While associations can be viewed on the edit screen for each person (just like facts), the Association view provides a way to see all your associations in a single list. The list includes the relationship type, the two individuals in the relationship and their role, and the date and place of the relationship.

*You can sort the list* by clicking the header of the column you wish to sort by.

*You can filter individuals* by typing the name of either person in the association.

*You can edit either person in the highlighted association* by clicking on the Edit person 1 or Edit person 2 button.

*You can edit the actual association* by clicking on the Edit relationship button. You will be able to edit the association type, the individuals, the date, place, and note for the association. You can also edit any association from the edit screen for either of the people. In that case you can also edit any sources, media, or tasks attached to the association.

## THE SIDE PANEL

The side panel is on the right side of the screen and contains six different panels: information, index, Life Summary, bookmarks, history, and groups. The information panel is at the top of the side panel, while the other 5 are in the lower half, each selectable by clicking on its icon.

### The Information Panel

The Information panel displays basic information about the currently selected person. As you move from person to person on any of the views, this panel will be updated.

The panel displays the name, primary photo, birth, marriage, and death date and place, and any relationship to the selected person in the Set Relationship command.

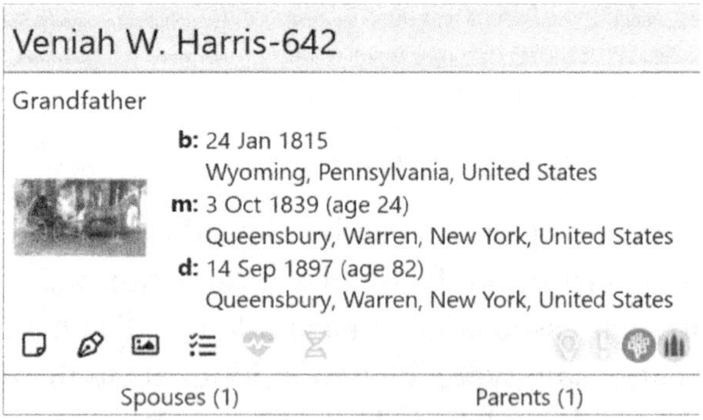


It will also display 2 sets of icons across the bottom of the panel. The first set of icons shows whether the current person has notes, source citations, media, tasks, and health or DNA entries. If an item exists, the icon will be darkened. As you widen the side panel, the icons can also display the count for each item. The second set of icons indicates whether the person has WebHints, problem alerts, is linked to FamilySearch or has an LDS status.

Directly under the icons are buttons which show how many spouses and sets of parents the current person has. Clicking either button will show you a list of the spouses (or parents). You can click one to make them the current spouse or parents of the selected person.

## The Index Panel

The index panel is simply a list of every person in your database. When you select a person in the index list, RootsMagic will change to that person in whatever main view (pedigree, family, etc.) you currently have selected.

Clicking the "Options" button (3 dots) will let you display alternate names in the index or display the person's record number next to their name.

You can quickly filter the index by typing a name (last name, then comma, then first names). You can also choose to filter the list to only include people in a group by selecting the group from the drop list directly below the search field.

## The Life Summary

The Life Summary displays the facts and family members of the person currently highlighted in the main view. Each of the 3 sections (events, spouses / children, and parents / siblings) can be collapsed by clicking the arrow in front of the section header. The current person can be edited by clicking the pencil button in the header.

Each person in the family sections will have a drop arrow to the right of their name. Clicking this menu button will give you the following options:

- Go To - make this person the new current person
- Edit - opens the Edit Person form for the spouse
- Unlink - lets you unlink the person as a spouse, parent or child
- Delete - lets you delete the person from the database

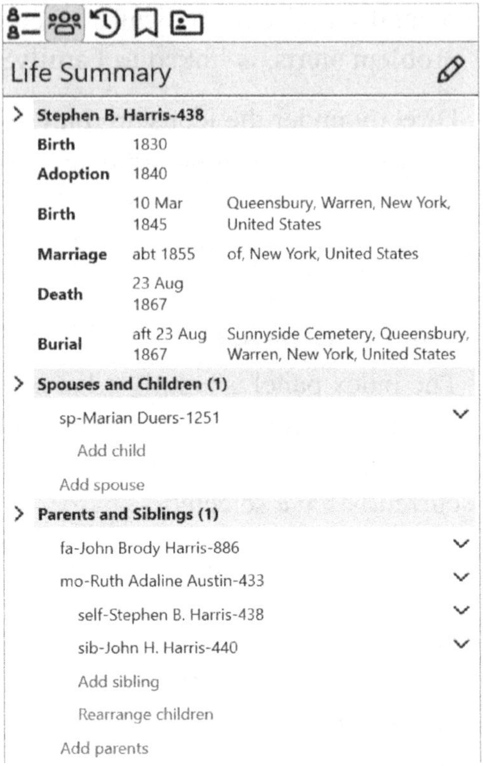


Links in each family section let you add additional spouses or parents to the person, children to a family, or rearrange the children or spouses.

## The Bookmark Panel

Often it is necessary to work with one person (or a small group of people) on a regular basis. RootsMagic makes it easy to bookmark and return to a person.

If you want to add the person to the Bookmark list, click the plus button in the header panel.

Later, when you want to return to a bookmarked person, highlight the person in the Bookmark list, and click the right

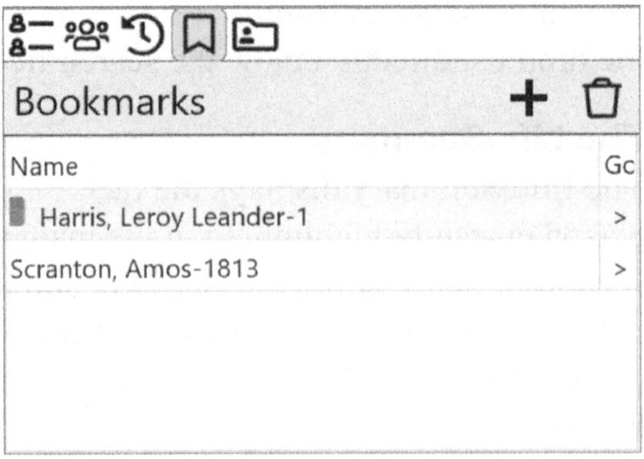

arrow next to their name. You can also remove a bookmarked person by clicking the trash can icon.

## The History Panel

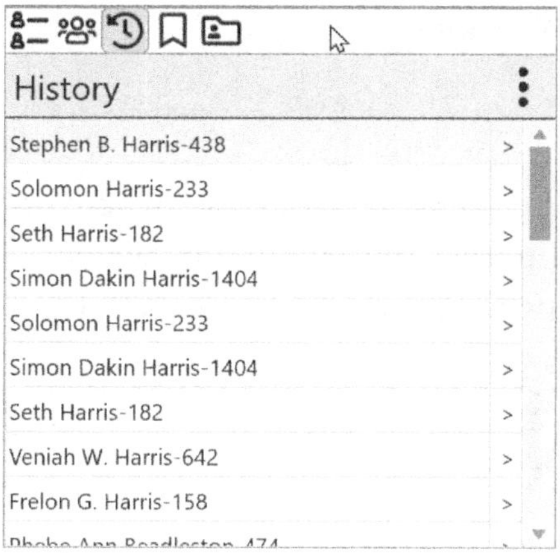


As you move through your database, RootsMagic keeps a list of the people you have visited during that session. That list is displayed in the History panel of the side list. You can click on any name in that history list to immediately jump to that person on the main screen.

## The Groups Panel

RootsMagic makes it possible to select a group of people in your database and give each of those groups a name. For example, you can select everyone born in California and call that group "Born in California". You can then select that group by name to use in reports, exporting, etc.

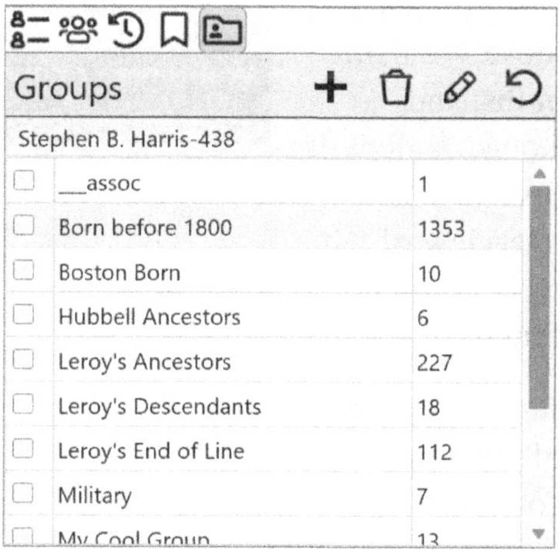


The groups panel provides a quick way to add or remove people from groups. The panel displays a list of all groups you have created. As you move between people in the People views, RootsMagic will show you which groups the selected person is in by displaying checkmarks in front of those groups. You can simply check or uncheck any group on the Groups panel to add or remove the person from that group.

To quickly create a new group, click the + button above the list and enter a name for the new group. If you want to delete a group, highlight the group and click the trash can button. If you want to edit a group, click the edit (pencil) button. More details on this are on page 100 in the chapter "Editing People".

## WEBHINTS

You know there are records out there for your family, but where do you start looking for them? WebHints are tiny light bulbs which will appear next to a person in the pedigree or family views to let you know that there may be records for your person on either FamilySearch, Ancestry, MyHeritage or FindMyPast. RootsMagic searches for these records in the background, and displays the WebHint bulb as it finds them.

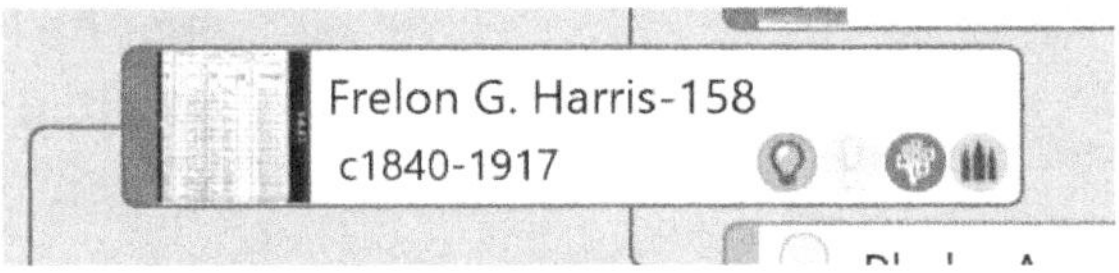


A yellow bulb means there are records you haven't yet checked to confirm or reject, while a blue light bulb means there are records that you have confirmed are related to your person.

Click on one of those WebHint bulbs, and RootsMagic will give you an overview of the records it has found for you.

Just click on any of the hint counts and RootsMagic will display more details about the hints. Many of these hints will even have scanned images of the actual document.

You can choose which types of WebHints you want from the Settings > WebHints page. These options can vary depending on the record provider. MyHeritage lets you adjust the confidence level and whether to use their Record Matches, Smart Matches, or both.

FamilySearch requires you to be logged in to see hints, so you'll need to enter your FamilySearch user name and password on the Settings > WebHints page so that RootsMagic can log in for you to retrieve any hints.

Ancestry WebHints are generated for Ancestry trees, so your RootsMagic file must be connected to an Ancestry tree before you can see any hints. The chapter Ancestry TreeShare describes this in more detail.

## Problem Alerts

When Problem Alerts are turned on, RootsMagic will display a warning sign (a red circle with an exclamation mark) next to any person who has a potential problem in their data. These problem alerts will be visible in both the Pedigree and the Family views.

You can hover your mouse over the alert to see a count of the problems. Just click on the problem count and RootsMagic will display the list of problems for the person. The problem alerts can also be seen in the information section of the right side panel of the People page.

## People Menu

The menu on the People page has a number of tools specific to working with people. The Edit and Tools menus contain commands described in the chapter Building the Family Tree (page 71). The Lists menu lets you access lists described in their own sections in this book (fact types, association types, and AI prompts).

## AI PROMPT BUILDER

The AI Prompt Builder lets you create and save customized prompts that can be used with AI engines. It doesn't interface directly with any specific AI, so you are free to use any AI you choose (or none).

An AI prompt is simply a set of instructions or requests that you provide to an AI, which then generates a response for you. RootsMagic helps you build prompts that can include details about the person you currently have selected in your file, so the AI has context for its response.

### Opening the Prompt List

When you open the AI Prompt Builder, you will see a list of all the prompts you have created. Each prompt in the list can be reused, edited, or duplicated, making it easy to build a library of prompts for different purposes. You can open the prompt builder from the Lists menu on the People page, or by right clicking a person and selecting AI Prompt Builder from the popup menu.

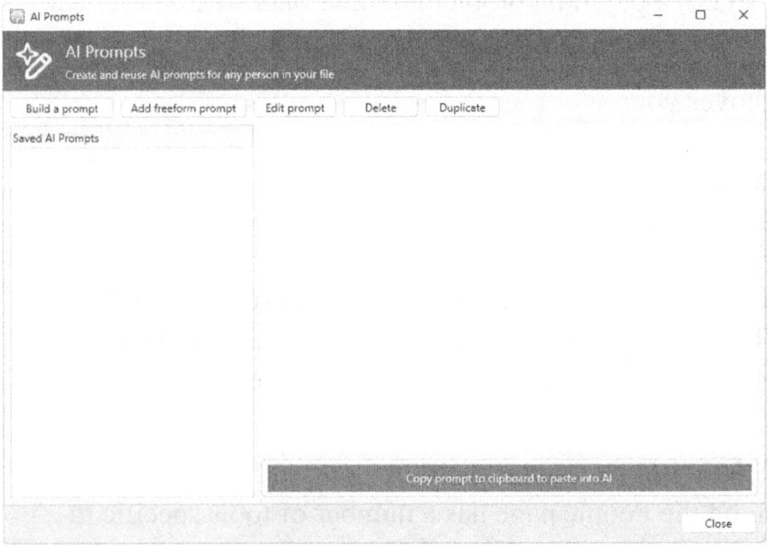


### Creating Prompts

You have two ways to create a prompt, the Prompt Builder, and freeform.

### *Prompt Builder*

Click Build a prompt to let RootsMagic help you design a prompt.

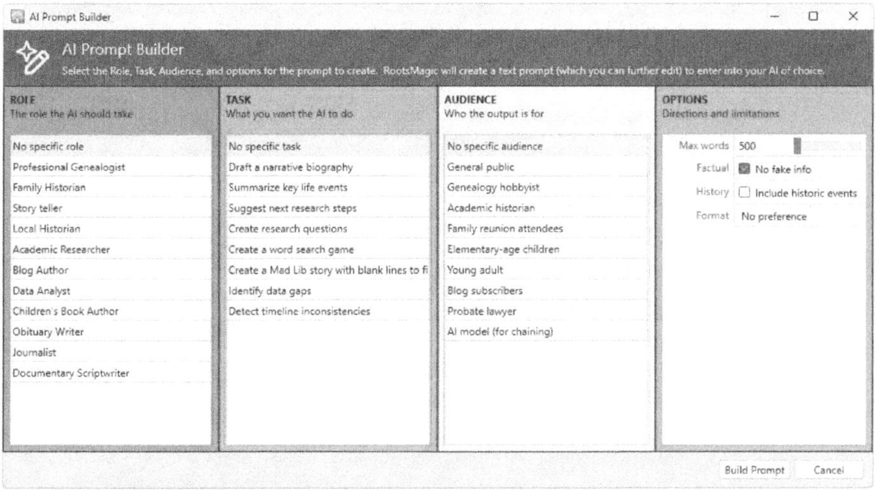


Choose options such as:

- Role: Who the AI should act as (e.g., historian, biographer, researcher).
- Task: What you want the AI to do (e.g., write a narrative, suggest research steps, draft an obituary).
- Audience: Who the AI is writing for (e.g., family members, researchers, children).
- Options: Additional controls, such as maximum length, output format, or whether to include historical context.

RootsMagic will use your selections to generate a ready-to-use prompt, and display that prompt in the prompt editor (which is also used when you want to create a free-form prompt).

### *Add Freeform Prompt*

Click Add freeform prompt to type in your own custom instructions into the AI Prompt Editor.

This is useful if you want complete control over the wording of the prompt. RootsMagic will still allow you to include information about the highlighted person if you wish.

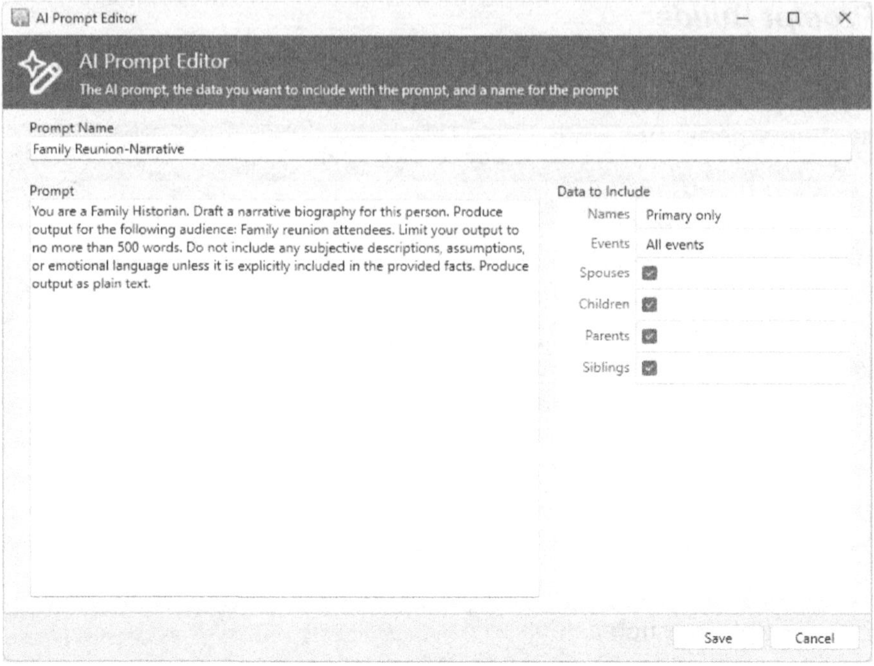


## Managing Prompts

Once you've created prompts, they will be displayed in the prompt list where you can manage them using these buttons:

- Edit Prompt – Make changes to a saved prompt at any time.
- Delete – Permanently remove a prompt you no longer need.
- Duplicate – Create a copy of a prompt that you can modify without changing the original. This is helpful if you want to make variations of a prompt.

## Using Your Prompts

After creating or editing a prompt, you can copy it and paste it into the AI engine of your choice. RootsMagic does not send prompts directly to an AI—this feature is designed to help you easily build accurate, detailed prompts for external use.

## ADDING PEOPLE TO YOUR DATABASE

As with most database programs, RootsMagic allows you to enter new information from the keyboard or by importing data from existing files.

> **Note**
>
> If you are lucky enough to already have data in a GEDCOM, Family Tree Maker, PAF, Legacy, TMG or Family Origins file, then you will want to read the chapter titled "Sharing Data with Others".

To add individuals to your RootsMagic database, click the Add menu.

*The* Add > Individual *command* simply lets you add an unlinked person to your database. The first person you add to a database must be added this way, since there is nobody to add parents, spouses, or children to yet.

*The* Add > Parents *command* adds parents to the person who is highlighted on the main screen. You can add more than one set of parents to each person.

*The* Add > Spouse *command* adds a spouse (or unmarried partner) to the person who is highlighted on the main screen. You can add multiple spouses to each person.

*The* Add > Child *command* adds a child to the person who is highlighted on the main screen. When adding children to a family, you may want to switch to the Family View to get a clearer picture of the family unit.

As you add a person to your database, RootsMagic will automatically link the person and add their name to the main views.

> **Note**
>
> The RootsMagic "Add" commands are consistent in that they **always** add to the highlighted person. For example, if you highlight a child in the Family View and do **Add > Child**, the child will be added to the highlighted person, and **not** as a child in the displayed family.

## Adding an Unlinked Individual

To add an unlinked individual, click Add on the People page menu and then select Individual. You can also just press Ctrl+Shift+I on the keyboard as a shortcut. This will bring up a screen where you can add the basic information for the person.

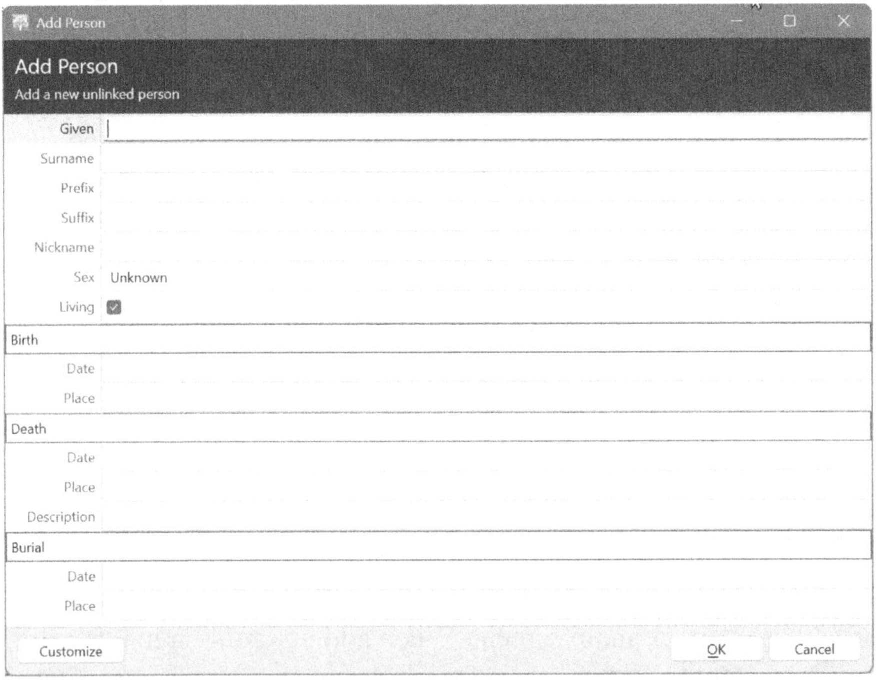


Simply fill in the blanks, using the Tab or Enter key to move on to the next field. If you don't know some of the information, just leave the field empty. If you make a mistake, you can move back to the previous field by pressing Shift+Tab or by clicking the mouse on the field you want to move to.

Enter the given names (first, middle, etc) in the Given name(s) field. Separate each name with a space, like: John Michael.

The Surname field is where you will enter the last name. If you are entering a female, you should enter their maiden (birth) name here.

Enter the person's sex in the Sex field by typing M or F as appropriate. RootsMagic also supports Unknown as an option.

You can also enter any prefix that should come before the name (like “Dr.”), any suffix that would come after your name (like “Jr.”), and any nickname you are known by (we won’t even go there).

You can also enter the birth date and birthplace. Enter the date in just about any format you want, and RootsMagic will convert it to the format you selected when you created the database. When you enter the birthplace, enter it from specific to general with a comma to separate each part of the place, like this:

Albuquerque, Bernalillo, New Mexico, United States

The death and burial fields work exactly the same way as the birth fields.

Although the Add Person screen only includes birth, death, and burial by default, you can click the Customize button to have RootsMagic include other fields as well.

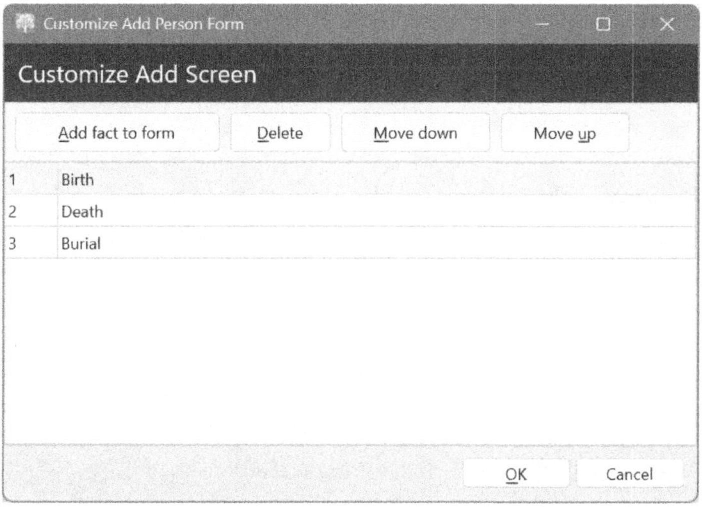

You can add other fact types to the Add Person screen, and rearrange the order those facts appear on the form. Select the fact types you want then click OK to return to the Add Person form. Any changes made will affect the Add Person screen from that point on (until you customize them again).

When you are ready to add the person, click the OK button. If RootsMagic thinks you may have already entered this person, it will display the following dialog, where you can continue adding the person, cancel, or link to the existing copy of the person (in cases where you are adding a spouse, parents, or child).

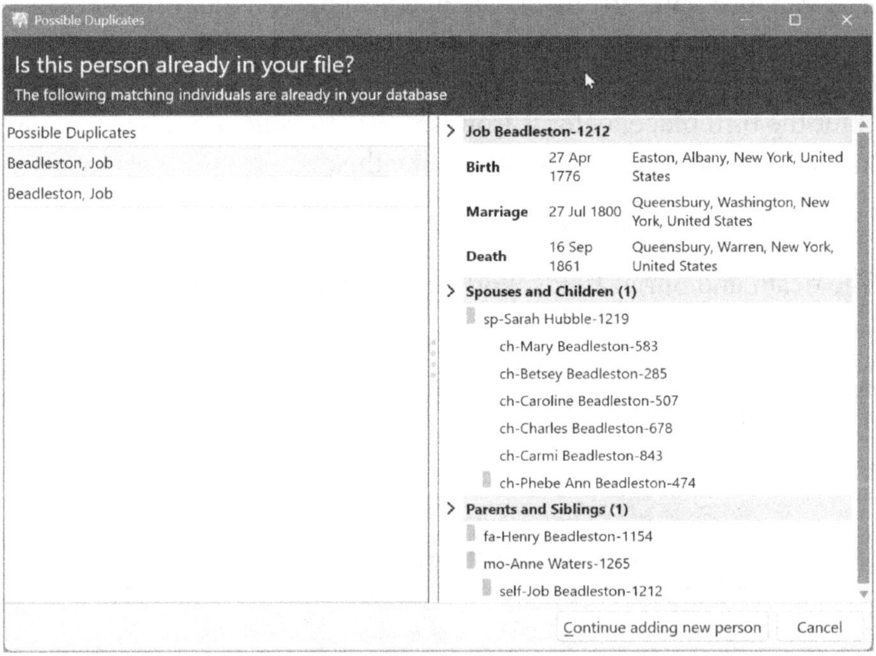


RootsMagic will then bring up the data entry screen for the new person, with the name, sex and birth, death and burial information filled out (if you entered them).

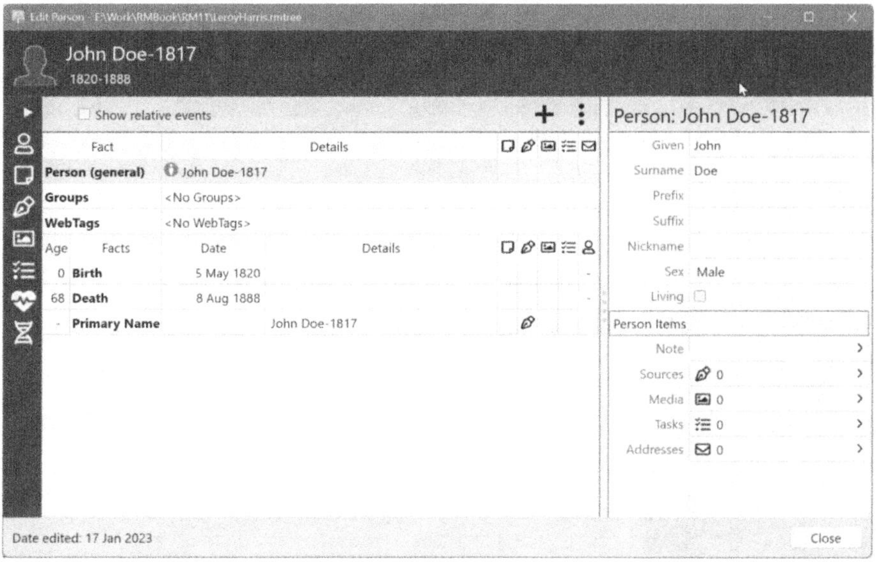


From this screen you can edit existing information, add other facts (like graduation, occupation, etc.), notes, sources (documentation), tasks, media, and a current address. Add as many items as you want, and if you forget anything, you can always come back later to add or change the information. This edit screen is described in more detail in the next chapter titled "Editing People" (page 97). When you are satisfied with your entries, click Close to finish adding the unlinked individual.

## Adding Parents, Spouses, and Children

One of the nice things about RootsMagic is that when you add a person to your database, it links the people together at the same time.

*To add parents to someone in your database*, highlight the name of the person on the main screen (by clicking your mouse on it), then press Ctrl+Shift+P on the keyboard, or select Add > Parents from the menu.

The following dialog box will appear to let you select how you want to add the father.

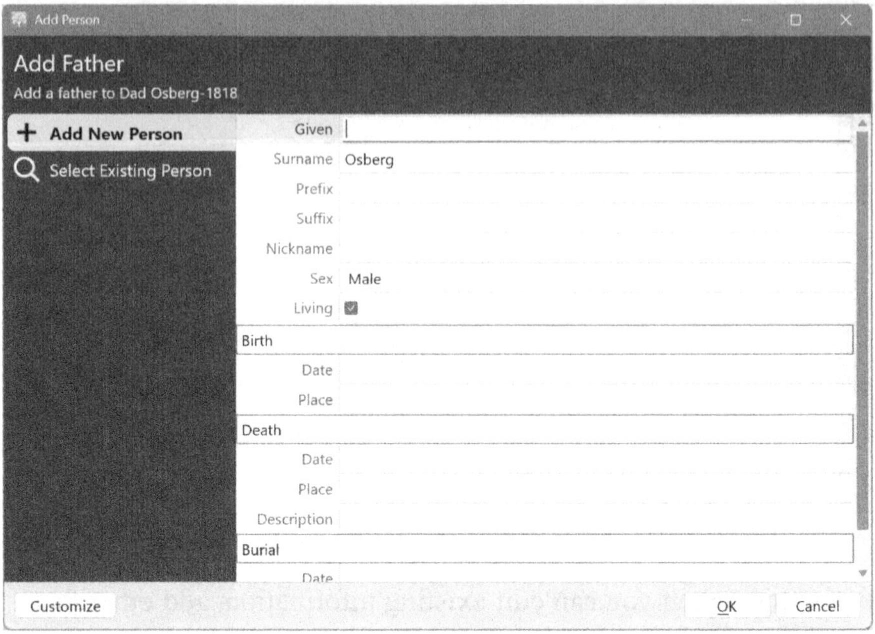


By default you add the father exactly the same way to add an unlinked individual. If the father has previously been entered into the file, you can click Select Existing Person on the side menu of the Add form and select the father from the list of people in the file.

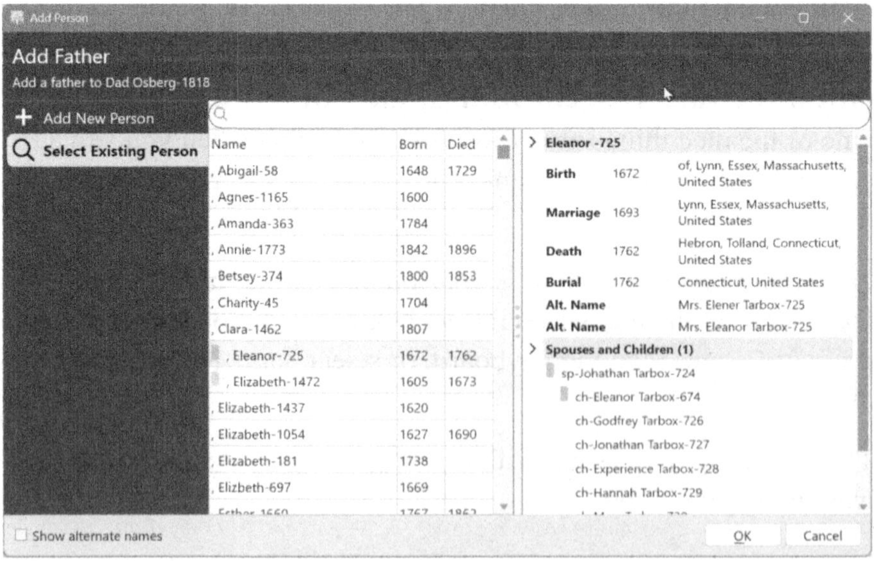

After you have added (or selected) the father, you will go through the exact same steps to add the mother. Once you have entered the parents, RootsMagic will ask if you want to add a marriage event for them.

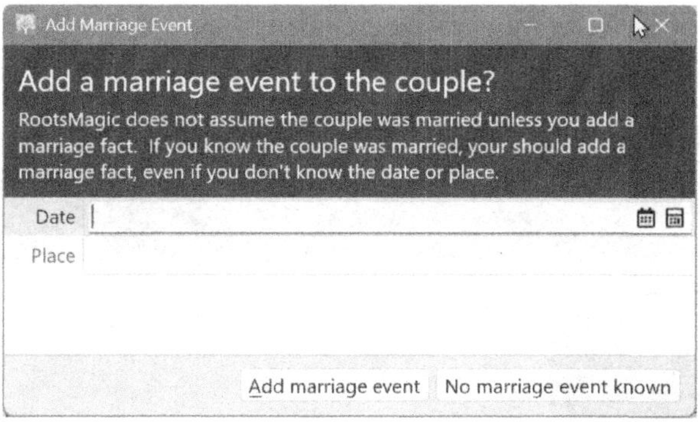


If the parents were married, select Add marriage event (even if you don't know the date, place, or anything else about the marriage). RootsMagic will never assume a couple is married unless you add a marriage event. If you don't add the marriage event here, you can always add it later.

You can add additional sets of parents to a person by repeating these steps. This allows you to track natural, adopted, foster, or any other types of relationships.

*To add a spouse (or unmarried partner) to someone in your database*, highlight the person you want to add the spouse to (by clicking your mouse on the person's name in the tree), then press Ctrl+Shift+S on the keyboard, or select Add > Spouse from the menu.

Adding a spouse is exactly the same as adding parents. You will get to choose between adding a new person or selecting an existing person. You will also be asked if you want to add a marriage event for this couple. If you want to add multiple spouses to a person, just repeat these steps for each spouse.

When you encounter a situation where a couple has children but are not married, you will still use the Add > Spouse command but just won't add a marriage event.

*To add a child to someone in your database*, highlight either the father or the mother, then press Ctrl+Shift+C on the keyboard, or select Add > Child from the menu.

Once again, you will get the option to add a new person, or select an existing person. This time the dialog will look a little bit different.

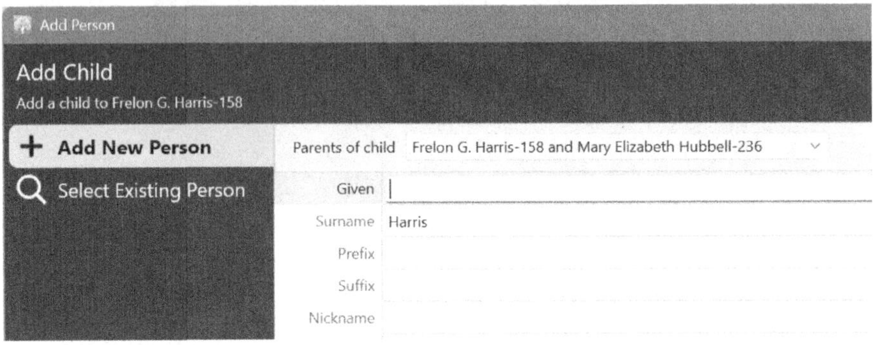


Since the person may have more than one spouse, the add child dialog will also ask which family to add the child to, and will also provide an option to add the child to the person and a new spouse. Choose which family to add the child to and then add the new child or select an existing child.

When you finish adding a child, RootsMagic will bring up a list of the children in the family, and will ask you to arrange them in the proper birth order. Just use your mouse to drag and drop the children into the proper order, then click the OK button.

This child order is used when RootsMagic prints family group sheets, books, and other printouts where the children in a family are included.

## Deleting People and Families

If you ever add someone to your database that you really didn't mean to, RootsMagic provides two commands to help you remove them.

*To delete a person*, highlight the person's name on the main screen, then select Edit > Delete > Person from the menu. RootsMagic will ask if you want to delete the person.

When you delete a person, RootsMagic will unlink the person from all families and will remove the person's record, including facts, notes, source citations, multimedia links, and tasks.

*To delete a family*, highlight either the father or the mother on the main screen, then select Edit > Delete > Family from the menu.

If you select Delete, RootsMagic will delete both parents and each child from the database.

## Unlinking People from Each Other

There will come a time when you will link a person into your family the wrong way. It is not uncommon to accidentally link a person as his own grandfather.

*Unlinking a person from their spouse* unlinks them as a parent in the currently displayed family. Highlight the person you want to unlink, making sure that the spouse you want to unlink from is also displayed on the screen. Then select Edit > Unlink > Unlink from Spouse from the menu. Only the link to the currently displayed spouse and children will be broken. All other links will remain intact, including links to parents and other spouses.

*Unlinking a person from their parents* unlinks them as a child in the currently displayed family. Highlight the person you want to unlink, making sure that the parents you want to unlink from are also displayed on the screen. Then select Edit > Unlink > Unlink from Parents from the menu . Only the link to the currently displayed parents will be broken. All other links will remain intact, including links to spouses and other sets of parents (if any).

*Unlink the family members from each other.* Highlight either parent, then select Edit > Unlink > Unlink family members from the menu. No other links will be broken, and the people will not be removed from the database. For example, the parents will still be linked to their parents and other spouses, and children will still be linked to their spouses and children. RootsMagic will also delete any marriage facts or notes associated with the family.

> **☺ Tip**
>
> If you ever encounter a situation in your database where a person has an "Unknown" spouse that you can't seem to get rid of, bring up the family with the unknown spouse in the Family View on the main screen, highlight the parent that isn't "Unknown" and do the Unlink Family command. RootsMagic will remove the "Unknown" spouse.

## Swapping Husbands and Wives

This isn't what it sounds like. There are times when you may enter a husband and wife backwards. This may be a situation where you couldn't tell the sex based on the name (Kim and Terry Smith), or it may just be accidental. RootsMagic has a command which will let you switch the husband and the wife in a family without having to unlink them first. Just highlight either the husband or wife, select Edit > Swap father and mother from the menu.

## Rearranging Children

To rearrange the children in the family, highlight either parent, select Edit > Rearrange > Rearrange Children from the menu.

The children in the list can be rearranged by clicking your mouse on the first column in front of a child's name, and while holding the mouse button down, dragging the child's name into the proper position. You can also rearrange a person by highlighting the person, then clicking the Move up or Move down buttons. Repeat this for each child that needs to be rearranged, and then click the OK button to close the child list.

You can also click the Sort by birth date button to have RootsMagic automatically rearrange the children by their birth date.

## Rearranging Spouses

To rearrange a person's spouses, highlight the person, select Edit > Rearrange > Rearrange spouses from the menu. A list of spouses similar to the list of children in the previous section will appear, and you can rearrange them in the same manner.

## Merging Duplicate Records

Sometime you may find that you have the same person entered more than once in the same database. This is especially common after importing a GEDCOM file into an existing database.

RootsMagic helps you clean up these duplicate records by providing a "merge" capability. Merging lets you combine two records for a person into a single record. RootsMagic allows you to manually merge duplicate records (one at a time), or it can search for duplicates for you. In addition, it also provides a number of different automatic merge options.

> **Warning**
>
> You should always make a backup before a session of merging, so that if you accidentally merge the wrong records, you can restore your database from a backup.

## Manual Merge

*To merge duplicate records one at a time*, highlight one of the duplicate records on the main screen, then select Tools > Merge > Manual merge from the menu, or click the right mouse button and choose Manual merge from the popup menu. RootsMagic will open the manual merge dialog.

Before you can merge records, you must select the records you want to merge. The merge screen will display the two records side by side, including names, sex, facts, and all immediate family members. The person who was highlighted on the main screen will already be selected on the left side of the dialog (the "primary" record).

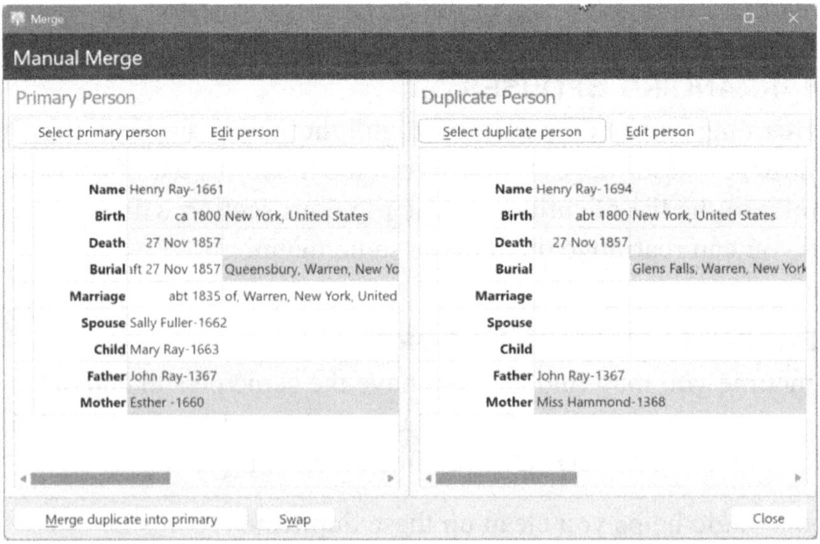

Click the Select duplicate person button and RootsMagic will bring up the search screen for you to select the duplicate record. Select the person, and his or her data will be displayed on the right half of the merge screen.

> ☺ **Tip**
>
> RootsMagic will use color to help you with your decision. Think of the colors like a stop light; green means the two pieces of data match, yellow means they "kind of" match, and red means they don't match.

If you want to switch the position of the two records, simply click the Swap button before performing the merge.

When you are sure you want to merge the two records together, click the Merge duplicate into primary button. RootsMagic will copy all of the information (including family links, facts, notes, and sources) from the record on the right to the record on the left. If both records contain facts that are identical, RootsMagic will not duplicate the fact in the resulting merged person. RootsMagic will then delete the record on the right.

### Duplicate Search and Merge

Although the manual merge is handy at times, it can also be tedious to search for the duplicate records one at a time.

RootsMagic can do a "duplicate search", which means it analyzes your database, and tries to find records that it thinks might be duplicates. It compares the names of the individuals in your database and finds individuals with closely matching names (the names don't have to be an exact match). These potential matches are then checked to make sure they are the same sex, and to check other information that you choose.

*To do a duplicate search and merge*, click the Tools menu on the People page and choose Merge > Merge duplicates.

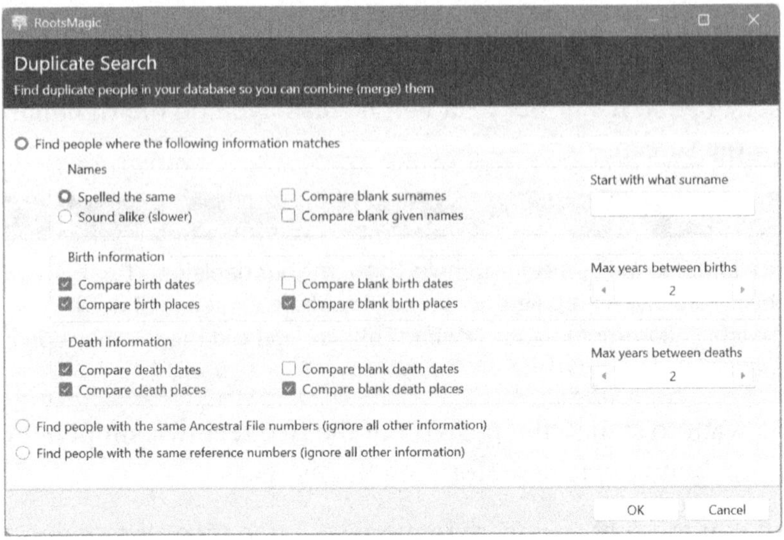


RootsMagic offers three different kinds of duplicate searches.

*Find people where the following information matches* lets you set options to have RootsMagic compare people using.

- **Names:** lets you tell RootsMagic how people's names must match to be considered duplicates. You can specify whether matching names have to match exactly, or if they just need to sound alike. You can also choose whether blank names (both given and surnames) will be considered as matches with non blank names. Checking these boxes often leads to many false duplicates.
- **Start with what surname:** lets you tell RootsMagic where in the database to start the duplicate search. If you leave this blank, then RootsMagic will search the entire database for duplicates. If you enter "D", then RootsMagic will start with surnames beginning with the letter "D". If you enter "Jones", then RootsMagic will start with people with the last name "Jones".
- **Birth information:** tells RootsMagic whether to compare birth information of people when checking for duplicates. You can choose to compare birth dates and / or birth places. You can also enter a maximum number of years between birth dates. If you set this value to 0, RootsMagic will only

consider two individuals duplicates if they were born the exact same year. A value of 5 means that two individual's birth dates can be 5 years apart and still be considered duplicates. The smaller this number, the fewer duplicates RootsMagic will find. You can also tell RootsMagic whether you want to consider individuals without birth dates or birth places as possible duplicates. If you don't check these boxes, RootsMagic will not consider any individuals whose birth date (or place) is blank, even if they match in other ways.

- **Death information:** works the same as the birth options (except with death data of course).

*Find people with the same Ancestral File Numbers* finds individuals with matching Ancestral File numbers. All other criteria are ignored.

*Find people with the same reference numbers* finds individuals with matching Reference numbers (REFN). All other criteria are ignored.

After you have made your choices and clicked the OK button, RootsMagic will search through your database for records that might be duplicates and displays them in a list.

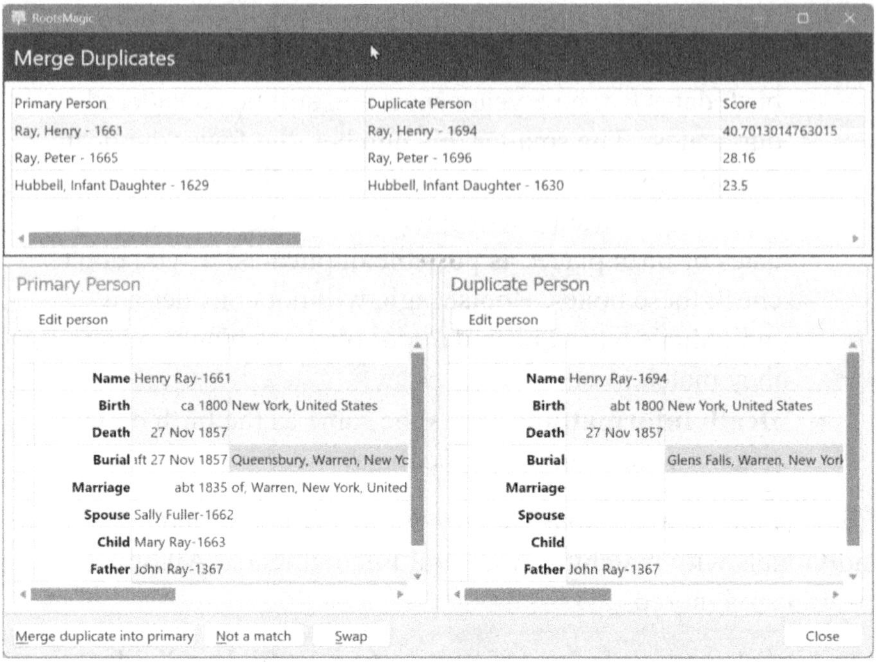


The list is sorted so that the most likely matches are at the top of the list. As you scroll down through the list of possible duplicates, the lower half of the dialog will display the full information about the two highlighted records.

*If the two records on the row are duplicates*, click the Merge duplicate into primary button and RootsMagic will merge the two records.

*If the two records on the row are NOT matches*, you can click the Not a match button and RootsMagic will remove the pair from the merge list, and will not display them as matches in any future duplicate search merges. You can select Not duplicate list from the Tools menu to see a list of all pairs you have marked as not duplicates, and you can remove pairs from that list.

RootsMagic also provides buttons on the merge list to edit both the primary and duplicate records.

> ☺ **Tip**
>
> When you merge duplicate records, you may find that the resulting record has two spouses, which happen to be the same person. This is because the spouse records are also duplicated. When you merge the duplicate spouse records, this situation will correct itself. *Don't* just delete the extra spouse, or you will end up with two families, one with an "unknown" spouse.

## Automatic Merges

RootsMagic offers several automatic merge options when you select Merge > AutoMerge from the Tools menu. The following dialog box will appear where you can select any or all of the merges offered.

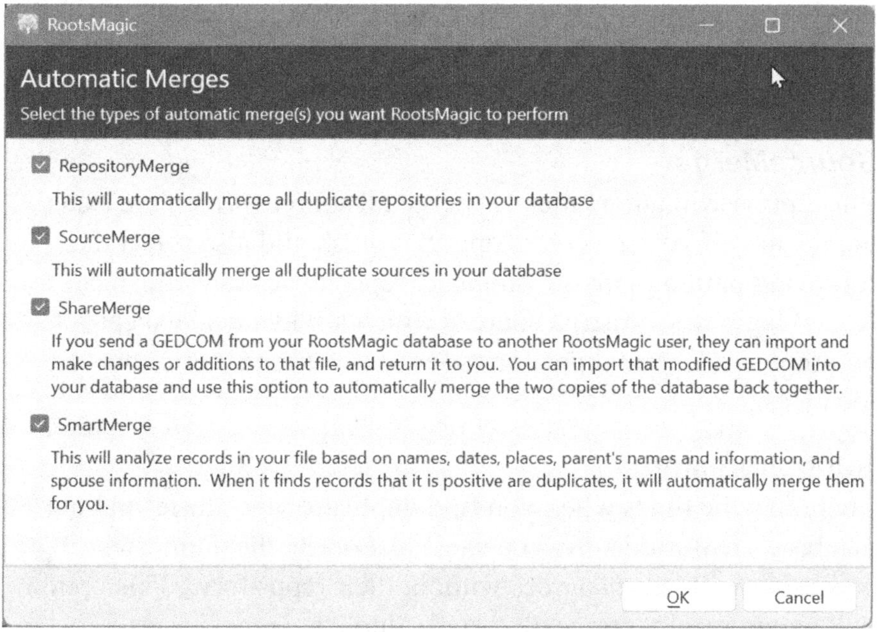


### *SmartMerge*

SmartMerge will search for duplicates, and will assign a "score" to each pair of potential matching records based on: names, birth, christening, death, and burial, parent data, and marriage data. If the matching records "score" high enough, SmartMerge will automatically merge the records for you. Any conflicting data in any of the above fields will disqualify the records from being SmartMerged.

This is very useful as a first pass in doing a merge, then you can run the duplicate search and merge to pick up the duplicate records that automatic SmartMerge missed.

SmartMerge may reject records that appear to be exact duplicates, but this is usually because there is not enough information for SmartMerge to base its score on. In these cases, SmartMerge errs on the side of safety.

#### *ShareMerge*

This is one of the most useful merge options available if you intend to share data with family members who are also using RootsMagic. This option is explained in more detail in the following section "Collaborating With Family Members".

#### *SourceMerge*

This option will automatically merge all sources which are exact duplicates. If you select this option, you should also select the following option to merge duplicate repositories as well, since RootsMagic won't merge sources which are identical except for pointing to different repositories (even if the repositories are identical).

#### *RepositoryMerge*

There may be times when you find duplicate repositories in your database. Unfortunately, you can't just delete the duplicates because it will leave sources without their repository. This option will automatically merge all exactly duplicate repositories.

### Collaborating With Family Members

One of the biggest problems facing families doing genealogy, is how to share their data back and forth without having to resort to long merge sessions.

Even when multiple family members start with the same original database, they may each enter different people, or make modifications to the same person. Then when you try to consolidate that information, you must either sit through a long merge session, or evaluate each database, picking and choosing which data is different and which is the same. RootsMagic offers several features that greatly simplify this process.

> **Warning**
>
> Both users need to be using RootsMagic for this feature to work. If one user is using a different program, it may throw away the unique ID number required for this feature.

**Globally Unique ID:** Any time you create a new person in RootsMagic, that person will be assigned a "hidden" ID number, which is unique to that person. This number is unique to that person… no other person (in any database) will ever receive that same unique ID number. If you export your database to a GEDCOM file, that unique ID number will travel with that person. And when you import that GEDCOM file into a RootsMagic database, that unique ID will come in with the person.

*So what does this mean to me?* Let's say you have a "master" database that you would like to share with family members. Simply create a GEDCOM file of your data and send it to them. When they import that GEDCOM file into their copy of RootsMagic, each person will have the same "unique ID" as the corresponding person in your master database.

You can now add, edit, or make other changes to people in your database, and they can do the same in their database. It is not necessary to keep the two databases "in sync".

I can already hear you asking *"how will we ever get those two databases combined into a single complete database"?*

Simple, just have your family member send you a GEDCOM file of their database, and import it into your database (remember… only do this if you are *both* using RootsMagic). At this point you will have a large number of duplicates, some of which are identical, and others that may differ a little bit. But RootsMagic knows which people are *really* the same, since their "unique ID" traveled with them.

So… select Merge > AutoMerge from the Tools menu, and leave all four options selected. RootsMagic will automatically merge the duplicate repositories and sources that exist. Then it will automatically merge everybody in the database who has the same unique ID. If there is conflicting information in the two people's data, RootsMagic will keep both copies of that data. For example, if the birth date of a person was changed in one of the databases, RootsMagic will keep both birth facts for the person.

## Setting the Living Flag

When you import a GEDCOM file you may often have individuals with no birth or death dates, or other means for RootsMagic to know how to apply the "Living" flag for the person.

The "Set Living" function lets you set (or clear) the living flag for any group of people in your database. Select Set living from the Tools menu and RootsMagic will bring up a dialog asking if you want to set the living flag to true or false for a group of people. Choose the desired setting and click OK. RootsMagic will then bring up the selection screen for you to choose the individuals whose living flag you want to change.

## Setting Relationships to a Person

RootsMagic can display relationships of the highlighted person in the information view in the side panel. You can choose which person to base these relationships on. Select Set relationships from the Tools menu and RootsMagic will bring up the following dialog.

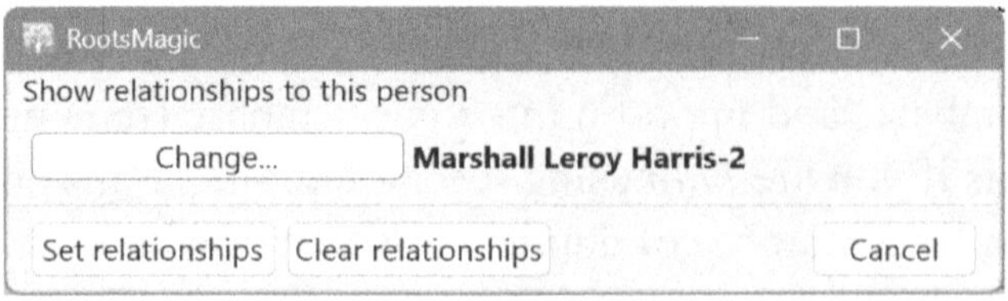

RootsMagic will default to the currently highlighted person, but you can click Change to select a different person. Click Set relationships to set the current relationships to that person. If you later add more related people you may need to re-run this command.

From that point on (until you change it), RootsMagic will display the relationship of the highlighted person on the main screen to that person. For example, if you set relationships for yourself, then when your 3rd great grandfather is highlighted, the information view will display "third great grandfather".

## Color Coding People

Have you ever wanted to be able to quickly tell whether a person in your database is part of a particular group? RootsMagic makes this easy by letting you color code any group of people. Select Color coding from the Tools menu and RootsMagic will bring up the following dialog.

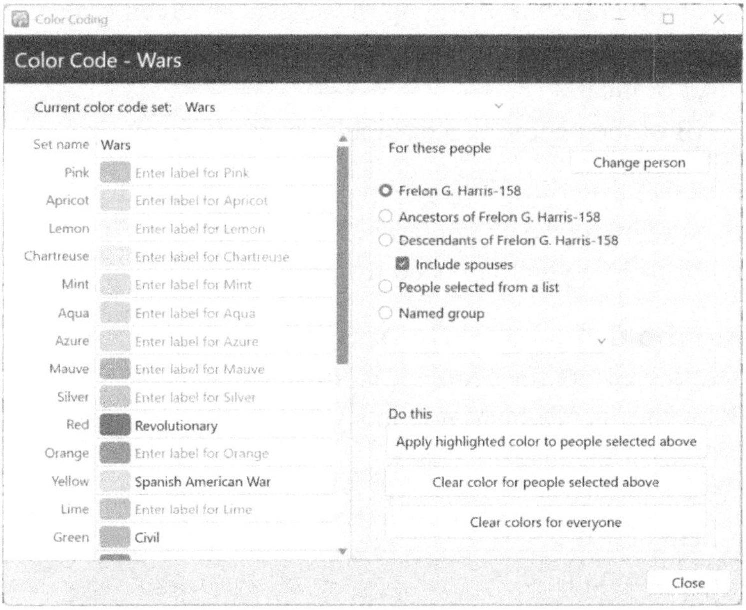

### Setting the Color for People

You can set or clear the display color for any group of people. Click on any color on the left to select that color, then:

- **Apply highlighted color to people selected above:** Lets you set the group of people to the highlighted color.
- **Clear color for people selected above:** Lets you clear the highlighted color for any group of people.
- **Clear colors for everyone:** Lets you clear (reset) the color for the entire database.

You can perform these operations for:

- The current highlighted person on the screen. You can change this person by clicking the Change person button.
- Ancestors of the current person.
- Descendants of the current person. You can also choose whether to include the spouses of descendants.
- People selected from a list. If you choose this option, RootsMagic will bring up the selection screen (page 294) for you to choose the individuals whose color you want to set or clear.
- All of the people in a particular named group.

When you set the color for a group of people, it sets the color for people matching those characteristics at that instant. If you later add or edit people you may need to re-run the color coding.

### Naming the Colors and Color Set

When setting colors for people it is important to remember what each color means. RootsMagic lets you name each color to handle this. Just click on any color on the left and enter a name for the color. For example, let's say you are color coding people based on the war

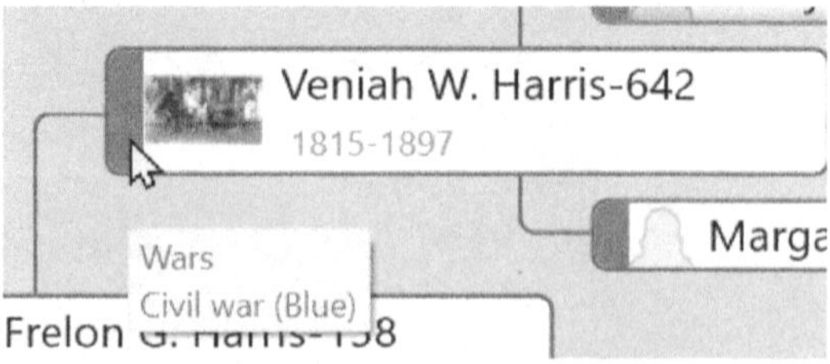


they served in. You might name Red as "Revolutionary war", and Blue as "Civil war". You can also name the color set itself to remind you what the colors represent. In this example you might click on "Set name" and enter "Wars".

When you hover over the color in either the pedigree or family view, RootsMagic will show you the name of the color set, as well as the color.

### Using Multiple Color Sets

You may often find yourself wanting to use color coding for something other than what you are currently using it for. Rather than having to clear the color coding and start over, RootsMagic lets you create up to 10 different color sets.

On the color code form, you can select these sets from the "Current color code set" drop list. When you switch to a different set, you can name that set and the individual colors just like you did with the first set.

Then at any time, you can switch to another color set from the drop list, and when you click Close RootsMagic will switch to using that new color set. So you can have one set for wars, another for family lines, and still use others for temporary uses without disturbing your other color codes.

## THE DATE CALCULATOR AND CALENDAR

*The date calculator* lets you calculate dates and the amount of time between dates. Selecting Date calculator from the Tools > Calculators menu will bring up the date calculator. The date calculator can also be brought up when you are entering dates for facts (like birth, death, etc.).

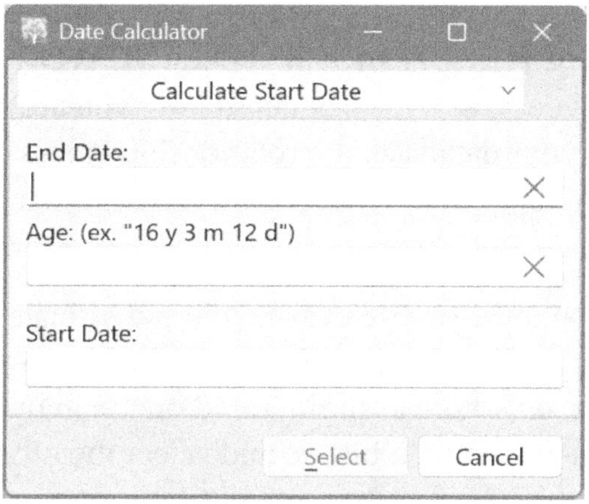


Choose what you want to calculate, then fill out the top 2 fields and

RootsMagic will display the result in the 3rd field.

When you are using the date calculator while entering facts for a person, it contains a button labeled Select which will copy the result into the fact's date field, and will then close the date calculator.

> **☺ Tip**
>
> The date calculator is the perfect tool for determining an approximate birth date from a tombstone inscription like "Died 12 March 1942 at the age of 82 Years, 10 Months, and 2 Days".

*The calendar* (select Calendar from the Tools menu) shows a calendar where you can look up dates to see what day of the week they fell on. You can click the arrows to move back and forth by months or years. The longer you hold the arrow down the faster RootsMagic cycles through the months or years.

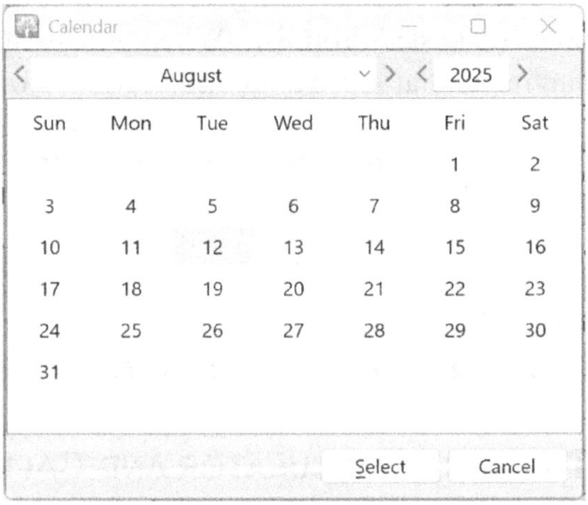


## The Relationship Calculator

If you have ever wondered how you are related to another person in your database, the relationship calculator is the quickest way to find out. Simply select Relationship calculator from the Tools > Calculators menu.

You must first select the two individuals whose relationship you want to know. Person 1 will already contain the name of the person who was highlighted on the main screen. Click on the Select person 2 button and select the other individual. RootsMagic will remember Person 2 until you change the person. Finally, click the Calculate button and RootsMagic will tell you how the two people are related, and who the common ancestors are.

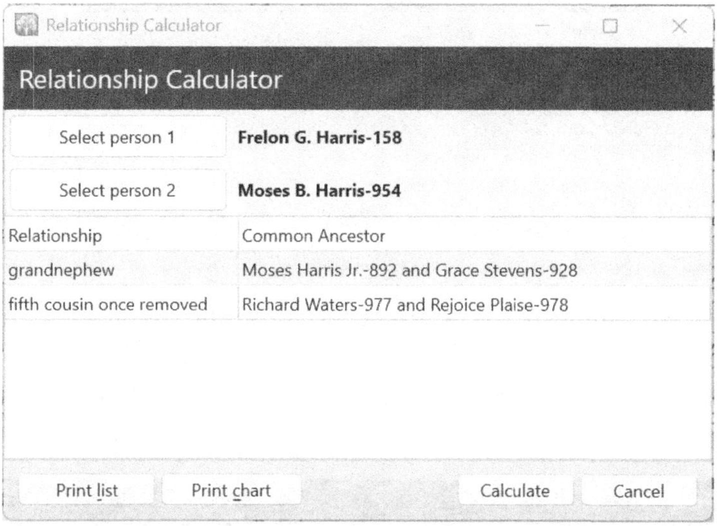


> ☺ **Tip**
>
> You can print the result list, or print a Relationship Chart (described on page 277) for any of the found relationships. RootsMagic also provides a supercharged version of the Relationship Calculator called the Kinship List. The Kinship List will print out every relative of a person and list their relationship to that person.

## The Soundex Calculator

The Soundex calculator simply calculates the Soundex code for any name you type into it.

*To access the Soundex calculator*, select Soundex calculator from the Tools > Calculators menu. There are no buttons to click; it calculates the code as you type it in. You can backspace and type in other names to find their Soundex code as well. When you are done, simply click the Close button.

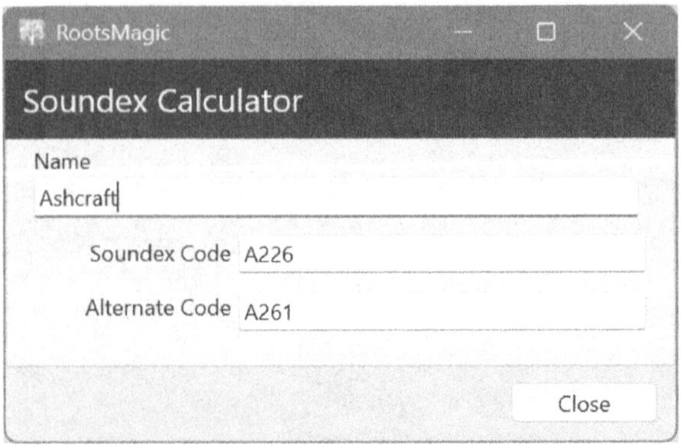


Many census and other types of records use the Soundex method to group similar sounding names together. For example, "Smith" and "Smythe" both have the same Soundex code "S530", so grouping by Soundex would keep all the Smiths and Smythes together.

**Note**

Some genealogical records (most notably census records) use a slightly modified algorithm when calculating the Soundex code. Although only a few names actually end up with different codes, RootsMagic supports both algorithms. If RootsMagic calculates two different Soundex codes, make sure you check under both codes.

# EDITING PEOPLE

The RootsMagic edit screen is the place where you will enter everything you know about a person. To edit a person, simply double click on the person's name on one of the People views. You can also highlight the person on the People page and press the Enter key to bring up the edit screen.

If you want the edit screen to be a little larger, you can resize it by clicking the edge of the edit screen and dragging it.

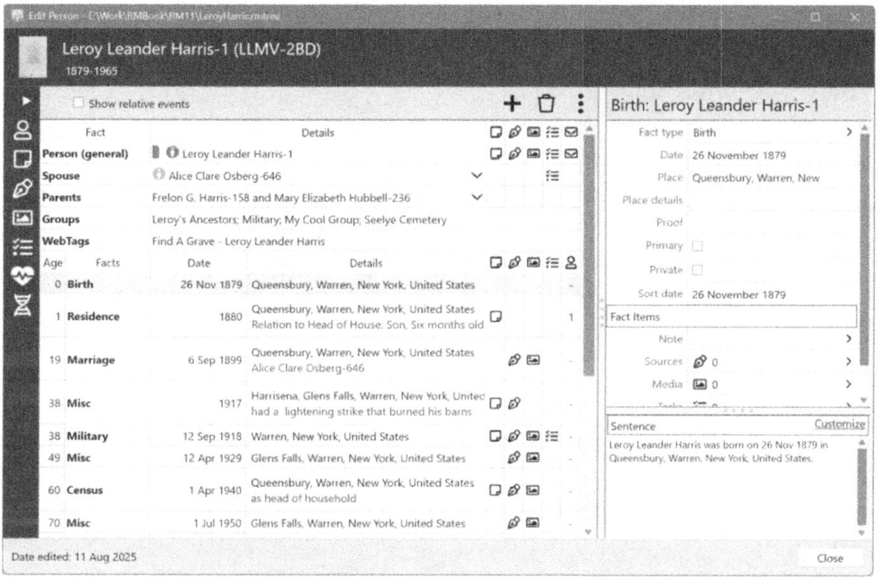


The edit screen is divided into two main sections, with a header at the top and a side menu on the far left. The left half of the screen is a list of all the pieces of information you have for the person. This list can include the person's name, spouses, parents, events, alternate names, events from immediate relatives, and more. The right half of the screen is a live-edit panel. When you select an item in the list on the left, RootsMagic will display an edit panel for that type of information on the right.

## NAMES, TITLES AND SEX

Selecting the "Person" row lets you type in the person's name, titles and sex. When you finish filling in one field, you can move to the next field by pressing the Enter or Tab key. If you make a mistake, you can press Shift+Tab to move back to the previous field. You can also click your mouse on any field to move the cursor there for editing.

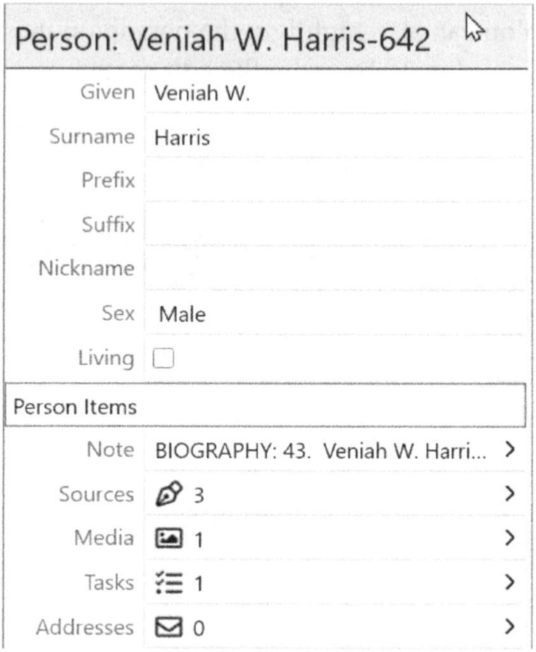


*The Given field* is where you enter the person's given names (first, middle, etc). You should separate each given name with a space, like this: John Michael.

*The Surname field* is where you enter the person's last name. If the person is female, you should enter their maiden (unmarried) name here.

*The Prefix field* provides a place to enter titles that come *before* the person's name, such as *Dr.* John Smith.

*The Suffix field* provides a place to enter titles that come *after* the person's name, such as John Smith *Jr.*

*The Nickname field* provides a place to enter a nickname that the person was (or is) known by.

*The Sex field* is a list that you can select "Male", "Female" or "Unknown" from. You can click your mouse on the list and select the sex, or press the first letter of the sex (M, F, or U).

*The Living checkbox* lets you mark whether the person is still living. This is used if you choose to "privatize" data for living people when creating GEDCOM files or websites. This is useful if you know the person is deceased and you don't have a death date.

## Spouses

RootsMagic will add a row for each spouse you have entered for the person. When you highlight a spouse in the list you will be able to set the label used for the person and spouse. This is mainly just for reports, but you can choose from Father, Husband, Mother, Wife, or Partner. There is also an option "Other", that if selected will let you type in your own label.

You can also optionally choose whether you feel you have proven this relationship with the "Proof" setting. You can choose from:

- Proven – this fact has been proven true (to some criteria)
- Disproven – this fact has been proven false
- Disputed – this fact is disputed in some circles
- Proposed – this is a theory or hypotheses

If you select one of these proof values for a piece of information, the icon will be displayed to the right of the label for that row.

## Parents

There are many different relationships a child can have with their parents, and RootsMagic allows you to set that relationship for each of the child's parents. Highlight the parents row on the edit screen and choose from birth, adopted, step, foster, related, guardian, sealed or unknown.

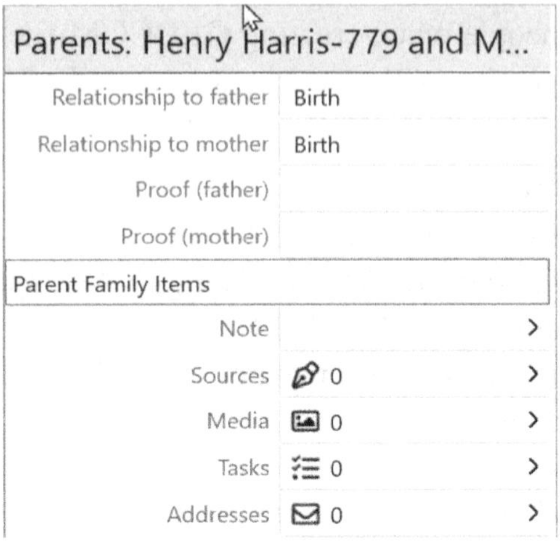


As with the spouse row, you can also select a proof for the relationship to either parent.

## Groups

RootsMagic makes it possible to select a group of people in your database and give each of those groups a name. For example, you can select everyone born in California and call that group "Born in California". You can then select that group by name to use in reports, exporting, etc.

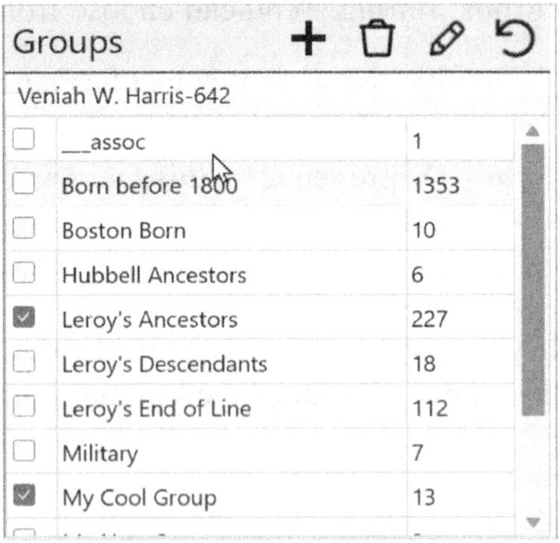


The "Groups" row on the edit person screen displays the groups the current person belongs to. When you highlight the Groups row RootsMagic will display a list of all groups you've created, with checkmarks next to any groups the person is in. Just mark the checkbox for any groups the person should be in (or unmark those they shouldn't).

*To create a new group*, click the + button above the list and RootsMagic will display the Add Group screen.

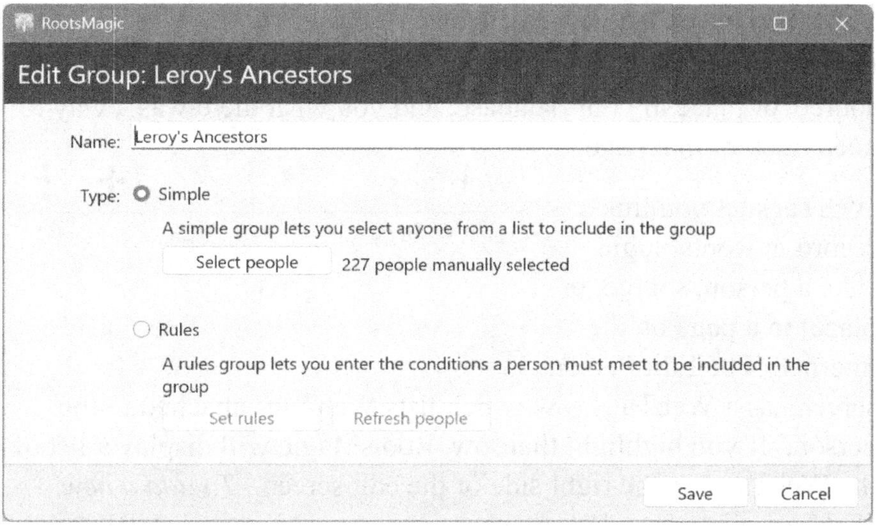


In addition to the name of the group, you can also choose between two types of groups.

- **Simple groups** simply let you select the people in the group from a list. You can click the "Select people" button to bring up a list of everyone in your file that you can select from for the group (described on page 218).
- **Rules groups** let you enter rules to select people (like when doing an Advanced Search on page 203). RootsMagic will mark all the people who match those rules and include them in the group. Only people who match the rules at that moment are included in the group.

*To edit an existing group*, highlight it in the list and click the edit (pencil) button. RootsMagic will display the same screen as when adding, and let you make any changes.

*To delete a group*, highlight it in the list and click the trash can button. You will be asked to confirm that you really want to delete the group.

If you add or edit people who might belong in a group (or who might need to be removed from a group), you can highlight the group in the list and click the refresh button (circular arrow) to update the group without having to re-enter the criteria.

## WebTags – Online Links

Often you will find a web page with information about a person, source, or place in your database, and you wish there was a way to keep track of that page.

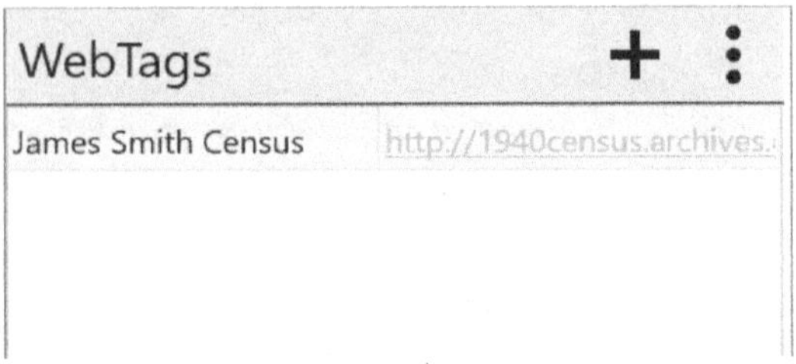


WebTags let you link a record in RootsMagic (like a person, source, or place) to a page on the internet. The Edit Person screen has a WebTags row which lists WebTags attached to the person. If you highlight that row, RootsMagic will display a list of the WebTags on the right side of the edit screen. *To add a new WebTag*, click the + button where you can add a name, URL, and note for the new WebTag.

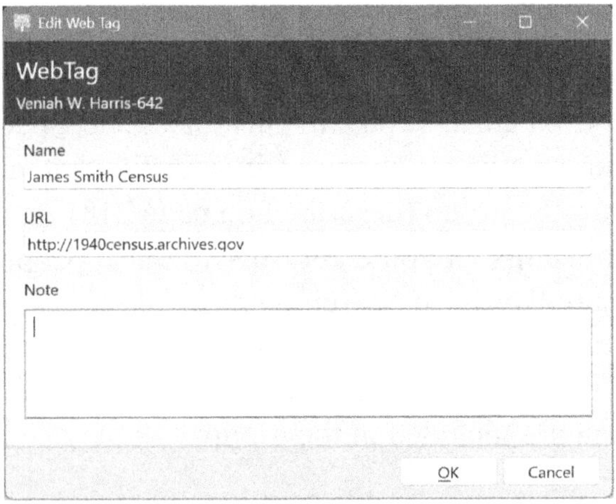


*To visit a WebTag site*, just click the link in the list.

*To edit the WebTags* for a person, click the options (3 dot) menu.

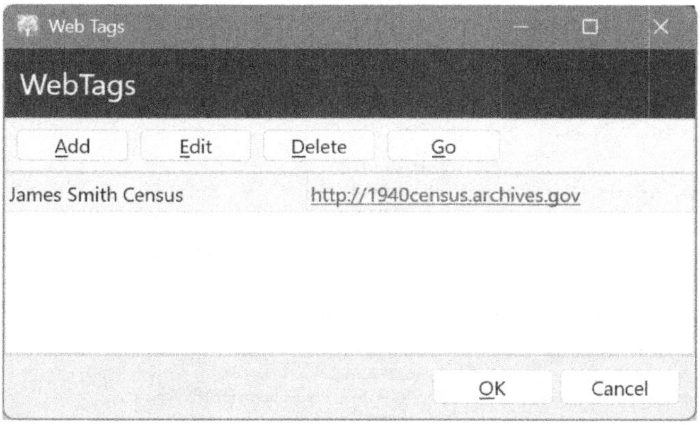


From this list you can also add, edit, delete, or go to a WebTag.

## FACTS AND EVENTS

RootsMagic allows you to enter unlimited facts to each person. A fact can be *an event* like a birth or death, *a phase in the person's life* like an occupation or military service, or *a descriptive item* like an ID number or physical description.

A fact can contain a date (or date period), a place, a description if necessary, a note and unlimited source citations.

You can enter multiple copies of each fact type, so you can, for example, enter all 10 occupations in Uncle Joe's life. By adding all these facts (along with fact notes and fact sources) you are building a complete personal history for each person in your database.

### Adding a Fact to a Person

*To add a fact to an individual*, click the "+" button on the person's edit screen, or press Alt+A as a shortcut key. RootsMagic will display a list of fact types that you can choose from.

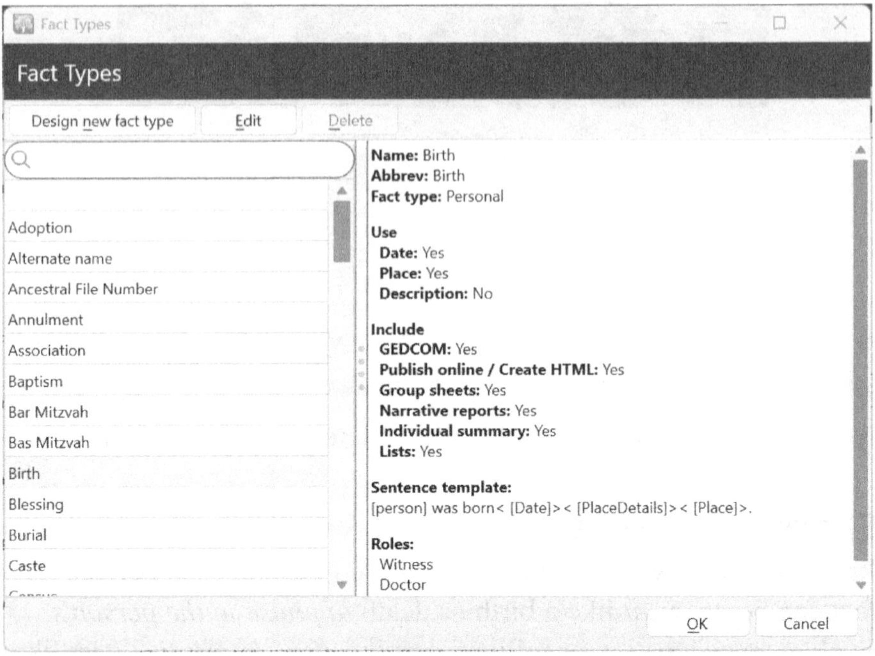


Simply highlight the type of fact you want to add. As with any list in RootsMagic, you can use the arrow keys to highlight the item, or can just begin typing the fact name and RootsMagic will filter the list to any fact types matching the text you type.

> **Note**
>
> If you want to add a fact that isn't in the list, you can create your own fact types. This is discussed in the next chapter titled "Facts and Events".

Once you have highlighted the type of fact you want to add to the person, just click the OK button and RootsMagic will add a blank fact of that type to the person's edit screen where you can enter the details for the new fact. You can enter the date and place for the fact, as well as a note and sources.

Simply fill in the information you know then click the Save button to save the new fact. Don't worry if you don't know some of the information. Just enter as much as you can. You can always come back to make changes or add more information.

If you have “conflicting” information about a fact (for example, two different birth dates), you can enter two different birth facts to the person, and use the “Primary” checkbox to tell RootsMagic which fact is the main one to use.

RootsMagic will show you what a sentence using that data with that fact will look like. You can click the Customize button to change the sentence for that single fact.

*For more information on facts and how they work*, see the next chapter titled "Facts and Events".

### Editing a Person's Facts

To edit a fact for a person, bring up the person's edit screen, click your mouse on the fact you want to edit, then begin editing the information on the right side of the screen. You can change any information or add new information. When you are satisfied with the changes, click the Save button to save the changes.

### Deleting a Person's Facts

To delete a fact from a person, bring up the person's edit screen, click your mouse on the fact you want to delete, then click the Delete (trash can) button. RootsMagic will ask you to confirm that you really want to delete the fact. Click Delete to remove the fact from the person's list or Cancel if you change your mind.

### Showing Relative’s Facts

RootsMagic gives you the option to display the basic (birth, death, marriage) events for immediate family members. Simply click the Show relative events checkbox in the header above the fact list.

### Copying and Moving Facts to Other People

RootsMagic provides the ability to copy or move a fact from one person to another. These commands are under the Options (3 dot) menu on the Edit Person form.

**Copy selected fact:** Select one or more people from the selection screen (page 218) and RootsMagic will copy the fact to each of those people. The fact will remain with the current person and be added to each selected person.

**Move selected fact:** Select a single person from the selection screen, and RootsMagic will be removed from the current person and added to the newly selected person.

## ASSOCIATIONS

Although associations share a number of attributes with facts and events (date, place, notes, etc.), they serve a very different purpose.

It is often helpful to our research to track friends, neighbors and other associates of our own ancestors. An association lets you specify the relationship between two people who aren't necessarily related by family. In addition, associations can also be used to track non-family relationships such as those between an enslaver and enslaved person.

To add an association, click the + toolbar button and select "Association" from the fact type list. RootsMagic will open the Add Association form.

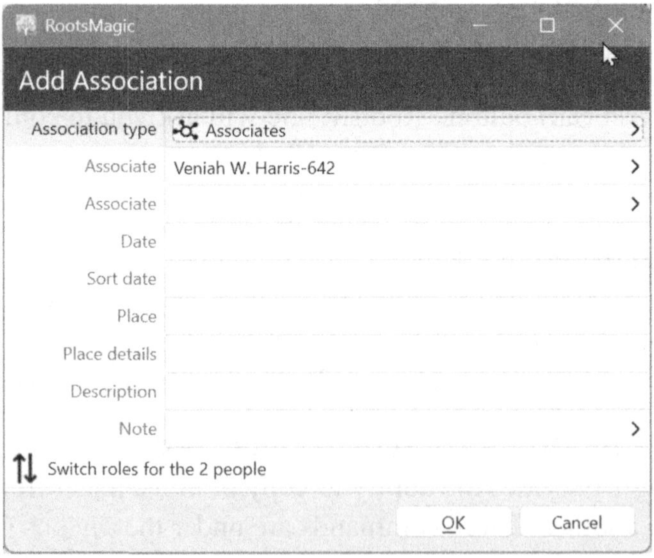


You can enter the type of association, the two people, and other information similar to other facts you might add. Once you save the association, you can edit or delete an association in the fact list in the same manner as any other fact, highlighting the association and editing it in the side panel.

## ALTERNATE NAMES

Many people don't go by the same name their entire life. For these people RootsMagic lets you add "Alternate name" facts. You add them just the same way you add any other fact to a person (by clicking the "Add" button) and selecting "Alternate name".

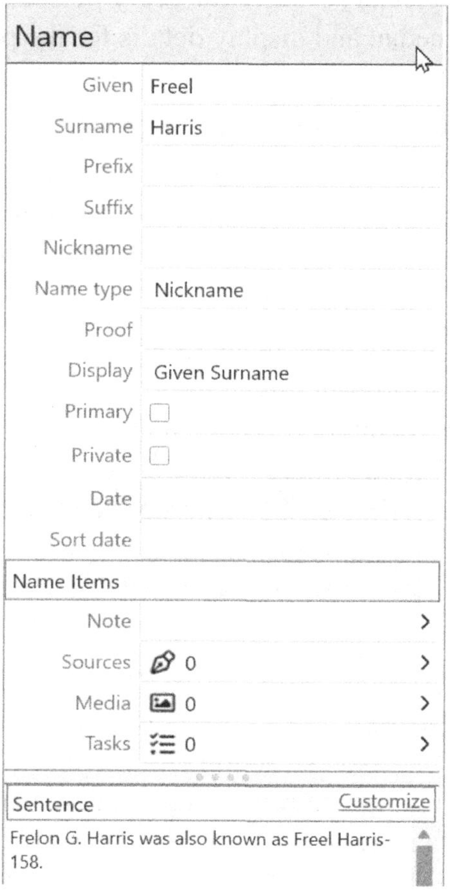


In addition to "Alternate Names", RootsMagic will also display a "Primary Name" row which works exactly the same. This "Primary Name" row is the same name as when editing the main person row, except that it also lets you enter notes, sources, etc. for the primary name (the notes, sources, etc. for the main person row are for the person, not the name).

The live edit panel on the right will display name fields for an alternate name fact. You can even enter a date or date range in case the person only went by that name during a particular period in their life.

You can also select what type of name the alternate name is; AKA (also known as), birth, immigrant, maiden, married, nickname, or other spelling. Just select the type from the list, although you can just leave it blank too if you want.

In some cultures, a person's name is written with the family name (surname) first. If you enter a name like this, just change the "Display" field for the name to "Surname Given" and RootsMagic will display it that way on the screen, reports, and anywhere else it appears.

As a special case, RootsMagic will always include an entry for "Primary Name" for every person. This lets you add citations, media, and display details for the person's primary name as well.

## Additional Information

Most items in the Edit Person list (people, families, facts, associations, etc.) can have additional information associated with it, such as notes, source citations, media, addresses, tasks, or other people the item may be shared with.

Simply click the buttons to add or edit this information. If there is already additional information for a person or fact, a symbol will be displayed in the list on the left.

> ☺ **Tip**
>
> Here's a shortcut for editing these items. Instead of highlighting a fact and clicking the **"Note"** button, simply click on the little box next to the fact in the note column. This also works for editing fact sources.

### Notes

The "Notes" button lets you enter and edit the note for the highlighted row. This is a note that is associated with that person, family, or fact. For details on notes, see the chapter titled "Notes – Telling Your Story".

### Sources

The "Sources" button lets you enter and edit the sources for the highlighted row. These are sources that are associated with that person, family, or fact. For details on sources, see the chapter titled "Sources and Citations".

### Media

The "Media" button in the edit panel shows the media for the selected fact. You can add photos for a person, family, or fact, and attach documents, sound and video clips. Photos attached to a person can be printed in many of RootsMagic's reports and charts. If you would like to see all media attached to a person, click the media item on the left side menu of the Edit Person screen to open the person's Media Album. For more information on the media album, see the chapter titled "Pictures, Sound, and Video".

### Address

The "Address" button lets you enter and edit the current addresses for the highlighted person or family. You only need to enter an address for the head of a household, not for each person in the household. This address is intended only for the "current" address. You can add "Residence" facts to the person if you want to track all the places the person ever lived. These addresses can be printed in the form of an address list or address labels, or can be exported to a mail-merge file that you can import into your word processor.

### Tasks

The "Tasks" button shows the task list for the highlighted person, family, or fact. The task list provides a place to save all those tasks you need to accomplish. For details on tasks, see the chapter titled "Tasks".

## Edit Person Options

The Edit Person screen has several options under the Options (3 dot) menu.

**Delete fact:** same as clicking the trash can icon to delete the currently highlighted fact.

**Copy FamilySearch ID**: If the person has been matched to a person on FamilySearch, this command copies the FamilySearch ID (FSID) to the clipboard.

**Options:** this opens the Options form for Edit Person.

**Copy selected fact:** copies the highlighted fact to another person or persons. The Explorer will open for you to select everyone to copy the fact to.

**Move selected fact:** moves the highlighted fact from this person to another person. You select the person with Explorer.

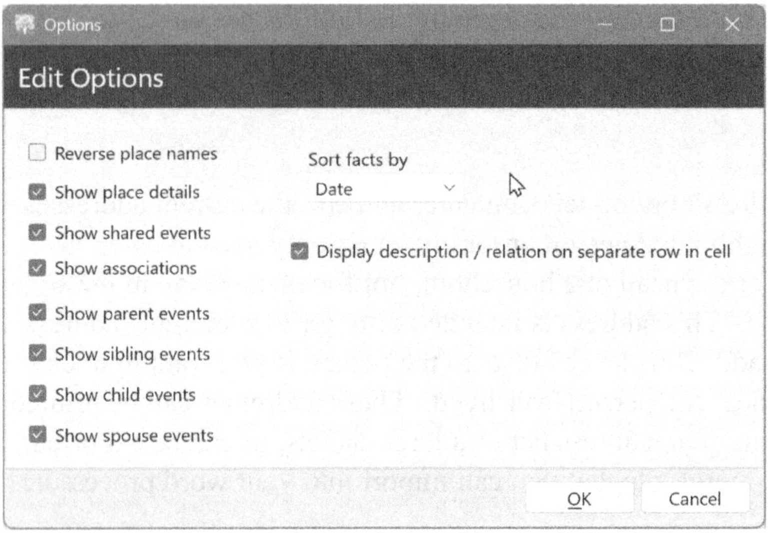


- **Reverse place name:** this lets you display place names in reverse (Country, State, County, City). This is useful to see events grouped geographically.
- **Show place details:** displays place details in the fact list.
- **Show shared events:** displays any shared events (shared by others) in the fact list.
- **Show associations**: displays any associations that have been added for the person.
- **Sort facts by:** select the order to display facts in the list.
- **Display description / relation on separate row in cell:** this displays facts using 2 rows each. This takes more screen space but shows more information.
- **Show parent / sibling / child / spouse events:** this determines which family member event will be displayed when you choose "Show relative events" on the fact list.

## Navigating Other Family Members

Although RootsMagic can open 3 edit person screens at the same time, there may be times you just want to quickly view or edit a family member. Next to each spouse and set of parents is a down arrow that you can click to see a list of all immediate family members in that family. Click on any name in the menu to switch the edit screen to that relative.

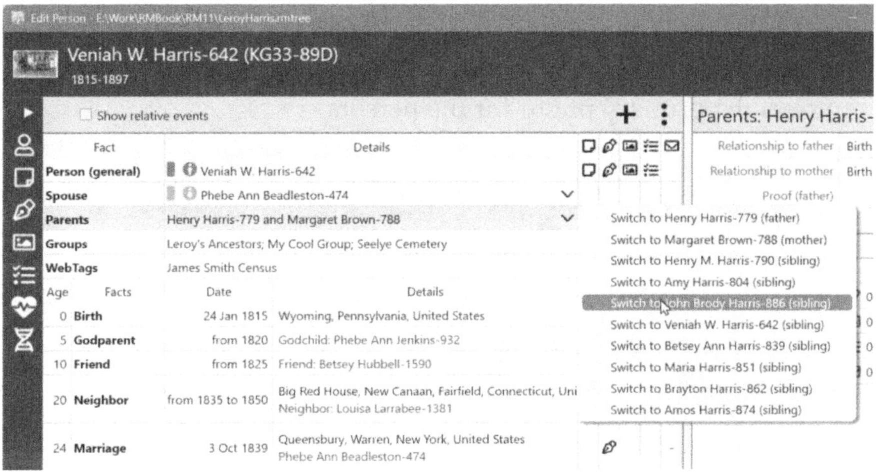


You will then be able to view or edit any information for that relative. Once you are ready to return to the original person, click the left arrow in the header and RootsMagic will return to the original person.

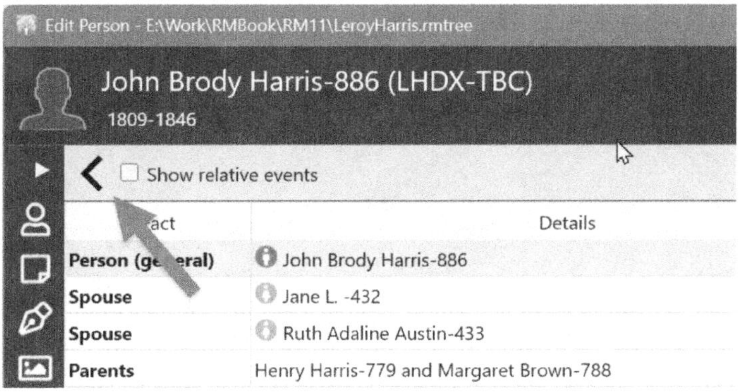

## Changing the Primary Photo

The primary photo for the person will be displayed in the header of the Edit Person screen in front of the name and lifespan. To view or change the primary photo,

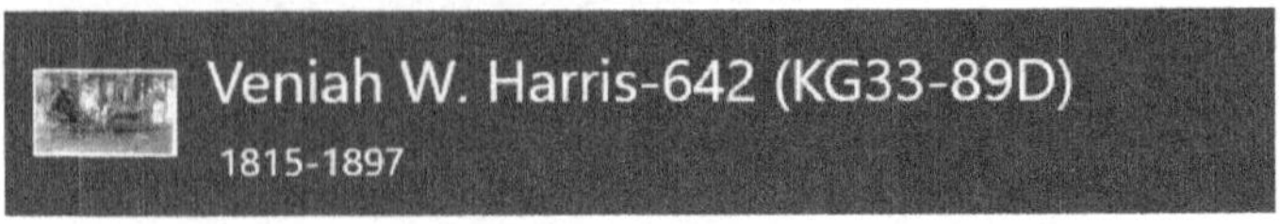


simply click the image in the header.

RootsMagic will open a form to let you zoom in or out on the photo, as well as select a new (or different) photo, or clear (remove) the primary photo for the person.

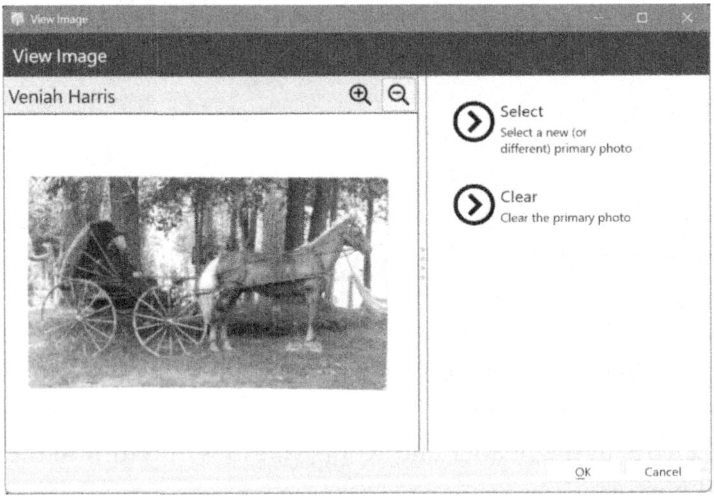

## EDIT PERSON SIDE MENU

The side menu on the Edit Person form lets you switch between the main edit screen (which we've been talking about), and several other screens, some with additional data (like DNA and Health History), and others which let you view and edit data in a more direct manner (notes, sources, media, and tasks). The currently selected view will be highlighted in the menu, and the menu may be collapsed to only show only the icons by clicking the arrow above the menu.

## NOTES VIEW

The notes view offers a more direct way to edit all the notes attached to a person. Although you can access the notes from the main edit screen, it is limited to viewing only the note for one piece of information at a time. For example, if you highlight the birth, you can view the birth note. The notes view lets you view all the notes attached to the person, their facts, names, associations, and even families.

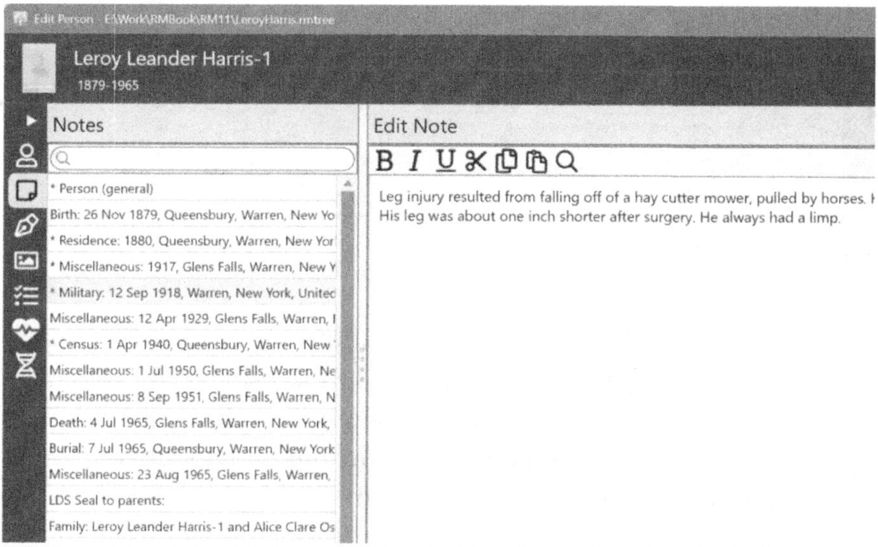

Select the information you want to edit the note for, and edit it in the panel on the right (see Note Editor, page 135).

If a piece of information has a note already, an asterisk will be displayed in front of that row. A search box above the list will filter the list to just the notes containing the text you enter.

## Sources View

Like the notes view, the sources view displays all citations attached to the person, facts, names, and families. It works a little differently than the notes view because each piece of information can have more than one citation. In addition to being able to edit an existing citation directly, you can also add, delete, memorize, and paste citations with the + and trash can buttons above the list. These features are described in detail in the section Entering Sources for People or Facts (page 160).

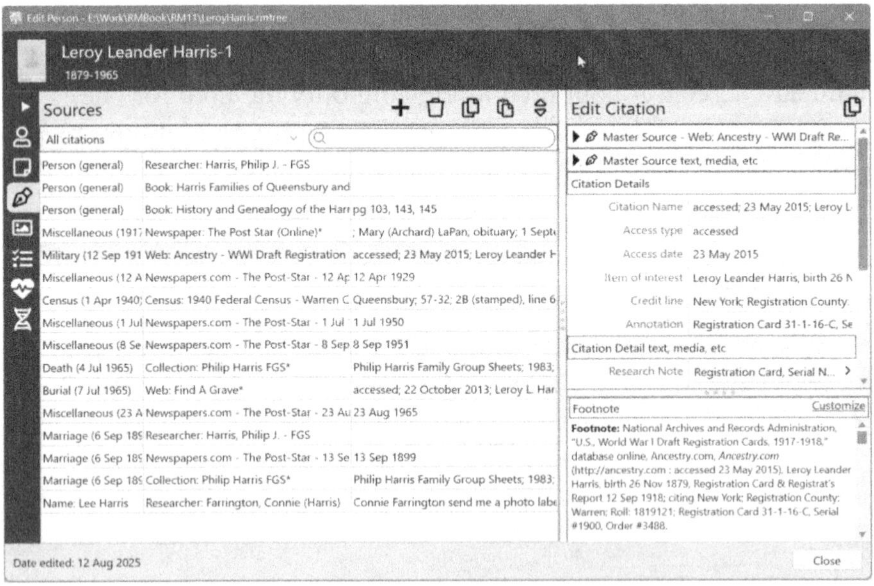


By default, RootsMagic displays all citations attached to the person, facts, etc., but a combo box above the list lets you filter the list to show only the citations for a single item. When the list is

filtered like this, the up/down arrow button will let you rearrange the citations for that item.

## Media Album

The media album lets you view and edit all the media attached to the person, family, their facts, and even citations attached to facts.

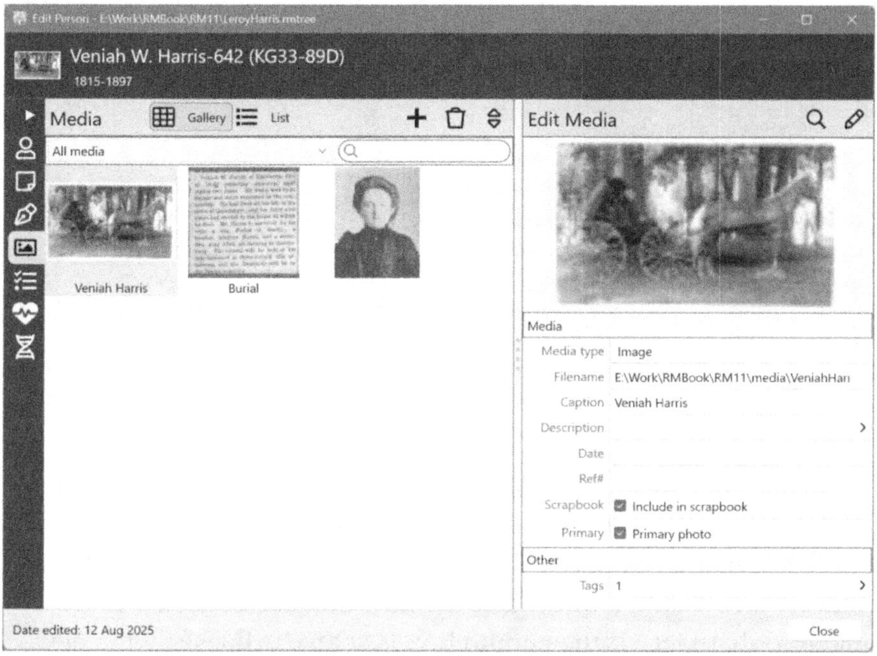


This media album page is discussed in more detail in the chapter Media Album (page 178).

## Tasks View

While tasks can be attached to most any type of record, the tasks view lets you see all tasks for a person in a single list. A combo box above the list lets you filter the list to show only the tasks for a single item.

You can add, edit, and delete any task for the person directly from this view.

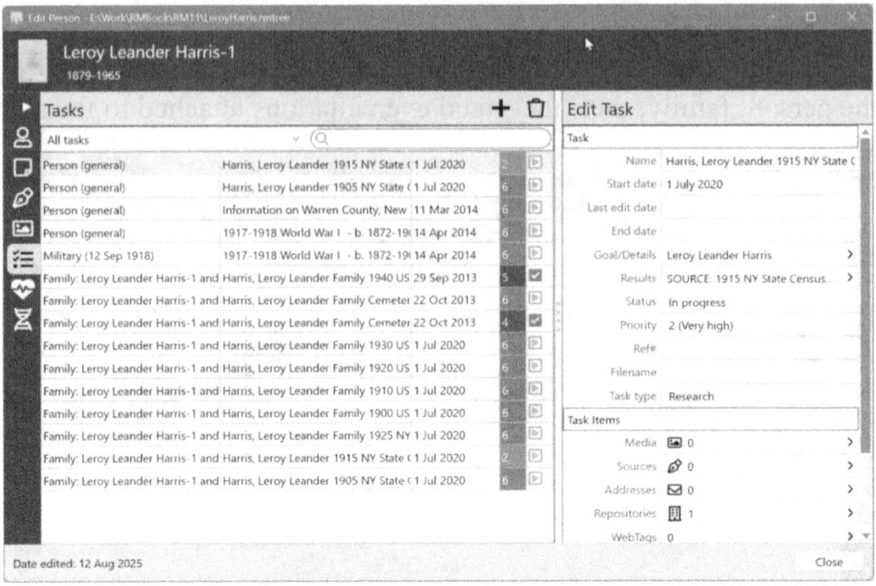


When adding a task, RootsMagic will create the new task (or use the selected task), and then link the new or selected task to whatever record the combo box is filtered to. For example, if the combo box is set to a birth fact, the new or selected task will be linked to that fact. If the combo box is set to "All tasks", the new task will be linked to the person as a general task.

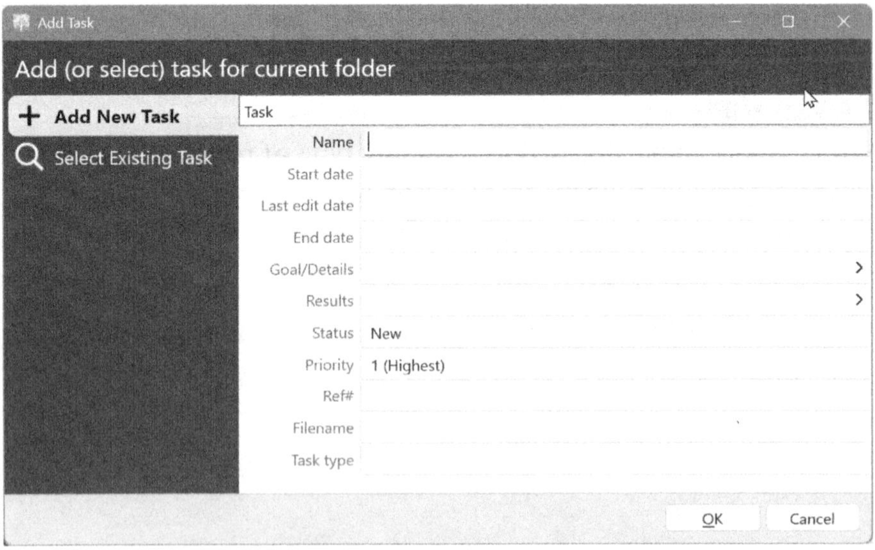

## Health History

RootsMagic lets you create a complete health history for any person in your file. You can track unlimited health conditions (illness, disease, accidents, etc.), including the onset date and unlimited notes for each condition. You can print Family Health History reports based on the information you enter.

To enter health conditions for a person, open their Edit Person screen, and then click the "Health" menu on the left side. The left side of the Health page is a list of all the health conditions you enter for the person, and the right side is an edit panel where you can modify the currently highlighted condition.

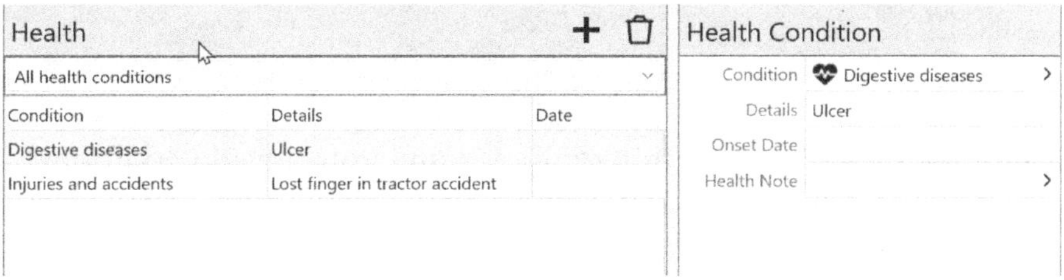


For each condition you enter, you can include a general category for the condition, as well as a brief detail description. You can also include the onset date for the condition, and unlimited notes to go into as much detail as desired.

To add a new condition, just click the + button above the list, and RootsMagic will ask you to select the category for the condition.

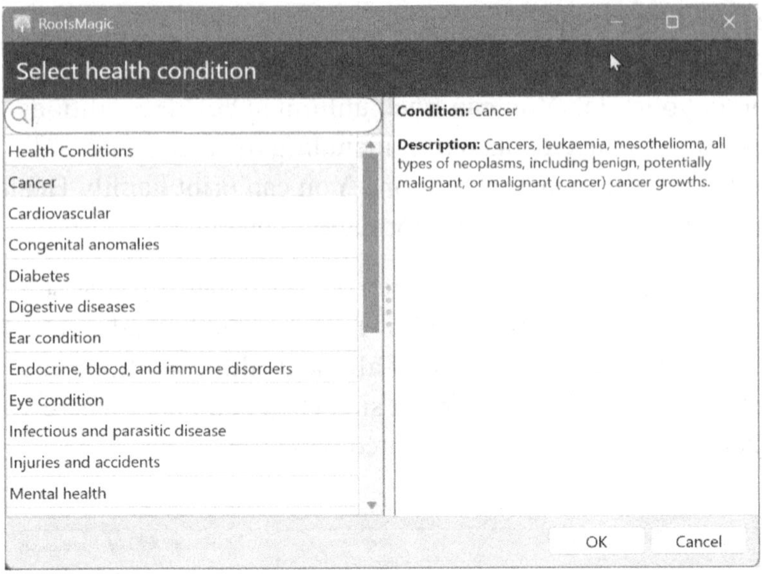


It will then add the condition to the list and you can add additional information in the edit panel.

## DNA Matches

RootsMagic lets you track unlimited DNA matches for any person in your file, including provider, shared cM, test dates, unlimited notes and other information. You can print DNA Kinship lists and Leeds Method cluster reports based on the information you enter.

To enter DNA matches for a person, open their Edit Person screen, and then click the "DNA" menu on the left side. The left side of the DNA page is a list of all the matches you enter for the person.

Each row in the list will display the provider, person, shared centimorgans, and other information which you enter for the match. It will also show both the relationship as entered into the RootsMagic tree, and the predicted relationship based on the DNA match.

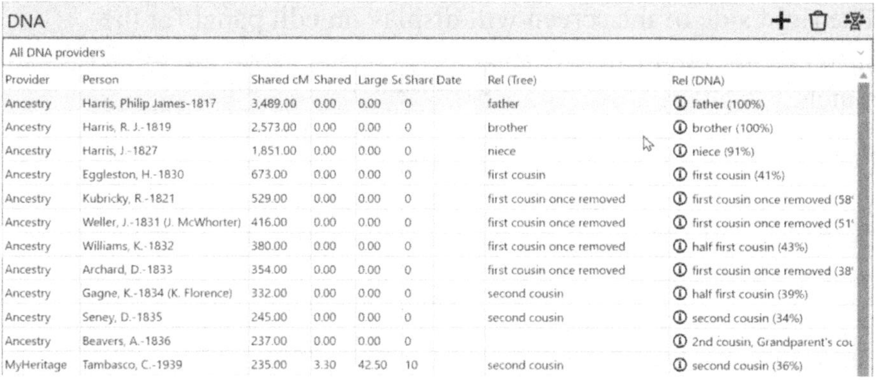

DNA

All DNA providers

| Provider | Person | Shared cM | Shared | Large Se | Share | Date | Rel (Tree) | Rel (DNA) |
|---|---|---|---|---|---|---|---|---|
| Ancestry | Harris, Philip James-1817 | 3,489.00 | 0.00 | 0.00 | 0 | | father | father (100%) |
| Ancestry | Harris, R. J.-1819 | 2,573.00 | 0.00 | 0.00 | 0 | | brother | brother (100%) |
| Ancestry | Harris, J.-1827 | 1,851.00 | 0.00 | 0.00 | 0 | | niece | niece (91%) |
| Ancestry | Eggleston, H.-1830 | 673.00 | 0.00 | 0.00 | 0 | | first cousin | first cousin (41%) |
| Ancestry | Kubricky, R.-1821 | 529.00 | 0.00 | 0.00 | 0 | | first cousin once removed | first cousin once removed (58 |
| Ancestry | Weller, J.-1831 (J. McWhorter) | 416.00 | 0.00 | 0.00 | 0 | | first cousin once removed | first cousin once removed (51 |
| Ancestry | Williams, K.-1832 | 380.00 | 0.00 | 0.00 | 0 | | first cousin once removed | half first cousin (43%) |
| Ancestry | Archard, D.-1833 | 354.00 | 0.00 | 0.00 | 0 | | first cousin once removed | first cousin once removed (38 |
| Ancestry | Gagne, K.-1834 (K. Florence) | 332.00 | 0.00 | 0.00 | 0 | | second cousin | half first cousin (39%) |
| Ancestry | Seney, D.-1835 | 245.00 | 0.00 | 0.00 | 0 | | second cousin | second cousin (34%) |
| Ancestry | Beavers, A.-1836 | 237.00 | 0.00 | 0.00 | 0 | | | 2nd cousin, Grandparent's cou |
| MyHeritage | Tambasco, C.-1939 | 235.00 | 3.30 | 42.50 | 10 | | second cousin | second cousin (36%) |

The predicted DNA relationship in the list will show the highest probability relationship, but if you click the info icon in front of the DNA predicted relationship, RootsMagic will display a full list of relationship probabilities for the match.

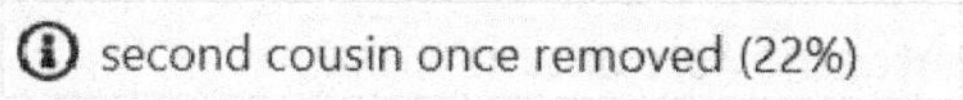


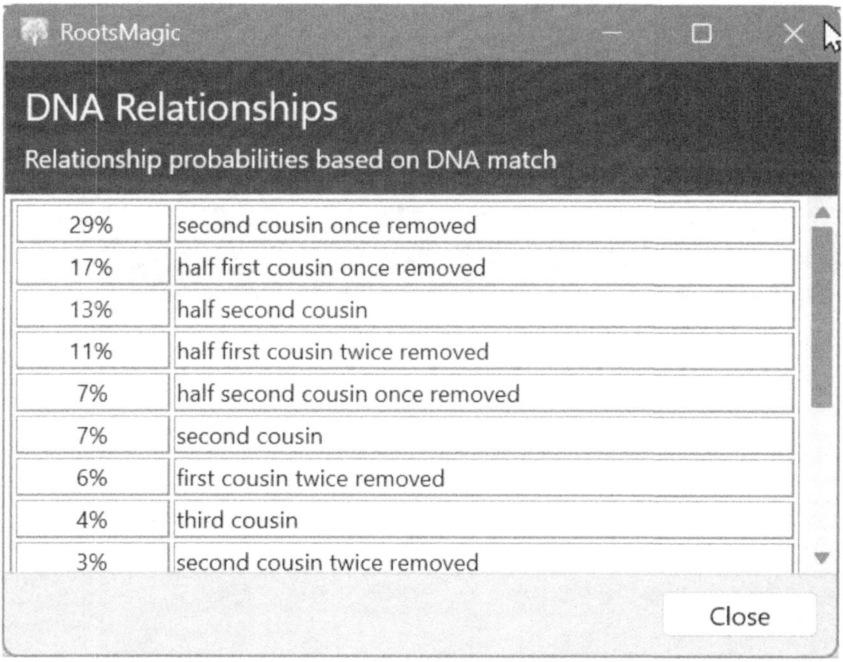

RootsMagic

DNA Relationships

Relationship probabilities based on DNA match

| | |
|---|---|
| 29% | second cousin once removed |
| 17% | half first cousin once removed |
| 13% | half second cousin |
| 11% | half first cousin twice removed |
| 7% | half second cousin once removed |
| 7% | second cousin |
| 6% | first cousin twice removed |
| 4% | third cousin |
| 3% | second cousin twice removed |

Close

The right side of the screen will display an edit panel for the currently highlighted match.

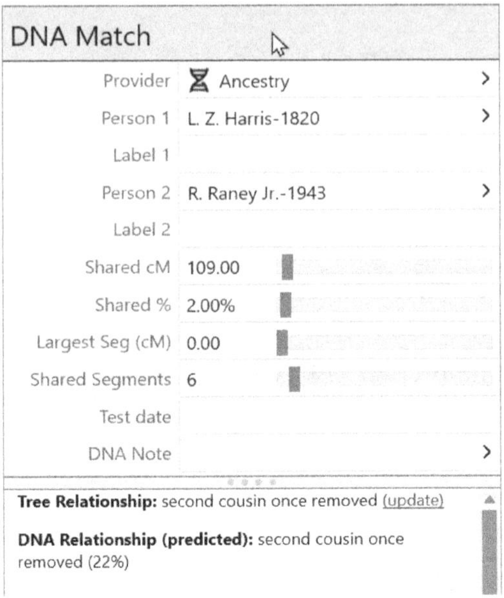


For each match you enter, you can enter the provider, the two people for the match, as well as the number of shared centimorgans, the percentage shared, largest and number of shared segments. You can also enter the test date if desired, and unlimited notes on the individual test.

## Adding a DNA Match

To add a DNA match to a person, click the + button above the list. RootsMagic will display the Add DNA Match form.

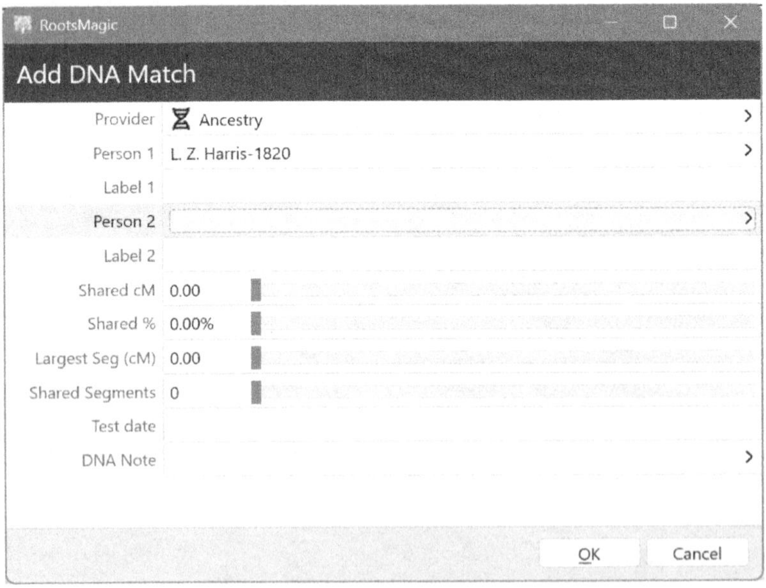

Since you will often be entering matches from the same provider, the form will default to the last provider you entered, and Person 1 will default to the current person.

You can enter the second person by clicking Person 2 and selecting (or entering) the person from the list that appears. Each match also provides fields called `Label 1` and `Label 2`, which is where you can enter the person's identifier on the provider website (since it is often not the full name of the person).

## Viewing Shared Matches

As you begin entering more DNA matches for individuals in your RootsMagic file, you will want to be able to view shared matches between people. To view shared matches between 2 people, open the DNA page for one person, and highlight the other person in the DNA list. Then click the Shared Matches button to the right of the delete (trash) button, and RootsMagic will display all shared matches between the two people.

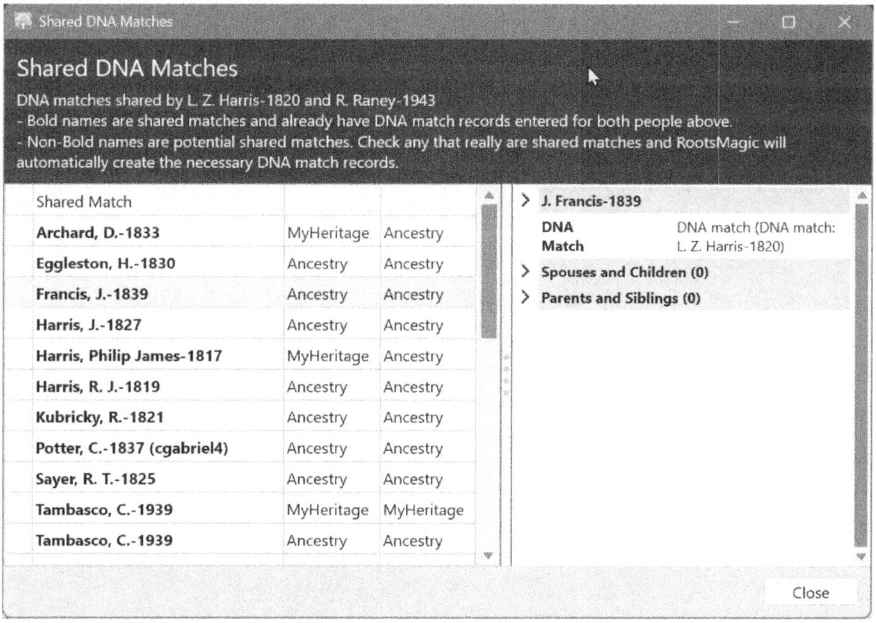


Shared matches which have been entered for both people will be displayed in bold in the list. In the example above, J. Francis is a shared match with both R.M. Harris and R. Raney because their name is bold in the list. Individuals who only have a match entered with one of the people will be displayed non-bold, and will display which provider the match is with for the first or second person.

Rather than forcing you to manually enter shared matches, RootsMagic will let you put a check in front of any matches which are shared with the other person. You can then click the disk icon and RootsMagic will automatically create the corresponding DNA match record for the other person.

# FACTS AND EVENTS

## WHAT IS A FACT?

RootsMagic allows you to track every detail in a person's life in the form of "facts". A fact can be *an event* like a birth or death, *a phase in the person's life* like an occupation or military service, or *a descriptive item* like an ID number or physical description.

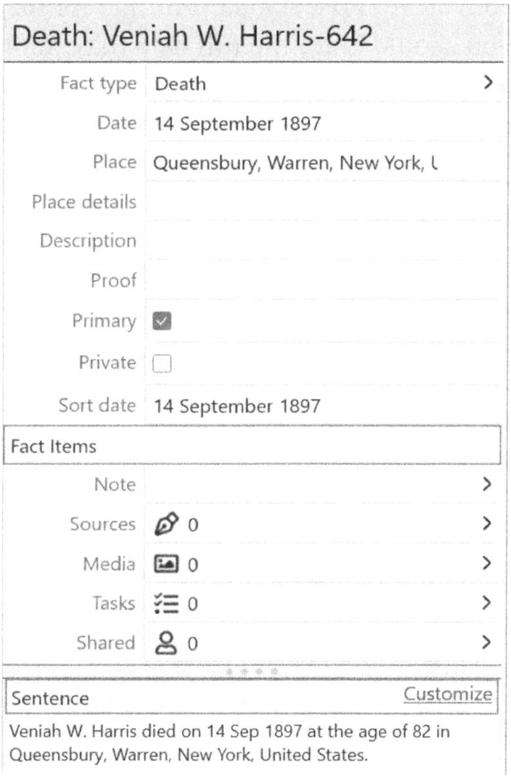


When you highlight a fact on a person's edit screen RootsMagic will display a live-edit panel where you can enter the information for the fact. A fact can contain any or all of the following parts: a date (or date period), a place (including details), a description, a note, media, tasks, and unlimited source citations.

You can also choose whether a fact is a primary or private fact. *A primary fact* is useful when you have multiple facts of the same type (like more than one birth fact when you have conflicting information). *A private fact* is one you may not want included in reports or other uses. A lock icon will be displayed next to any private fact. Most reports offer the option to print or ignore private facts.

You can also optionally choose whether you feel you have proven this fact with the "Proof" setting. You can choose from:

- Proven ✓ – this fact has been proven true (to some criteria)
- Disproven ⃠ – this fact has been proven false
- Disputed ! – this fact is disputed in some circles
- Proposed – this is a theory or hypotheses

## Dates

RootsMagic will accept just about any date you type, and will convert it into a standard format for displaying and printing. While you should enter the full date (day, month and year) if you know it, RootsMagic will also accept partial dates, like `Feb 1780`, `13 Feb`, `Feb`, or `1780`. You can even use BC if you are lucky enough to have information back that far.

### *Double Dates*

RootsMagic also supports double dates, which were used in England prior to the adoption of the Gregorian calendar. You would enter these double dates with a slash separating the two years, like `13 Feb 1729/30`.

### *Quaker Dates*

RootsMagic has built-in date support for Quaker dates. Quaker date are written referring to days of the weeks and months of the year by their number rather than the names which were based on "pagan" gods.

RootsMagic accepts these dates as "12day 5month 1588" or "12da 5mo 1588", and displays them as "12da 5mo 1588". Note that Quaker dates before 1752 were based on the Julian Calendar, so the first month refers to March, not January.

### *Date Modifiers*

RootsMagic provides *date modifiers*, which you can add to your dates to alter their meaning. You can use them with full dates, partial dates, or a combination of the two. Here is a list of the date modifiers supported by RootsMagic.

| Modifier | Description | Example |
|---|---|---|
| Before | Before a date | before 1 Jan 1900 |
| By | Happened by this date | by 1 Jan 1900 |
| To | End date of an unknown period | to 1 Jan 1900 |
| Until | Until a date | until 1 Jan 1900 |
| From++ | Start date of an unknown period | from 1 Jan 1900 |
| Since | Since a date | since 1 Jan 1900 |
| After | After a date | after 1 Jan 1900 |
| Between/And | A date which is between two dates. | between 1 Jan 1900 and 5 Jan 1900 |
| From/To | A date period. Useful for spans like the period of time a person held an occupation. | from 1 Jan 1900 and 5 Jan 1900 |
| - (dash) | Date period | 1 Jan 1900-5 Jan 1900 |
| Or | Conflicting dates | 1 Jan 1900 or 5 Jan 1900 |
| About | Near a date | abt 1 Jan 1900 |
| Estimate | An estimated date | est 1 Jan 1900 |
| Calculated | A calculated date | calc 1 Jan 1900 |
| Circa | Near a date | ca 1 Jan 1900 |
| Say | An estimated date | say 1 Jan 1900 |
| Certainly | Little doubt about the date | cert 1 Jan 1900 |
| Probably | More than likely date | prob 1 Jan 1900 |
| Possibly | Some evidence supports the date | poss 1 Jan 1900 |
| Likely | Odds favor the date | lkly 1 Jan 1900 |

| | | |
|---|---|---|
| Apparently | Presumed date | appar 1 Jan 1900 |
| Perhaps | Could be the date | prhps 1 Jan 1900 |
| Maybe | Date might be correct | maybe 1 Jan 1900 |

### Sort Dates

The sort date is a "non-printing" date which you can enter to force RootsMagic to sort the facts in the order you want.

When you enter the normal date for the fact, RootsMagic will automatically fill the sort date, but you can change it if you want. This is useful in situations like when you have a death fact with a place but don't know the date. Instead of putting in a fake date like "after 1 Jan 1900" in the date field, you can go ahead and leave the date field blank but put in a sort date to force the fact into the position you desire.

**☺ Tip**

If you happen to have multiple events which happened on the same date you can use the sort date to force them into the desired order. You can enter the actual date in the sort date, but append a number to force the sort order between them. For example, if you have a death and burial both on 15 Jun 1850, you can enter:

15 Jun 1850 - 1 for the death sort date

15 Jun 1850 - 2 for the burial sort date

### Places and Place Details

RootsMagic facts allow you to enter the place where the fact or event occurred. When you enter a place, separate each part with a comma, and enter it from specific to general like this:

Albuquerque, Bernalillo, New Mexico, United States

By separating each part of the place with a comma, RootsMagic can abbreviate the place when it needs to fit the place name in a tight area of a report.

> ☺ **Tip**
>
> When entering place names, it is best to spell out the different parts. While abbreviations (like the post office abbreviations for states) are standard in their country of origin, they are not standard throughout the rest of the world.

Every time you enter a new place, RootsMagic adds the place you enter to a master place list. Whenever you need to enter a place, RootsMagic will autofill the place as you type. As you type each letter of the place name, RootsMagic tries to match the letters you've typed with existing names in the place list. Just continue typing characters until the correct place appears.

You can also click the "Place list" button (which looks like a globe on the right end of the place field) to bring up a list of previously entered places to choose from. The master place list is described on page 145.

The Gazetteer button (magnifying glass) will open the gazetteer to let you look for a place from RootsMagic's 3.5 million place name database.

RootsMagic also provides a second field called the "Place Details". This is where you can enter more specific information about the place, like the hospital, cemetery, or street address where the event took place. You can click the button at the right end of the place details field to open the place details list.

### Descriptions

Some facts have what is called a "description". This is where you enter a specific detail about a fact. For example, in the Occupation fact, you would enter the actual occupation (for example teacher).

## Shared Facts

You will often come across facts or events that are actually shared by more than just the person you add the fact to. For example, you may have a census record which includes a father, mother, and a number of children. You don't want to have to retype that fact over and over into each person's edit screen, so RootsMagic offers a feature called "Shared facts".

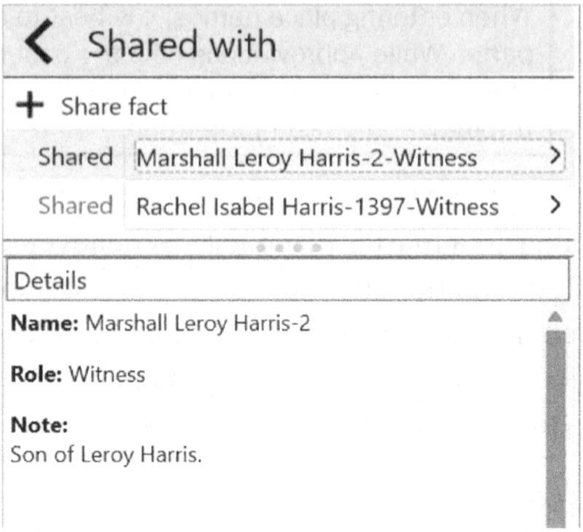


This is also useful for facts like Residence, and can also be used to add "witnesses" to events, like the best man for a marriage event, or a witness to a baptism.

Any time you are highlighting a fact in a person's edit screen, the live edit panel on the right will have a button called "Shared". Click that button and RootsMagic will allow you to select other people who will share that particular fact.

### Adding a Shared Fact

You can click "Share fact" to add the person who shares this event. You can choose someone who is in the database (by selecting them from a list) or you can select the Just type name menu on the left and type in the name of a person (this is useful for neighbors and others that you don't actually want to enter into the file).

*You can also add multiple people* at once who share the fact on this same screen by checking the boxes in front of the names you want to share with, and use the Mark and Unmark buttons above the list to select multiple people just like when using the RootsMagic Explorer (page 218).

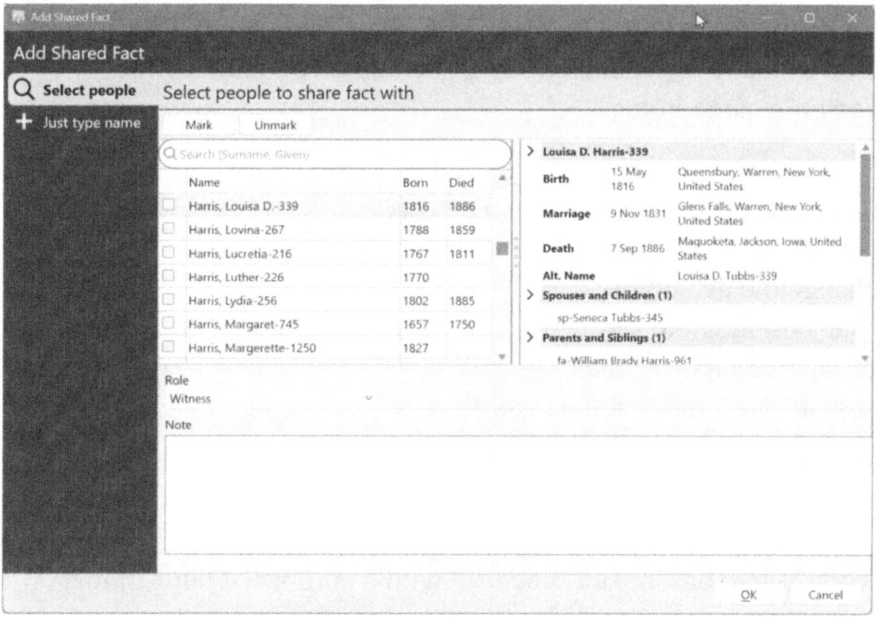


Once you have selected the person (or people), there are two extra pieces of information you can enter:

1. **The person's role in the event.** For example, if the shared fact was a census, the role might be "Spouse", "Child", "Boarder", or any other role you might want to include. Just select the role you want from the list. These role types aren't all automatically built in, so there is an item in the list called "Add new role type". Select that item and you can create a new role. Just enter a name for the role, and an optional sentence template. The sentence template is used to write the sentence in books when a person with this role is talked about.
2. **A note about the person's role in the event.** This optional note is a place where you can put more details about this person's specific role in this event.

If you select multiple people at once, it will assign the same role and note to each member of that group.

### Editing or Deleting a Shared Fact

You can also make changes to a shared fact by clicking the person's name in the list.

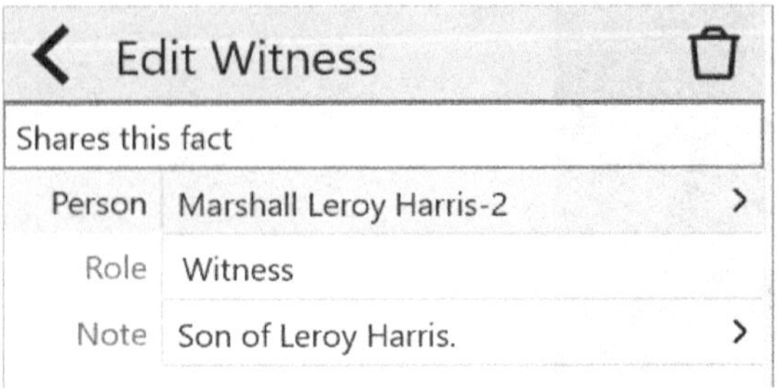


RootsMagic will open a panel where you can change the person or role, edit the note for the shared fact (for that person), or remove the person from the shared fact by clicking the trash can icon at the top of the panel.

## THE FACT TYPE LIST

RootsMagic has a "fact type list" with a number of built-in fact types that are already defined and include the appropriate fields. You can also create your own fact types that RootsMagic will add to the fact list. A description of each of the built-in facts can be found in the Quick Summary at the end of this book.

You can get to the fact type list in two different ways: 1) by clicking the Add button on a person's edit screen, and 2) by selecting Lists > Fact type list from the People page menu. You can scroll through the list of fact types and see details about the highlighted fact type on the right side of the Fact Type List.

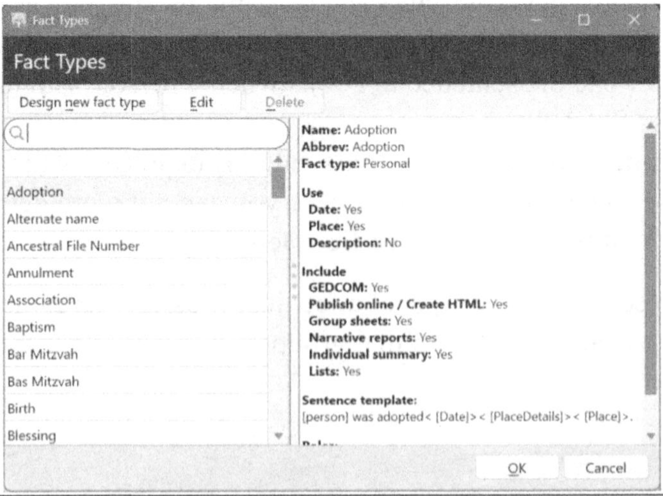

### Creating a New Fact Type

To create a fact type that isn't already in the list, click the Design new fact type button. The following screen will appear so you can tell RootsMagic whether the new fact type will be attached to people (like birth, death, etc), or to families (like marriage, divorce, etc.).

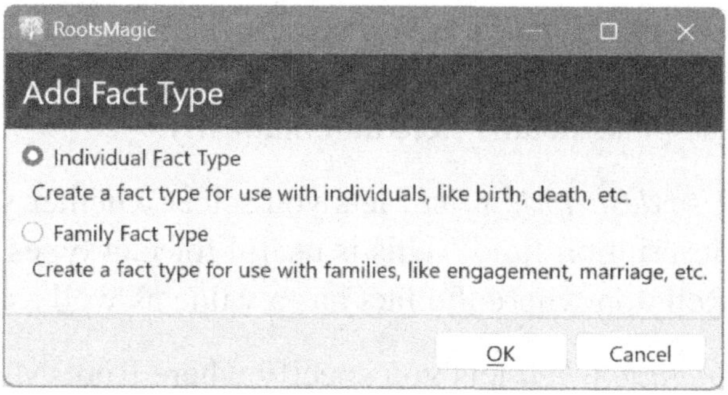


RootsMagic will then display the following dialog so that you can enter the details for the new fact type you want to create.

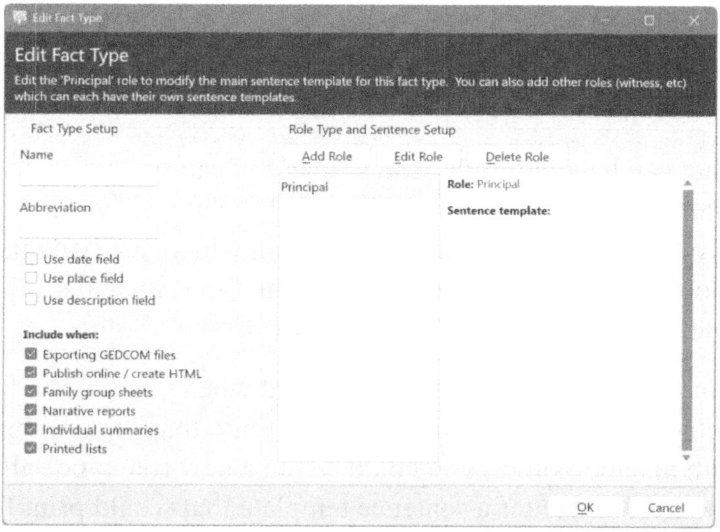


*Name* is where you enter the name for the new fact.

*Abbreviation* is where you enter a short version of the fact type name.

*Use date field* lets you select whether your fact type needs a date. Although you might not think your fact needs this field, you might want to add it anyway. For example, a physical description might not be thought of as needing a date, but you might have facts stating that Aunt Peggy was a brunette from 1960 to 1985, but was a blonde from 1985 to 1987.

*Use place field* lets you select whether your fact type needs a place. If you include the place field, RootsMagic will also include the place details field automatically.

*Use description field* lets you select whether your fact type needs a description field. This is useful for fact types like Occupation or Religion where the fact has a value as well as a date and place.

*Include when* lets you specify where RootsMagic uses your new fact. If you uncheck an item in this area RootsMagic will ignore the fact when performing that function. For example, if you uncheck Family group sheets, RootsMagic will not print that fact in family group sheets.

*Role Type and Sentence Setup* is where you enter "sentence templates" to tell RootsMagic how you want this fact type to appear when printing books or creating websites.

Each fact can have multiple "roles" that you can write a sentence template for. Every fact has a role called "Principal" which is the sentence that will be printed for the person who actually owns the fact. So if you add a birth fact to a person, the Principal sentence template is the one that will print for that person's birth.

You can also add other roles that are used when you share a fact with someone else. So if you wanted to share that person's birth fact with his godmother, you could create a new role type called "Godmother" and enter a sentence template that would print for the godmother in her paragraph in the book.

*To create a sentence template* you need to tell RootsMagic how to put a fact's information together to create a readable sentence. Edit a role to create the sentence template for that role.

To create the templates you can use field names which RootsMagic provides for the different kinds of information. For example [person], [date], and [place]. Notice that field names have square brackets around them. Simply put these field names together and include any additional words or punctuation you want between them. For example:

[Person] was born [Date] [Place].

When RootsMagic has to write that sentence, it will replace [Person] with the person's name, [Date] with the date entered for the fact, and [Place] with the place entered for the fact. So when the actual sentence is printed it will look something like this:

John Doe was born on May 1, 1820 in Avon, Polk, Iowa.

Notice that when RootsMagic replaces [date] with the date, it adds the word "on" or "in" as appropriate, so you don't need to take that into account in your template. Also, when RootsMagic replaces [place] with the place, it adds the word "in" so that you don't have to add the word "in" to the sentence template. This ensures that the sentence will still read properly even if the date or place are blank for a particular fact.

There are dozens of different fields you can use in a sentence template, with modifiers to change how the fields work, and switches which let you handle any situation you can think of.

Let's say you wanted to create a sentence template for an occupation. You might enter something like this:

[person] was a [desc] [date] [place].

But what if you had information that a person was working but didn't know what the job was? If you left the description field blank your sentence would look like this:

John Doe was a from 1820 to 1830 in Avon, Polk, Iowa.

RootsMagic lets you use angle brackets < > to tell the source template not to print something unless the user actually fills in the field. It even lets you put a bar | separator in to have a default value if the field is blank. So if you did this:

[person] was <a [desc]|employed> [date] [place].

those angle brackets tell RootsMagic to only print the description if it isn't blank, otherwise print "employed". So the sentence would look like either:

John Doe was a farmer from 1820 to 1830 in Avon, Polk, Iowa.

or

John Doe was employed from 1820 to 1830 in Avon, Polk, Iowa.

There are a *ton* of other things you can do with sentence templates (way too many to talk about here). There is an appendix at the end of the book (page 369) which describes the entire template language available.

## Editing an Existing Fact Type

To edit an existing fact type, highlight the name of the fact you want to edit, and click on the Edit button. RootsMagic will display the "Edit Fact Type" dialog with the current settings for the fact. If you are editing one of RootsMagic's built-in fact types, some of the fields will be disabled so that you can't change them. Make any changes you want, then click the OK button to save the changes.

## Deleting an Existing Fact Type

To delete a fact type from the fact list, simply highlight the fact name in the fact list, and click the Delete button. RootsMagic will ask if you really want to delete the fact type. You can only delete fact types that you have added yourself. RootsMagic won't let you delete any of the built-in fact types.

## Notes – Telling Your Story

If names, dates and places are the bones of your family history, notes are the meat on those bones. *A note* is where you enter stories or more details about a person, family, or fact. For example, a birth note might include the name of the doctor that delivered the person, who witnessed the birth, how much the person weighed at birth, or other stories about the birth.

Notes can be associated with people, families, or facts in a person's life.

- *Individual notes* are tied to a person. These notes are where you enter information about a person that won't fit in one of the facts for the person. To enter or edit an individual note, open the person's edit screen, highlight the first row (their name) and click the "Notes" button.
- *Family notes* are tied to a family. These notes are where you enter information about a family that you don't want to enter separately for the father, mother and children. To enter or edit a family note you can open the person's edit screen, highlight the row with the desired family, and click the Notes button.
- *Fact notes* are tied to a fact in a person's life. These notes are where you enter more detailed information about the fact. To enter or edit a fact note open the person's edit screen, highlight the fact, then click the Notes button.

## Note Editor

When you edit a note, the note editor will slide into the current panel so that you can still tell what fact the note belongs to. You can just begin typing in the note.

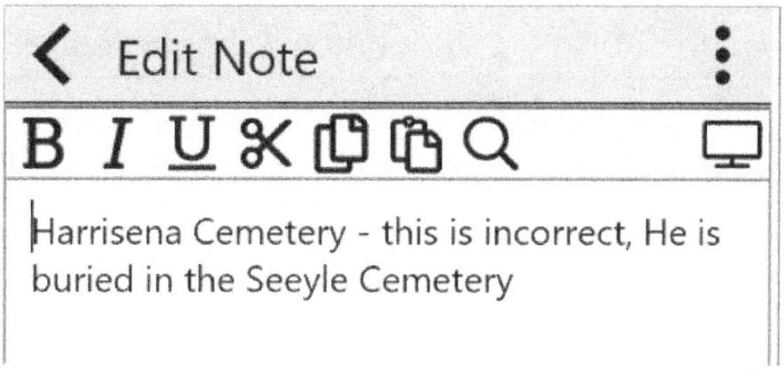


You can access the edit commands from

the editor toolbar, by clicking the Options (3 dot) menu, or by right clicking the mouse button.

| Edit Command | Command Description | Hot Key |
|---|---|---|
| Cut | Places the marked text on the clipboard, then removes the marked text from the note. | Ctrl+X |
| Copy | Places the marked text on the clipboard. | Ctrl+C |
| Paste | Inserts text from the clipboard to the note at the position of the blinking cursor. | Ctrl+V |
| Paste as plain text | Same as paste, except strips formatting before pasting the text. | Ctrl+Shift+V |
| Undo | Undoes the last editing command. | Ctrl+Z |
| Undo all | Undoes any changes since the note was opened. | |
| Find | Lets you search for text within the note. | Ctrl+F |
| Find Next | Repeats the last search. | |
| Open in new window | Opens the note in a separate resizable window | |
| Spell check | Spell checks the current note. | |
| Bold | Bolds the selected text. | Ctrl+B |
| Italics | Italicizes the selected text. | Ctrl+I |
| Underline | Underlines the selected text. | Ctrl+U |
| Character map | Opens the character map to let you select special (accented) characters. | Ctrl+T |

When you are finished editing the note, click the Save button and RootsMagic will save the note and attach it to the appropriate person, family, or fact.

If you would like to edit the note in a larger separate window, click the screen button (shown on the left) and RootsMagic will open the note in a separate resizable window.

> ☺ **Tip**
>
> *To quickly edit a fact note*, just click your mouse in the note column of the fact list next to the desired fact.

## Spell Checking

RootsMagic provides a built-in spell checker, and includes the ability to add your own words to its dictionary (which is especially important for family names).

*To spell check the text in a note*, select "spell check" from the Options menu, or click the right mouse button in the note editor and select Spell Check from the menu. RootsMagic will begin spell checking the note text.

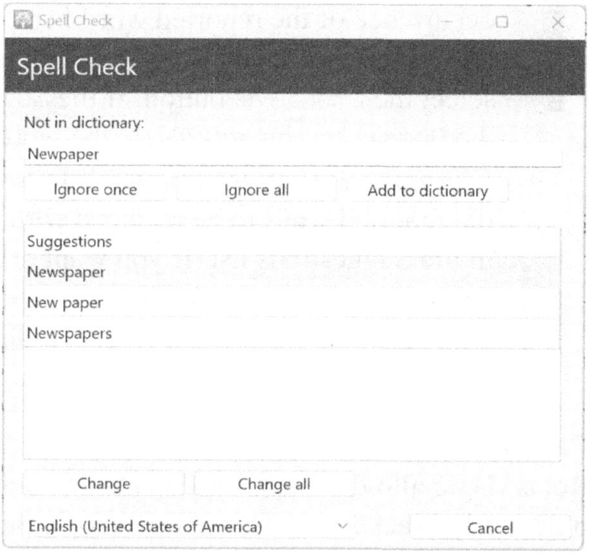


*When an unknown word is found*, RootsMagic will display the Spell Check dialog with the unknown word. You can type in the correct spelling, or you can select one of the suggested replacements from the Suggestions list.

- **Ignore Once:** Causes this occurrence of the misspelled word to be skipped. If the same misspelled word appears later, it will be reported.
- **Ignore All:** Causes this and all further occurrences of the misspelled word to be skipped. You might use this button if

the word reported as a misspelling is actually spelled correctly. If the word is one you use frequently, you may wish to ignore it permanently by selecting the Add to dictionary button.

- **Add to Dictionary:** Causes the reported word to be added to the dictionary. Use the Add to dictionary button if a correctly spelled word you use often is reported as a misspelling (e.g., your family name). If the word is not used frequently, you may want to select the Ignore once or **Ignore All** buttons instead. RootsMagic uses the operating system's native spell check engines (Windows or Mac), so the dictionary file is that one that the operating system already uses.
- **Change**: Causes the reported word to be replaced with the highlighted word in the Suggestions list. Only this occurrence of the reported word is replaced. If you want this and all following occurrences of the word replaced, select the Change All button. If the Suggestions list is empty, the Change button will delete the word.
- **Change All:** Causes this and all following occurrences of the reported word to be replaced with the highlighted word in the Suggestions list. If you want only this occurrence of the word to be replaced, use the Change button.
- **Cancel:** Exits from the spell check dialog without making any more changes.

## Private Notes

RootsMagic allows you to make parts of your notes private. Just place curly brackets { } around any text in the note that you want to be considered private.

When you print reports, export GEDCOM files, or create websites, RootsMagic will give you the option to include or ignore private notes. If you don't include private notes, RootsMagic will strip out everything between the curly brackets, including the brackets themselves.

If you do include private notes, you will also have the option whether to strip out the brackets when printing.

For example, if you have the following note:

This is a line of text.{ This is a private note.} This is another line of text.

choosing to ignore private notes would result in:

This is a line of text. This is another line of text.

Including private notes would result in either:

This is a line of text.{ This is a private note.} This is another line of text.

or

This is a line of text. This is a private note. This is another line of text.

depending on whether you chose to strip the brackets.

# ASSOCIATIONS

## WHAT IS AN ASSOCIATION?

Although associations share a number of attributes with facts and events (date, place, notes, etc.), they serve a very different purpose.

It is often helpful to our research to track friends, neighbors and other associates of our own ancestors. An association lets you specify the relationship between two people who aren't necessarily related by family. In addition, associations can also be used to track non-family relationships such as those between an enslaver and enslaved person.

## ADDING AN ASSOCIATION

There are two ways to add an association to someone in your database, from the Edit Person form (just like adding an event), and on the Association list view on the People page.

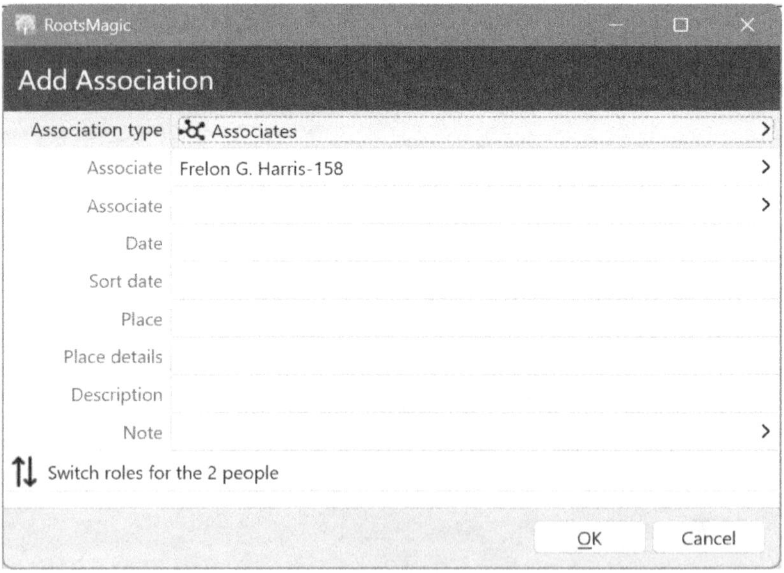


You can select the type of association, the two people, as well as the date, place, description and other information similar to other facts you might add as described in the previous chapter.

Below the data entry fields is a button Switch roles for the 2 people. This button will swap person 1 and person 2 on the data entry form. So for example, if the association type is Education, switching roles will switch the two people back and forth between "teacher" and "student".

## Creating and Editing Association Types

When you click to change the association type, RootsMagic will bring up the Association Type list to select from.

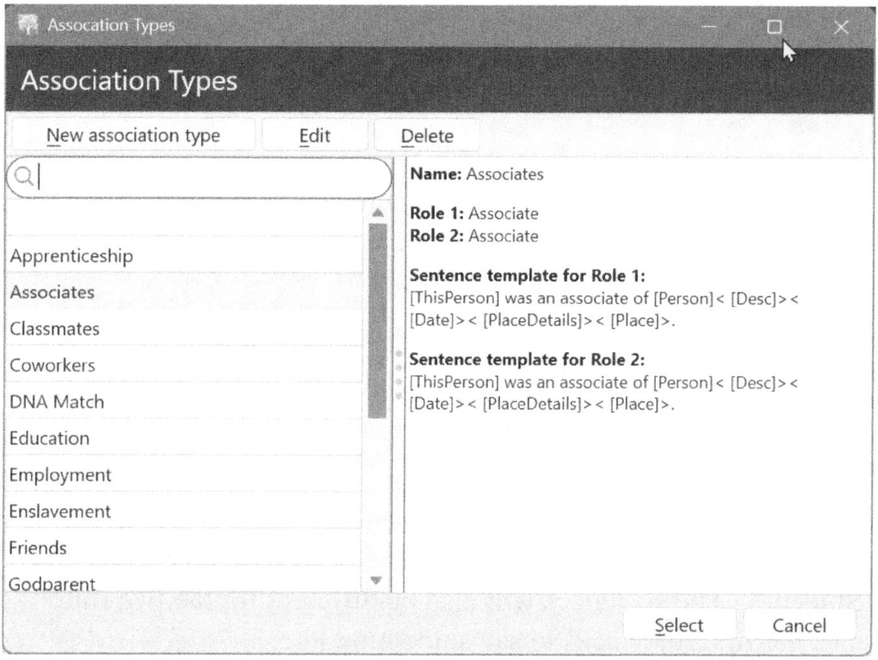


The list will include all the built-in association types, but you can add your own to the list as well.

*To add a new association type*, click the "New association type" button and RootsMagic will let you enter the information needed.

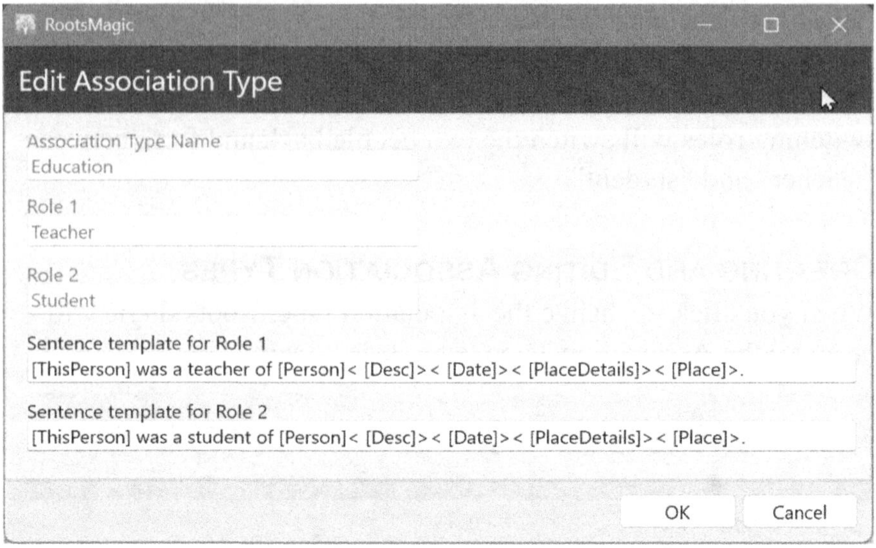


Each association type consists of a name, which describes the association, two role names (one for each person), and two sentence templates (one for each role).

With some association types, the role names (and role sentences) may be the same for both roles (for example, for the association type "Friends", both roles are "Friend" and the sentence templates are the same for both.

However, some association types require two different roles, such as the case with "Education". Role 1 is "Teacher" while role 2 is "Student". The sentences will also be different for the two roles, since the first role needs to say something like:

Person 1 was the teacher of Person 2

while the second role needs to be:

Person 2 was a student of Person 1

Sentence templates are created using the sentence template language described in the Appendix.

*To edit an association type*, highlight the type in the list and click the "Edit" button. RootsMagic will display the same screen to let you edit the information. You can edit any part of the association type for user defined types, but you will only be able to edit the sentence templates for any built-in types.

*To delete any user defined types,* just highlight the type and click the “Delete” button. If you delete an association type that is currently in use by any associations, those associations will be reset to the default association type “Association”.

## The Associations View

The Associations view is one of the views in the People page. While associations can be viewed on the edit screen for each person (just like facts), the Association view provides a way to see all your associations in a single list. The list includes the relationship type, the two individuals in the relationship and their role, and the date and place of the relationship.

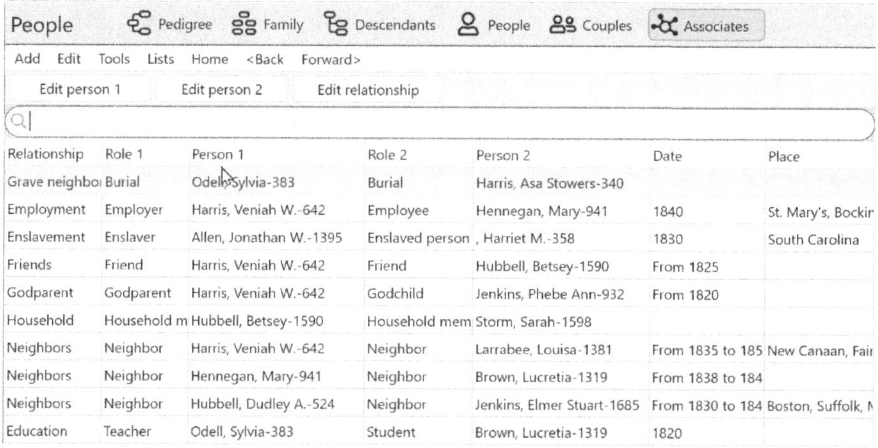


| Relationship | Role 1 | Person 1 | Role 2 | Person 2 | Date | Place |
|---|---|---|---|---|---|---|
| Grave neighbo | Burial | Odell, Sylvia-383 | Burial | Harris, Asa Stowers-340 | | |
| Employment | Employer | Harris, Veniah W.-642 | Employee | Hennegan, Mary-941 | 1840 | St. Mary's, Bockir |
| Enslavement | Enslaver | Allen, Jonathan W.-1395 | Enslaved person | , Harriet M.-358 | 1830 | South Carolina |
| Friends | Friend | Harris, Veniah W.-642 | Friend | Hubbell, Betsey-1590 | From 1825 | |
| Godparent | Godparent | Harris, Veniah W.-642 | Godchild | Jenkins, Phebe Ann-932 | From 1820 | |
| Household | Household m | Hubbell, Betsey-1590 | Household mem | Storm, Sarah-1598 | | |
| Neighbors | Neighbor | Harris, Veniah W.-642 | Neighbor | Larrabee, Louisa-1381 | From 1835 to 185 | New Canaan, Fair |
| Neighbors | Neighbor | Hennegan, Mary-941 | Neighbor | Brown, Lucretia-1319 | From 1838 to 184 | |
| Neighbors | Neighbor | Hubbell, Dudley A.-524 | Neighbor | Jenkins, Elmer Stuart-1685 | From 1830 to 184 | Boston, Suffolk, M |
| Education | Teacher | Odell, Sylvia-383 | Student | Brown, Lucretia-1319 | 1820 | |

*You can sort the list* by clicking the header of the column you wish to sort by.

*You can filter individuals* by typing the name of either person in the association.

*You can edit either person in the highlighted association* by clicking on the Edit person 1 or Edit person 2 button.

*You can edit the actual association* by clicking on the Edit relationship button. You will be able to edit the association type, the individuals, the date, place, and note for the association. You can also edit any association from the edit screen for either of the people. In that case you can also edit any sources, media, or tasks attached to the association.

## Association Reports

While associations can appear in regular RootsMagic reports like narrative reports, there are also two reports specifically for analyzing associations: the Association Report and the Association List. These are both described in the chapter "Printing Reports".

# PLACES - MAPPING, GEOCODING, AND GAZETTEERS

One of the most important pieces of information you will need to keep track of are the places where your ancestors lived and worked. RootsMagic provides a Places page to assist with this. Just click “Places” on the side menu to display this page.

## PLACE LIST

Whenever you enter a place for an event in RootsMagic, that place is added to the place list so that you can reuse it over and over.

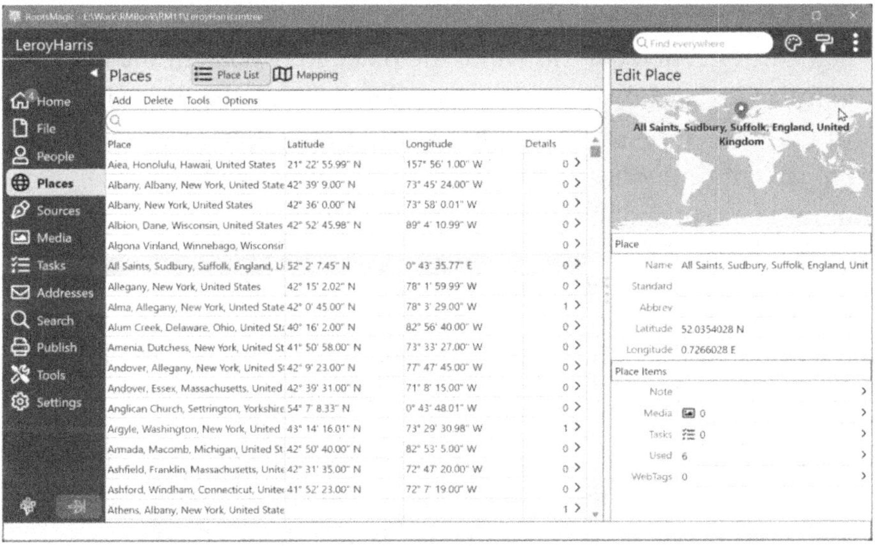


The list of places includes the name of the place, the latitude and longitude of the place (if entered), and the number of place details for the place. Place details are specific locations within the place, like hospitals, cemeteries, home addresses, or the like.

You can click on the count in the “Details” column to slide in a list of the place details for that place. The place details list also contains the latitude and longitude, as well as the number of events using that particular place detail.

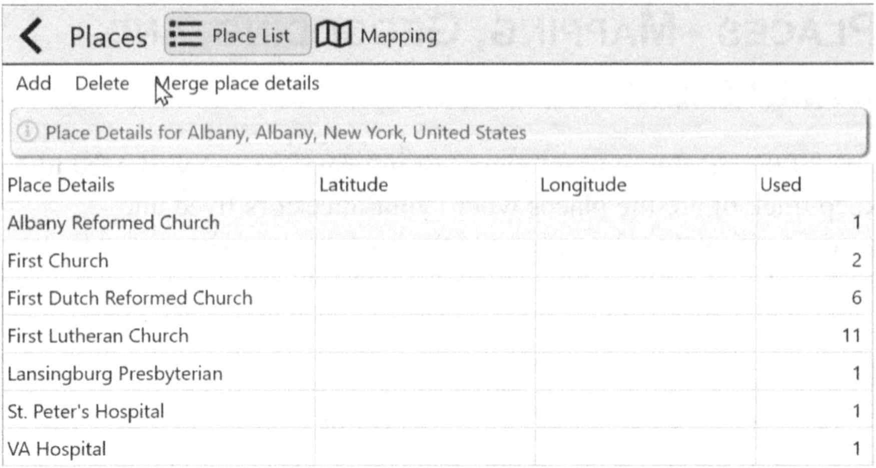


Place details are the specific locations you might have entered when editing a person. So while the place may contain the city, county, state, and country, the place details might be the name of a hospital, cemetery, or other specific location within that place. You can edit individual place details, including the latitude, longitude, note, and media items for the detail.

*If you want to see where a place (or place detail) is used*, click the Used button in the edit panel to bring up a list of every fact using the place. You can click the Edit (pencil) button above the list to open the edit screen for the person with the highlighted fact.

*To delete a place in your place list*, highlight the name of the place in the list, then click the Delete menu. RootsMagic will ask if you really want to delete the place name. If you do delete the place name, any facts that happened in that place will have their place field erased.

*To view a list of places in your place list which aren't being used* by any event, select Options > Show unused places from the menu. You can delete any unused place from this list.

*To see any tasks which are using a particular place*, select Tools > Show tasks for selected place from the menu.

*If you want to see the places grouped geographically*, select Options > Reverse places from the menu and RootsMagic will display the list with each place name reversed (from general part to the specific part of the place). This will group places by country, then state, then county, etc.

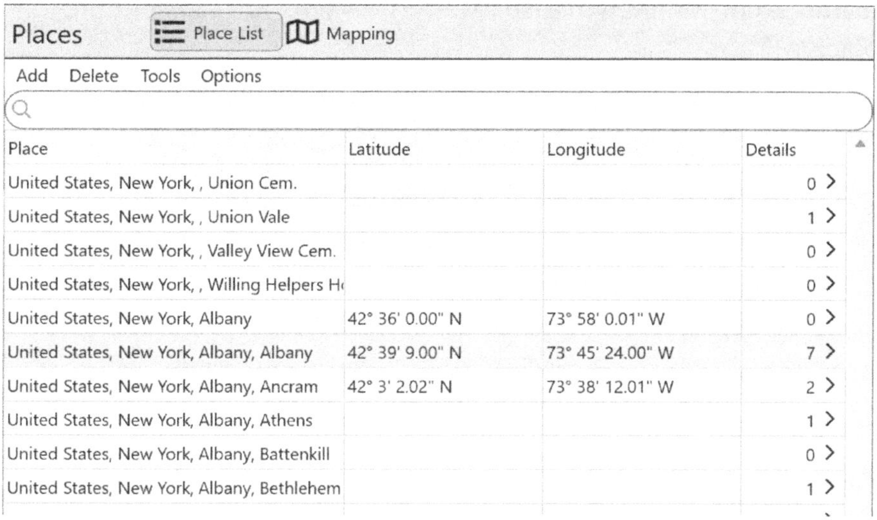


## Editing Places

*RootsMagic lets you make changes to the Place or Place Detail lists* by highlighting any place in the list and editing them in the panel on the right. You can edit the place name, the latitude and longitude for the place, a "standardized" or abbreviated place name, a note or place history for the place, media items (pictures) of the place, tasks, and links to web pages about the place. All items except the actual place name are optional.

Just change the place name the way you want, then click the Save button to save the modified place name. Every fact that uses that place name will be adjusted to use the modified place name.

You can also click the "Media" or "Tasks" buttons to add or view any media or tasks associated with the place. This is useful for adding a picture of a home, cemetery plot, or other landmark to a place.

The WebTags button lets you add links to web pages which may have histories or other details about the place.

You may find places in your place list that you would like to split into a place and separate place details. You can do this by highlighting the place and selecting Split place from the Tools menu. RootsMagic will display a form where you can split the place.

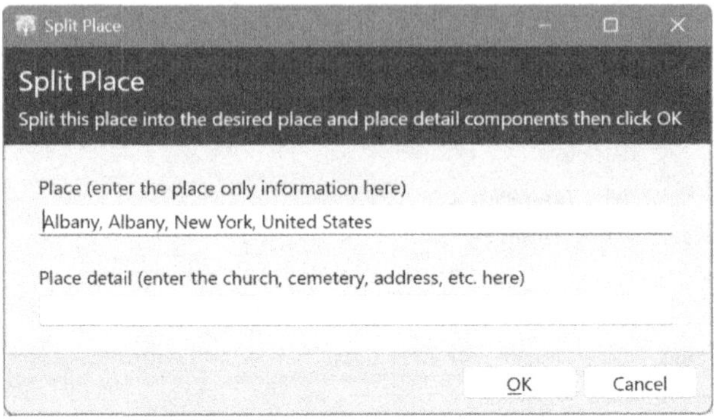


## Searching for Places

*To filter the list of places to find a specific location*, just begin typing in the search box above the place list. As you type, RootsMagic will filter the list to only include places which contain what you type. So, for example, if you type *New York*, RootsMagic will only display places containing the text *new york* anywhere within the place. If you want to only show places that start with new york, simply type a quote " before typing the text. For example, if you only want to show places that start with new york, just type "new york.

*You can also select "Search and replace"* from the Tools menu to make changes to multiple places at once. Just note that if you end up with duplicate places you will need to use the merge places feature described later to consolidate them.

## Geocoding Places

If you want RootsMagic to automatically fill in the latitude, longitude, and standardized place name, you can do it one place at a time, or all at once. From the Tools menu select either Geocode selected place or Geocode all places. RootsMagic will search its 3.5 million name place database for the place or places and use the information to populate the latitude, longitude and standardized place name.

After doing Geocode all places, RootsMagic will bring up a list of any places that it was unable to match.

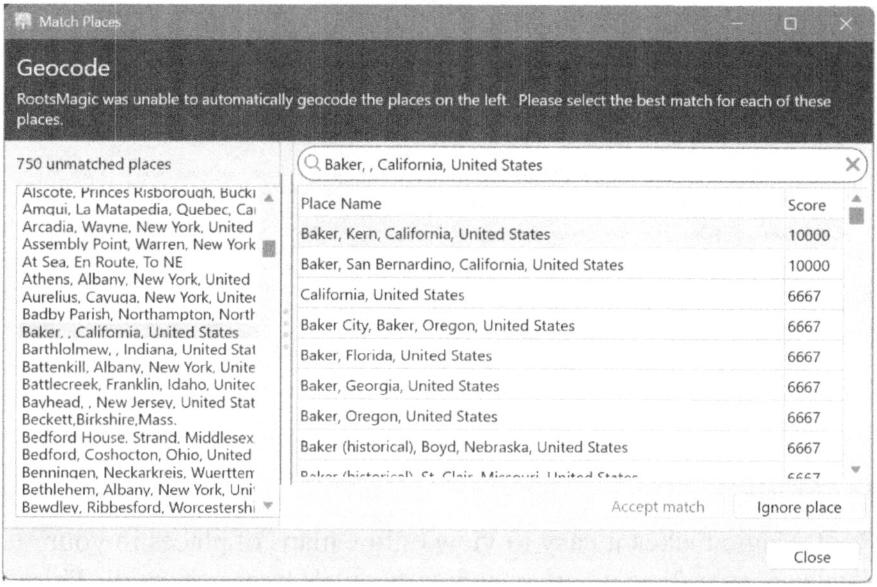


You can select any place in the list and RootsMagic will display a list of possible matches that you can select from. If you select a match and click Accept match, RootsMagic will use that match to geocode that particular place.

## Merging Duplicate Places

At some point you may find your place list cluttered with multiple copies of the same place, each spelled just a little differently. This is especially common after importing information from a GEDCOM file. Highlight the place you want to keep and select Tools > Merge places from the menu.

RootsMagic will display a list of the places in your file. Just put a checkmark next to the places you want to merge into that place and click the OK button.

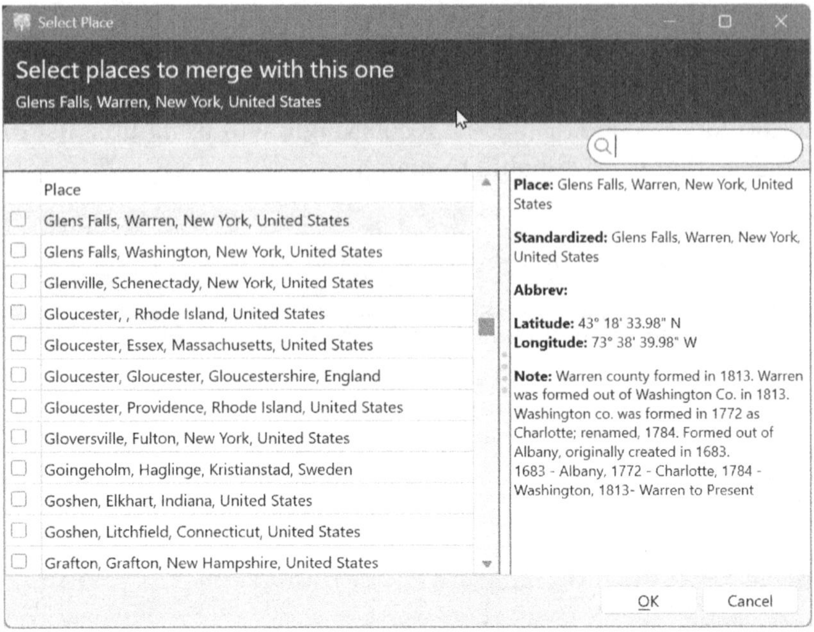


## MAPPING

RootsMagic makes it easy to view online maps of places in your database, as well as where events in people's lives occurred. This feature requires an internet connection. Select the Mapping button on the Places page and the RootsMagic Mapping screen will appear.

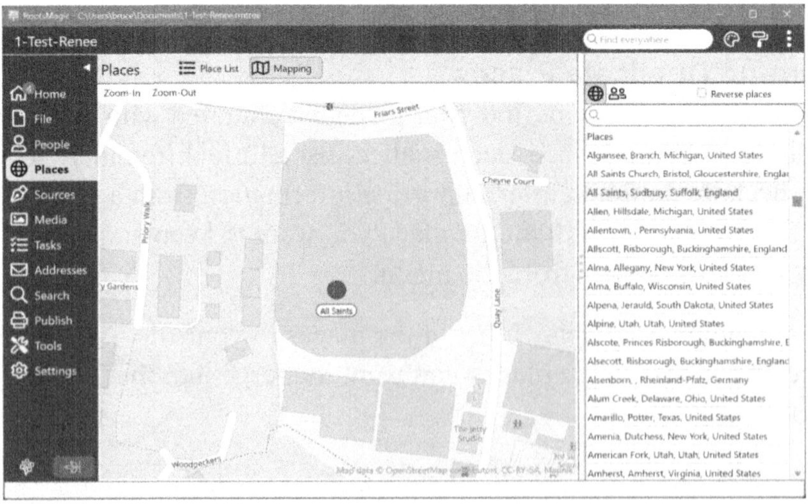

The map view is shown on the left side of the mapping display, and the right side is a list to tell RootsMagic what to display on the map.

## Mapping a Single Place

By default, the list contains all the places in your database. Just click on a place in the list and RootsMagic will display the map of that place.

You can zoom in or out to see more or less detail using either the mouse wheel, or the zoom options on the menu.

You can also check Reverse places to display the places reversed, so instead of:

City, County, State, Country

Each place would be displayed

Country, State, County , City

This has the effect of grouping places together in the list geographically.

## Mapping Events for Multiple People

*To see where events in a person's life occurred*, click the people icon above the list of places.

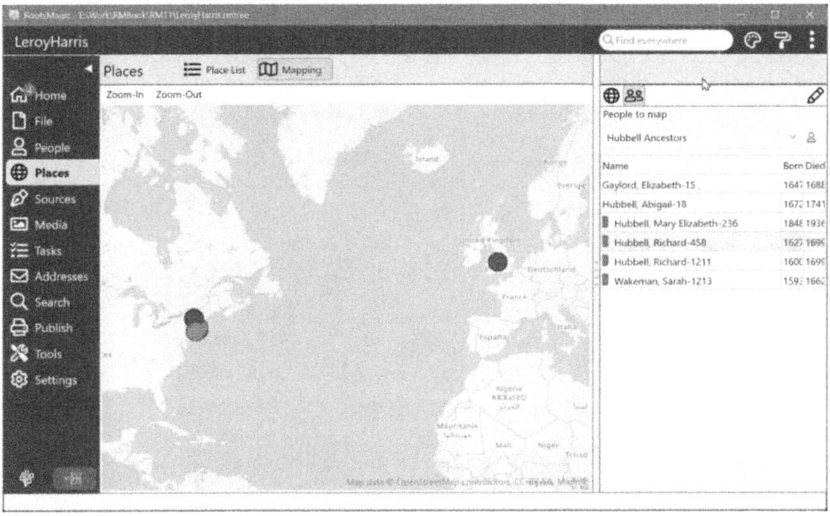

RootsMagic will change the list to display people in your database. A drop list at the top will let you choose which people to show in the list (by default it is set to Nobody). If you have any groups defined, you can directly select a group of people to display. Otherwise you can choose Select from a list and RootsMagic will let you select the group of people you want in the list.

Once you have selected a group of people, RootsMagic will display all the events for all of those people on the map with blue markers.

Just click on a person in the list and RootsMagic will change that person's event markers to red. You can move your mouse over any of those pins to see a list of the events that happened in that location.

## GAZETTEER

The Gazetteer is an easy way to look up places around the world. Select Tools > Gazetteer from the Places page menu, then enter part of a name to search for (it can be a city, state, country, etc.). The gazetteer will display places in the world which match what you entered.

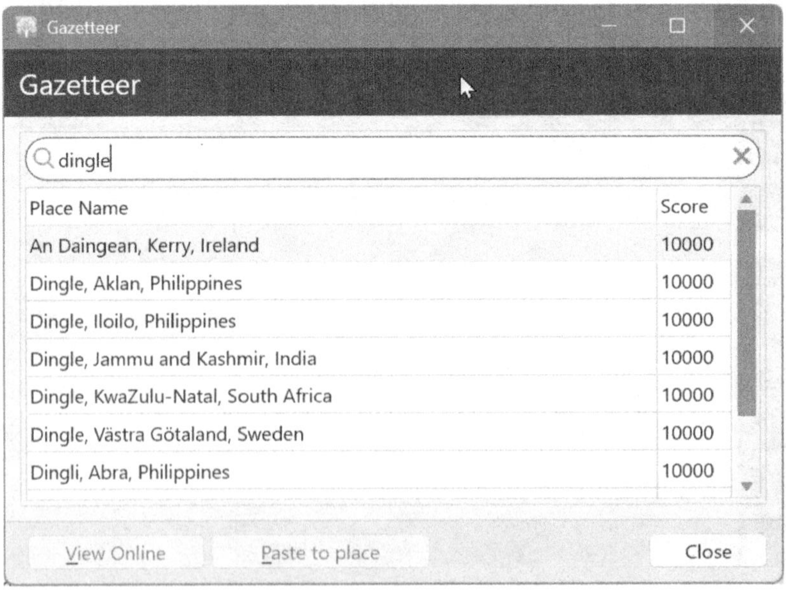

You can view an online map showing where in the world that place is located. When the Gazetteer is called from the Edit Person screen, you can paste the highlighted place into the place field for the fact.

## CountyCheck

RootsMagic's CountyCheck feature uses a different (specialized) database than the other place features. CountyCheck can tell you whether a county, state, or country existed on a particular date. Currently the CountyCheck feature is limited to places in the USA, Canada, United Kingdom, and Australia.

### *CountyCheck Explorer*

The CountyCheck Explorer lets you enter the name of a county or state, and will list possible matches. You can open this by selecting Tools > CountyCheck Explorer from the Places page menu.

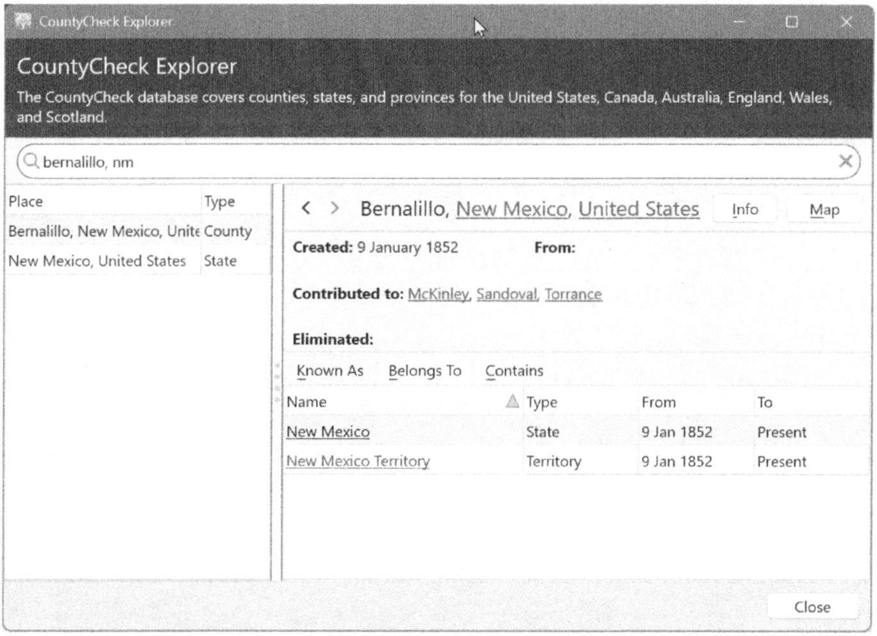


Highlight any of the possible matches and RootsMagic will display information about that place, including other names it may have been known by, places it contains, and places it belongs to.

You can also click the Info button to view more information about the place online, or you can click Map to view a historical boundaries map for the place.

### *Live CountyCheck*

As you enter events, CountyCheck will look at the date and place of the event and let you know whether the county, state or country existed on that date. If possible, RootsMagic will offer a suggestion for you to use. You can turn the live CountyCheck feature on or off in the Settings page (Program settings).

### *CountyCheck Report*

If you prefer to see all of CountyCheck's recommendations all at once, you can choose the CountyCheck report. This report is described in the chapter "Printing Reports".

## Cleaning Places

RootsMagic provides a special tool to help you clean and fix place names. This tool called PlaceClean is described in the chapter "Tools".

# SOURCES AND CITATIONS

One of the most important things you can do when researching your family history is to document your information. Without proper documentation, the data you hand down to your descendants will probably have to be checked all over again.

*Sources* allow you to document where your information about a person, family, or fact came from. For example, a birth source might be a birth certificate, a baby announcement, or a family bible with details of the person's birth.

## SOURCES AND CITATIONS

To use sources to document your family, you need to understand the difference between a Source and a Citation.

*A Source is* the actual paper or document that provides information about your family. For example, a source might be a birth certificate, a book, or a tombstone. When you enter a source, you will enter information about the source, like a description, title, author, publisher, etc. You can also select one or more "Repositories", which is just a fancy word for the place where the source is stored (like a library, courthouse, or even your own home).

*A Citation is* a reference to a source. By "citing" a source, you can allow a source to be entered just once, but cited many times. For example, if you cite a book as a source, you only enter the details about the book once (title, author, publisher), but you can cite it as many times as you want. The citation includes both the source, and also "source details" that are specific to that reference, such as the page number, volume, or film number. Like a source, a citation may be reused multiple times for different pieces of information.

*A citation link* is a link between a citation and the person, fact, or family using the citation. A citation link is not reusable.

As an example, if a person's birth were mentioned on page 93 of a book:

- The source would be the book, and you would enter the title, author and publisher of the book for the source.
- The citation would reference the source (book), and the citation details would also include page 93.
- The citation link would connect the person's birth with the citation above.

Citations for other people or facts might also cite the same citation if they were mentioned on the same page. Other people or facts that are mentioned on other pages would use the same source (book), but would link to a different citation using the different page numbers.

You can also enter actual text and comments from both the source and citation.

## Where Can I Use Sources?

Sources can be associated with individuals, families, or facts in a person's life.

- *Individual sources* are tied to a person. These sources are where you enter information about a person that won't fit in one of the facts for the person
- *Family sources* are tied to a family. These sources are where you enter information about a family that you don't want to enter separately for the father, mother and children
- *Fact sources* are tied to a fact in a person's life. These sources are where you enter more detailed information about the fact

## Sources Page

As you add sources, RootsMagic adds them to the Sources page, which is accessible by clicking "Sources" on the main screen side menu. The left side of the Sources page is the master source list, which is a list of all sources entered for the file.

## Source List

Each source in the list contains the source name and the number of citations using the source. As you highlight a source in the list, RootsMagic will display the details about the source in the edit panel on the right side of the screen.

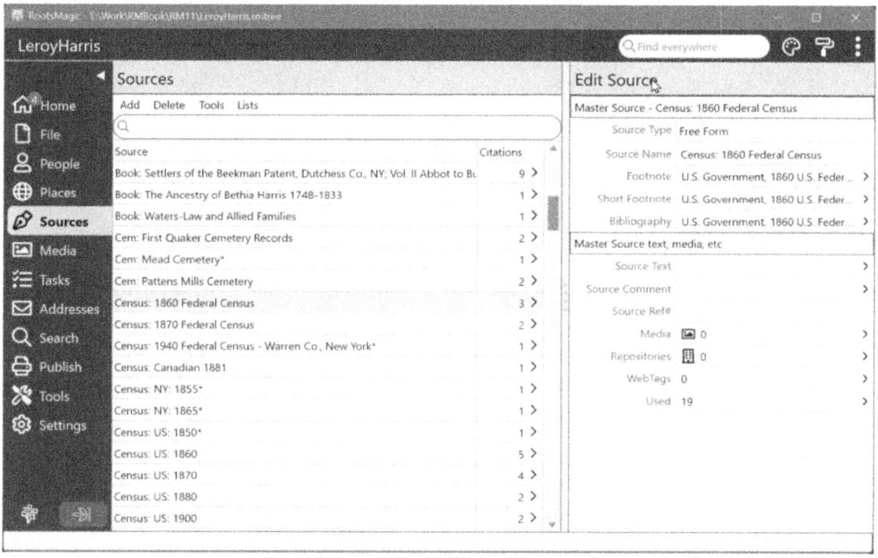

The top half of the edit panel lets you enter or change the information about the source itself. The fields available to edit will depend on what type of source you are entering.

The bottom half of the source panel lets you enter text from the source, comments about the source, and an optional reference number in case you have a special filing system for your sources.

You can also add or modify media, repositories, or WebTags attached to the sources.

The final item on the edit panel is "Used", which is a count of the number of times this source is used. Keep in mind that the "Used" value is usually not the same as the citation count, since citations can be reused over and over.

## Citation List

When you want to see a list of all the citations for a particular source, click the value in the Citations column to the right of the source names. RootsMagic will slide in a list of all the citations for the selected source. The source name will be in the header above the citation list.

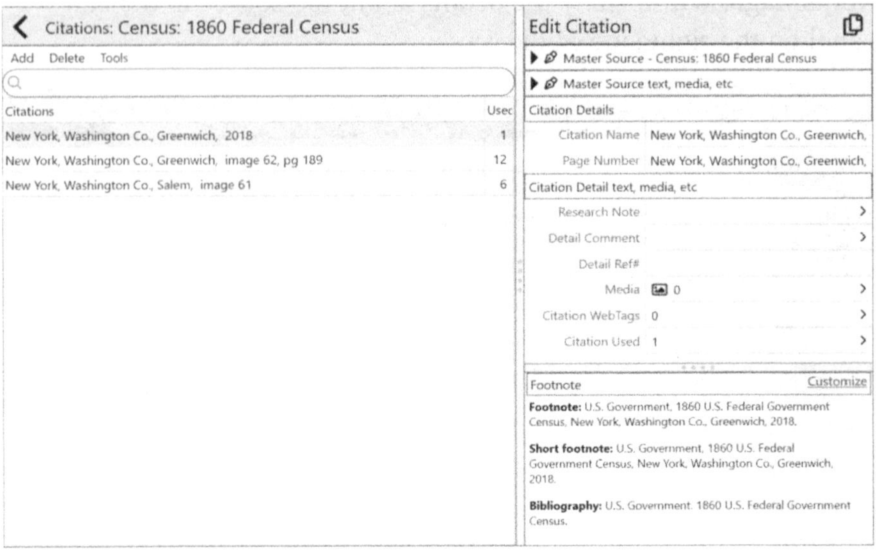


When you select a citation in the list, RootsMagic will display a citation edit panel on the right.

The top two sections of the citation edit panel contain the master source for the citation. They can be expanded by clicking on the arrow at the left of the headers. You can edit the master source here, but keep in mind that those changes will affect every citation using that same source.

The next two sections let you enter or edit details for the highlighted citation, as well as text, media, or WebTags for the citation.

You can also see how many times the highlighted citation is used. Clicking that count will display a list of every place the citation is used. Many other pages have a very similar "Used" list: media, addresses, repositories, places and tasks.

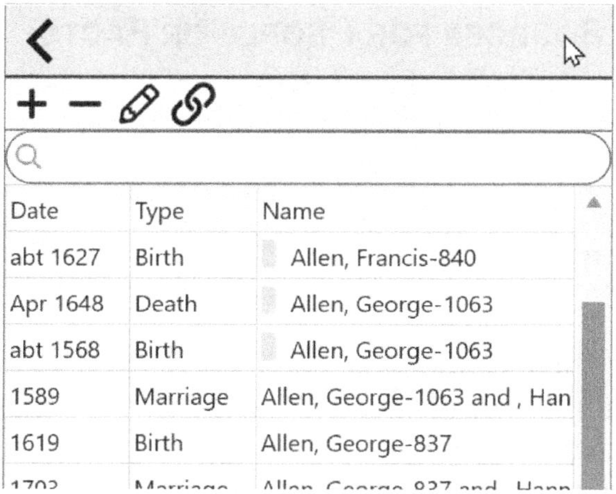


- Click the + button to add another person, family or fact to this citation.
- Click the – button to remove the highlighted person, family, or fact from the address.
- Click the pencil button to edit the person, family, or fact.
- Click the link button to change the person, family, or fact linked to the address.
- Filter the list by type or name using the search box above the list.

The bottom section of the edit panel shows you what the footnote, short footnote, and bibliography will look like with the data you have entered for the source and citation. They are generated based on the source template you used for the source. If you didn't use a source template, they will be whatever you type in the footnote, short footnote and bibliography fields of the free-form source.

If you want to customize the footnote, short footnote, or bibliography, you can click the "Customize" link and enter exactly what you want.

## Entering Sources for People or Facts

When you are on the Edit Person screen and click the Sources button for a person, fact or family, RootsMagic will slide in the list of citations for that item. This screen is a list of all the sources that have been cited (referenced) for that item.

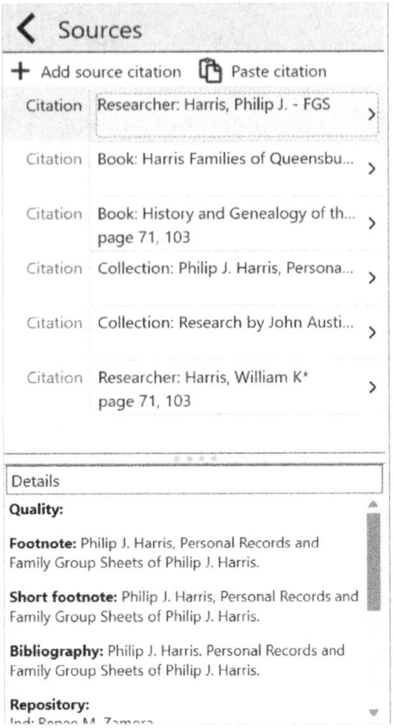


If you click on the word "Citation" in front of a citation, RootsMagic will display the details (footnote, short footnote, bibliography, repository, etc.) for that citation.

If you click on the citation itself, RootsMagic will slide in the citation edit panel for that citation. The edit panel will look exactly like the citation edit panel in the previous section, except that it will include a button in the header to "Copy" the citation to the clipboard to be used with the "Paste citation" feature. You can also click the trash can button on the citation edit panel to remove the citation from the person, fact or family.

### Citation Quality

The citation edit panel will also include 3 fields to define the "Quality" of the citation for the specific fact it is being used for. This quality follows the standards set down by the Board for Certification of Genealogists (BCG). Rather than just a "good" or "bad" type of quality rating, RootsMagic lets you choose the quality of

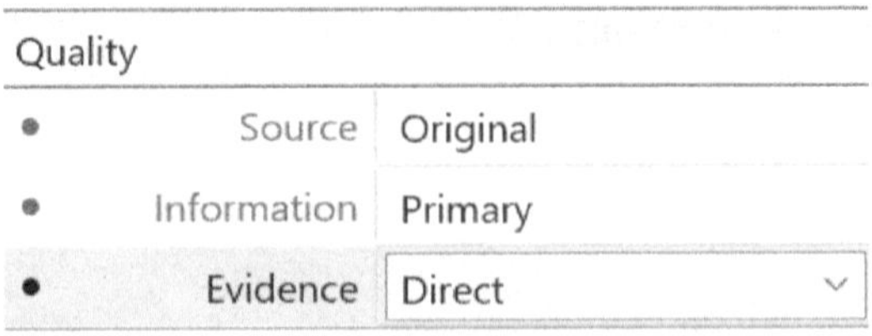

the source itself, the information in the source, and the evidence the source is attempting to answer.

Source

- **Original:** This source is in its first recorded form
- **Derivative:** This source is extracted, transcribed or otherwise derived from the original
- **Authored:** This source is an historical narrative. Information comes from other materials, but the author's conclusions form a new creation
- **Don't know**

Information

- **Primary:** This information was provided by someone with firsthand knowledge of the person or fact
- **Secondary:** This information was provided by someone with secondhand knowledge of the person or fact
- **Undetermined:** This source does not provide enough information to determine whether it is primary or secondary.
- **Don't know**

Evidence

- **Direct:** This source answers the research question by itself
- Indirect: This source is relevant, but needs additional information
- **Negative:** This source is missing information that it should contain
- **Don't know**

The quality is at the citation use level, since the same source (or even the same citation) can have a different quality depending on what it is used for. For example, a birth certificate could have a different quality depending on whether it was used for the person's birth, or used for the father's place of birth.

## Adding a Citation to a Person, Fact, or Family

When you are viewing the list of citations for a person, family or fact there will be two buttons above the list: Add source citation and Paste citation. The first button, which lets you enter or select a source and citation to add is described in the next chapter "Adding a New Source or Citation".

The second button lets you paste a memorized (copied) citation to the current record. It will display the memorized citation, and offer two different ways to paste that citation to the person, fact, or family.

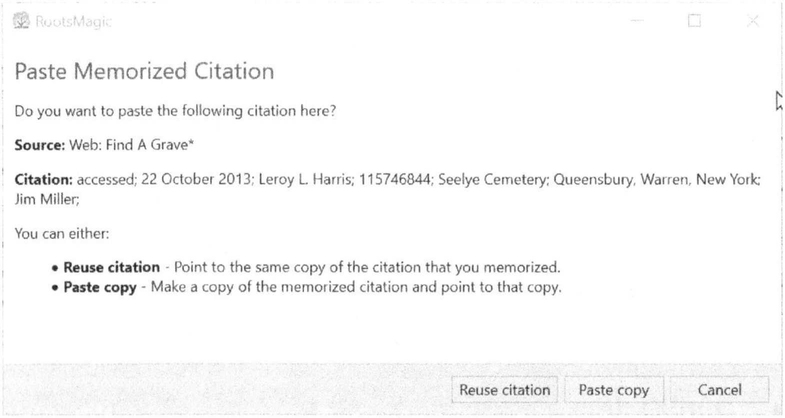


**Reuse citation** adds the actual memorized citation to the record. That means that if you later modify the citation, it will be modified for every fact that uses that same citation.

**Paste copy** makes a copy of the memorized citation, and then adds that copied citation to the record. This option is useful when you want to add a citation that is really close to an existing one but you may want to make a few specific changes.

## Adding a New Source or Citation

You can add a new source or citation from either the Sources page, or from the citation edit panel on the Edit Person screen.

To add a new source or citation:

1. Click the Add button on the source or citation list in the Sources Page.
2. Click the "Sources" button on the Edit Person screen for any fact or family. Then click the "Add source citation" button.

RootsMagic will display the "Add Source" screen, which is actually a wizard which steps you through adding (or selecting) a source and/or citation.

*On the Source page*, the screen will simply let you add a new source or citation (depending on whether you're on the source list or citation list).

*On the Edit Person screen*, RootsMagic will also let you select an existing source (or citation) as well as adding a new one. It will have a menu on the side to switch between Adding or Selecting sources or citations. If the source (or citation) already exists in the file, click the "Select existing" button and just choose the desired source (or citation) from the list.

### Adding a Source

When adding a new source, the first screen will be a list of source types to select from. Select the type of source you want to enter, and RootsMagic will display the appropriate fields for you to fill in.

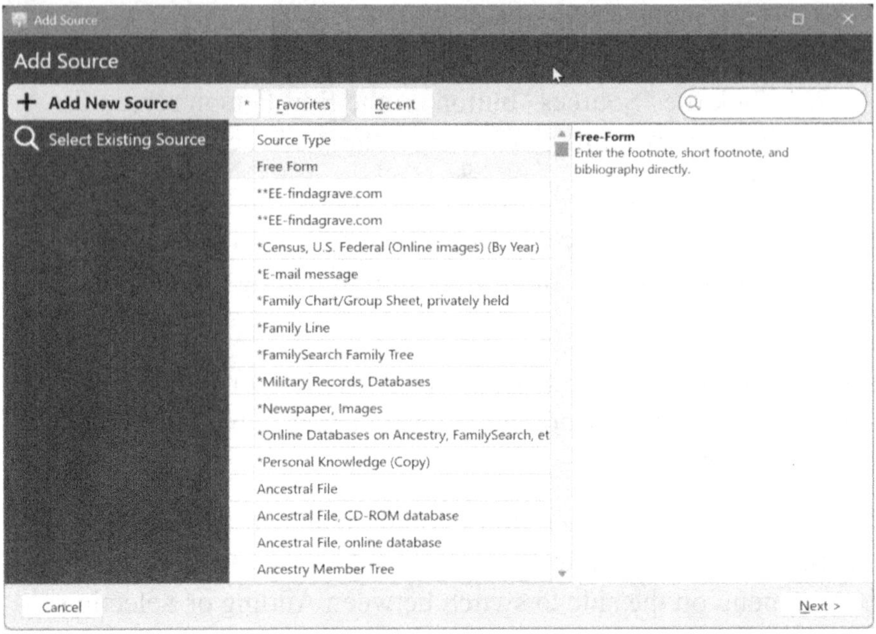


Notice that the first source type in the list is called "Free Form" (even though that isn't alphabetical like the rest of the list). It is a little different from the other source types.

*If you select a free form source*, RootsMagic will let you enter the footnote, short footnote, and bibliography directly for that source.

*If you select one of the source types (those that aren't free form)*, RootsMagic will provide specific fields for you to fill in for that source type. Just fill in the blanks and RootsMagic will write the properly formatted footnote, short footnote, and bibliography for you.

Rather than scroll through the long list of source types, enter what you are looking for in the search box in the upper right corner. RootsMagic will filter the list down to only those source types that match what you are looking for. For example, if you want to enter a birth certificate, type "birth certificate" into that field and the list will filter to only those source types.

Although there are over 400 different source types built in, most of us will only use a very small number of them. When you find a source type you think you will be using on a regular basis, highlight it in the list and then click the asterisk button in the header to make it a favorite. RootsMagic will place a star in front of the source type to indicate that. You can then select that source type quickly by clicking the Favorites button rather than scrolling through the long list.

Any time you use a new source type, RootsMagic will keep track of it. You can access these recently used source types by clicking the Recent button.

As you scroll through the list of source types, RootsMagic will display information about that source type on the right side of the screen, including the reference that the source type is based on. Here is a list to tell you which reference each of those cryptic codes refers to.

- EE = Evidence Explained
- E! = Evidence
- CYS = Cite Your Sources
- QS = Quick Sheet
- AQS = Ancestry Quick Sheet

*Free form sources* require you to enter the footnote, short footnote, and bibliography directly. If you want your sources to be entered in a proper format, this does require you to have some knowledge of how to put together a footnote or bibliography entry.

*A footnote is* a note of text which cites a source for something in the report. The footnote can appear at the bottom of a page (which is why it is called a "footnote"), but it can also be at the end of the report, in which case it is often called an "endnote". It is usually tagged to the text in the report with a superscript number.

*A bibliography* is an alphabetical list of the sources used in a report that appears at the end of the report. A source is only listed once in the bibliography regardless of how many times it is "cited" in the report.

But what if you don't know how to write a footnote or bibliography? The SourceWizard is RootsMagic's tool that will write properly formatted sources for you. When you choose a non-freeform source, you just choose the type of source, fill in the blanks, and RootsMagic writes the footnote, short footnote and bibliography.

SourceWizard source types are based on a number of different references: Evidence Explained, Evidence! and the various Quick Sheets by Elizabeth Shown Mills, and Cite Your Sources by Richard Lackey. The actual fields will differ based on the source type you selected.

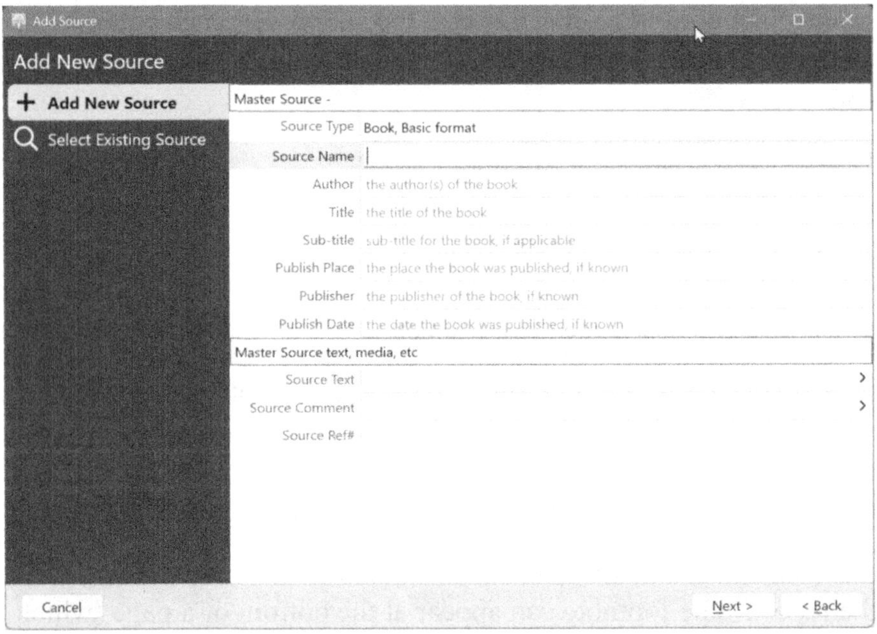


In addition to the fields that make up the source, you can also enter text or comments which apply to the source itself. Actual text from the source might be a transcription of the preface of a book. Any comments would apply to the book as a whole, such as a description of the quality of the book.

You can also enter an optional source reference number to tie your master source to your physical filing system. If you assign file numbers to the hard copies of your certificates, books, and other sources, you can enter that number here.

Just fill in the information you know for the source, then click the Next button. If you are entering a source on the master source list, the screen will close and RootsMagic will create the new source. If you are entering a new source and citation on the Edit Person screen, RootsMagic will create the source and then take you to a screen to add a citation using that source.

## Adding a Citation

Adding a citation for a source is very similar to adding the original source itself. If the citation you want already exists in the file, click the "Select Existing Citation" button on the left and just choose the desired citation from the list.

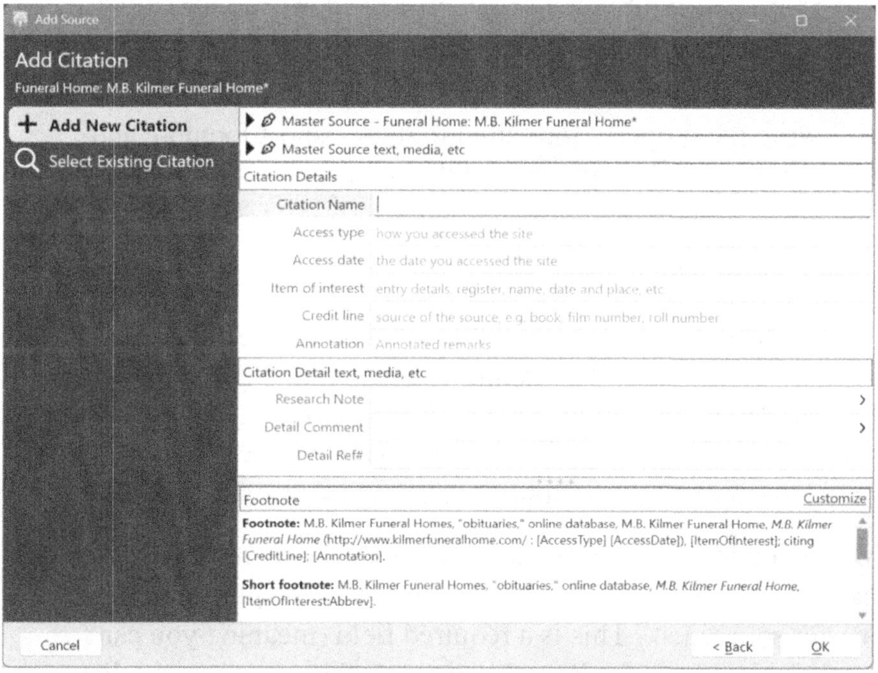


The top two sections contain the master source for the citation. They can be expanded by clicking on the arrow at the left of the headers. You can edit the master source here, but keep in mind that those changes will affect every citation using that same source.

The next two sections let you enter or edit Research notes and comments for the highlighted citation. You might want to enter a summary, transcription, or extraction of the part of the source you are using in this instance. You can also enter any comments about the research notes as well.

Entering a detail reference number on this page lets you tie this detail to your physical filing system. This is useful if (for example) you assign file numbers to page numbers within books, rather than just to the book itself.

The bottom section of the edit panel shows you what the footnote, short footnote, and bibliography will look like with the data you have entered for the source and citation. They are generated based on the source template you used for the source. If you didn't use a source template, they will be whatever you type in the footnote, short footnote and bibliography fields of the free-form source.

As you fill in the fields in the citation section, the SourceWizard will write the properly formatted footnote, short footnote and bibliography on the right side of the screen.

Each field will have a gray text hint in the field to let you know what kind of data it is expecting.

As you enter text in various fields you will notice the fields are actually quite smart. For example, a name field (like author) knows how to display the name as "John Doe", "Doe", or even "Doe, John" depending on how it needs to be formatted. But you only have to enter it as "John Doe".

When you save the new source, RootsMagic will ask you to enter a name for the source. This the text you want displayed in the master source list. This is a required field (meaning you can't leave it blank). Since RootsMagic sorts the master source list alphabetically, you can use this name to make the sources sort the way you want. For example, you could enter the names of census sources so that they group in an understandable fashion, like:

Census, Iowa, 1870

Census, Iowa, 1880

Census, Iowa, 1900

Census, New Mexico, 1910

Census, New Mexico, 1920

Census, Utah, 1910

## Source Options

RootsMagic provides a number of options when working with sources on the Source page.

### Printing Your Sources

If you want a report of which people, families, and facts are citing a particular source, select Tools > Print Sources from the menu on the Sources page. RootsMagic will print up the report dialog for the Source list.

### Adding a Source to a Group of People

If you have a source that you need to add to more than one person, highlight the citation in the Citation view of the Sources page, then select Tools > Add this citation to multiple people. RootsMagic will bring up the selection screen so that you can mark all the people you want to add the source to. RootsMagic will add the citation as a general citation to everyone you select.

### Copying a Source or Citation

You may find a need to add a source (or citation) that is very similar to another source (or citation) already entered. In this case you can highlight the similar source (or citation) in the list and select Tools > Copy selected source (or Tools > Copy selected citation) from the menu. RootsMagic will make an exact copy of the source (or citation) which you can edit. The new source or citation will have the same name as the original except with (copy) added to the end of the name.

## Merging Duplicate Sources

There may be times when you find multiple copies of the same source. This sometimes happens when importing a GEDCOM file that came from a program that doesn't allow you to reuse sources. RootsMagic offers two options for merging duplicate sources.

1. To merge all exact duplicate sources into a single source open the Sources page, then select Tools > Merge all duplicate sources from the menu. RootsMagic will merge all the exact duplicate sources in your database. If there is any difference in the source footnote, short footnote, bibliography, actual text or comments field, the sources will not be merged.
2. To merge two sources (even if one is a little different from the other), highlight the primary source in the source list and select Tools > Merge sources from the menu. You can then select the duplicate source and click the OK button. RootsMagic will ask if you want to merge the duplicate source into the primary source. RootsMagic does not combine the text from the two sources. It only keeps the text from the primary source and merges citations of the duplicate source into the primary source.

## Merging Duplicate Citations

RootsMagic not only allows reusing source, but also lets you reuse citations. RootsMagic offers two options for merging duplicate citations.

1. To merge all exact duplicate citations into a single citation open the Sources page, then select Tools > Merge all duplicate citations from the menu. RootsMagic will merge all the exact duplicate citations in your database. If there is any difference in the citations fields the citations will not be merged.
2. To merge two citations (even if one is a little different from the other), select the citation list for the desired source and select Tools > Merge citations from the menu. You can then select the duplicate citation and click the "OK" button.

RootsMagic will ask if you want to merge the duplicate citation into the primary citation. RootsMagic does not combine the text from the two citations. It only keeps the text from the primary citation.

## Creating New Source Types

While RootsMagic provides over 400 different source types, there may be times when you want to create your own source type that isn't already built in. To see a list of all the built-in source types, select Lists > Source template list from the menu on the Sources page.

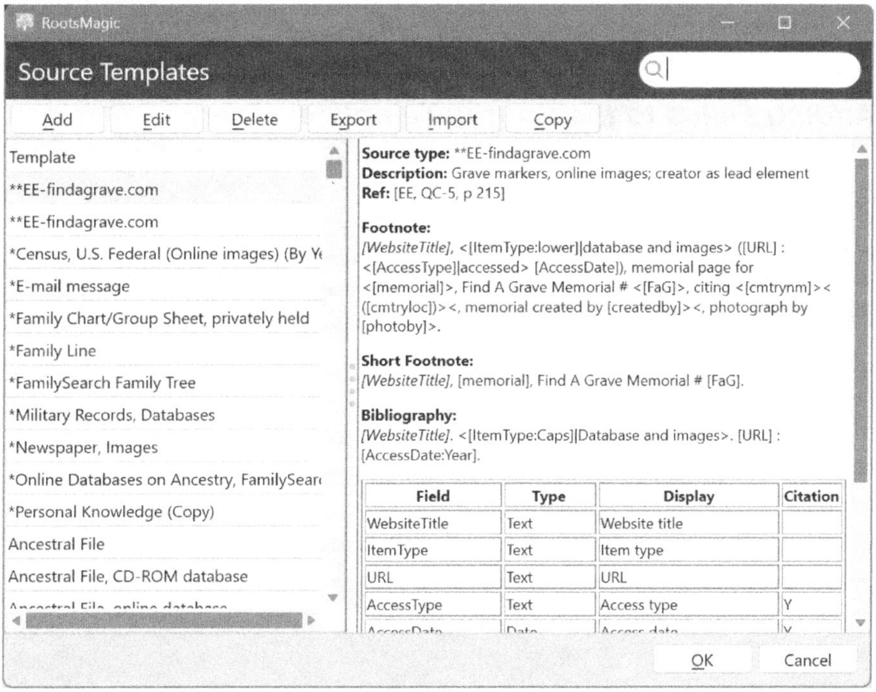

### Adding a New Source Type

To create a new source type, click the Add button to open the Source Template Editor.

There are two steps to creating a new source template; adding the fields which the user will fill in with data, and telling RootsMagic how to put those fields together to make a proper source citation.

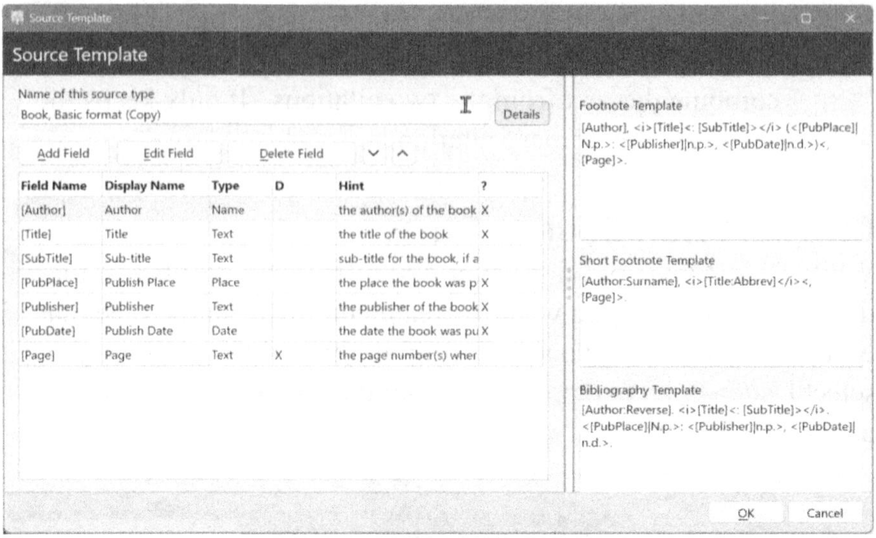


### ***Adding Fields to the Source Template***

To add a field, click the Add Field button and fill in the screen that appears.

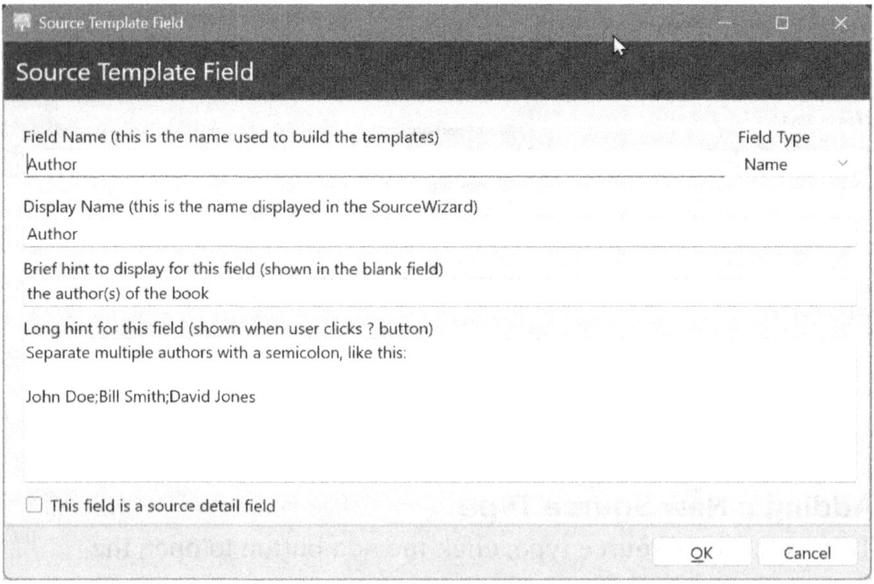


There are several pieces of information you need to enter for each field:

- **Field Name:** This is the name that you will use when creating the templates. It can't contain any spaces, and you might want to keep it kind of short but readable.
- **Field Type:** Choose from Text, Name, Date, or Place. This determines what features RootsMagic will apply to this field.
- **Display Name:** This is the name of the field as it is displayed in the SourceWizard when entering a source of this type.
- **Brief Hint:** This is the gray text which is shown in the field when it is blank. Try to keep it short so it will fit and display in the field.
- **This field is a source detail field:** This is a very important option. It tells RootsMagic whether this field is part of the Master Source, or part of the source details. This is useful for fields like page numbers which are different for each use of that source.

You can edit or delete fields from the Source Template Editor, as well as rearrange the order of the fields using the up and down arrow buttons.

### *Creating the Source Templates*

After you have added the fields for your new source type, you need to tell RootsMagic how to put them together to create the footnote, short footnote, and bibliography. The Source Template Editor has 3 fields for you to do just that.

To create the templates, you can use the fields you created in the first step (put them in square brackets) and include the punctuation you want between them. For example:

[Author], [Title] ([PubPlace]: [Publisher], [PubDate]), [Page].

When RootsMagic has to put that source together, it will replace [Author] with whatever you enter into the author field on the source screen, [Title] with whatever you enter into the title screen, and so on.

Now of course that is a very basic template, and you will want to fix it up some more. Since you would want the title to be displayed in italics you can put <i> and </i> around it, like this:

[Author], <i>[Title]</i> ([PubPlace]: [Publisher], [PubDate]), [Page].

Those two little symbols tell RootsMagic to turn italics on and then off.

But what if there were cases where a page number (the [Page] field) might not be entered by the user? RootsMagic lets you use angle brackets < > to tell the source template not to print something unless the user actually fills in the field. So if you did this:

[Author], <i>[Title]</i> ([PubPlace]: [Publisher], [PubDate])<, [Page]>.

those angle brackets tell RootsMagic not to print the comma or the [Page] field unless the [Page] field actually contains something.

There are a *ton* of other things you can do with source templates (way too many to talk about here). There is an appendix at the end of the book which describes the entire template language available.

### Editing and Deleting Source Types

You can click the Edit button to edit a source type that you have created. You can't edit one of the built-in source types since they are custom designed based on *Evidence Explained*, *Evidence!*, and several other standard formats.

> **☺ Tip**
>
> If you want a source type that is very much like one of the existing ones, highlight that source type and click the "Copy" button. RootsMagic will make an exact copy of that source type which you can then edit (and rename so that you know it is yours).

When you edit a source template, you will use the exact same screens and techniques described in the previous section (Adding a New Source Type).

*If you want to delete one of your own source templates*, highlight it in the list and click the "Delete" button. As with editing, you can't delete any of the built-in source types.

### Importing and Exporting Source Types

RootsMagic makes it possible to share a source template you have created with other people. Just highlight the template in the list and click the Export button. RootsMagic will open the standard File Save dialog so that you can save that template to a file.

You can then give a copy of that file to another RootsMagic user and they can click the Import button on the Source Types list to import that new source type into their file.

# Media - Pictures, Sound, and Video

As accessibility to scanners, digital cameras and smartphones have increased it becomes easier to add photos or video to your computerized genealogy. RootsMagic lets you attach media items to different record types: people, facts, families, names, sources, citations, places, tasks and associations.

## Media Page

As you add media items (images, videos, sound clips, or just plain old files), RootsMagic adds them to the Media page, which is accessible by clicking "Media" on the main screen side menu.

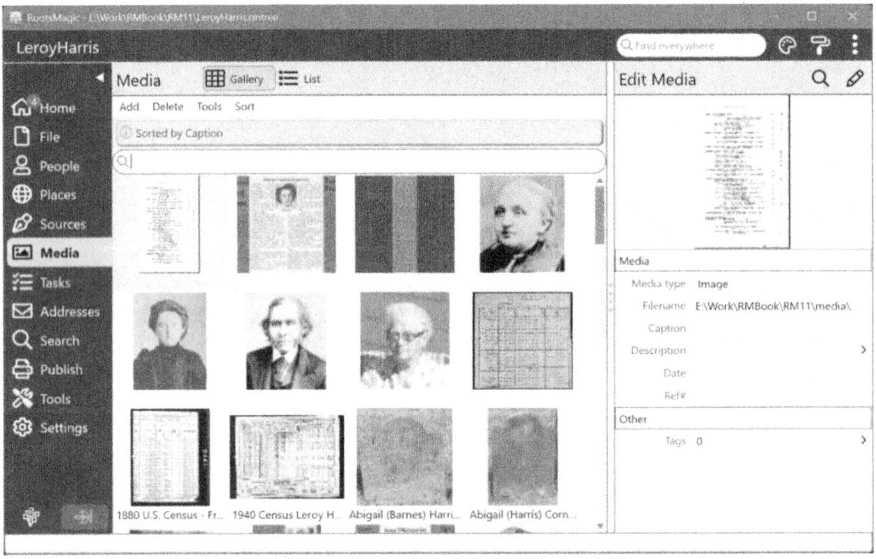


The Media page displays thumbnails of all the media items you have added to the database. You can also select the list view icon above the thumbnail gallery to instead view the images in a list format. The list format shows more details for each item, at the expense of a smaller thumbnail. It's easy to just switch back and forth as needed.

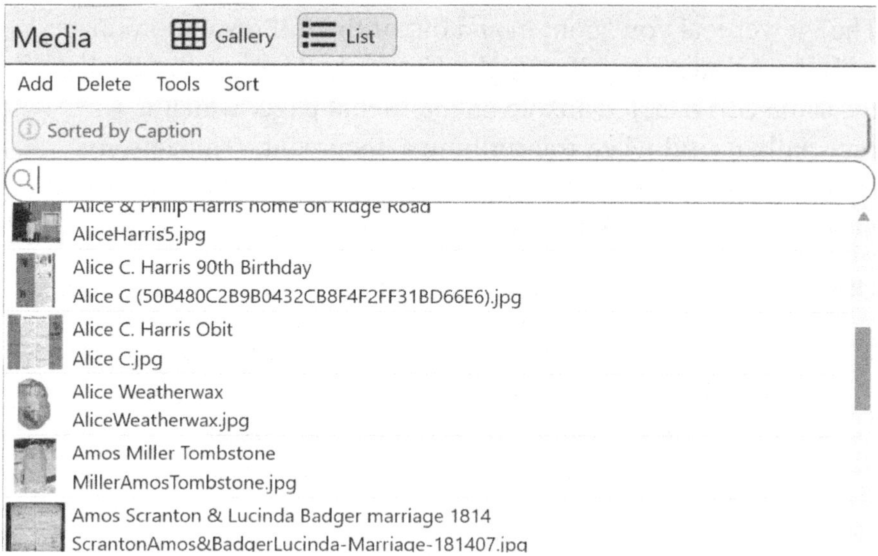


As you select a media item in the thumbnail or list view, RootsMagic will display the details about the media item in the edit panel on the right side of the screen.

The upper section of the edit panel is a copy of the image, with two buttons above it. The magnifying glass button will open the image in the built-in RootsMagic image viewer.

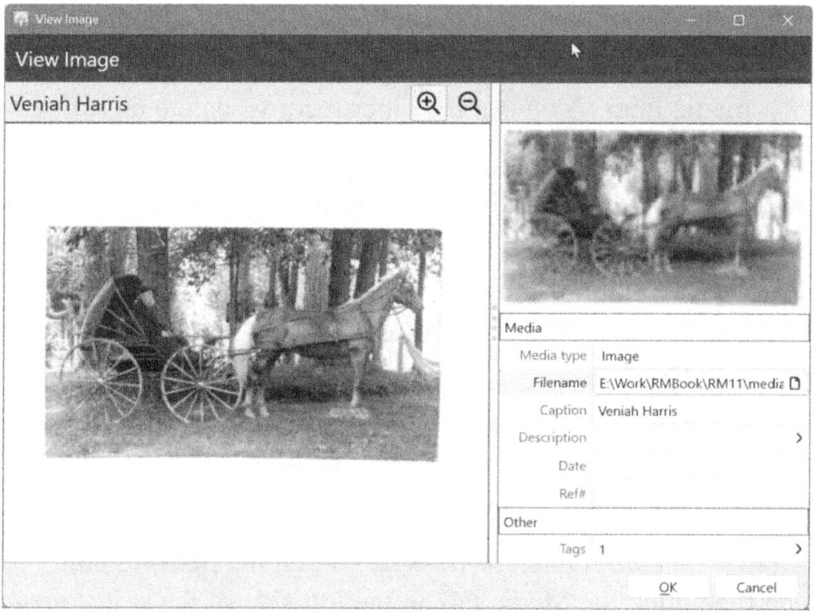

The viewer lets you zoom in and out of the full resolution image with the + and – magnifying glass buttons. The viewer also has the same edit panel available on the Media page, which is especially useful when transcribing a document. This lets you zoom into an image for a better view as you type the transcription into the description field of the media item.

Other items you can modify in the edit panel for a media item are:

- *Media type* lets you specify whether the media is an image, sound clip, video clip, or file (like Word, PDF, etc.).
- *Filename* let you select the media item itself.
- *Caption* is one line of text you can use to display under the image in some reports.
- *Description* is a note where you can enter transcriptions, descriptions of a picture, or any other text associated with the media item.
- *Date* lets you enter an optional date for the picture. This could be the date a picture was taken, the date you added it to RootsMagic, or any other date you want.
- *Ref#* is an optional reference number to use for any purpose needed.
- *Tags* is the number of places the media is used. Clicking the Tags button will bring up a list of every use of the media item. You can tag other records, delete tags, or edit the owning record itself from the list.

*You can filter the list of media items* by typing what you want to find in the search box above the thumbnail view. It will display items whose Caption or Filename contain the text you enter.

## Media Album

RootsMagic also provides a Multimedia Album for each person, family, fact, source, citation and place in your database. This album can hold scanned photos, files, sound clips, and video clips.

*To view the media album for a person*, open the person's edit screen then click the Media tab on the left side of the edit screen.

The media album will display all media attached to the person, their facts, and families.

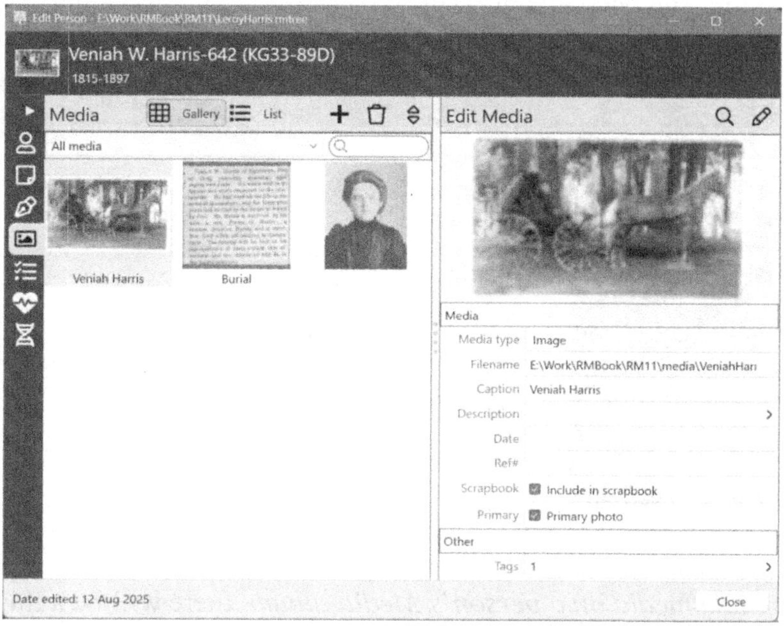


The media album for a person looks and works almost exactly the same way as the media page, except that it is limited to only the media items associated with the current person.

You can filter the media album to only show the media items for a single fact or family by clicking the drop list labeled "All media" above the images. You will see not only the person (general), but all facts and families for the person, as well as all citations for them. Any item that has media attached to it will have an asterisk * in front of the item in the drop list. Select any item from the drop list to see the media specifically attached to that item.

## Adding Media

*You can add new media from both the Media page and a person's media album* by clicking the Add + button. RootsMagic will open the "Add Media" form, which will have either 2 or 3 ways to add a new media item.

*When you add media on the main Media Page*, there will be two ways to add the media: selecting it with open file, or drag and drop it into the Add Media page.

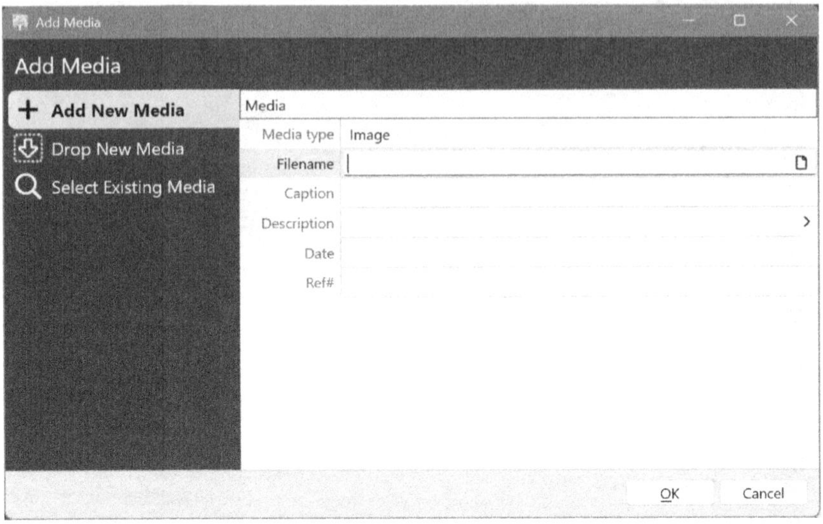


*If you add media on a person's Media album*, there will be a third way; selecting existing media that has previously been added.

## Entering the Media Properties

The default option when adding media is to select it directly. You can select the media type (image, sound, video, or file), and enter the filename of the media. When you click the filename field, a button will appear to the right that you can click to select the media via the Open File dialog.

**Caption:** allows you to enter a one line description of the photo, like John on his first birthday.

**Description:** allows you to enter a more detailed description of the photo. This is especially useful for listing the names of all the people in a family photograph.

**Date:** lets you enter a date for the media. This can be the date the photo was taken.

**Ref#:** lets you enter a personal file number which ties this record to your own filing system.

Once you have everything entered the way you want, click the OK button and RootsMagic will add the photo.

If you ever want to change the caption, description, or other settings for the photo, simply click on the photo in the album and edit the information in the edit panel.

### Adding Media Items the Fast Way

RootsMagic also lets you quickly add multiple media items to an album by dragging and dropping them. Select "Drop New Media" from the menu on the left side, and you can select multiple media items from your desktop, file manager, or other location, then using your mouse drag them to the drop target. You can then select the individual media items in the album to edit their caption or description, or tag them to other records.

### Adding a Previously Added Media Item

To reuse a previously added media item click the **"Select Existing Media"** menu on the left. This will show all the media items you have added to the current database. Just highlight the desired item and click the "OK" button.

## Tagging Media Items

RootsMagic knows that a picture can contain more than just a single person, place or thing. RootsMagic lets you "tag" a picture or media item with the person, family, event, source, citation, task, association, or place the media item refers to. A media item can have more than one tag, so you can, for example, tag a census image with the people and family mentioned in the image, the source or citation for the census, and the place the census image refers to.

To tag a picture, click the "Tags" button on the edit media panel. RootsMagic will display a list of all items using the media item. From this list you can add, edit, or delete tags, or even edit the original record itself.

To add a tag, click the + button above the list and RootsMagic will display the Add/Edit Tag form.

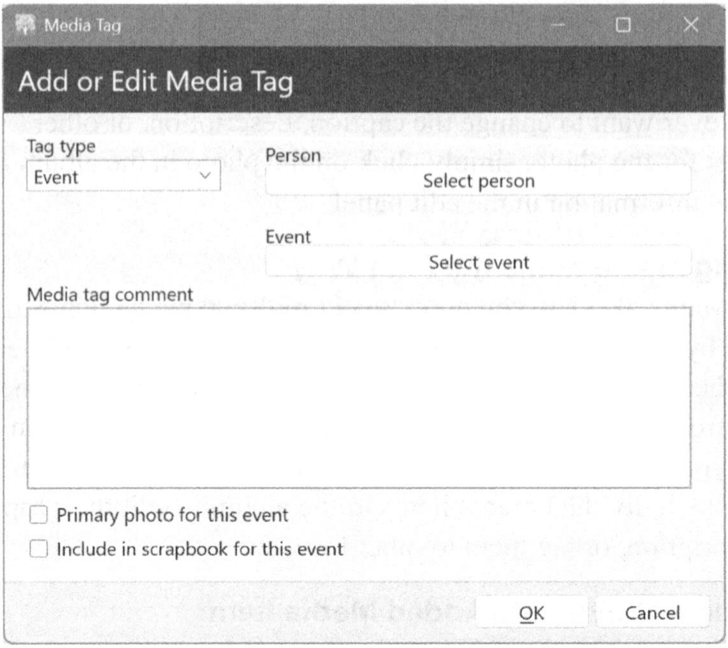


Select the type of item you want to tag the media with and then select the item itself. You can enter a comment for the tag to provide more details about that particular item in the picture.

*"Primary photo"* lets you tell RootsMagic which photo in an album is the one that you want printed on charts, since RootsMagic allows you to add unlimited photos to an album. The primary photo is also displayed on the main screen for the person.

*"Include in scrapbook"* lets you tell RootsMagic whether you want this photo to be included when you print the scrapbook.

**Warning**

RootsMagic only stores links to multimedia items, not the items themselves. Therefore, moving the items to another directory will cause RootsMagic to lose track of them and report the links as invalid.

If this happens, open the Media page, and select **Tools > Fix broken media links** from the menu.

## REMOVING MEDIA

To remove an item (photo, document, sound or video clip) from RootsMagic, highlight the item, then click the Delete (trash can) button. RootsMagic will ask if you really want to remove the item. Click on Yes to remove the item.

*When removing an item from a person's edit screen*, RootsMagic simply removes the link to the item. It doesn't actually remove the image, document, sound or video file from the hard drive itself.

*When removing an item from the Media page*, RootsMagic will not only remove the media item from the file, but will also remove all tags for the media item.

## REARRANGING MEDIA IN AN ALBUM

Since you may not always add your photos in the same order you want them displayed or printed, RootsMagic allows you to rearrange them any way you want (for example, from baby picture to 100th birthday photo). Just click the rearrange button (up/down arrows) on the album, and RootsMagic will bring up a list of all media attached to the current record, which you can drag and drop into the desired order.

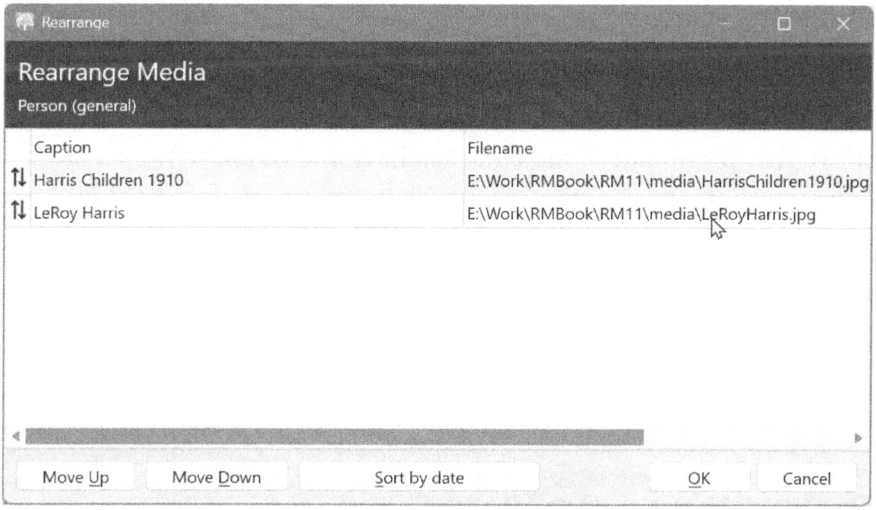

This is only available from the Edit Person media album, and not from the general media page. It will let you arrange the order of the media for the specific item it is attached to. If you try to rearrange while showing "All media", RootsMagic will only rearrange the General media, since it's only possible to arrange media attached to a single record.

## Printing Scrapbook Photos

RootsMagic allows you to print your photos in a variety of ways.

*If you simply want to print a single photo*, open the Media page, click on the photo you want to print, then select Print from the Tools menu.

*If you want to print your photo with data*, just choose any of the RootsMagic printouts that offer a checkbox to include photos, and make sure that box is checked. RootsMagic will print photos in books, individual summary, family group sheet, scrapbooks, or photo tree.

## Viewing and Editing a File

When you add a file to an album, RootsMagic displays the icon for the file type in the album.

*To view a file*, select the media item in either the Media page or Edit Person media album, then click the magnifying glass button above the thumbnail in the edit panel. RootsMagic will open an image with its internal viewer, or a non-image file using the program which is associated with that file type in your operating system.

If you click the Edit (pencil) button when selecting an image, RootsMagic will open the image in whatever program is associated with images in your operating system.

## Playing Sound and Video Clips

When you add a sound clip or video clip to an album, RootsMagic displays the icon of the media type. *To play a sound or video clip,* select the media item in either the Media page or Edit Person media album, then click the magnifying glass button above the thumbnail in the edit panel. RootsMagic will open the file using the program which is associated with that file type in your operating system.

# TASKS

Although RootsMagic is designed to store information you have already collected, it can also assist you in your research by helping track your research tasks.

## TASK PAGE

*The Task page* provides a place to save all those tasks you need to accomplish. It lets you enter an unlimited number of "tasks", which include information like goals, results, and dates, and lets you attach records to a task like people, families, events, sources, citations, places, media, and more. You can group tasks in folders, or filter the entire list of tasks in any manner desired.

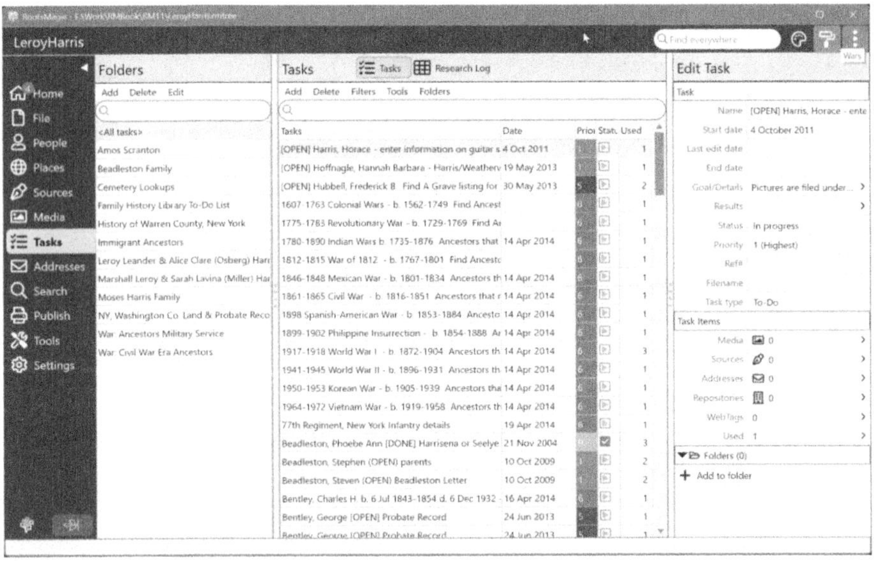


### Task List

The task list (the center column) will display all the tasks in your file. It will include the task name, open date, priority, status, and a count of how many places the task is used (or linked to). You can sort the list in different ways by clicking the header of the column you want to sort by. The "Used" column is the one column that you can't sort by since it is calculated on the fly in the list.

When you highlight a task in the list, RootsMagic will display the details about that task in the edit panel to the right of the list.

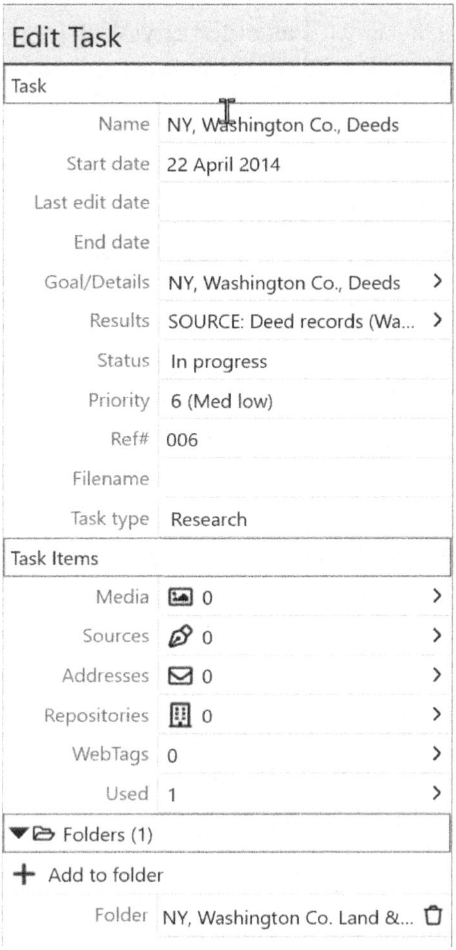


- *Name* is a one-line description of the task.
- *Start date* lets you enter the date you created this task.
- *Last edit date* lets you enter the most recent date you worked on this task.
- *End date* lets you enter the date you finished this task. Although many people will just delete a task they have finished, others want to keep a record of the tasks.
- *Goals / Details* is a note field that lets you enter full details on the task and what needs to be accomplished.
- *Results* is a note field where you can enter any results related to your task.
- *Status* lets you specify whether the task is still open or whether it has been completed. You can also denote if there is a problem with the task.
- *Priority* lets you specify how urgent this task is from 1 (highest priority) through 9 (lowest)
- *Ref#* lets you enter a number or text to tie this task to your paper records.
- *Filename* lets you link the task to a file on your hard drive. This could be a file which provides more information about the task.

- *Task type* lets you choose whether the task is research, to-do, or correspondence.

You can also link media, sources, addresses, or repositories to the task, as well as enter any WebTags (links) for the task. You can also click the "Used" button to see a list of any other records which are linked to the task (people, families, events, etc).

The bottom section of the edit panel shows you what folders the task is in. A task can be in more than one folder, and you can add or remove tasks from folders in this panel.

### Task Folders

The left side of the Task page is the folder list. A folder is basically a way of grouping together tasks that belong together for any reason. You can create a folder for example to hold all the tasks related to a particular family. Or perhaps you wish to use a folder to hold tasks that are related to a specific research task (basically a "research log").

You can add, edit, and delete folders using the buttons in the header of the folder list. Once you've created a folder, you can add tasks to the folder by highlighting the task and clicking the "Add to folder" button at the bottom of the edit panel.

When you want to see all the tasks in a folder, just click the name of the folder in the list and the Task list will filter to show only the tasks in that folder. Click on <All tasks> in the folder list to restore the task list back to all tasks.

If you want to temporarily hide (and show) the folders list (to make more room for the tasks), click the folder button above the task list.

## Research Log View

When displaying the tasks in a folder, RootsMagic offers another view of the tasks, called the Research Log view.

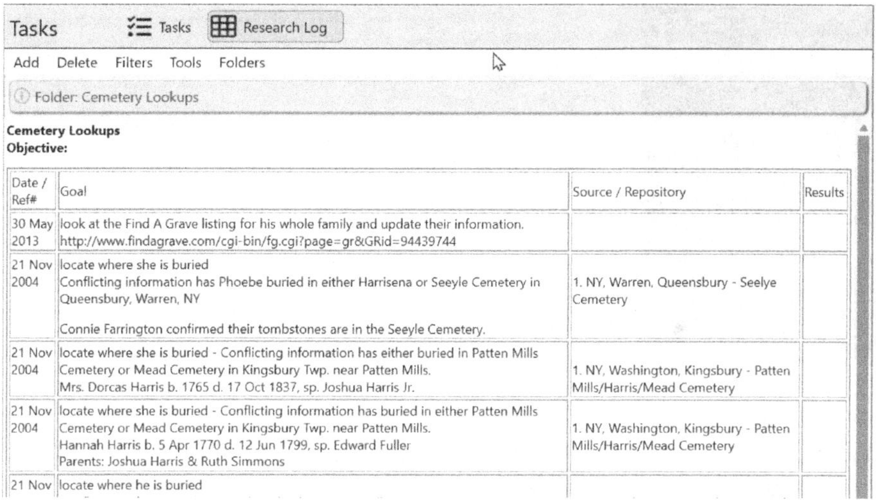


This view displays the tasks in a table in the form of a research log, which lets you treat a folder as a research log. Selecting the research log view when you are displaying all tasks (not a folder) will display a message that the research log view requires you to select a folder.

## ADDING A TASK

You can add a task to RootsMagic in two different ways: first by clicking the Add menu in the Tasks page, and second by clicking the Tasks button and then Add Task in an edit panel (like when editing a fact in the edit person screen, or any other edit panel which supports tasks).

The Add Task form will include the same fields in either case, and will be the same as when editing a task as described in the previous chapter. When adding a task in an edit panel, the Add Task form will have a side menu which will let you either add a task, or select an existing task. When adding a task from the Tasks page, there will be no option for "selecting" a task.

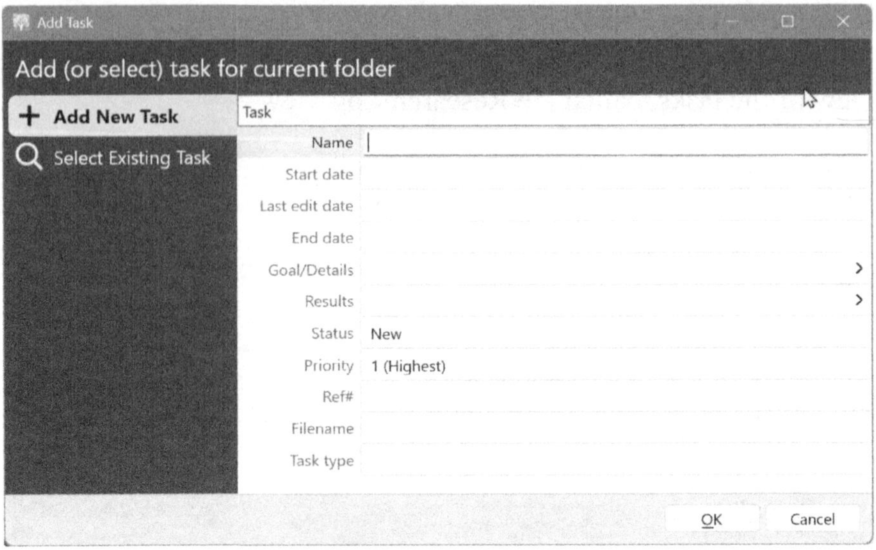


When adding a task on the Tasks page, RootsMagic will create the new task and display it in the list.

When adding a task in an edit panel, RootsMagic will create the new task (or use the selected task), and then link the new or selected task to the record the edit panel is for. For example, if you are editing a fact in the Edit Person screen, and choose to add a task, the new or selected task will be linked to that fact.

## Filtering Tasks

While it's nice to be able to create unlimited tasks in your file, the real power of tasks comes in the ability to filter the list to only show the tasks you are interested in.

To create a filter, select Filters > Filter tasks from the menu. You can create and apply a filter, and then use the "Clear filter" option from the same menu to restore the list back to all tasks in the file.

The filter form has two sections of filter options: filtering based on the content of the task itself, and filtering based on records the task is linked to.

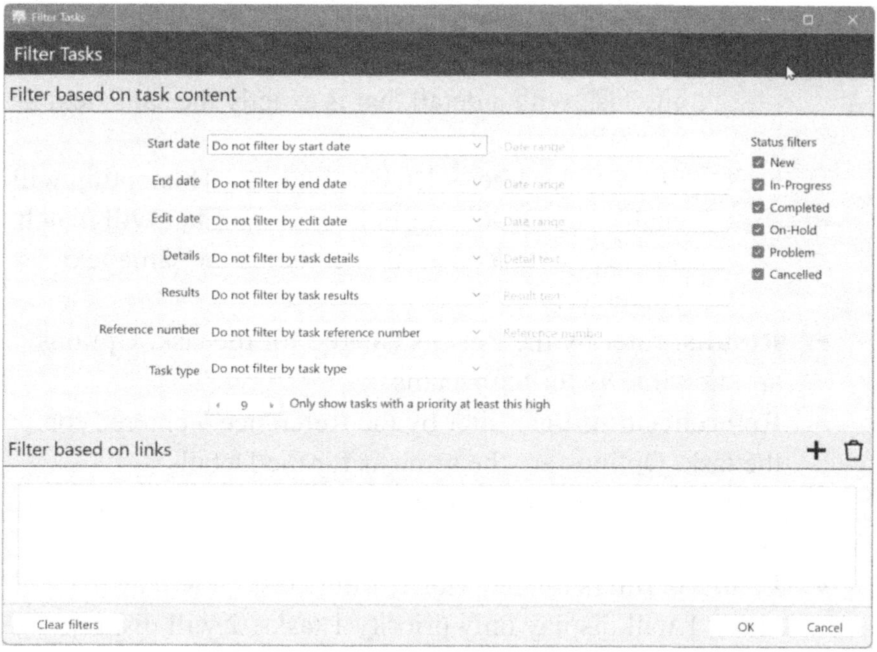


## Filtering by the Task Content

The top half of the filter form lets you create a filter based on the contents of the task itself. You can filter by:

- **Start date**: filter by the start date of the task. Options are:
    - Do not filter by start date
    - Only show tasks with no start date
    - Only show tasks with a start date of - Selecting this option will enable the "Date range" field. You can enter a single date, a date range (like "between 1920 and 1930"), or an open range (like "before 1920" or "after 1920").
- **End date**: filter by the end date of the task. Options are the same as for the Start date
- **Edit date**: filter by the edit date of the task. Options are the same as for the Start date
- **Details**: filter by the Details / Goals entered for the task. Options are:
    - Do not filter by task details

    - Show tasks where details equals - This option will enable the Detail text field, and the filter will match any task with a detail that is exactly the same text as you enter.
    - Show tasks where details contains - This option will enable the Detail text field, and the filter will match any task with a detail that contains the same text you enter.
- **Results**: filter by the Results entered for the task. Options are the same as for the Details
- **Reference number**: filter by the Reference # entered for the task. Options are the same as for the Details
- **Task type**: filters by the task type (to-do, research item, or correspondence)
- **Priority**: filters by the priority of the task. 9 will display all tasks, 1 will display only priority 1 tasks, 2 will display priority 1 and 2 tasks, etc.
- **Status:** Enter checks for any statuses you want to display. Remove checkboxes from any statuses you want filtered out.

You can mix and match the filter criteria above. Just be aware that all criteria you select must match for a task to be displayed.

### Filtering by Records Linked to the Task

In addition to the filters above, you can also add filters based on what the task is linked to. These filters work together with the filters above and can be mixed and matched. Click the + button in the section header to add a link filter.

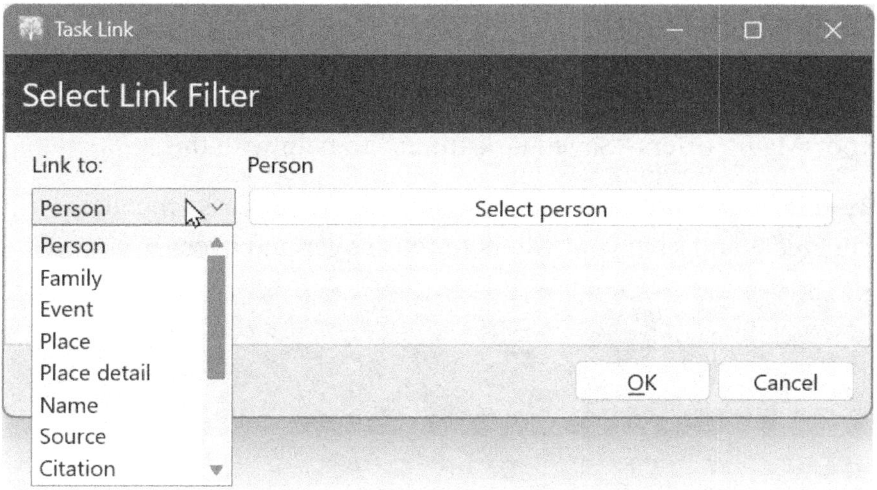


When adding a link filter, you must select:

- The type of record - You can select a person, family, event, place, place detail, name, source, citation, address, repository, media, or folder
- The record itself - Once you select the record type, the drop list on the right side will let you select the record of that type.

Then just click OK and that item will be added to the filter.

### Quick Filtering by a Single Linked Record

Sometimes you may want to just quickly see the records attached to a single person, place, etc. RootsMagic makes this easy from the various pages. For example, if you want to see all the tasks attached to a person, select that person in any of the views of the People page, then select Tools > Show tasks for selected person from the menu. RootsMagic will switch to the Tasks page and automatically filter the list to only show those tasks attached to that person. If you want to clear that filter just select Filters > Clear filter from the Tasks page menu.

You can do the quick filter for people, places, sources, citations, media, addresses, repositories, folders, and associations.

### Saved Task Filters

Although RootsMagic's task filtering is extremely powerful, it can also be quite tedious to re-enter a filter multiple times. RootsMagic offers "Saved task filters" to help with this.

By selecting Filters > Saved task filters from the Tasks menu, you can create and save your filters to reuse over and over.

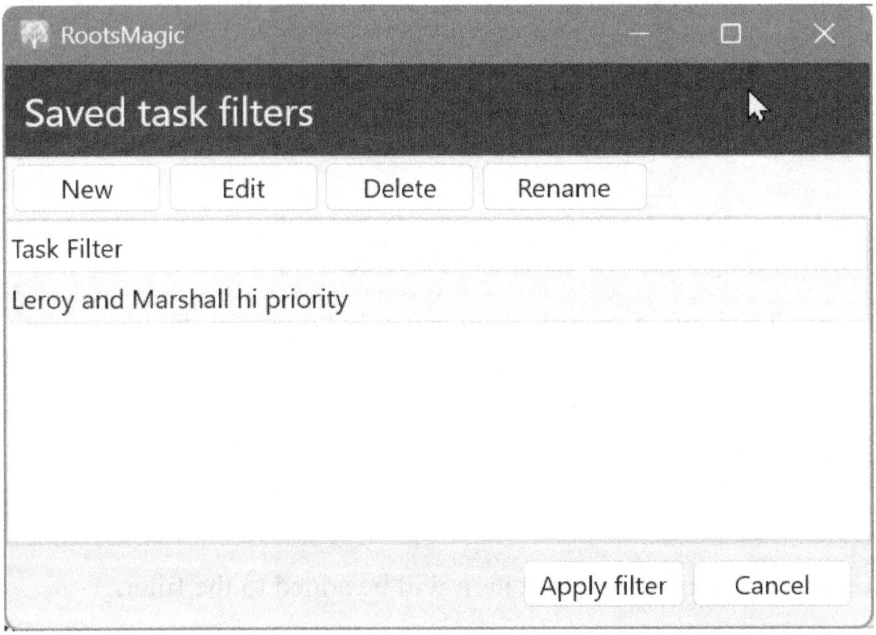


New lets you create a new task filter. You will be able to enter your filter settings exactly as usual, and then give that filter a name. RootsMagic will add your new filter to the Save task filter list. Once you have created a saved filter, you can edit, delete, or rename it from the same list.

When you want to use a saved filter, just open the saved filter list, highlight the desired filter, and click the Apply filter button on the bottom of the form.

# ADDRESSES AND REPOSITORIES

The Addresses page helps you keep track of both addresses and repositories in your file. While addresses and repositories are very similar in the information they contain (name, address, etc.), they serve very different purposes, and therefore have their own separate views in the Address page.

An address is a location for a person or family, or can be referenced by a task that needs to keep track of a person's address.

A repository is a location where a source is stored, or can be referenced by a task that needs to keep track of where sources may be stored.

## ADDRESSES

RootsMagic helps you keep track of the addresses of people (or families) in your file. This is primarily for the current addresses of living people, as they can be used when printing address lists and mailing labels.

> ☺ **Tip**
>
> If you want to keep track of locations where a person lived during their lifetime, you should use the "Residence" fact on the Edit Person screen. This lets you keep notes, pictures, and other documents related to the person's residence.

### Address List View

The Address view is a list of all the addresses you have entered into the file. Click Addresses on the side menu to view this list. As you move up and down the list, RootsMagic will display the address details on the right side of the screen, where you can directly edit them.

In addition to the basic name, address, and phone, you can also enter the person's email address, a website, and a note where you can keep more information about the person or address.

*To add an address*, click Add on the menu.

*To delete an address*, highlight the address in the list and click Delete on the menu. If you delete an address attached to a person, family, or task, the deleted address will be removed from that record.

The Tools menu will display options to print the list of addresses, automatically merge all duplicate addresses, or show you any tasks that are using the highlighted address.

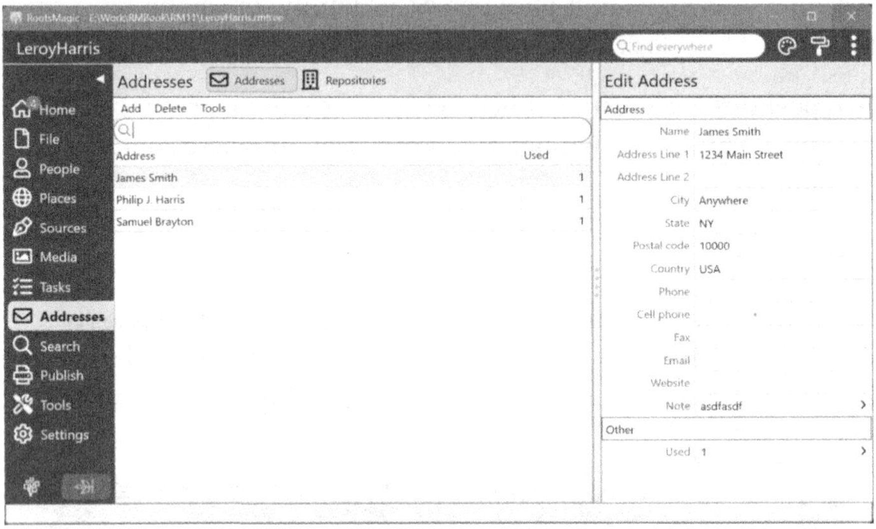


RootsMagic will also show you how many people, families, or tasks are using this address. If you click the "Used" button on the edit panel, RootsMagic will display an editable list of every use of the address.

## Working with Addresses

While you can add, edit, or delete addresses from the Address view, you will usually add addresses from the Edit Person screen. When you highlight the person row, or the spouse or parent rows when editing a person, the right side of the screen will have an Addresses button to let you add an address to the person or family.

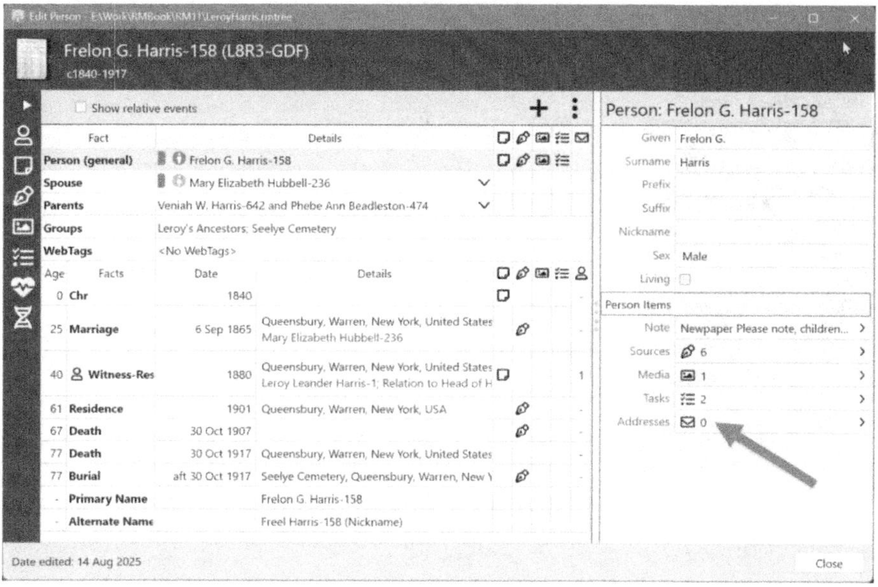


Clicking the Addresses button will display a list of any addresses for the person or family.

You can click an address to bring up the edit panel for that address. Any changes you make to the address will apply to anyone else who is using that same address as well.

You can also add an address to the person or family from this panel by clicking the + Add address button. You will be able to type in a new address, or select an existing address to attach to the person or family.

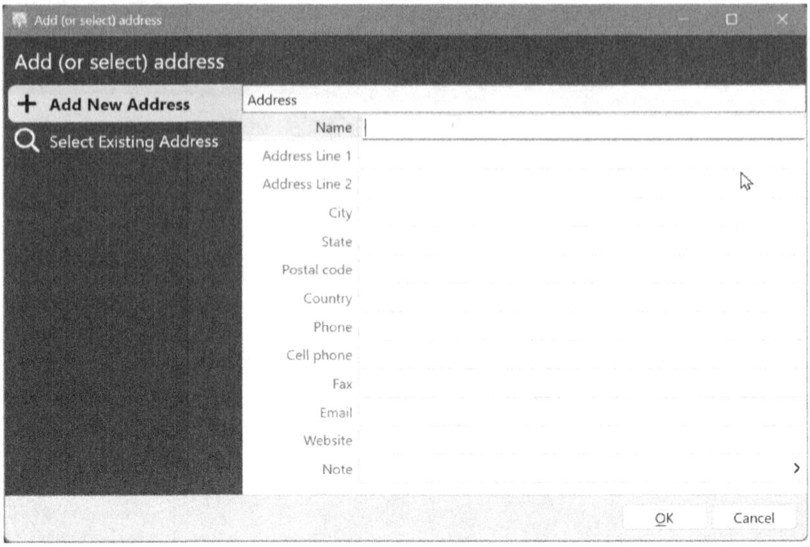


## REPOSITORIES

Almost as important as documenting where you found your information, is where that information is located. These locations, whether they be libraries, archives, courthouses, or even your own home, are called "repositories".

### Repository List View

The Repository view is a list of all the repositories you have entered into the file. Click Addresses on the side menu and then click the "Repositories" icon on the toolbar to view this list.

Editing and manipulating repositories works exactly like the address view in the previous section.

## Working with Repositories

While you can add, edit, or delete repositories from the Repository view, you will often add addresses from the Sources page. When you highlight a source in the source list, the right side of the screen will have a Repositories button to let you add a repository to the source.

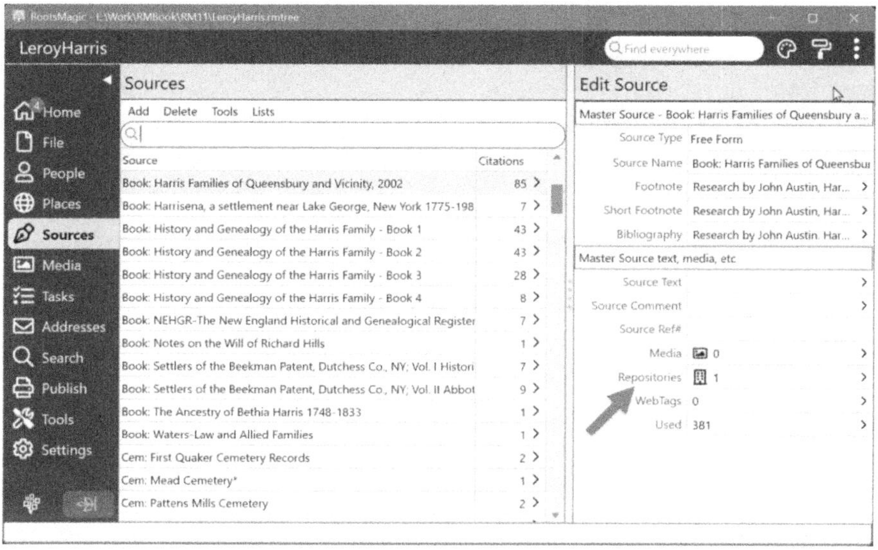


Clicking the Repositories button will display a list of any repositories for the source.

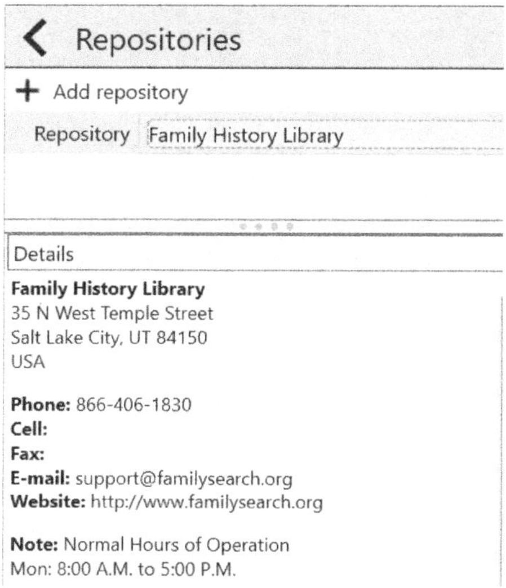


You can click a repository to bring up the edit panel for that repository. Any changes you make to the repository will apply to any other sources using that same repository.

You can also add a repository to the source from this panel by clicking the + Add repository button. You will be able to type in a new repository, or select an existing repository to attach to the source. When adding or editing a source, you can enter multiple repositories for the source.

# SEARCHING FOR INFORMATION

Although you can move through your family on the various views, there are times when you need to find someone buried deep in your database.

*To find a person in your database*, simply click Search on the side menu to display the Search page.

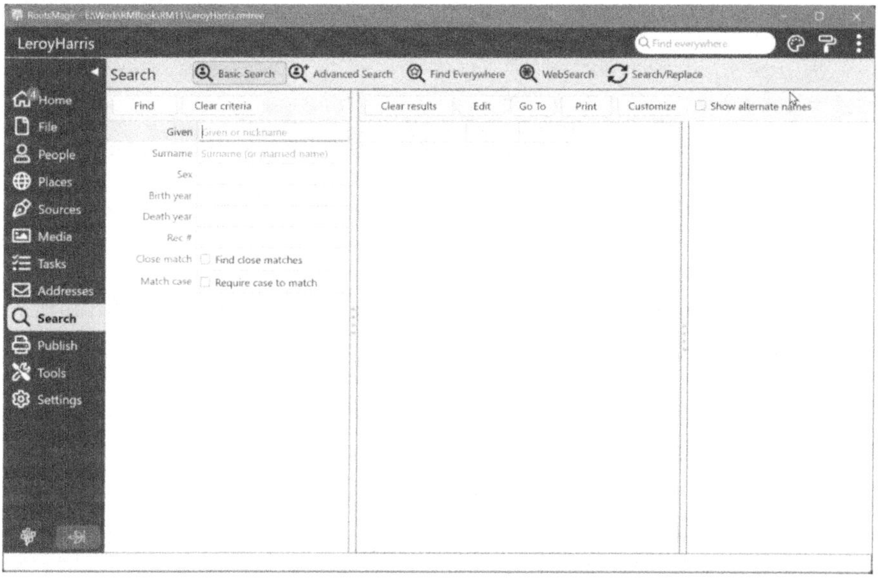


## BASIC SEARCH

To find a person (or persons) when you know their name, select Basic Search and enter any of the basic information asked for. You can enter the given name, surname, sex, birth and death year, or the record number. Then click the "Find" button and RootsMagic will display a list of matching people on the right.

The nice thing is that it doesn't just search for the name entered in a person's edit screen. It will also search for married names as well. So if you search for Mary Smith, it will find Mary Ann Jones if she is married to William Smith.

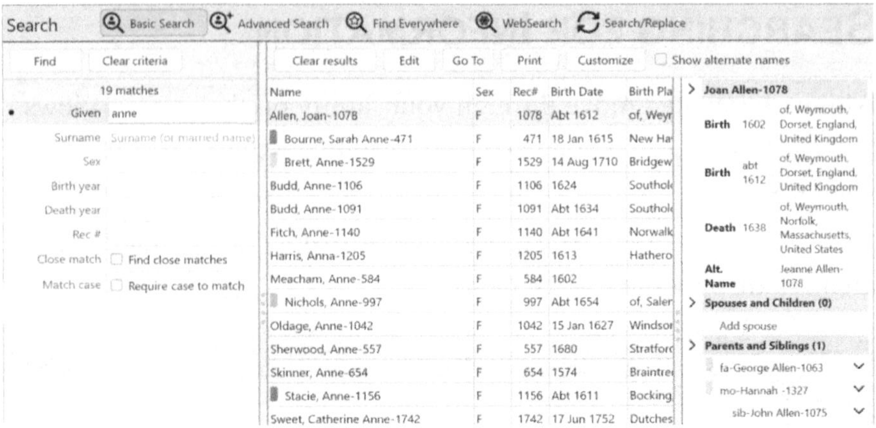


*To find a specific person*, enter both a given name and surname.

*To list everyone with a particular given name,* enter just the given name and leave the surname field empty.

*To list everyone with a particular surname*, enter just the surname and leave the given name field empty.

When the results are displayed, you can see more information about the highlighted person in the information panel on the far right. There are a number of things you can do with the buttons above the results.

- Edit – Open the edit screen for the highlighted person
- Go To – Go to the highlighted person in the People page. You can do any other work anywhere in the program, and when you return to the Search page the results will still be there so you can pick up where you left off.
- Print – Print the results. This will also let you save the results to Excel or .CSV file.
- Customize – Customize the result columns. This works exactly like customizing the Person List view (page 59).
- Show alternate names – Display alternate names for results.

You can sort the results by any column by clicking the header for that column.

## ADVANCED SEARCH

To find a person (or group of people) when you don't know their name, select Advanced Search, and then click the Find button to enter the search rules (described in the next section). RootsMagic will display the rules you enter in the left panel, and the results on the right. The results panel for the advanced search works exactly like the results panel for the basic search, with one addition: a Group button above the results will let you create a rules based group from the results by simply entering a name for the new group.

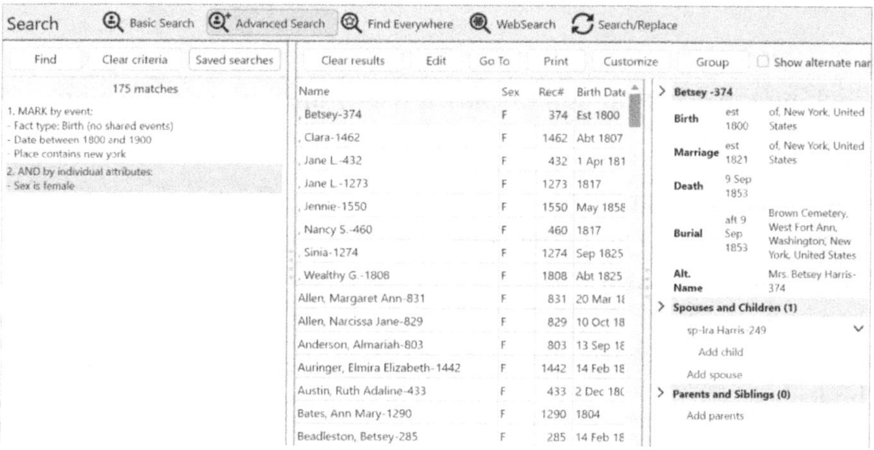


### Search Rules

Search Rules let you tell RootsMagic how to search or select a group of people. A rule lets you find people in various ways. The Search Rules form lets you add, delete, or rearrange the order of these rules.

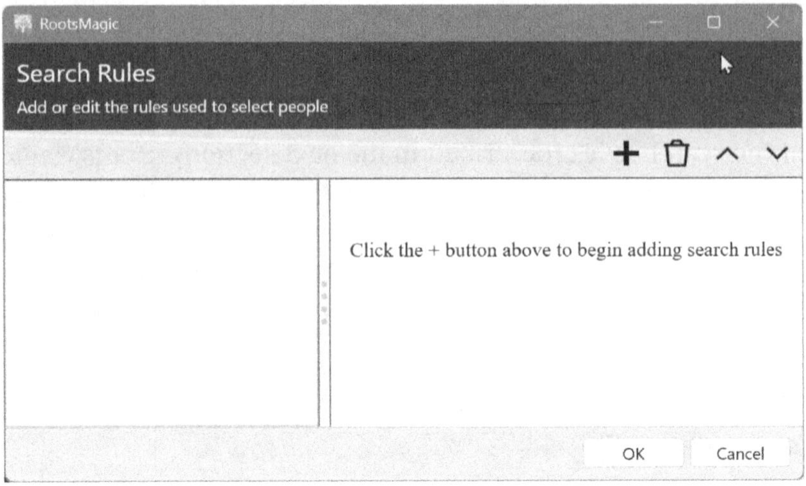


Clicking the + button will display a list of the various ways you can find people.

Just select the desired rule type from the list. Some rule types (such as Everyone) will simply add the rule to the Rules list on the left. Other rule types will let you select a starting person, and will then add the rule to the Rules list.

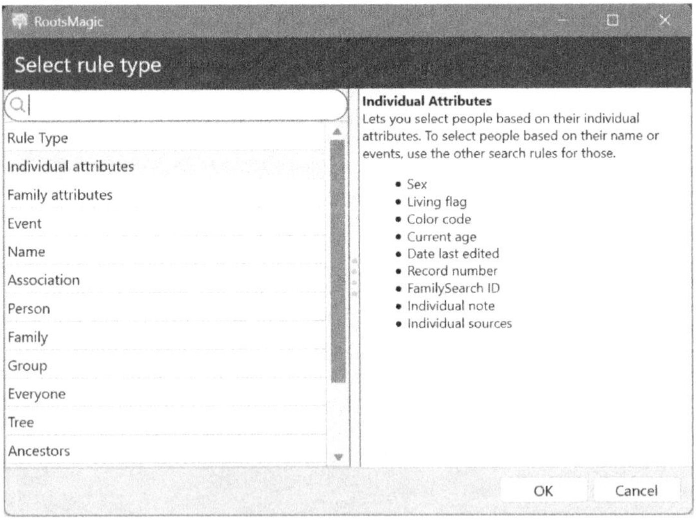


As rules are added to the Rules list, you can select a rule to see the options on the right side of the screen. The first rule in your list will select every person that matches the rule. For the remaining rules you will select whether to "And", "Or", or "But Not".

And – every person who matches the rule will be selected, but ONLY IF that person was already selected.

Or – every person who matches the rule will be selected (regardless of whether they were already selected)

But Not – every person who matches the rule will be un-selected (cleared)

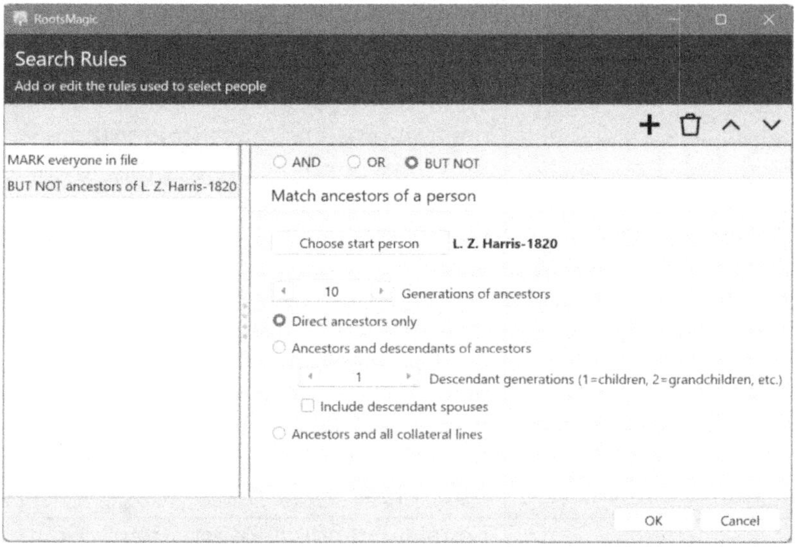


### *Individual Attributes*

This rule type matches people based on attributes like their sex, color coding, whether they are living, and more. Choose the value for the attributes you want to match. If you don't care about a particular attribute, just leave the value as "ignore".

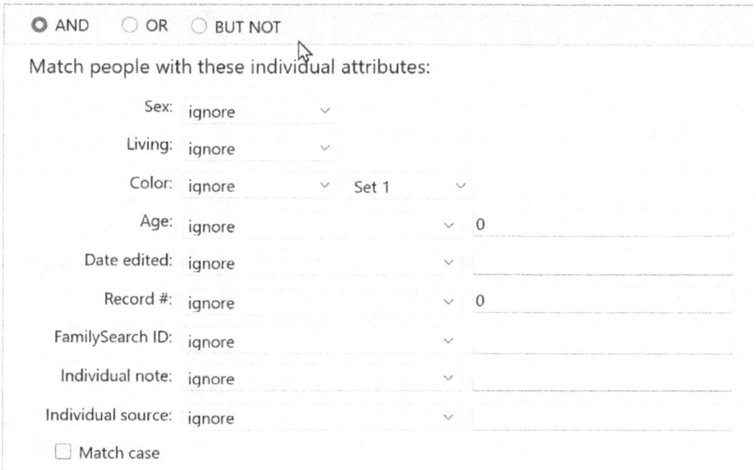

Each attribute can be searched in a number of different ways, depending on the data type.

| If search field is a... | You can compare in these ways... |
|---|---|
| Date | equal to, not equal to, is before, is after, is blank, is not blank, contains, does not contain, is between |
| Place, Name, or Text | equal to, not equal to, contains, does not contain, less than, greater than, less than or equal, greater than or equal, sounds like, is blank, is not blank |
| Proof | Is blank, is proven, is disputed, is disproven, is proposed, is not blank, is not proven, is not disputed, is not disproven, is not proposed |
| Note | Contains, does not contain, is blank, is not blank |
| Number | equals, not equal to, less than, greater than, less than or equal, greater than or equal |
| Source | Exists, does not exist, contains / does not contain / is blank / not blank (for each part of the source or citation) |
| Sex | Is male, is female, is unknown, is not male, is not female, is not unknown |
| Color coding | Is black/red/blue/etc., is not black/red/blue/etc. for each color code set |

### *Family Attributes*

This rule matches people based on attributes about their families, such as the count of children, spouses, etc.

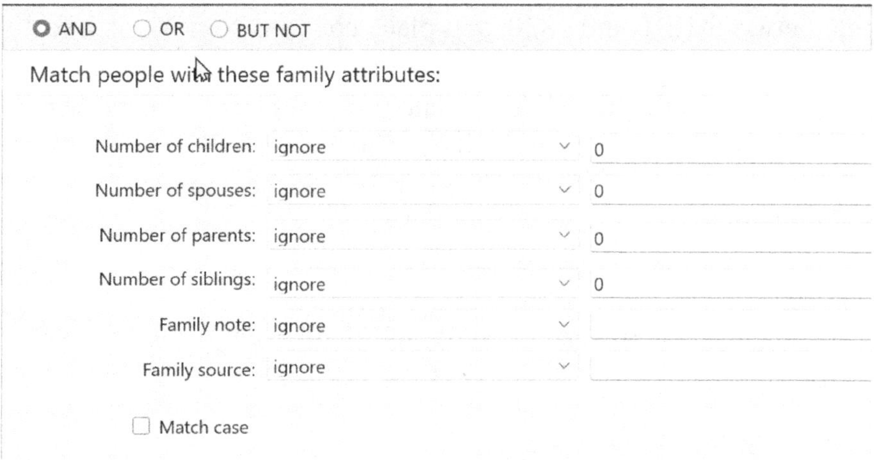


### *Event*

This rule matches people based on an event in their life. It can match on a specific type of event (birth, death, etc.), or it can match on any fact. It can even match based on facts which have been shared with a person.

One special note, if you create an event rule with multiple attributes to search for, they must all match the exact same fact. For example, if you set the event rule to match Occupation, with date between 1810 and 1820, and place contains New York, a fact will only match if it matches all 3 of those items. If a person has one occupation that matches the date (but not place) and another that matches the place (but not date), the person will not be considered a match. This is different from earlier versions of RootsMagic.

### *Name*

This rule matches people based on their name (including alternate names).

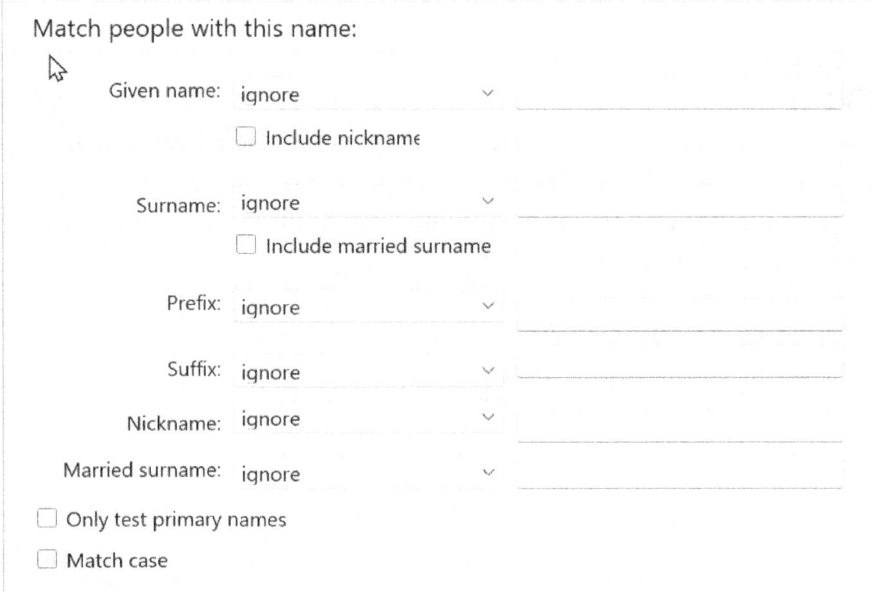


### *Association*

This rule works almost exactly the same as the Event rule, except that it searches associations instead of events.

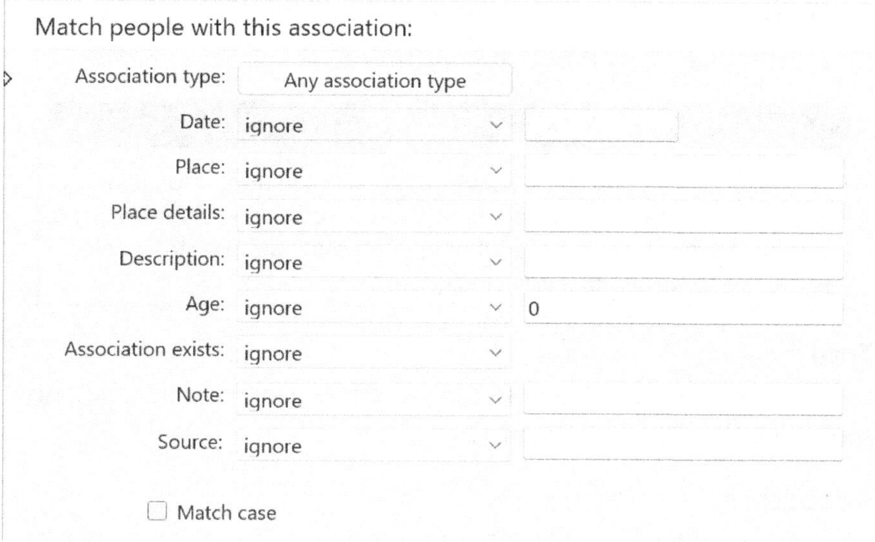


### *Person*

This rule matches a single person. The only option is selecting the person.

### *Family*

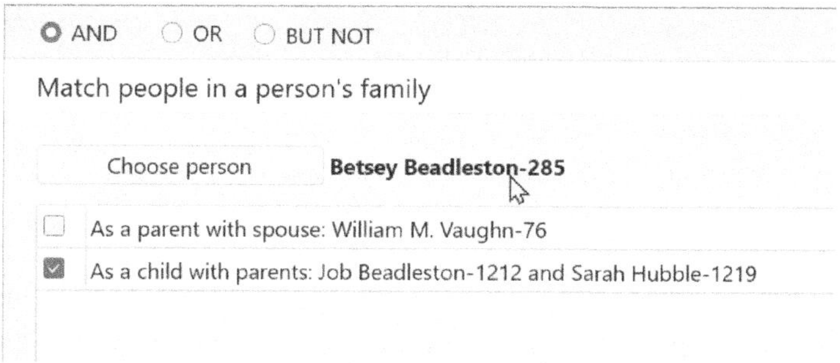


This rule matches one or more families of a single person. Select a person and click the checkbox in front of the families you want.

### *Group*

This rule matches everyone in a selected group. The only option is selecting the group.

### *Everyone*

This rule matches everyone in your file.

> ☺ **Tip**
>
> The Everyone option is especially useful when you want to include everybody except for a certain few. You can include everyone in your database, then use the other options with "But not" to unselect those few that you don't want included.

### *Tree*

This rule matches everyone in the same tree as a person. The only option is selecting the person.

### *Ancestors*

This rule matches the ancestors of a single person. Select a person and choose the options you want.

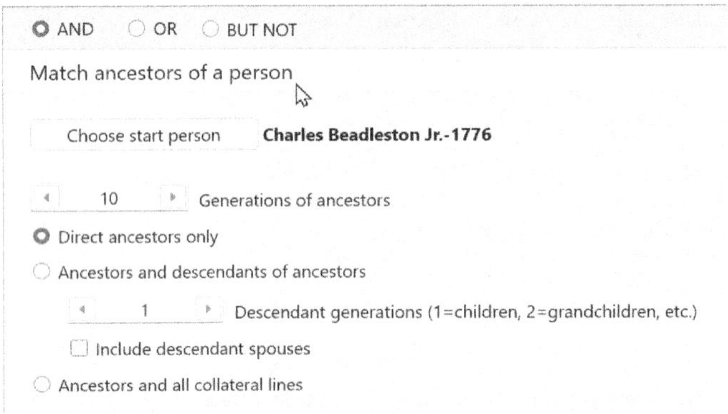


You can choose the number of generations to consider, and whether to include the children of each ancestor as well. You can also choose to print the collateral lines which tries to select all ancestors and their families.

Make your choices, then click OK and RootsMagic will mark or unmark the highlighted person and his or her ancestors.

### *Descendants*

This rule matches the descendants of a single person. Select a person and choose the options you want.

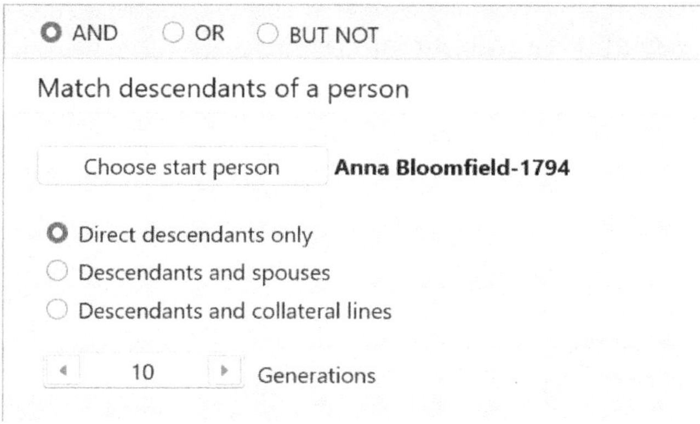


You can choose the number of generations to consider, and whether to include the spouses of each descendant as well. You can also choose to print the collateral lines which tries to select all descendants and their families.

Make your choices, then click OK and RootsMagic will mark or unmark the highlighted person and his or her descendants.

### *Genetic*

This rule matches everyone in the same genetic line as a single person.

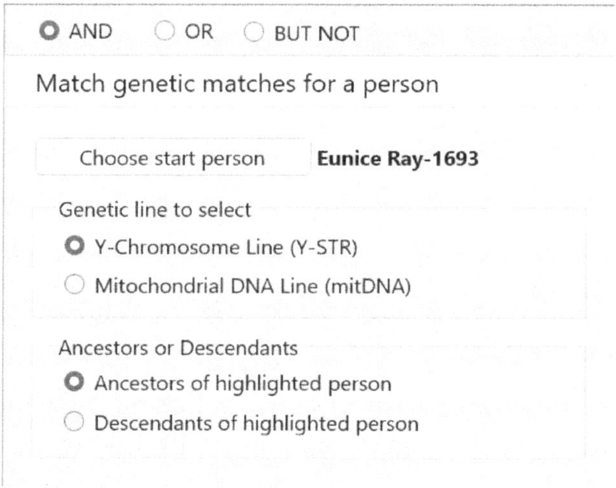


You can choose whether to follow the Y-Chromosome or the Mitochondrial line for the person, in either the ancestor or descendant direction.

Make your choices, then click OK and RootsMagic will mark or unmark the highlighted person and his or her descendants.

### *Special*

This rule offers a few special match conditions. Just select the one you want.

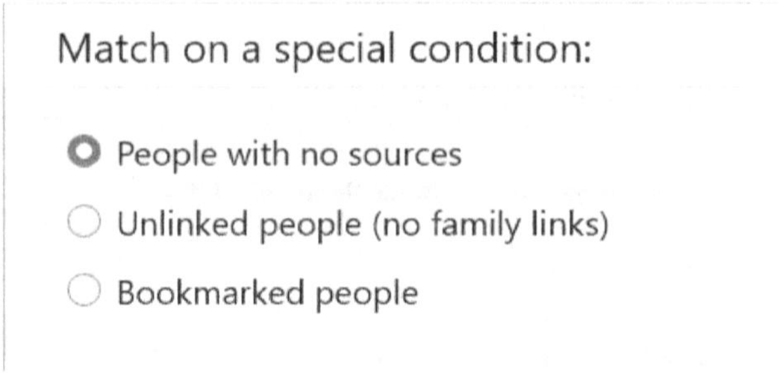


### Saved Searches

If you enter a set of rules that you are likely to use again, you can save that criteria by clicking the "Saved searches" button on the advanced search view. RootsMagic will display a list of any searches that you have saved.

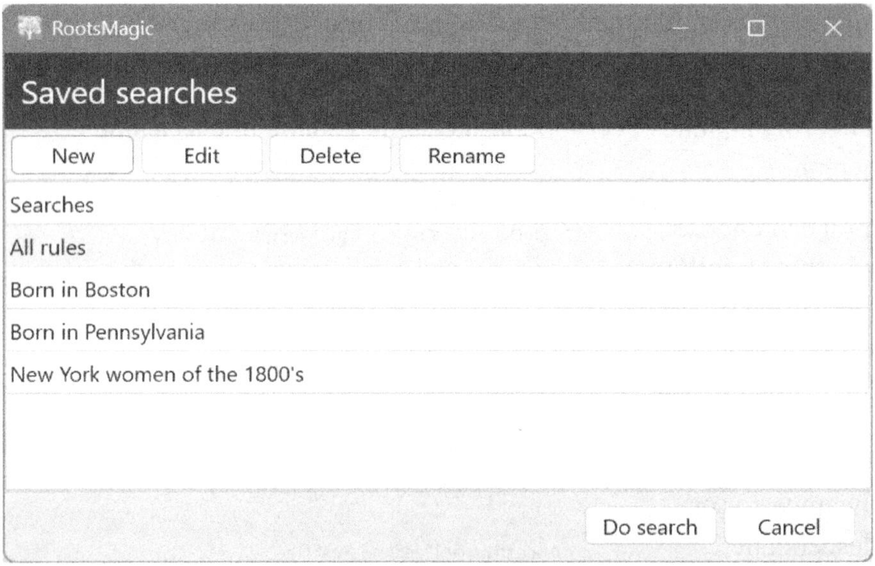


*To create a new saved search*, click the New button on the Saved Search screen and RootsMagic will display the search rules form for you to fill. If you already had a search active, the rules form will be pre-filled with that search. Enter the rules you want, click OK and enter the name for your saved search.

You can modify the rules for a saved search with the Edit button, and can rename the saved search with the Rename button. Finally, if you will no longer be needing a saved search, you can delete it from this screen as well.

*To use a saved search*, just click the "Saved Search" button on the Advanced Search view, highlight the search you want and click the "Do search" button.

## FIND EVERYWHERE

Sometimes it isn't enough to just search for a person or family. You may occasionally want to find every item in your file that contains some text. To do this, select Find Everywhere on the Search page.

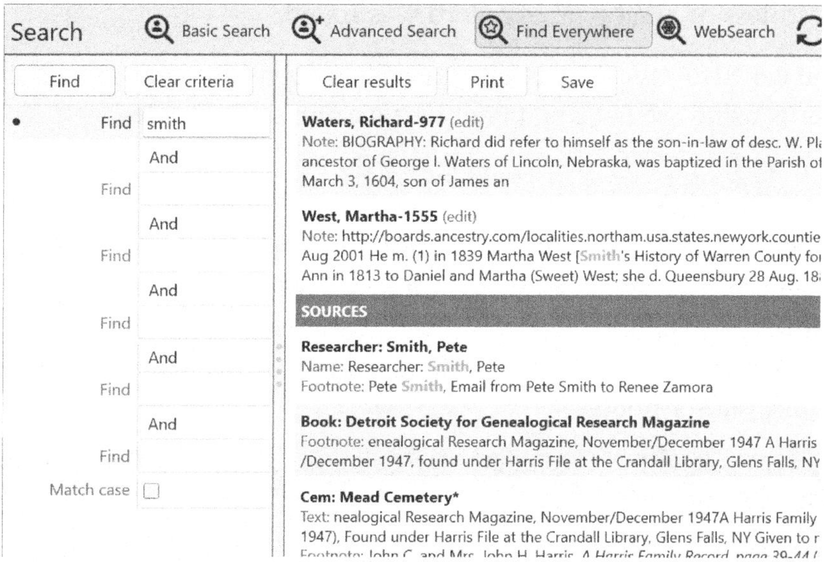


Enter the text you want to search for on the left side of the screen and then click the Find button. RootsMagic will search for the exact word or phrase that you enter. If you want to search for words or phrases that aren't right next to each other in the record, you can enter those words in separate fields and then use the AND or OR option to tell RootsMagic how to search for the different terms.

So, for example, if you wanted to find every record that had the words Smith and Jones in it, you would type Smith into the first field and Jones into the second field, and leave the AND option set for them. On the other hand, if you wanted every record with Smith or Jones, you would type Smith in the first field and Jones in the second field and change the option to OR. If you want the capitalization to match as well, you can mark the Match case checkbox.

When you click OK, RootsMagic will search every record in your file (people, families, events, notes, sources, tasks, multimedia, places, and more) and display the results on the right side of the screen.

Each result will be displayed with the search text highlighted in red, and a blue hyperlink will allow you to edit the found record, regardless of what type of record was found.

You can also save your results to a file (in html format) or print the results using the Save and Print buttons above the results.

## WEBSEARCH

WebSearch helps you find more information about your family on the internet. It works a lot like your regular web browser, except that it is able to automatically search various websites for your family members. Keep in mind that some of these search engines require subscriptions.

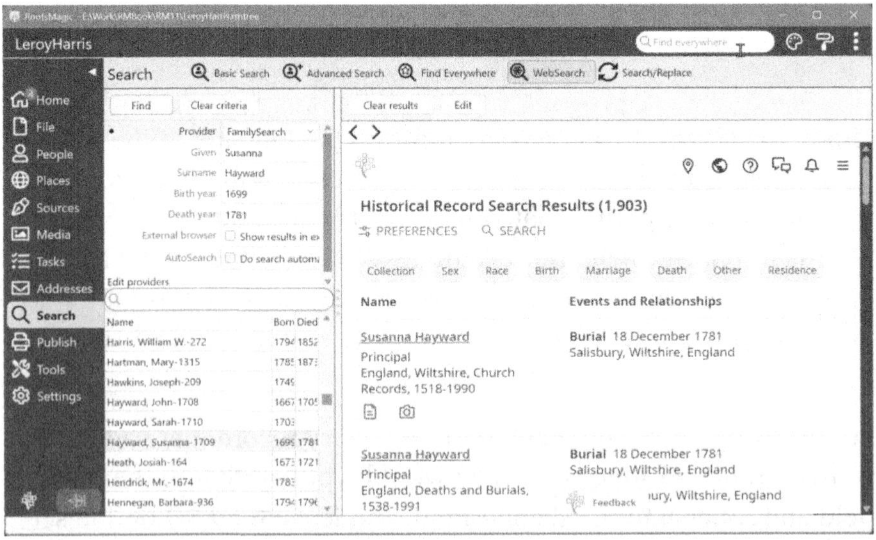

The first thing you need to do is choose the website you want RootsMagic to search. Click the "Provider" field and select one from the list. Once you have chosen a search engine, you can select a person from the list on the left side of the screen (or just fill in the search fields) and then click the Find button to actually do the search.

But if you're lazy like me, you may want to just check the Autosearch checkbox so that RootsMagic won't make you click that button every time you select a new person. If you want to compare the results with your own information, the Edit button button above the results will open the edit screen for the highlighted person in the list.

There may be times you want to have RootsMagic use a browser other than the one built in. If you mark the checkbox "External browser", then RootsMagic will open up the search using whatever browser is selected as the default on your computer.

Finally, you can select which search providers you want to show up in the list, as well as add your own providers to the list by clicking the "Edit providers" button just above the list of names in the left panel.

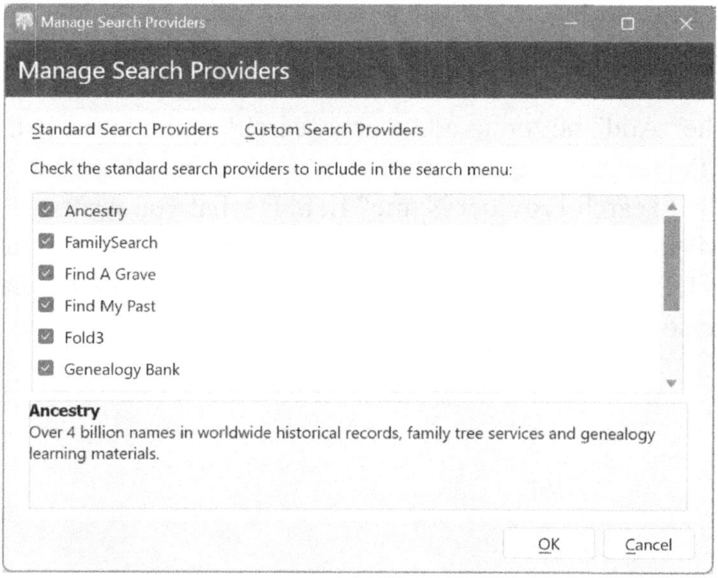

## Standard Search Providers

There are 2 tabs on the Search Providers form, the first of which is just a list of checkboxes to tell RootsMagic which of the built-in search engines you want to show in the menu. Check or uncheck them as desired.

## Custom Search Providers

The second tab Custom Search Providers lets you add other search engines to the WebSearch list.

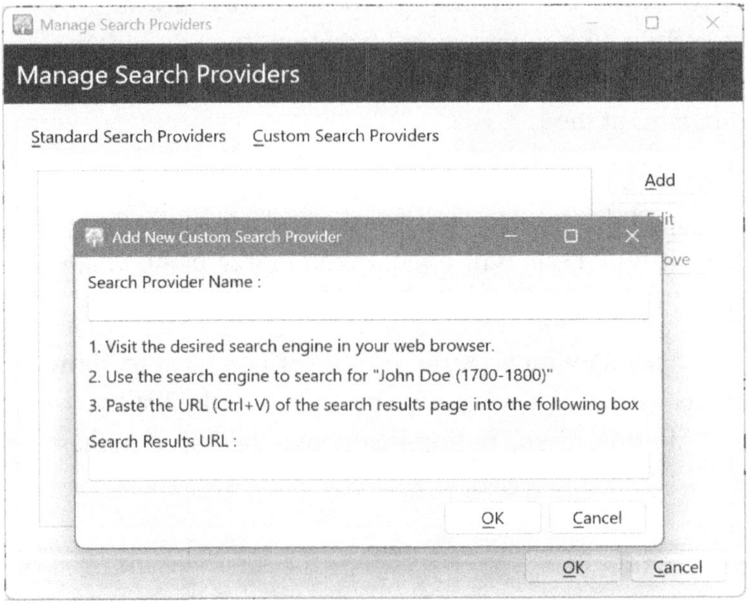


Click the "Add" button to add a new search engine to the list. Just follow the instructions on screen to add a new search engine to the list. The "Search Provider Name" field is what you want RootsMagic to display in the list of search engines. The "Search Results URL" is where you tell RootsMagic how it should search for a person.

## SEARCH AND REPLACE

One very powerful data manipulation feature in RootsMagic (and one of the most dangerous to your data if used improperly) is global search and replace. *To do a global search and replace*, select Search/Replace on the Search page.

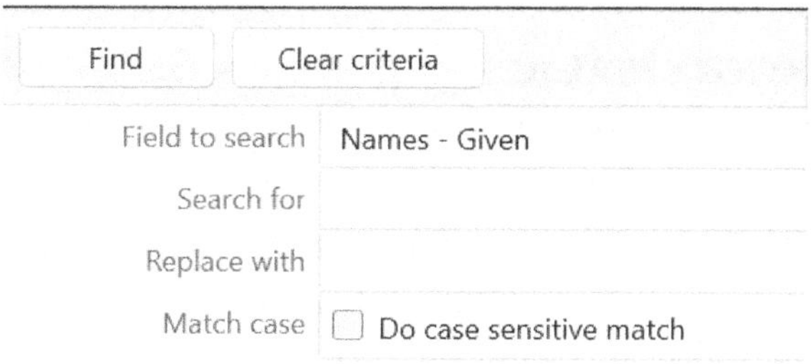


RootsMagic will display options on the left side of the search screen.

RootsMagic doesn't simply search and replace any and every piece of data. You must tell it what type of data you want to search and replace by selecting from the Field to search drop list. You can search and replace in a number of different fields, including names, places, media, notes, sources, citations, and facts.

Just type in the text you want to search for, and the text you want to replace it with, and click Find. RootsMagic will bring up each item to replace one at a time for you to confirm. You can Replace or Skip the item and go onto the next item, or you can Replace all items without confirmation.

**☺ Tip**

Keep in mind that if you want to search for every instance of Stafford in place names and wanted to change them to Staffordshire, the replace all option would also change Stafford, Stafford, England to Staffordshire, Staffordshire, England. So you want to take account of all punctuation and spaces. So to replace Stafford correctly, you would search for Stafford, England and replace it with Staffordshire, England.

*Search and replace can also be used as "Search and Delete"* by just leaving the Replace with field blank. RootsMagic will then search for each occurrence of the text you enter, and replace it with nothing (thus deleting it). Be careful with this new knowledge.

Although search and replace can be used to update broken media links, it is easier to open the Tools page and select Fix broken media links to have RootsMagic fix them automatically.

## ROOTSMAGIC EXPLORER – SELECTING PEOPLE

Many places within RootsMagic require you to select a person (or multiple people) for a particular feature. RootsMagic Explorer is the list which is used for this. The selection screen has a list of everybody in the file on the left side, and the right side displays information about the currently highlighted person. But the main purpose of the selection screen is to select people.

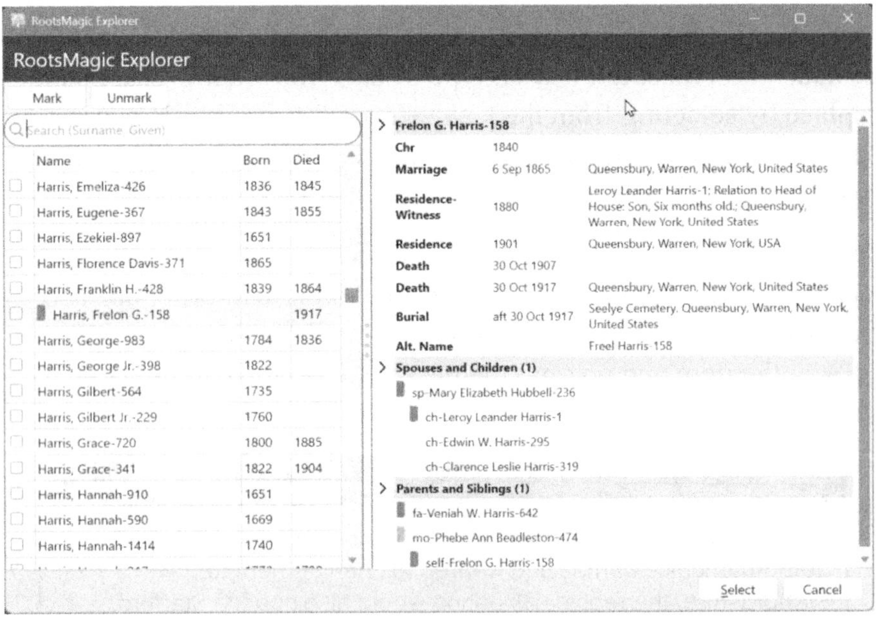


*If the feature you have selected only needs a single person*, the list will not have checkboxes in front of the names in the list, and will *not* include the Mark and Unmark buttons above the list.

*If the feature can apply to multiple people,* the selection screen lets you "mark" and "unmark" people to include in your custom report. When a person is marked, a check appears in front of their name in the list. When you unmark a person, the check is removed from in front of their name. You simply mark and unmark people until you have a check next to every person you want to include, then click "Select".

There are two buttons at the top of the selection screen, Mark and Unmark. Clicking each button will display a menu of ways you can mark (or unmark) people in the list. You can mark or unmark people in the following ways: single person, family, group, everybody, tree, ancestors, descendants, genetic line, or by criteria. These options are described on page 203 in the section "Search Rules".

The one option that works differently in Explorer from search rules is family selection. In search rules, you simply select the families, and all members of the families are selected. In Explorer, you can select the entire family, but can also unmark individuals in the family if desired.

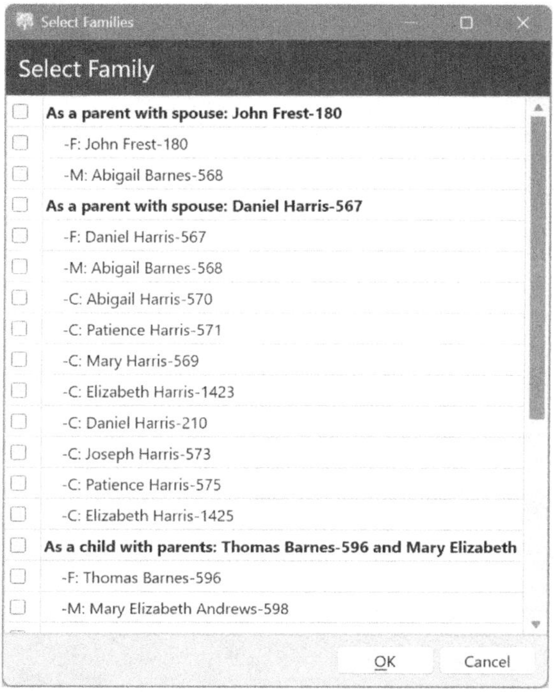


Three additional options in Explorer that are not included in the "Search Rules" are Living and Deceased (they can be done from the Criteria option in Search Rules), and Saved searches.

*To mark or unmark living people*, select Living people from the "Mark" or "Unmark" menu.

*To mark or unmark dead people*, select Deceased people from the "Mark" or "Unmark" menu.

*To mark people based on a search which you have saved,* choose Saved searches from the Mark or Unmark menu. RootsMagic will let you select (or create) a saved search to mark or unmark people that match. The section “Advanced Search” (page 203) provides more details on creating a saved search.

# PRINTING REPORTS

One of the main reasons a person buys a genealogy program is to print out their family on paper. Not surprisingly, everybody wants his or her family displayed in a different format.

*To print a report* in RootsMagic, click on "Publish" in the side menu, then select "All reports and charts". RootsMagic will display a list of available reports, with a drop list above it to choose how you want the list formatted.

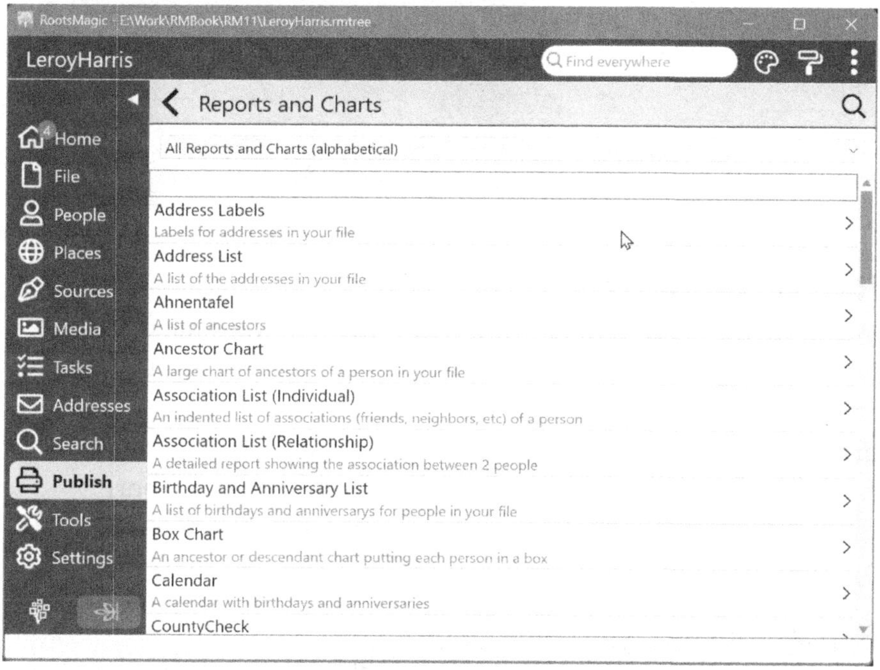


You can have the list displayed alphabetically, or choose to group the reports by category. You can also choose to only view the reports in a single category. To select any report, just click the report in the list and RootsMagic will open the report viewer for that report type. The left side of the report viewer is a list of options for that report. You can set any options, then click the "Generate Report" button below the options. RootsMagic will generate and display the report on the right side of the viewer.

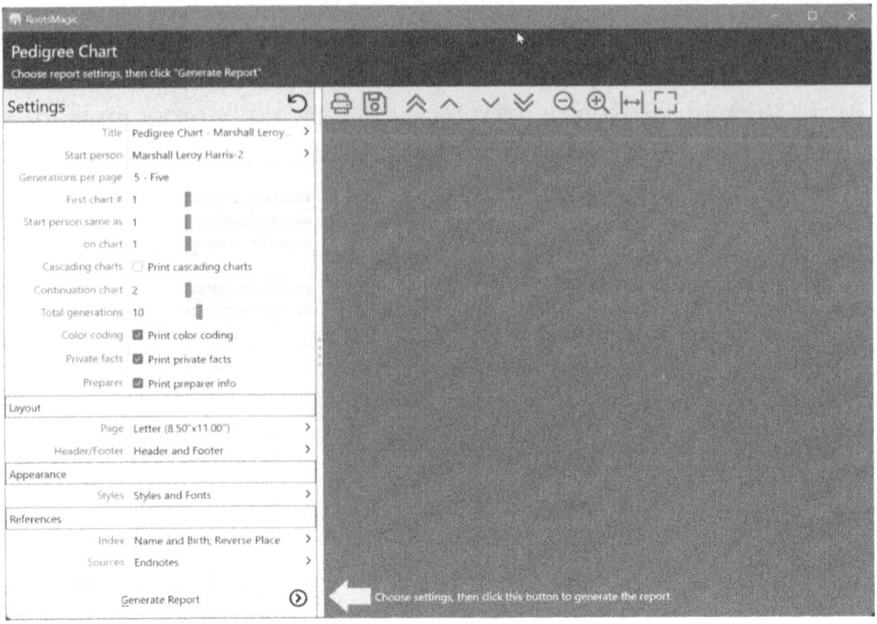


## REPORT OPTIONS

While each type of report will have its own options, most report types will use some or all of the following options. Rather than repeatedly discuss these options for each and every report, we'll mention them here. Of course, the "Reset" button in the upper right corner of the option pages is to reset the various report settings back to their default, so have fun experimenting with the options.

### Report Title

Several reports allow you to customize the title for the report. You can click the "Title" field to change or reset the title.

### Page Layout

Many of the various printout dialogs have a button that lets you change the margins, headers and footers, page orientation and starting page number for the selected report type. For example, if you change the page layout for group sheets, it doesn't affect the page layout of pedigree charts. Clicking the “Page” button under “Layout” will display the following options.

*Page Size* lets you select the size of the page. You can choose from a list of preset sizes, or enter a custom width and height.

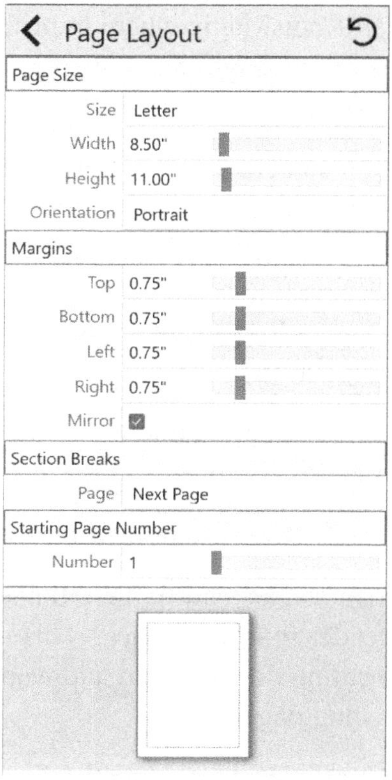


*Orientation* lets you tell RootsMagic which direction to print on the paper. Portrait prints the standard way on the page, while landscape prints "sideways" on the page.

*Margins* lets you enter the top, bottom, left and right margins for the printout. There is a checkbox to choose whether to "mirror" the margins on odd and even pages.

*Section Breaks* lets you choose where a new section (like the endnotes or indexes) will start. They can start on the next page, or the next odd or even page.

*Starting Page Number* lets you select the starting page number for the report. This can be useful if you are combining multiple reports together.

## Header and Footer

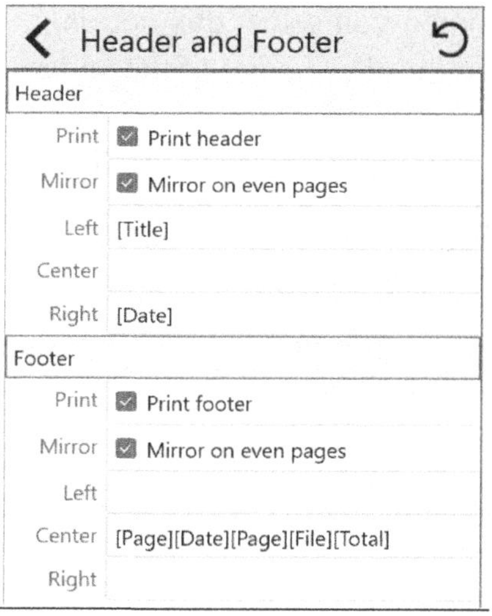


To change the header or footer for the report, click the Header/Footer button under the Layout options.

Check the "Print" box (in the Header section) if you want RootsMagic to print a header at the top of each page. The header will consist of the text entered in the Left section, Center section, and Right section along with a separator line. These "sections" tell RootsMagic where to print the text within the header. For example, anything entered in the "Center section" will be centered in the header.

You can enter text into any section, or special "codes" that RootsMagic will convert when printing. These codes are:

[Date] - RootsMagic will replace this with the current date.

[Page] - RootsMagic will replace this with the current page number.

[Title] - RootsMagic will replace this with a title designed specifically for this printout.

[File] - RootsMagic will replace this with the name of the database.

You can also swap the left and right header sections (mirror header) on even pages. This is useful for example when you are printing double sided and want the header to be a mirror image on facing pages.

The footer works exactly the same way as the header, except that it is printed at the bottom of each page.

### Selecting the Appearance of the Report

*"Styles"* lets you select the styles and fonts that RootsMagic will use for the selected report. When you select this option you will see a list of the styles used by the report. You can click on any style to modify it.

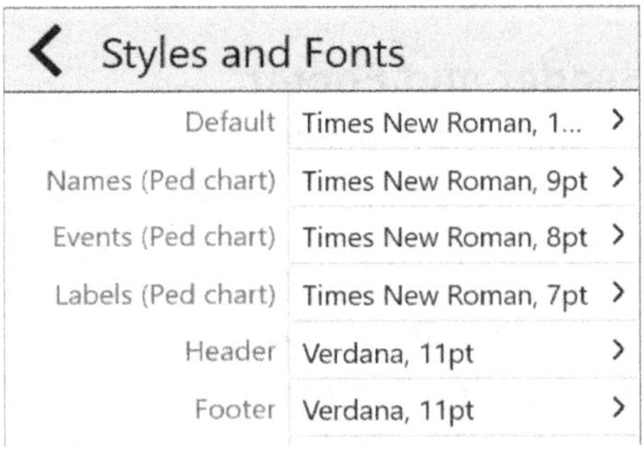


When you select any style, RootsMagic lets you edit not only the font, but other parts of the style as well, including text alignment, colors, indentation, spacing and margins.

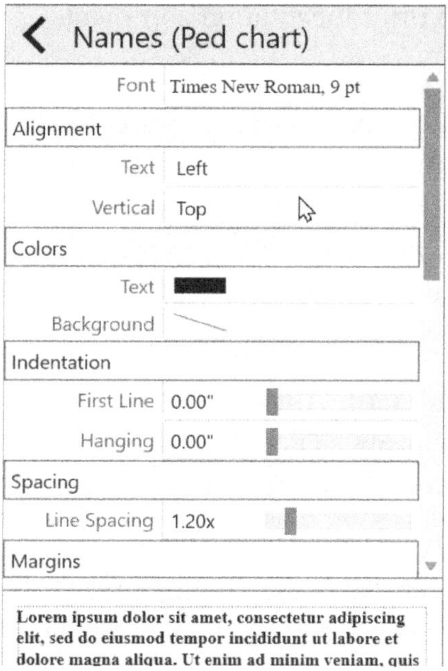


As you modify the style, RootsMagic will display the style in the panel below the settings.

The first style for any report will always be the "Default" style. While all the other styles for the report can be completely different, they are initially based off of this style. So for example, if the Default font is Times New Roman and you change it to Arial, any of the other styles which were Times New Roman will also change to Arial (but will keep their other unique properties like font size, etc.).

## Source Options

Many of the reports let you print your sources as part of the report. RootsMagic provides a lot of options for you to customize the way those sources will print. For those reports you can click the "Sources" button under "References".

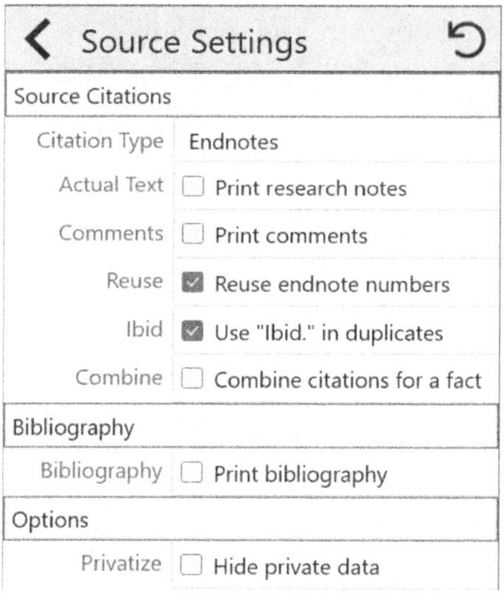


*The Citation Type* lets you choose where you want the sources to print; Endnotes will print at the end of the document, while footnotes will print at the bottom of each page. You can also choose to just not print any sources at all for the report.

*Print research notes* tells RootsMagic to print the research notes after the source.

*Print comments* tells RootsMagic to print the citation comments following the source.

*Reuse* causes RootsMagic to not print exact duplicate sources over and over when using endnotes. If RootsMagic encounters an exact citation that it has already printed, it will reference the already printed citation again. This has no affect when printing footnotes since the previously printed footnote would likely not be on the same page.

*Ibid* tells RootsMagic to use the Latin term "Ibid." when multiple exactly the same citations appear in a row. The first time the full citation will be printed, but each consecutive identical citation will use "Ibid.".

*Combine citations for a fact* will combine all the citations for each fact into a single citation. This can greatly reduce the number of footnotes or endnotes that are printed. Be careful combining this with the "Reuse endnote numbers" option above, because combined citations will rarely be exactly the same as other combined citations.

*Bibliography* will print an alphabetical list of all the sources used in the report. This is independent of the footnotes and endnotes, and can be printed in addition to or instead of them.

*Hide private data* tells RootsMagic whether to hide private information in certain sources when they are printed. Some of the source templates provide the ability to have certain sensitive data (like personal addresses) replaced with privacy text like "ADDRESS FOR PRIVATE USE". This option tells RootsMagic whether to print that sensitive data or to print the privacy text.

### Indexes

Many reports offer the option to print an index at the end of the report. You can print a name index, which is a list of the people who are in the report, or a place index, which is a list of the places mentioned in the report. For those reports you can click the "Index" button under "References".

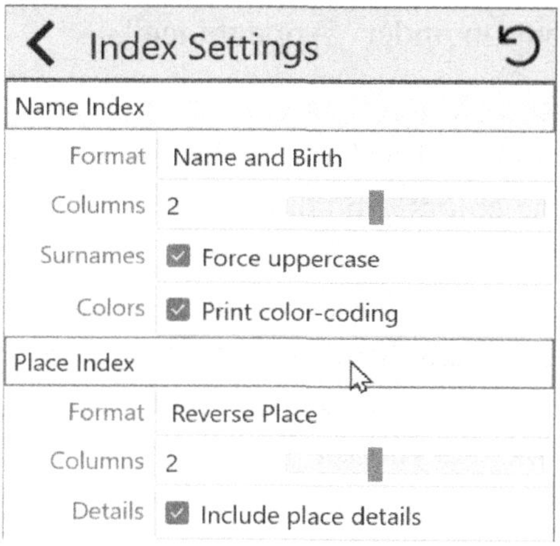


*The name index is a list of the people* mentioned in the report. There are several different formats you can choose from. You can also choose how many columns to print for the index.

You can specify whether you want the surnames in the index uppercase. This is useful to make the surnames stand out better. And finally, you can tell RootsMagic whether you want to color code the names in the index. If you choose this option, RootsMagic will print the index using any color coding you have set for the people in the index.

*The place index is a list of the places* mentioned in the report. You can choose whether to reverse the place names in the index. When you reverse the places it groups them together geographically and makes it easier to find a place in the index. You can also choose how many columns to use for the place index.

### Borders

A few reports offer the option to print information in boxes with borders. For those reports click the "Box border" button under "Appearance".

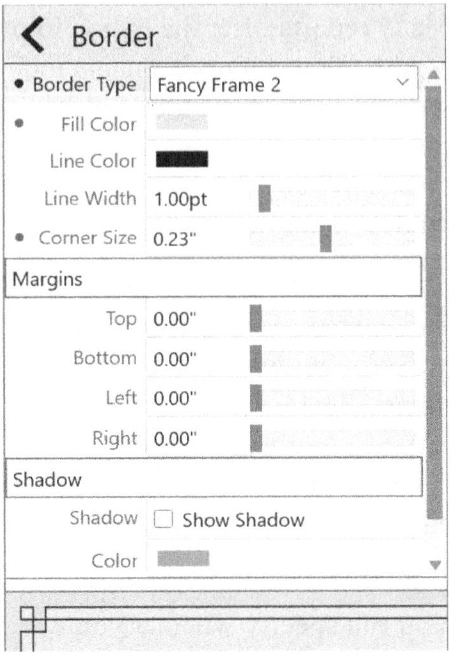


RootsMagic lets you edit not only the border type, but also the colors, line thickness, corner size, and margins. You can even choose whether to include a drop shadow on the border, including its color and size. As you modify the border, RootsMagic will display the border in the panel below the settings.

## THE REPORT VIEWER

When you create any report, RootsMagic will open it in the Report Viewer. This preview lets you step through the entire report, zoom in or out, and print, or save your report. The left side of the Report Viewer are the report options, while the right side is the generated report, including a column of thumbnails for each page in the report. You can click on any thumbnail to change to that page of the report.

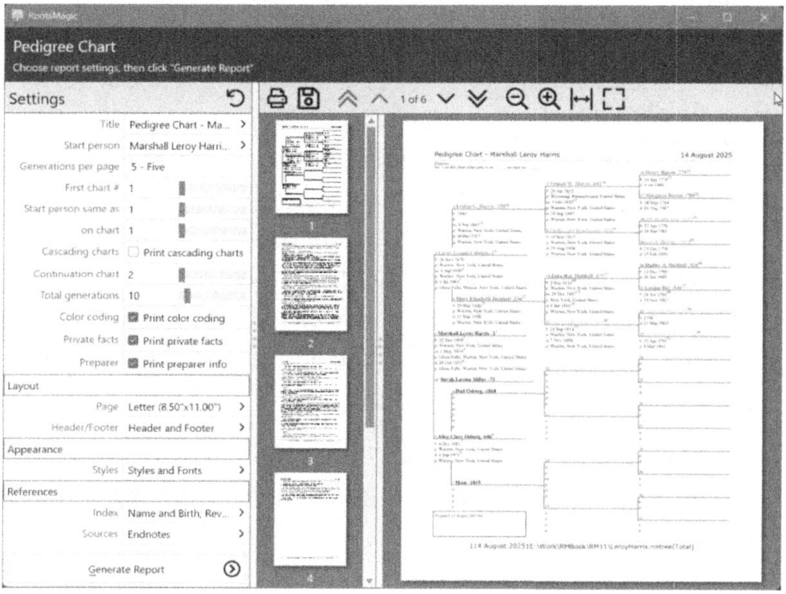


## Modifying the Report

Sometimes you will create a report and find out you didn't use the exact settings you wanted. Simply change the settings on the left and click “Generate Report” again and the report will be updated.

## Printing a Report

To print the displayed report, just click the "Print" button. You will be able to select from the standard print options.

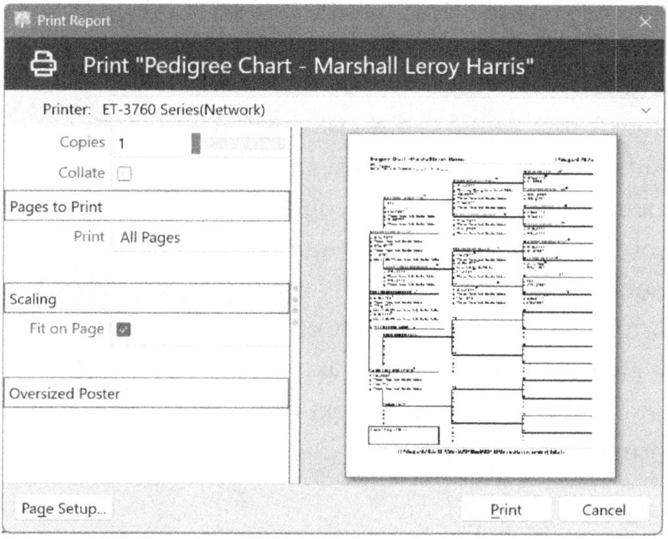

- **Copies:** the number of copies to print
- **Collate:** check to have the pages collated when you print multiple copies
- **Print:** Printing the entire document, the currently displayed page, or a range of pages.
- **Fit on Page:** For large format charts, you can choose whether to fit the chart on the paper size.
- **Oversized Poster:** If you uncheck "Fit on Page" for a large format chart, you can select the amount of overlap and cut marks for printing on multiple pages.

You can also click the "Page Setup" button to change paper size and other options from the print setup form for your operating system.

### Saving a Report to File

If you want to save the displayed report to a file, click the "Save" button on the Report Viewer. RootsMagic supports a number of different file formats, but some may not be available depending on the type of report.

- Microsoft Word (DOCX) is a word processing format that preserves the formatting of the file, such as fonts, tabs, indents, superscripts, etc. Most current word processors can read DOCX files, so this is a good way to get a RootsMagic report into your word processor for extra editing.
- Microsoft Excel (XLSX) is a spreadsheet format that is useful for saving table (row and column) information to be opened in a spreadsheet program.
- Acrobat PDF is a (mostly) non-editable format that is very useful for sending to family members. It retains all formatting, images, etc. and can be printed by the recipient to look exactly as if you had printed it yourself.
- Text files will retain the text itself, but will lose most formatting.

- Comma separated (CSV) is a text format broken into fields. This format can be useful for importing into databases or spreadsheets.

## Pedigree Charts

The pedigree chart is a visual display of the direct ancestors of the person on the far left of the chart. It is one of the most commonly used charts in genealogy.

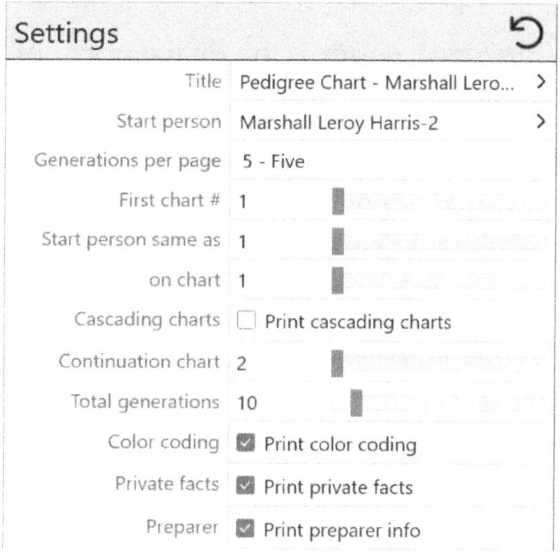


To generate a pedigree chart for a person, highlight the start person on the main screen, then select Pedigree Chart from the report list. The following options are available for this report:

*Start person* is the person who the pedigree chart will begin with. You can click the "Start person" button to change this person.

*Generations per page* lets you print 4, 5, or 6 generations of ancestors on each page of the printout.

*First chart #* is the number of the first chart printed (usually 1).

*Start person same as* and *on chart* let you specify whether the starting person is already on a chart you have previously printed. These are usually both 1.

*Cascading charts* makes RootsMagic create a series of pedigree charts that span more generations than will fit on a single page. RootsMagic will still use the generations per page selected, but will print additional pages as necessary and number the pages. Each person in the farthest right generation of a chart will become person number 1 on subsequent charts.

If you select cascading charts, the following options become available. Although you should usually just use the default values, RootsMagic allows you to change them in case you need to print continuation charts for ones you have printed previously.

*Continuation chart* is the number of the second chart printed (usually 2).

*Total generations* is the total number of generations for all charts combined.

*Color coding* lets you print any color coding you may have applied to people in your database. If you mark this checkbox, RootsMagic will print the name of each person in the same color as they are color coded on screen.

*Private facts* lets you choose whether RootsMagic should include any facts (birth, marriage, or death) that you have marked as "private".

*Preparer* tells RootsMagic whether you want your name and address printed on the pedigree chart. You can enter that address information in the Settings page.

## FAMILY GROUP SHEETS

The Family Group Sheet is probably the most heavily used printout in genealogy. It is essentially a table that lists all of the facts for a father, mother, and children in a family.

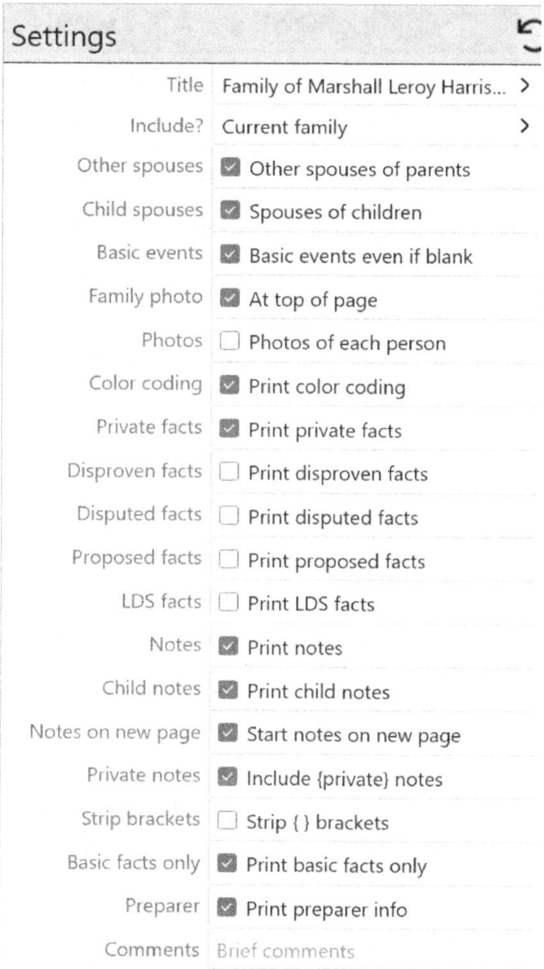


To generate a family group sheet, highlight the father or mother of the family on the main screen, then select Family Group Sheet from the report list.

*Include?* lets you decide if you want to print a single group sheet for the current family, or if you want to print a bunch of group sheets all at once. If you pick the second option, RootsMagic will bring up a list of every family in your database to choose from.

*Other spouses of parents* lets you specify whether RootsMagic should print other spouses of the parents on the group sheet.

*Spouses of children* lets you specify whether RootsMagic should print spouses of each child on the group sheet.

*Basic events even if blank* determines whether RootsMagic will print birth, marriage, death and burial facts for each person even if they are blank. If this box is unchecked, RootsMagic will only print facts that have been entered for the person. If a person doesn't have a death fact entered, RootsMagic will not print a blank one for them.

> ☺ **Tip**
>
> It is possible to turn off certain facts from ever printing in the family group sheet. Select **Lists > Fact type list** from the menu on the People page and a list of every fact type will appear. Select the fact type you want to disable and click Edit. You can then uncheck the Family Group Sheet checkbox for that fact and RootsMagic will not print that fact on any group sheets.

*Family photo at top of page* tells RootsMagic whether to print a family photo above the group sheet. You need to add a photo to the family's scrapbook before RootsMagic can print it.

*Photos for each person* tells RootsMagic whether to print individual photos for each person on the right side of the group sheet.

*Print color coding* lets you print any color coding you may have applied to people in your database. If you mark this checkbox, RootsMagic will print the name of each person in the same color as they are color coded on screen. Color coding is described on page 91.

*Print private facts* lets you choose whether RootsMagic should include any facts (birth, marriage, death, etc.) that you have marked as “private”.

*Print disproven (disputed, proposed) facts* lets you filter out facts which are not proven.

*Print LDS facts* lets you choose whether RootsMagic should include any LDS facts (baptism, endowment, sealings, etc).

*Print notes* determines whether RootsMagic will print any notes with the group sheet. If this box is checked, RootsMagic will print all the family, individual, and fact notes associated with the family. You can select whether the notes will begin on a separate page following the group sheet, or whether they will immediately follow the last child on the group sheet. You can also disable printing of the children's notes, in case you are printing multiple group sheets and don't want to duplicate the children's notes on multiple group sheets.

*Print private notes* and *Strip brackets* let you choose whether RootsMagic should print any private notes you have entered. Private notes are described in more detail on page 138.

*Basic facts only* lets you print a group sheet with only basic facts like birth, death, and burial.

*Print preparer and comments* allows you to enter text that will be printed at the bottom of the family group sheet. The preparer information will also be included.

## Narrative Reports

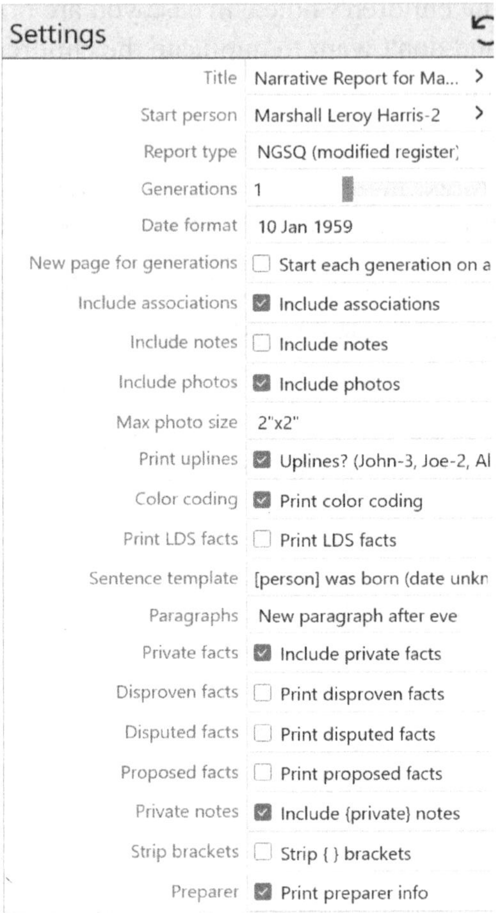


Narrative reports allow you to print a family history of a person, where RootsMagic writes the sentences for each fact. The narrative report can include the ancestors of the person (parents, grandparents, etc.) or the descendants (children, grandchildren, etc.).

*Start person* is the person the report will begin with. You can click the "Start person" button to change this person.

*Report type* lets you select what type of book you want to print.

- **Ancestors only:** Prints a narrative history of the starting person and his/her ancestors. Only direct ancestors are included in the book.
- **Ancestors and children:** Same as the ancestor book, except that children of each ancestor are also included.
- **Modified Register:** Prints a narrative history of the starting person and his/her descendants. The book is broken into chapters by generation.
- **Register:** Prints a narrative history of the starting person and his/her descendants. The book is broken into chapters by generation.
- **Outline (indented):** Prints a narrative history of the starting person and his/her descendants grouped by family.

Many non-genealogists find this book format easier to follow. Each generation is indented from the previous generation, and is numbered in an outline format (I, A, 1, i, a, etc).

- **Henry (indented):** Same as the indented outline descendant book, except that the numbering system follows the Modified Henry format. The first person is number 1, and each generation receives an additional digit stating the order of that child in that generation. If there are more than 9 children in a family, the modified Henry system uses the letters of the alphabet. For example, the person with Henry number 1.b.3 is the third child of the eleventh child of the starting person.
- **D'Aboville (indented):** The D'Aboville numbering format is similar to the Henry format, except that a period is added between generations, so that digits instead of letters can be used beyond 9. For example, the person with D'Aboville number 1.11.3 is the third child of the eleventh child of the starting person.

*Generations* lets you specify how many generations you want to include in your report.

*Date format* lets you select how RootsMagic will print dates in the report. Month names can be abbreviated or fully spelled out.

*Start each generation on a new page* specifies whether RootsMagic will start each new generation (chapter) on a new page.

*Include associations* tells RootsMagic whether to include an associations for the person.

*Include notes* specifies whether RootsMagic will include notes in the report. If notes are included, RootsMagic will insert them in the text. For example, a birth note would immediately follow the sentence about the person's birth date and place.

*Include photos* specifies whether RootsMagic will include photos of individuals in the report. RootsMagic will use the primary photo for the person. You can also choose the size RootsMagic should print the photos. Photos are not included when printing to a text file.

*Print uplines* is only available when printing Modified Register or Register reports. This option will print a list of ancestors (and generations) following the name of each descendant in the report. For example:

John Doe (David-3, Samuel-2, William-1) was born in 1820.

*Print color coding* lets you print any color coding you may have applied to people in your database. If you mark this checkbox, RootsMagic will print the name of each person in the same color as they are color coded on screen. Color coding is described on page 91.

*Print LDS facts* lets you choose whether to include LDS ordinances (baptism, endowment, etc.) on the right side of the group sheet.

*Sentence template* lets you tell RootsMagic what to write for people with no facts. When creating the narrative report, RootsMagic will write sentences for each fact entered for a person. If a person has no facts, then RootsMagic can't normally write anything about the person. If you don't want anything written about the person, then you can leave this field blank. Some suggestions for this template are:

[person] was born.

[person] was born (date unknown).

No further information is known about [person].

*Paragraphs* lets you choose how to handle paragraphs. You can:

- Keep fact sentences in the same paragraph puts all the information about a person in a single paragraph.
- New paragraph after every fact will put each sentence (and its note) in separate paragraphs.

- New paragraph after facts with notes will keep fact sentences together unless they have a note. If a fact sentence has a note, RootsMagic will start the next sentence in a new paragraph.

*Private facts* lets you choose whether RootsMagic should include any facts (birth, marriage, death, etc.) that you have marked as "private".

*Disproven (disputed, proposed)* lets you filter out facts which are not proven.

*Private notes and Strip brackets* let you choose whether RootsMagic should print any private notes you have entered. Private notes are described in more detail on page 138.

*Print preparer* lets you specify whether RootsMagic should print the preparer's name and address at the bottom of the printout. You can set the preparer's name and address in the options screen (page 360).

> ☺ **Tip**
>
> When printing a report to a Word (DOCX) file RootsMagic will not actually build the index at the end of the report (since RootsMagic has no way of knowing how your word processor will paginate the report). Instead, RootsMagic will "mark" each person in the Word file so that your word processor can build the index itself. This is extremely useful in case you want to add more text, photos, or make other changes.
>
> RootsMagic will add instructions on how to generate the index to the Word document.

## Box Chart Reports

Box chart reports let you print ancestor or descendant box charts which can be used in books because they print on standard size pages. They can also be selected when publishing your information using the RootsMagic Publisher described later.

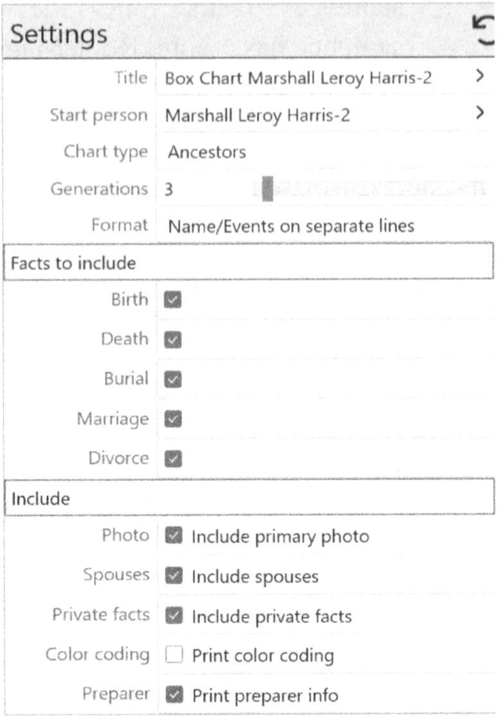


*Start person* is the person who the report will begin with. You can click the "Start person" button to change this person.

*Chart type* lets you select what type of chart you want to print.

- **Ancestors:** Prints a box chart of the starting person and his/her ancestors. Only direct ancestors are included in the chart.
- **Descendants:** Prints a box chart of the starting person and his/her descendants. Each generation is indented a bit to the right, and connecting lines are drawn to show the links between generations.

*Generations* lets you specify how many generations you want to include in your box chart.

*Format* lets you select how RootsMagic will print each person's information in the chart. You can choose from:

- **Single line:** RootsMagic will print the name of each person followed by their birth and death date on the same line.

This is intended to be a compact format and no boxes are drawn around the single line for each person.

- **Name and events each on a separate line:** RootsMagic will print the name of each person on a line, then print each fact type you choose to print on a separate line under the name.

- **Name and events word wrapped:** RootsMagic will print the name followed by the facts you choose word wrapped to fit inside the box.

*Facts to include* lets you choose which facts you want to include in each person's box. You can choose from birth, death, burial, marriage, and divorce.

*Include primary photo* specifies whether RootsMagic will include photos of individuals in the chart. RootsMagic will use the primary photo for the person. Photos are not included when printing to some file types.

*Include spouses* lets you choose whether spouses should be included in the descendant box chart. This option is not applicable when printing an ancestor chart.

*Include private facts* lets you choose whether RootsMagic should include any facts (birth, marriage, etc.) that you have marked as "private".

*Print color coding* lets you print any color coding you may have applied to people in your database. If you mark this checkbox, RootsMagic will color a person's box in the same color as they are color coded on screen. The boxes of non color coded people will be printed in the color chosen in the "Box style" dialog. Color coding is described on page 91.

*Print preparer* lets you specify whether RootsMagic should print the preparer's name and address at the bottom of the printout. You can set the preparer's name and address in the options screen (page 360).

> ☺ **Tip**
>
> If you want to print large charts with boxes, you should probably use the large format chart feature described in the next chapter.

## ADDRESS LABELS

RootsMagic will print mailing labels using any number of standard Avery labels.

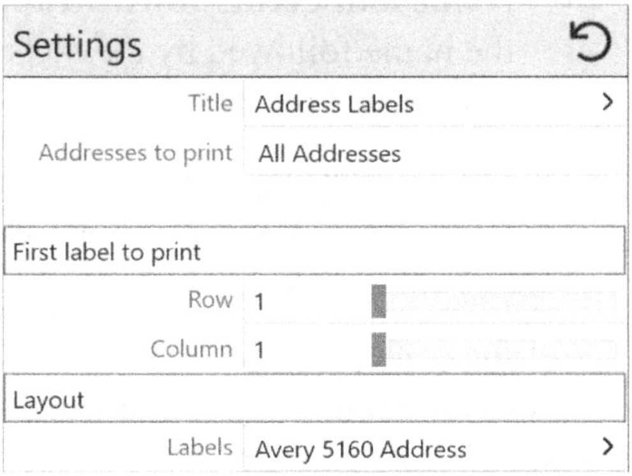


*Addresses to print* lets you decide which people you want to include in the list.

- All addresses – prints every address in the file
- People addresses – prints every address attached to a person
- Family addresses – prints every address attached to a family
- Selected people addresses – brings up a selection screen described in the chapter titled "Custom Reports" (page 294), and allows you to select the people you want to print labels for.

*First label to print* is especially useful when you have a partially printed label sheet, and need to start printing your labels somewhere in the middle of the sheet.

*Labels* lets you select what type (and size) label you want to print on. Just select the desired label type.

## LISTS

RootsMagic provides a large assortment of printable lists. Just select “All Reports and Charts” from the Publish page and select the desired list type. All lists offer the ability to print to the screen or printer, a text file, or a Word file.

## Address List

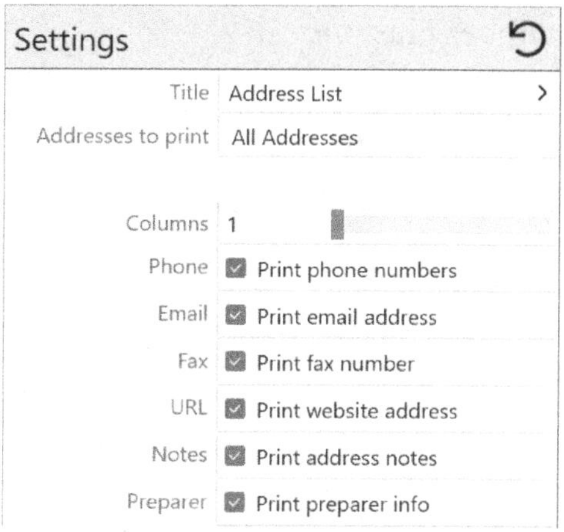


The address list allows you to print any or all of the addresses that you have entered for people.

*Addresses to print* lets you decide which people you want to include in the list.

- **All addresses:** prints every address in the file
- **People addresses:** prints every address attached to a person
- **Family addresses:** prints every address attached to a family
- **Selected people addresses:** brings up a selection screen described in the chapter titled "Custom Reports" (page 294), and allows you to select the people you want to print labels for.

*Columns* lets you choose how many columns to print the address list in.

The remaining checkboxes let you tell RootsMagic which additional address information (phone number, fax, etc.) you want to print for each person.

*Preparer* lets you specify whether RootsMagic should print the preparer's name and address at the bottom of the printout. You can set the preparer's name and address in the options screen (page 360).

## Ahnentafel

The Ahnentafel (which means "Ancestor Table" in German) is an ancestor report. The Ahnentafel is in narrative form, and each individual in the report is assigned an "Ahnentafel number." This numbering system makes it easy to determine a person's parents. The Ahnentafel number of a person's father is exactly twice the person's number and the mother's number is twice the person's number plus one.

*Person* is the person who the report will begin with. You can click the "Start person" button to change this person.

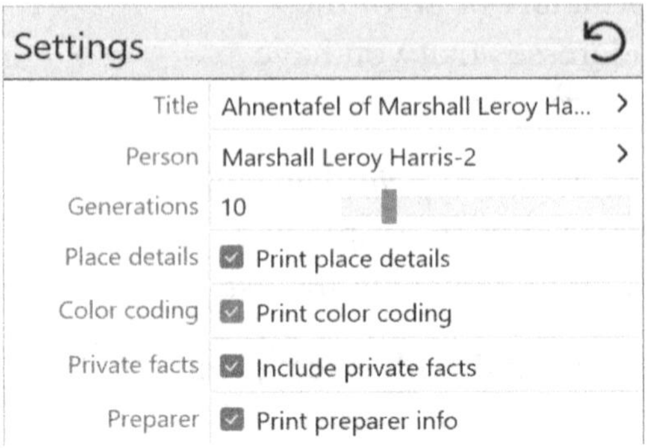


*Generations* lets you specify how many generations you want to include in your report.

*Print place details* lets you choose whether to print the place details for each event, or just the place field.

*Print color coding* lets you print any color coding you may have applied to people in your database. If you mark this checkbox, RootsMagic will print the name of each person in the same color as they are color coded on screen. Color coding is described on page 91.

*Include private facts* lets you choose whether RootsMagic should include any facts (birth, marriage, death, etc.) that you have marked as "private".

*Print preparer* lets you specify whether RootsMagic should print the preparer's name and address at the bottom of the printout. You can set the preparer's name and address on the Settings page.

## Association List (Individual)

The Association List (Individual) is an indented list which shows all the associations for a person, up to as many levels deep as desired. You can think of this report like a descendant list of associations for a person. An association is a relationship between two people who aren't necessarily related by family.

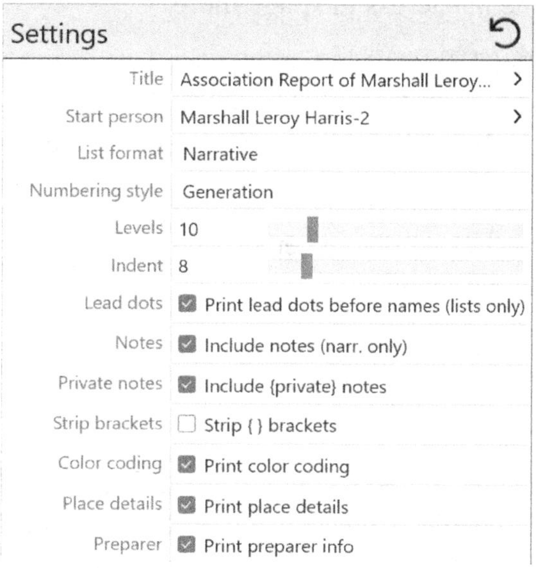


*Start person* is the person who the report will begin with. You can click the "Start person" button to change this person.

*List format* lets you print each person:

1. Name (role) date - place
2. Name/Role/Date/Place in columns
3. Narrative

*Numbering style* lets you choose what number to print in front of each person in the report. The outline, Henry, and D'Aboville numbering systems are described in Narrative Reports on page 236.

1. **Generation:** prints the generation the person is in
2. **Outline:** Outline numbering (I, A, i, a, etc.)
3. **Henry:** 1, 11, 111, etc.
4. **D'Aboville:** 1, 1.1, 1.1.1, etc.

*Levels* lets you specify how many levels of associations you want to include in your list.

*Indent* lets you specify how much each level will be indented to the right. If you make this number small, you can fit more levels across the page. If you make this number larger, you can spread the list across the page more.

*Lead dots* tells RootsMagic whether it should print a string of dots before each person's name in the list. This can sometimes make the list easier to read. Dots are only available in the non-narrative format.

*Notes* specifies whether RootsMagic will include association notes in the report.

*Include private notes and Strip brackets* let you choose whether RootsMagic should print any private notes you have entered. Private notes are described in more detail on page 138.

*Color coding* lets you print any color coding you may have applied to people in your database. If you mark this checkbox, RootsMagic will print the name of each person in the same color as they are color coded on screen. Color coding is described on page 91.

*Print place details* lets you choose whether to print the place details for each event, or just the place field.

*Preparer* lets you specify whether RootsMagic should print the preparer's name and address at the bottom of the printout. You can set the preparer's name and address in the options screen (page 360).

### Association List (Relationship)

The Association List (Relationship) is a list which shows how two people are connected by associations. The two people don't need to be directly connected by a single association. The report will trace through associations with other people to make the connection if necessary.

*Person 1 and Person 2* let you select the two people you want to find the relationship for. RootsMagic will bring up a list of everyone in your database for you to select from. By default, the first person will be set to the person who was highlighted on the main screen, but you can change to a different person if you want.

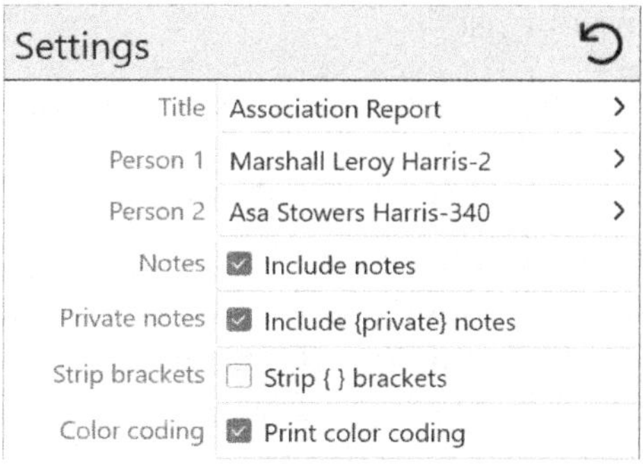


*Notes* specifies whether RootsMagic will include association notes in the report.

*Include private notes and Strip brackets* let you choose whether RootsMagic should print any private notes you have entered. Private notes are described in more detail on page 138.

*Color coding* lets you print any color coding you may have applied to people in your database. If you mark this checkbox, RootsMagic will print the name of each person in the same color as they are color coded on screen. Color coding is described on page 91.

## Birthday and Anniversary List

The birthday and anniversary list prints birthdays and / or anniversaries sorted by date. You can choose to include everyone in your database, or just selected individuals.

*Include?* lets you decide which people you want to include in the list. You can print everyone in the database, or select people from a list. If you check "Select from a list" RootsMagic will bring up a list of every person in your database.

This selection screen is described in the chapter titled "Custom Reports" (page 294), and allows you to select the people you want in your list.

You can choose to print a list of birthdays, anniversaries, or both.

You also have several options which can be used to filter out individuals, such as only including living people and including (or ignoring) marriages with divorces entered. You can also have RootsMagic print the preparer's name and address at the end of the list. You can set the preparer's name and address in the options screen (page 360).

## CountyCheck Report

The CountyCheck report is a list of events with place problems like a county which didn't exist on the date of the event.

*Include?* lets you decide which people you want to include in the list. You can print everyone in the database, or select people from a list. If you check "Select from a list" RootsMagic will bring up a list of every person in your database. This selection screen is described on page 218, and allows you to select the people you want in your list.

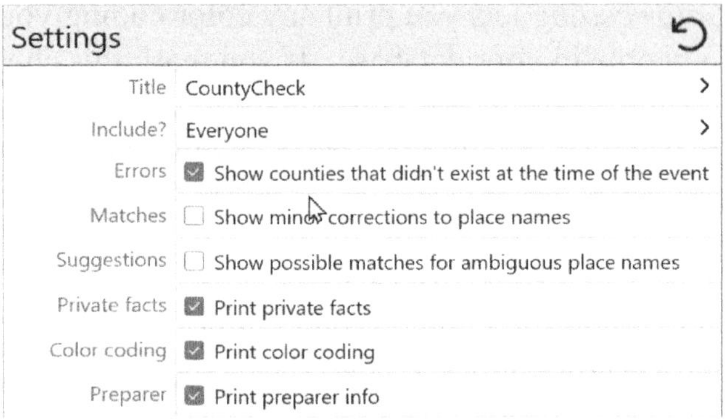


You choose which messages you want printed: errors (like a county not existing on a date), suggestions (for possible missing parts of the place), or matches.

*Print private facts* lets you choose whether RootsMagic should include any facts (birth, marriage, death, etc.) that you have marked as "private".

*Print color coding* lets you print any color coding you may have applied to people in your database. If you mark this checkbox, RootsMagic will print the name of each person in the same color as they are color coded on screen. Color coding is described on page 91.

*Preparer* lets you specify whether RootsMagic should print the preparer's name and address at the bottom of the printout. You can set the preparer's name and address in the options screen (page 360).

## Descendant List

The descendant list is an indented list of the highlighted person and his or her descendants (children, grandchildren, etc). Each person is printed on a single line and each generation is indented to the right of the previous generation. You can print this list with either one line per person, or full birth, marriage and death information on multiple lines.

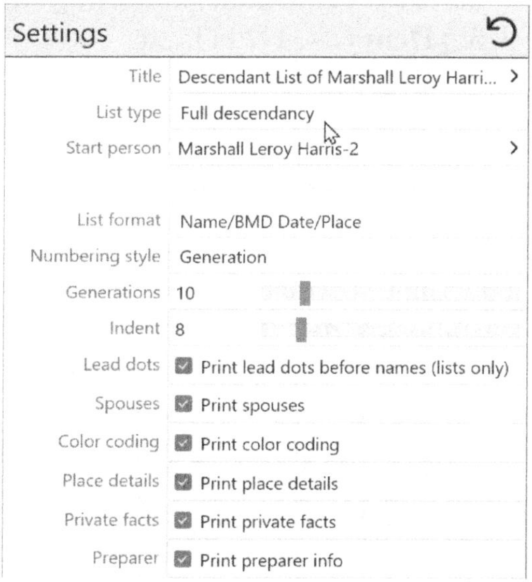


*List type* lets you choose whether to print a full descendancy (all descendants of the starting person), or a direct line descendancy (only those descendants from the starting person to a specific descendants).

*Start person* is the person who the report will begin with. You can click the "Start person" button to change this person.

*Descendant* only appears when you print a direct line descendancy, and lets you select the end person on the report.

*List format* lets you print each person:

1. on a single line with just their birth and death date
2. on a single line but with the name, birth dates and death dates in columns
3. on up to 4 lines for each person (name, birth date and place, marriage date and place, and death date and place)
4. on a single line with just the birth and death year
5. with the name, birth, marriage, and death date and place wordwrapped

*Numbering style* lets you choose what number to print in front of each person in the report. The outline, Henry, and D'Aboville numbering systems are described in Narrative Reports on page 236.

1. **Generation:** prints the generation the person is in
2. **Outline:** Outline numbering (I, A, i, a, etc.)
3. **Henry:** 1, 11, 111, etc.
4. **D'Aboville:** 1, 1.1, 1.1.1, etc.

*Generations* lets you specify how many generations you want to include in your list.

*Indent* lets you specify how much each generation will be indented to the right. If you make this number small, you can fit more generations across the page. If you make this number larger, you can spread the list across the page more. When printing wordwrapped format, this setting doesn't apply because the wrapped paragraphs have a hanging indent.

*Lead dots* tells RootsMagic whether it should print a string of dots before each person's name in the list. This can sometimes make the list easier to read. Dots are only available in the non narrative format.

*Print spouses* specifies whether RootsMagic should print the spouses of the descendants in the list.

*Print color coding* lets you print any color coding you may have applied to people in your database. If you mark this checkbox, RootsMagic will print the name of each person in the same color as they are color coded on screen. Color coding is described on page 91.

*Print private facts* lets you choose whether RootsMagic should include any facts (birth, marriage, death, etc.) that you have marked as "private".

*Preparer* lets you specify whether RootsMagic should print the preparer's name and address at the bottom of the printout. You can set the preparer's name and address in the options screen (page 360).

## DNA Kinship List

The DNA Kinship list will show the DNA predicted relationships of the highlighted person to anyone you have a DNA match for. It can also display the relationship based on how they are connected in your RootsMagic tree so that you can compare the entered and DNA relationships side by side.

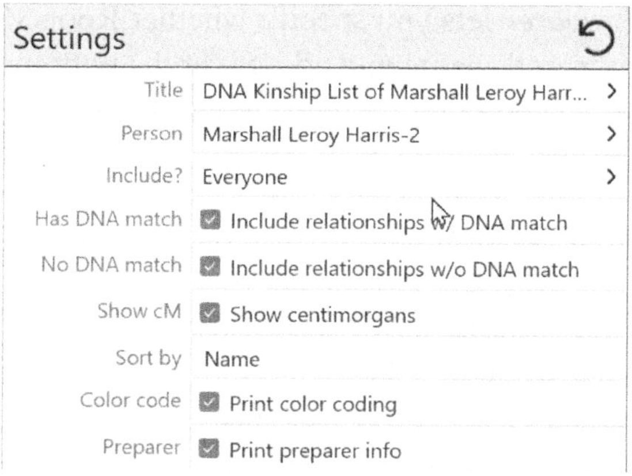


*Person* is the person who the report will find DNA matches for. You can click the field to change this person.

*Include?* lets you decide which people you want to include in the list (kind of like a filter). You can include everyone in the database, or select people from a list. If you check "Select from a list" RootsMagic will bring up a list of every person in your database. This selection screen is described on page 218, and allows you to select the people you want in your list.

*Has DNA match* lets you include people that you have a DNA match for.

*No DNA match* lets you include people that you do not have a DNA match for. If you check this box, you will get relatives in the RootsMagic tree that don't have a DNA match with the start person.

*Show cM* tells RootsMagic to display the number of centimorgans the start person shares with the DNA match.

*Sort by* lets you sort the resulting list either alphabetically or by relationship.

*Color code* lets you print any color coding you may have applied to people in your database. If you mark this checkbox, RootsMagic will print the name of each person in the same color as they are color coded on screen.

*Preparer* lets you specify whether RootsMagic should print the preparer's name and address at the bottom of the printout. You can set the preparer's name and address in the options screen (page 360).

## Duplicate List

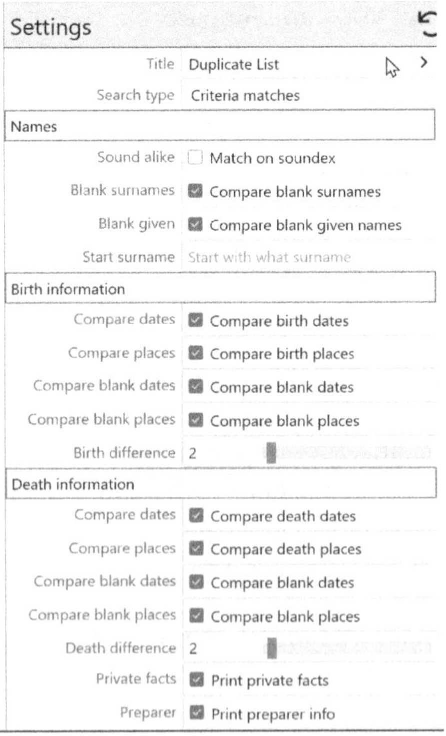


The duplicate list is a report of possible duplicate records in your database. The list will contain pairs of records that might be duplicates. This report is particularly useful when you want to merge individual records and want a list of records that need merging.

RootsMagic offers three different search types.

**Criteria matches** lets you set options to have RootsMagic compare people using:

- *Names* lets you tell RootsMagic how people's names must match to be considered duplicates. You can specify whether matching names have to match exactly, or if they just need to sound alike. You can also choose whether blank names (both given and surnames) will be considered as matches with non blank names. Checking these boxes often leads to many false duplicates.
- *Start surname* lets you tell RootsMagic where in the database to start the duplicate search. If you leave this blank, then RootsMagic will search the entire database for duplicates. If you enter "D", then RootsMagic will start with surnames beginning with the letter "D". If you enter "Jones", then RootsMagic will start with people with the last name "Jones".
- *Birth information* tells RootsMagic whether to compare birth information of people when checking for duplicates. You can choose to compare birth dates and / or birth places. You can also enter a maximum number of years between birth dates. If you set this value to 0, RootsMagic will only consider two individuals duplicates if they were born the exact same year. A value of 5 means that two individual's birth dates can be 5 years apart and still be considered duplicates. The smaller this number, the fewer duplicates RootsMagic will find. You can also tell RootsMagic whether you want to consider individuals without birth dates or birth places as possible duplicates. If you don't check these boxes, RootsMagic will not consider any individuals whose birth date (or place) is blank, even if they match in other ways.
- *Death information* works the same as the birth options (except with death data of course).

**AFN Matches** finds individuals with matching Ancestral File numbers. All other criteria is ignored.

**REFN Matches** finds individuals with matching Reference numbers (REFN). All other criteria is ignored.

*Print private facts* lets you choose whether RootsMagic should include any facts (birth, marriage, death, etc.) that you have marked as "private".

*Preparer* lets you specify whether RootsMagic should print the preparer's name and address at the bottom of the printout. You can set the preparer's name and address in the options screen (page 360).

## Fact List

The Fact List is one of the most useful printouts available in RootsMagic. It allows you to print lists of people associated with any fact in your database (including any user-defined facts you have created).

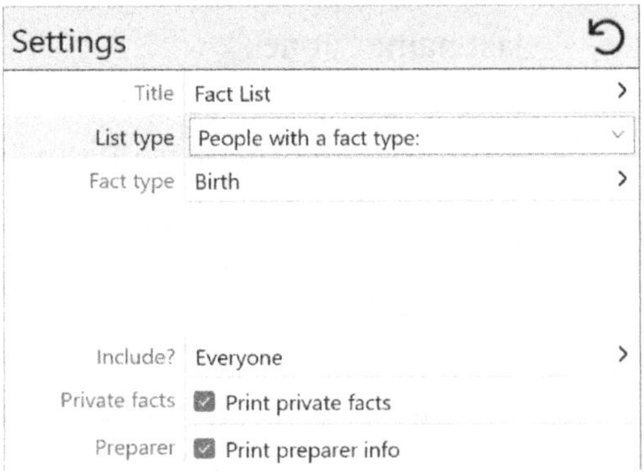


*You can print a list of people who have or don't have a specific fact.* Simply select the desired fact type from the drop list, and you can print a list of everyone with that fact, everyone without that fact, or everyone with more than one of that fact. For example, if you wanted a list of everyone in your database that you have not entered a birth for, select birth from the list, select People missing a fact type, and click "Generate Report".

*You can print a list of facts that have or don't have sources.* You can even print facts that have sources of a certain quality.

*You can print a list of facts with text dates.* These are dates that are either invalid dates, or are dates that RootsMagic can't figure out.

*You can print a list of private facts.* These are facts that you have marked the "private" checkbox for.

*Include?* lets you decide which people you want to include in the list. You can print everyone in the database, or select people from a list. If you check "Select from a list" RootsMagic will bring up a list of every person in your database. This selection screen is described on page 218, and allows you to select the people you want in your list.

*Print private facts* lets you choose whether RootsMagic should include any facts (birth, marriage, death, etc.) that you have marked as "private".

*Preparer* lets you specify whether RootsMagic should print the preparer's name and address at the bottom of the printout. You can set the preparer's name and address in the options screen (page 360).

### Health Conditions List

The Health Conditions list is an alphabetical list of any or all people in your file who have a specific health condition (or any health condition).

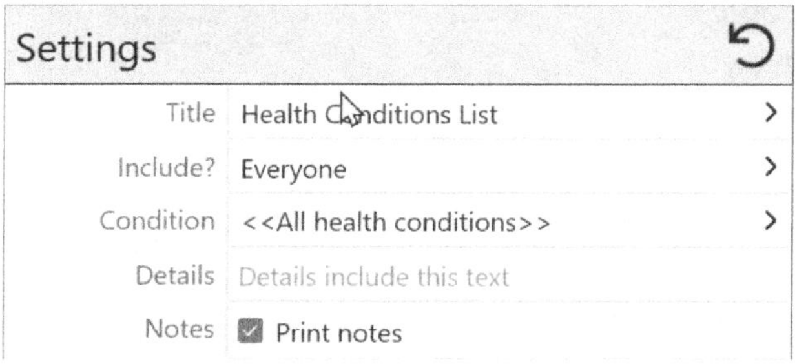


*Include?* lets you decide which people you want to include in the list. You can print everyone in the database with the desired condition, or select people from a list. If you check "Select from a list" RootsMagic will bring up a list of every person in your database. This selection screen is described on page 218, and allows you to select the people you want in your list.

*Condition* lets you choose which general health condition to print a list for, as well as an option to include anyone with any health condition. For example, if you select Cancer as the condition, then the list will contain anyone that you have entered a Cancer health condition for.

*Details* lets you narrow down your list even further. You can enter text which must be in the health condition details to be included. For example, if you select Cancer as the condition, and enter Lung in the details, only people who have a Cancer health condition with the word Lung in the details will be included.

*Notes* lets you choose whether to print any notes entered for the selected health condition.

## Individual List

The Individual list is an alphabetical list of any or all people in your database. It can be as simple as just the names of the individuals, or can include the facts, parents, spouses, and children for each individual as well.

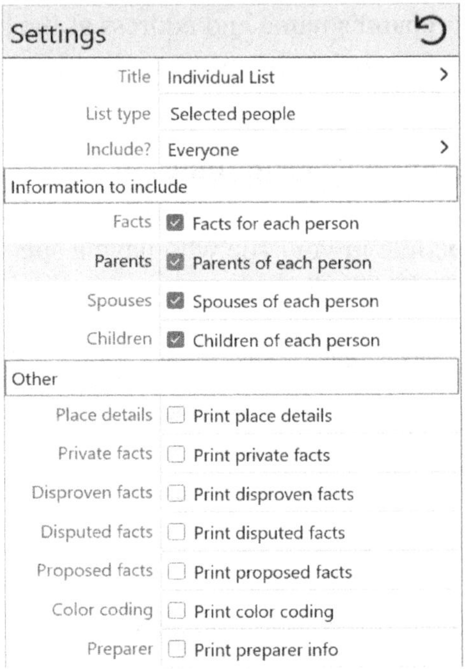


*Include?* lets you decide which people you want to include in the list. You can print everyone in the database, or select people from a list. If you check "Select from a list" RootsMagic will bring up a list of every person in your database. This selection screen is described on page 218, and allows you to select the people you want in your list.

You can also print several specialized lists, including people who have no parents entered in the database, people who have more than one set of parents entered in the database, and people who aren't linked to anyone else in the database (no spouses, children, or parents).

*Information to include* specifies what information you want printed for each person in the list, including facts for each person, or the parents, spouses, or children of each person.

*Place details* lets you choose whether to include place details for the facts that are included.

*Private facts* lets you choose whether RootsMagic should include any facts (birth, marriage, death, etc.) that you have marked as "private".

*Disproven (disputed, proposed) facts* lets you filter out facts which are not proven.

*Print color coding* lets you print any color coding you may have applied to people in your database. If you mark this checkbox, RootsMagic will print the name of each person in the same color as they are color coded on screen. Color coding is described on page 91.

*Preparer* lets you specify whether RootsMagic should print the preparer's name and address at the bottom of the printout. You can set the preparer's name and address in the options screen (page 360).

### Kinship List

One of the coolest lists in RootsMagic is the Kinship list. RootsMagic will print a list of every person in the database that is related to the highlighted person, and will display the relationship to that person. It will include all degrees of ancestors, descendants, siblings, aunts, uncles, and cousins (including how many times removed or half relationships). It will even get spouses of your relatives. Be prepared though, if you have a big database, this list can get pretty long!

*Person* is the person who the report will find relatives for. You can click the "Start person" button to change this person.

*Include?* lets you decide which people you want to include in the list. You can print everyone in the database, or select people from a list. If you check "Select from a list" RootsMagic will bring up a list of every person in your database. This selection screen is described on page 218, and allows you to select the people you want in your list.

*Sort by* lets you sort the resulting list either alphabetically or by relationship.

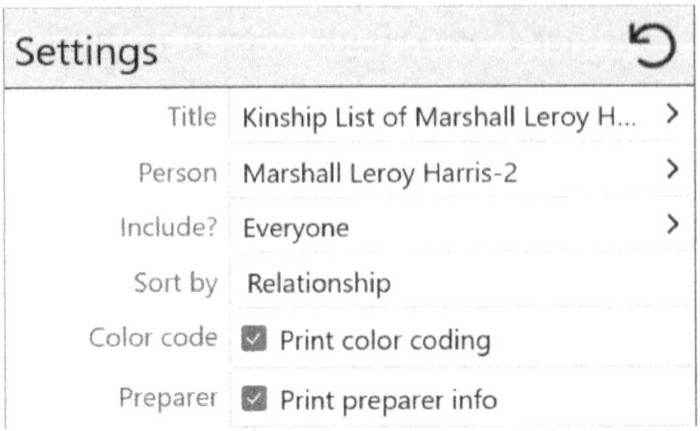


*Color code* lets you print any color coding you may have applied to people in your database. If you mark this checkbox, RootsMagic will print the name of each person in the same color as they are color coded on screen.

*Preparer* lets you specify whether RootsMagic should print the preparer's name and address at the bottom of the printout. You can set the preparer's name and address in the options screen (page 360).

### LDS List

The LDS list (there are actually two of them) will print LDS ordinance information for the people in your database. These will be the ordinances you actually have stored in the database (not the official ordinances up on FamilySearch). To see (and download) the official ordinances, see the FamilySearch chapter (page 326).

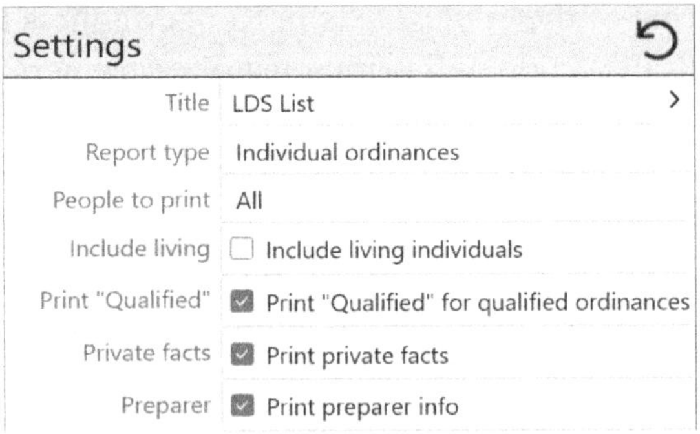


*Report type* lets you select which ordinance list to print.

- **Individual ordinances:** lists individuals and the dates for LDS baptism, endowment, and sealing to parents.
- **Marriage sealings:** lists families and the marriage date and sealing to spouse date.

*People to print* lets you select which individuals to include in the selected list.

- **All:** prints everyone in the database
- **Only those missing ordinances:** prints only individuals who are missing at least one ordinance
- **Only those with all ordinances completed:** prints only individuals who are not missing any ordinances
- **Only those with "submitted" ordinances:** prints only individuals who have at least one ordinance with a status of Submitted.
- **Only those with "qualified" ordinances:** prints only individuals who have at least one ordinance which is qualified for temple work.

*Include living individuals* gives you the option to ignore living individuals (since you can't do temple work for them anyways).

*Print 'Qualified' for qualified ordinances* will cause RootsMagic to print the word "qualified" for any ordinance that is qualified for temple work.

*Print private facts* lets you choose whether RootsMagic should include any facts (birth, marriage, death, etc.) that you have marked as "private".

*Preparer* lets you specify whether RootsMagic should print the preparer's name and address at the bottom of the printout. You can set the preparer's name and address in the options screen (page 360).

### Marriage List

The Marriage List is a listing of "couples" in your database. Having a marriage fact is not a requirement to appear in the list.

*Sort by* lets you sort the marriage list by the husband's name, the wife's name, marriage record number, the marriage date, or the marriage place.

You can have RootsMagic print couples with a marriage event, or those without a marriage event, or both.

*Print private facts* lets you choose whether RootsMagic should include any facts (birth, death, etc.) that you have marked as "private".

*Print preparer name and address* lets you specify whether RootsMagic should print the preparer's name and address at the bottom of the printout. You can set the preparer's name and address in the options screen (page 360).

## Missing Info List

The Missing Info List creates a list of individuals missing any fact(s) or part of a fact that you choose. You can select multiple fact types in a single report.

Click and highlight as many facts as you want RootsMagic to check for each person. Then select what part of the fact needs to be missing.

- *Are missing this fact* will print a person if any of the highlighted facts are missing for the person.
- *Have this fact but date is blank* will print a person if the fact exists, but the date is missing.
- *Have this fact but place is blank* will print a person if the fact exists, but the place is missing.

*Include?* lets you decide which people you want to include in the list. You can print everyone in the database, or select people from a list. If you check "Select from a list" RootsMagic will bring up a list of every person in your database. This selection screen is described on page 218, and allows you to select the people you want in your list.

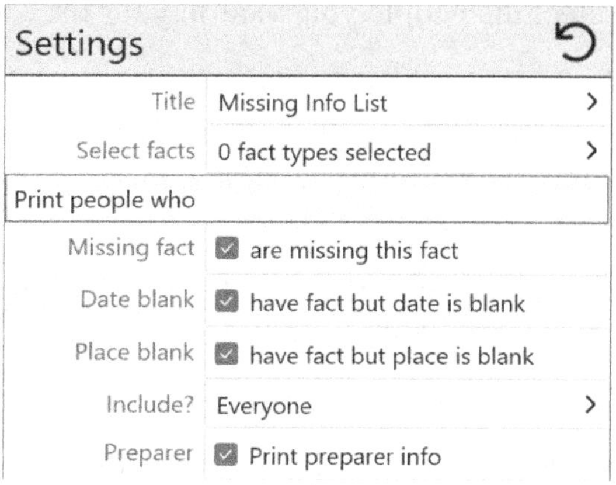


*Preparer* lets you specify whether RootsMagic should print the preparer's name and address at the bottom of the printout. You can set the preparer's name and address in the options screen (page 360).

## Multimedia List

Since RootsMagic links to multimedia items on your hard disk, it is possible to lose track of which photos, video and sound clips you are linking to. The multimedia list generates a printout of multimedia items your database is using, including the full path name and what the item is linked to.

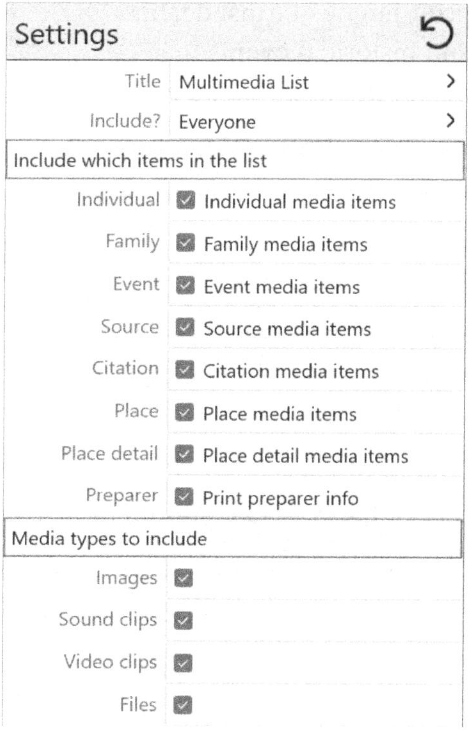


*Include?* lets you decide which people you want to include in the list. You can print everyone in the database, or select people from a list. If you check "Select from a list"

RootsMagic will bring up a list of every person in your database. This selection screen is described on page 218, and allows you to select the people you want in your list.

*Include which items in the list* lets you decide which multimedia items you want to include in the list. You can select any combination of multimedia items connected to people, families, sources, events, or places.

You can further filter the list by choosing whether to include any combination of image, sound clips, video clips, or files.

*Preparer* lets you specify whether RootsMagic should print the preparer's name and address at the bottom of the printout. You can set the preparer's name and address in the options screen (page 360).

### On This Day List

The "On This Day" report will list all the events from your database that occurred on a selected day. You can also choose to print famous births, deaths, and historical events that occurred on that same day.

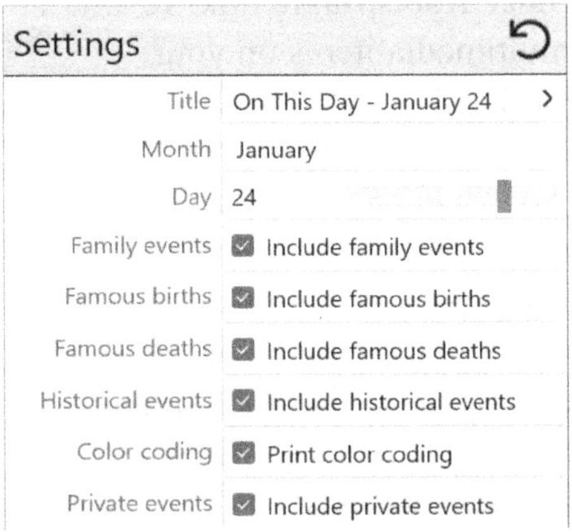


*Month and Day* let you select which date to print the events for.

The next 4 checkboxes let you select which items RootsMagic will include in the report.

*Color coding* lets you choose whether RootsMagic should display any of the people in "family events" using their color coding.

*Private events* lets you choose whether RootsMagic will print events from your database which you have marked as private.

## Place List

The place list can potentially be one of the longest reports you generate.

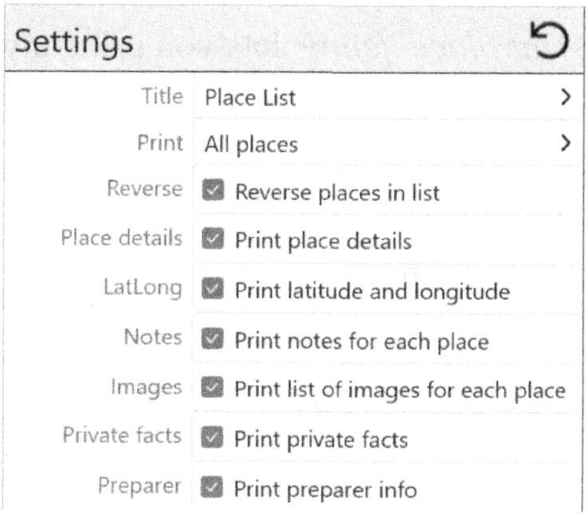


*Print* lets you select what you want to include in the list. Several of the options you can just select and click OK. Other options require you to enter some additional information.

1. *Print all places in database* will print a list of every place in your database.
2. *Print all places and events* will print a list of every place in your database, along with all the events which occurred in each of those places.
3. *Print events in a single place* will print a list of every fact in your database that occurred in the highlighted place. It will list the person's name, fact type, and date for each fact.
4. *Print events near a place* will print a list of every event which happened within a selected distance. For example, you can print every event which happened within 50 miles of Dallas, Texas.
5. *Print filtered places and Print filtered places and events* let you enter some text and RootsMagic will only include places which contain that text.

When places are printed, RootsMagic can reverse them so that the general part of the place name is first to sort places geographically. For example, if you mark the checkbox to reverse place names, places will be listed like:

New Mexico, Bernalillo Co., Albuquerque

New Mexico, Santa Fe Co., Santa Fe

Utah, Salt Lake Co., Draper

Utah, Salt Lake Co., Salt Lake City

Utah, Utah Co., Orem

Utah, Utah Co., Provo

*Print place details* lets you print any place details associated with each place in the list.

*Print latitude and longitude* will cause RootsMagic to print the latitude and longitude for each place that you have entered that information.

*Print notes for each place* causes RootsMagic to print any notes you entered for the place. You can also have RootsMagic print a list of any images the each place's multimedia scrapbook.

*Images* lets you print a list of any images attached to each place.

*Print private facts* lets you choose whether RootsMagic should include any facts (birth, death, etc.) that you have marked as "private".

*Preparer* lets you specify whether RootsMagic should print the preparer's name and address at the bottom of the printout. You can set the preparer's name and address in the options screen (page 360).

### Statistics List

The statistics list is a fun little list that will calculate various statistics about a group of people in your database. It will calculate the minimum, maximum, and averages for age at first marriage, age at death, marriages per individual, and children per marriage. It also breaks these categories down by sex.

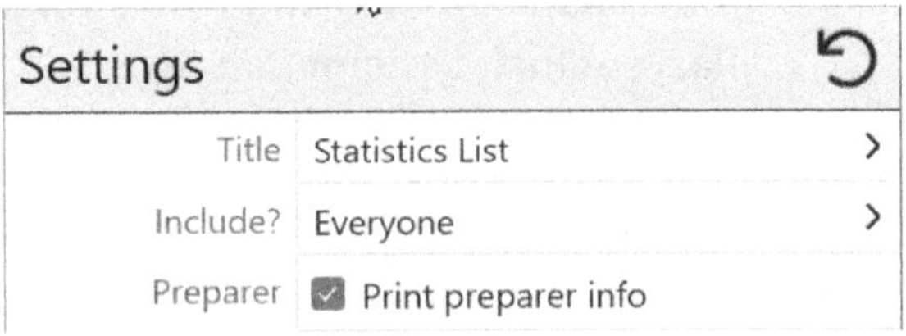


*Include?* lets you decide which people you want to include in the list. You can print everyone in the database, or select people from a list. If you check "Select from a list" RootsMagic will bring up a list of every person in your database. This selection screen is described on page 218, and allows you to select the people you want in your list.

*Preparer* lets you specify whether RootsMagic should print the preparer's name and address at the bottom of the printout. You can set the preparer's name and address in the options screen (page 360).

### Surname Statistics List

The Surname Statistics List prints a list of every surname in your database. Each surname is listed only once, along with the number of people with that surname (broken down by males and females), and the earliest year and most recent year the surname appears in your database.

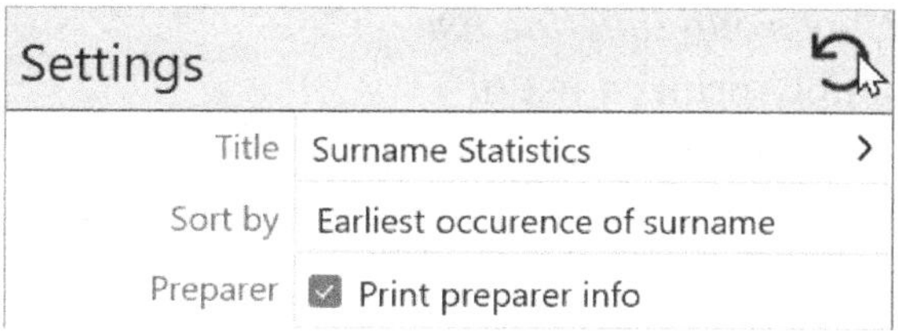


You can sort the surname statistics list: 1) alphabetically, 2) by the number of people with that surname (frequency), 3) by the number of males with that surname, 4) by the number of females with that surname, 5) by the earliest occurrence of the surname, and 6) by the most recent occurrence of the surname.

*Preparer* lets you specify whether RootsMagic should print the preparer's name and address at the bottom of the printout. You can set the preparer's name and address in the options screen (page 360).

### Timeline List

The Timeline list is actually two different lists that print a chronological list of events for a group of people (including your entire database if desired).

*The Individual timeline list* prints a chronological list of the events in the highlighted person's life, along with the birth, marriage, and death information for any other group of people that you select (but only those that fall within the lifetime of the primary person). By selecting the family members of the highlighted person, you can get an informative list of all family events which occurred within his or her lifetime.

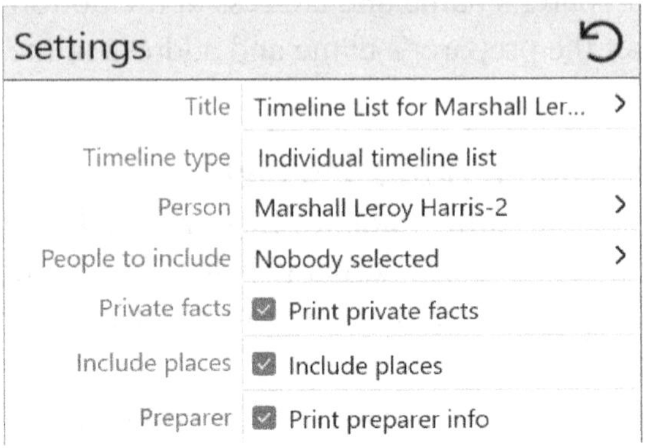


*The Group timeline list* simply prints a list of every event for any group of people you select. This is especially useful for printing a list of all events for a family.

*People to include* will display a list of all the people in your database, and you can select which people you want to include in your group timeline list. This selection screen is described in the chapter titled "Custom Reports" (page 294).

RootsMagic will then chronologically list all events in the selected person's lives (if they have a date).

*Include private facts* lets you choose whether RootsMagic should include any facts (birth, death, etc.) that you have marked as "private".

*Include places* tells RootsMagic to print the place for each event.

*Preparer* lets you specify whether RootsMagic should print the preparer's name and address at the bottom of the printout. You can set the preparer's name and address in the options screen (page 360).

## WebTags List

The WebTags list will print a list of any or all of the WebTags you have entered for your database. WebTags (described on page 102) are links from people, sources, and other record types to web pages online.

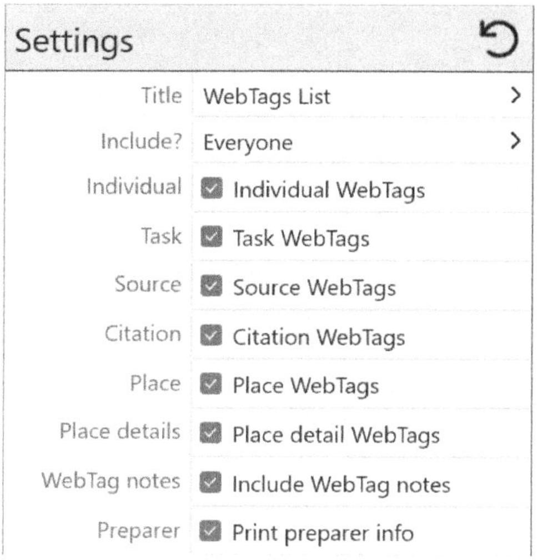


*Include?* lets you decide which people you want to include in the list. You can print everyone in the database, or select people from a list. If you check "Select from a list" RootsMagic will bring up a list of every person in your database. This selection screen is described on page 218, and allows you to select the people you want in your list.

**Individual:** Include WebTags attached to people.
**Task:** Include WebTags attached to tasks.
**Source:** Include WebTags attached to sources.
**Citation:** Include WebTags attached to citations.
**Place:** Include WebTags attached to places.
**Place details:** Include WebTags attached to place details.

*WebTag notes* lets you choose whether to include the notes entered for WebTags.

*Preparer* lets you specify whether RootsMagic should print the preparer's name and address at the bottom of the printout. You can set the preparer's name and address in the options screen (page 360).

## Who Was There List

The "Who Was There" list is a very powerful report that lets you see every person who was in a particular place at a particular time.

The report will print the name of each person who may have been in that place at that time, along with their birth and death date, and any events in their lives that occurred in that place.

*Place* is where you will enter the place to search in. This can be a city, state, or country.

*Date* is where you enter the date or time period to search. If you want to find everyone who may have been in the selected place regardless of the date, just enter a large date span like from 1500 to 2100.

*Avg life span* lets you enter an average life span for RootsMagic to use for people who are missing a birth or death date.

*Include?* lets you decide which people you want to include in the list. You can print everyone in the database, or select people from a list. If you check "Select from a list" RootsMagic will bring up a list of every person in your database. This selection screen is described on page 218, and allows you to select the people you want in your list.

*Minimum and Maximum age* lets you enter ages to filter the list by.

*Print married name on date* lets you choose whether to print the most likely married name for each female on the date selected.

*Print alternate names* lets you choose whether to print any alternate names entered for each person.

*Reverse place names* lets you choose whether to print places in reverse (Country, State, County, City).

*Print color coding* lets you print any color coding you may have applied to people in your database. If you mark this checkbox, RootsMagic will print the name of each person in the same color as they are color coded on screen.

*Preparer* lets you specify whether RootsMagic should print the preparer's name and address at the bottom of the printout. You can set the preparer's name and address in the options screen (page 360).

## Research Reports

Research reports is a special category of reports and lists which are research related.

### Repository List

The repository list will print either a single repository (libraries, archives, etc.) or all repositories in the database. You can also have RootsMagic include all the sources and tasks for each repository. This is especially useful if you want to print a list of things you need to do at a repository.

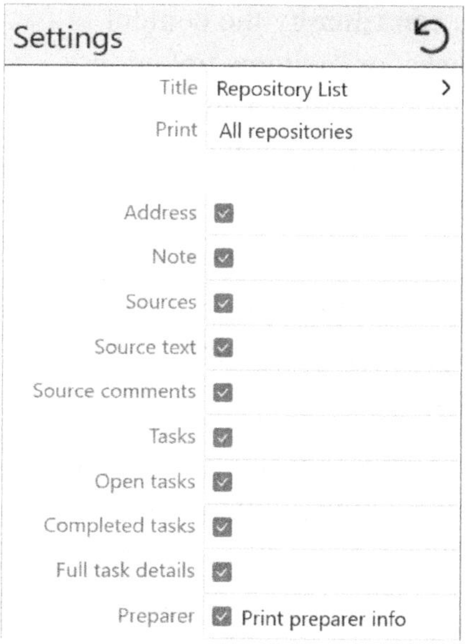


*Address* tells RootsMagic to print the full address for each repository.

*Note* tells RootsMagic to print any notes you have entered for each repository.

*Sources* will print all sources which reside in each repository. Additionally you can include the actual text and comments about each source.

*Tasks* will print all tasks for each repository. You can choose whether to print open or completed tasks (or both), and can ask RootsMagic to print the full details for each task.

*Preparer* lets you specify whether RootsMagic should print the preparer's name and address at the bottom of the printout. You can set the preparer's name and address in the options screen (page 360).

## Research Log

The research log will print all the tasks in a folder in a columnized format.

*Folder* lets you select which folder to print as a research log.

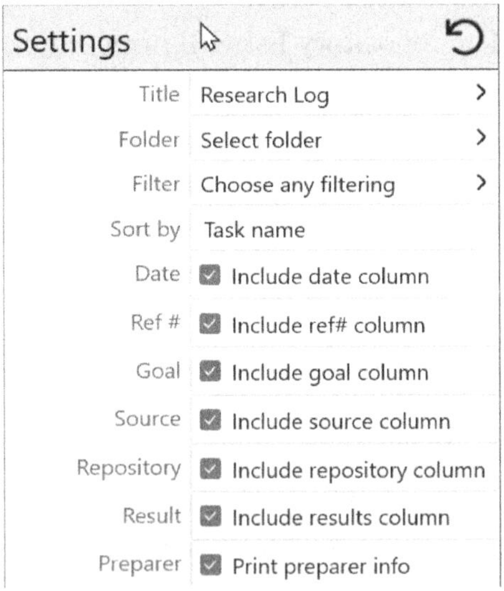


*Filter* lets you enter criteria to select which tasks to include. You can filter by the content of tasks, or by items linked to the task, or both. Details on task filters can be found on page 190.

*Sort by* lets you sort the task list by task name, start date, edit date, status, priority, or reference number.

The next 6 checkboxes let you choose which columns to include in your research log.

*Preparer* lets you specify whether RootsMagic should print the preparer's name and address at the bottom of the printout. You can set the preparer's name and address in the options screen (page 360).

## Research Notes

The research notes report will print the research notes and comments for every citation for a person or family.

*Print for* lets you choose whether to print the research notes for a person or a family. Your decision here will enable either the Person or Family field to select the desired person or family.

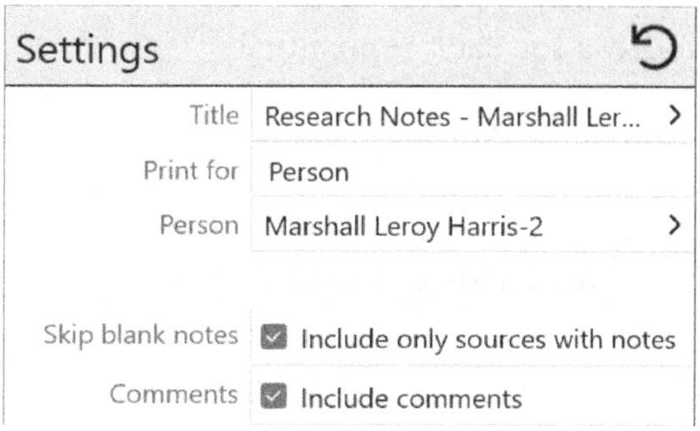


*Skip blank notes* lets you choose whether to include any citations that don't have research notes entered.

*Comments* lets you choose whether to include any comments you have entered for the citations.

## Source List

The source list will print either a single source, or a list of every source in the database. You can also have RootsMagic print every use (citation) of each source. If you print all sources you can also tell RootsMagic how to sort the printed sources.

*Short footnote* will print the short version of the source if it has been entered.

*Bibliography* will print the bibliography version of the source if it has been entered.

You can also choose to print the actual source text and comments about the source.

*Repositories* will print all repositories for each source in the list. You can also have RootsMagic print the full address for each repository.

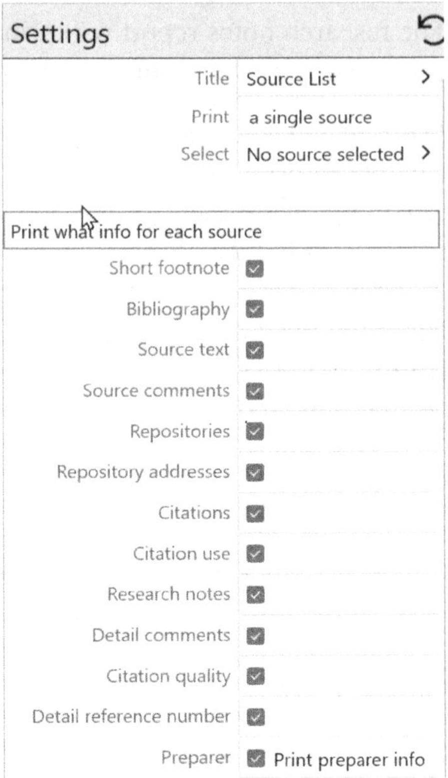


*Citations* specifies whether all citations for each source should be printed. The citation includes the person (or family) and the fact. You can also choose to include the research notes, detail comments, detail reference number and citation quality for each citation.

*Preparer* lets you specify whether RootsMagic should print the preparer's name and address at the bottom of the printout. You can set the preparer's name and address in the options screen (page 360).

## Task List

The task list will print a list of the tasks in your database. It will include the task description, the person the task is for, the soundex code for the person, the repository where the task needs to be done, and the date the task was created.

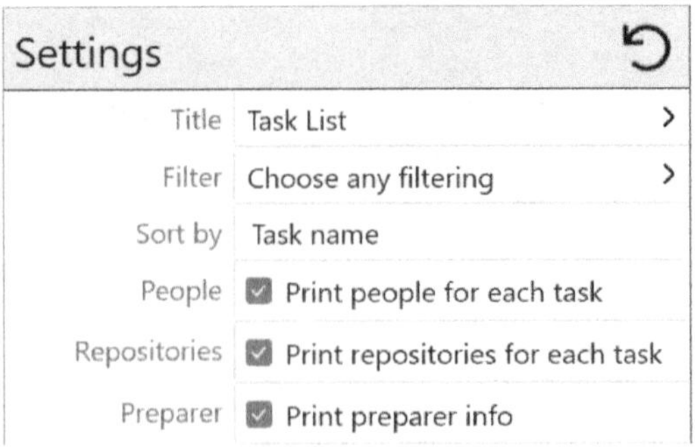


*Filter* lets you enter criteria to select which tasks to include. You can filter by the content of tasks, or by items linked to the task, or both. Details on task filters can be found on page 190.

*Sort by* lets you sort the task list by task name, start date, edit date, status, priority, or reference number.

*People* tells RootsMagic whether to print a list of people using each task.

*Repositories* tells RootsMagic to print the full street address for each repository.

*Preparer* lets you specify whether RootsMagic should print the preparer's name and address at the bottom of the printout. You can set the preparer's name and address in the options screen (page 360).

## CALENDARS

If you are always forgetting birthdays and anniversaries, then this is the report for you. You can print a calendar with birthdays and anniversaries for any month or year.

*Title* lets you enter a title for your calendar.

*Include?* lets you decide which people you want to include in the list. You can print everyone in the database, or select people from a list. If you check "Select from a list" RootsMagic will bring up a list of every person in your database. This selection screen is described on page 218, and allows you to select the people you want in your list.

*Month and Year* lets you select which month (or all months) and which year to print a calendar for. If you choose "All months" then RootsMagic will print a calendar for each month in the year you choose.

You can choose whether to print birthdays, anniversaries, or both. You can even choose to ignore anniversaries of marriages with divorces entered.

*Private facts* lets you choose whether RootsMagic should include any facts (birth, death, etc.) that you have marked as "private".

Several options ("Only living", "Married name", and "Include age") let you customize the information that is included on the calendar.

## Individual Summary

The Individual Summary prints just about everything you have entered for a person. You can print a summary for the highlighted person, or you can print multiple summaries all at once. If you choose "Select from a list", RootsMagic will display a list of all the people in your database, and you can select which people you want to include.

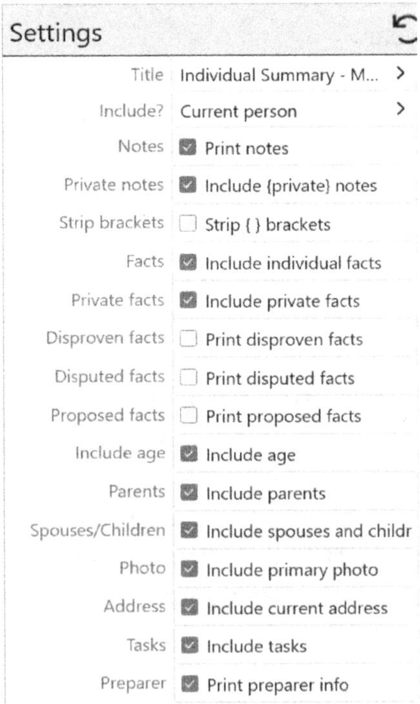


*Include?* lets you select which people to print summaries for. By default it will print a single summary for the currently highlighted person, but you can select a group of people to include. The options are described on page 293.

The remaining checkboxes let you select which items to print for the person. You can include notes, facts (birth, death, etc), the person's age at each event, parents, spouses and children, a photo, tasks, and the person's current address. You can also choose whether to print private notes or facts, and whether to filter out facts which are not proven.

*Preparer* lets you specify whether RootsMagic should print the preparer's name and address at the bottom of the printout. You can set the preparer's name and address in the options screen (page 360).

## FAMILY HEALTH HISTORY

A Family Health History lets you print a report for a person that includes one or all of their medical conditions, as well as the medical conditions of their close relatives (children, siblings, parents, grandparents, and aunts / uncles). This report is especially useful for providing to a health provider.

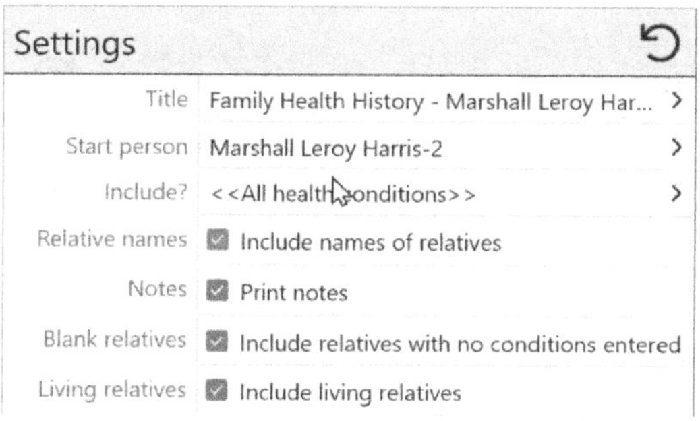


*Start person* is the person the health history is for. You can click the "Start person" field to change this person.

*Include?* lets you select which health condition you want a history for. You can select any of the built in conditions, or choose to include all medical conditions.

*Relative names* lets you privatize your family health history by replacing the names of all relatives with Private when unchecked.

*Notes* determines whether notes entered for medical conditions will be included in the history.

*Blank relatives* tells whether to include family members who have no matching health conditions entered. Unchecking this can reduce the size of the report, especially when a lot of family members do not have matching health conditions.

*Living relatives* lets you select whether you want living relatives included in the report.

## LEEDS METHOD (DNA CLUSTERING)

The Leeds Method is a process to help you sort DNA matches for a person into colorful clusters based on shared ancestors. The method was developed by Dana Leeds and is described in detail on her personal website (https://www.danaleeds.com/the-leeds-method/).

The Leeds Method results in a grid, where the first column is the names of the shared matches. Each additional column is a "cluster", where each cell is colored based on whether that match is in that cluster.

The Leeds Method is usually created manually using a spreadsheet. When the RootsMagic Leeds Method report is created in RootsMagic, it can then be saved directly to an Excel file if desired.

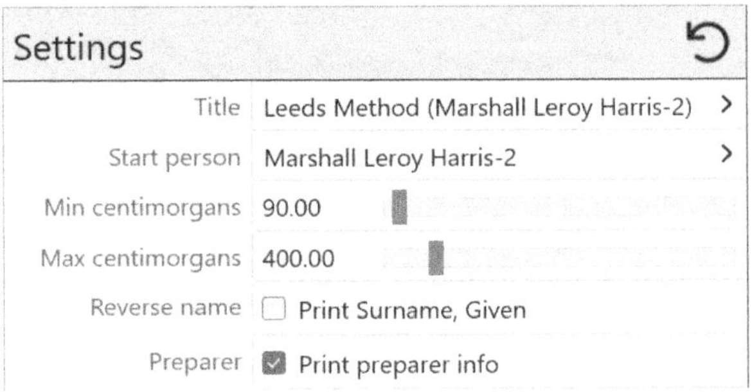


*Start person* is the person the Leeds Method finds DNA clusters for. You can click the "Start person" field to change this person.

*Min centimorgans and Max centimorgans* let you select which shared matches to include based on the number of shared centimorgans. The default values (90 and 400) will often give you 4 clusters (one for each grandparent). If you lower the minimum a bit you can get more clusters (great grandparents). Every person is different, so you can experiment with different values.

*Reverse name* lets you choose whether names are displayed with the given names first, or in reverse with the surname first.

*Preparer* lets you specify whether RootsMagic should print the preparer's name and address at the bottom of the printout. You can set the preparer's name and address in the options screen (page 360).

## RELATIONSHIP CHART

If you have ever wondered how two people in your database are related, then the Relationship Chart is the printout for you. Select the "Relationship Chart" in the report list. You can select any two people from your database, set some options, and RootsMagic will generate a box chart that shows you exactly how the two people are related.

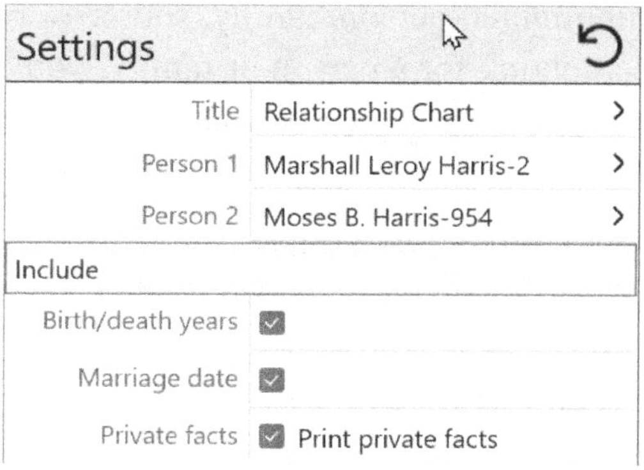


*Title* lets you enter the title you want printed at the top of the chart.

*Person 1 and Person 2* let you select the two people you want to find the relationship for. RootsMagic will bring up a list of everyone in your database for you to select from. By default, the first person will be set to the person who was highlighted on the main screen, but you can change to a different person if you want.

*Birth and death years* tells RootsMagic to print the life span for each person (like "1780 – 1843").

*Marriage date* tells RootsMagic to print the marriage date for each couple in the relationship chart.

*Print private facts* lets you choose whether RootsMagic should include any facts (birth, death, etc.) that you have marked as "private".

*Box border* (under Appearance) lets you choose the format of the borders RootsMagic draws around the photos. This is described in detail on page 228.

## LARGE FORMAT CHARTS (WALL CHARTS)

As you add more people to your database, you will find that the connections between people can become blurred in your mind.

Wall charts let you print huge family trees which can help you visualize these complicated relationships. While they are easy to create, RootsMagic provides numerous customization tools, so we will cover them in detail in the next chapter.

## SCRAPBOOK

The Scrapbook is designed to print all the photos for the highlighted person, family, source or place. If you print a scrapbook for a person or family, you can also choose whether you want to include photos attached to the facts for that person or family.

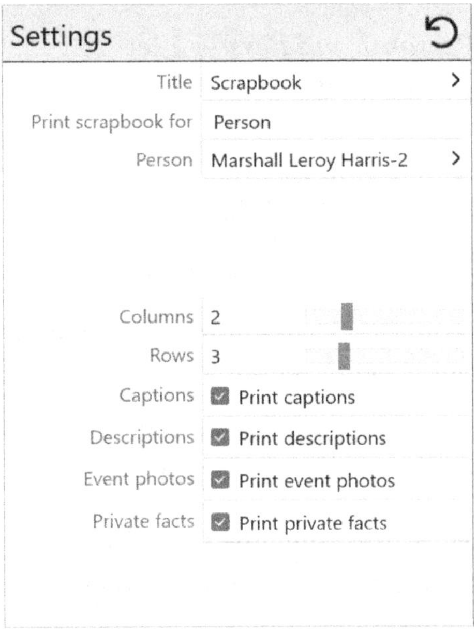


*Print scrapbook for* lets you select what type of record you want to print a scrapbook for. When you choose to print a scrapbook for a person, family, source, or place, you will be able to select the person, family, source or place by clicking the button below.

You can select how many rows and columns to print on each page, and whether you want to print the captions or descriptions for each photo. You can tell RootsMagic whether you want a photo included in the scrapbook when you add or edit it in on a person's media album.

*Private facts* lets you choose whether RootsMagic should include any facts (birth, death, etc.) that you have marked as "private".

*Box border* (under Appearance) lets you choose the format of the borders RootsMagic draws around the photos. This is described in detail on page 228.

## Photo Tree

The Photo tree will print a tree (with leaves) with three generations of photos superimposed on it. The tree includes the starting person, his parents, and grandparents. In addition, you can include the brothers and sisters of the start person at the base of the tree.

*Title* lets you enter the title you want printed at the top of the photo tree.

*Start person* is the person who the report will begin with. You can click the "Start person" button to change this person.

*Background* lets you select an image to be used instead of the default tree.

*Include siblings* tells RootsMagic to print all the children at the base of the tree. RootsMagic will reduce the size of the children's photos as necessary to fit them all in the space available.

*Box border* (under Appearance) lets you choose the format of the borders RootsMagic draws around the photos. This is described in detail on page 228.

## Custom Reports

Custom reports allow you to create your own lists. While they are easy to create, there are also sophisticated techniques that can be applied, so we will cover them in detail in their own chapter titled "Custom Reports".

# LARGE FORMAT CHARTS (WALLCHARTS)

While most printouts are limited to standard sized pages, RootsMagic large format charts  are designed to be as large as you need them to be (they aren't called *wall*charts for nothing).

Large format charts lets you print huge family trees which can help you visualize these complicated relationships.  You can create ancestor, descendant, hourglass or fan charts.  To create a large format chart, click "All reports and charts" on the Publish page, then select the desired chart. You can select "Charts (large format)" from the drop list above the list of reports to show just the large format charts.

## ANCESTOR CHARTS

An ancestor chart is a box chart of a person and their ancestors (parents, grandparents, great grandparents, etc.).

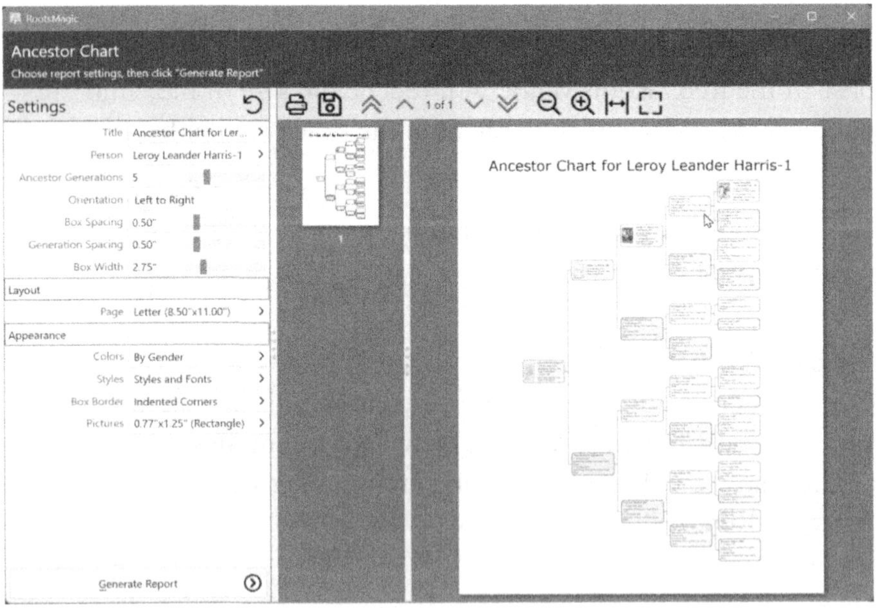


The two main settings you need to select are Person (the start person), and Ancestor Generations (the number of generations to print).

*Orientation* lets you choose the direction of flow for the chart. You can choose from:

- *Left to right* lets the chart flow from the start person from left to right (this is the direction shown in the image)
- *Right to left* lets the chart flow from the start person from right to left
- *Top to bottom* lets the chart flow from the start person from top to bottom
- *Bottom to top* lets the chart flow from the start person from bottom to top

The next 3 options let you select how to size and space the boxes in the ancestor chart. *Box spacing* lets you choose how far apart the closest boxes in the same generation will be. *Generation spacing* lets you choose how far apart boxes in different generations will be. *Box width* lets you choose how wide each box will be.

## Chart Layout

Clicking the "Layout" button in settings lets you choose the layout and background of the chart.

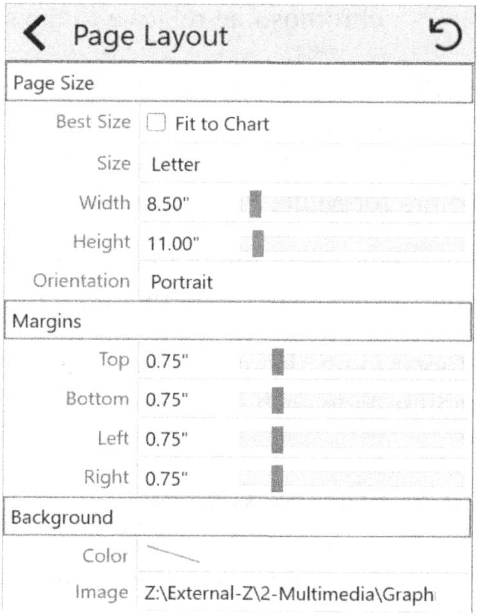


*Page Size* lets you choose the size of the page itself. If you choose "Fit to Chart", RootsMagic will just make the page large enough to hold the chart that is generated. If you don't select that option, you will need to specify the paper size and orientation you want.

*Margins* let you select the amount of space between the chart and the edges of the page.

*Background* lets you choose a background color or an image to be placed behind the chart. When color is displayed as a red line, it means there is no color selected for the background.

### Chart Appearance

The chart appearance section lets you choose the chart colors, font styles, box border, and the size of pictures in each person's box.

#### *Colors*

In addition to choosing the colors of lines, you can also choose how the boxes in the chart should be colored.

- **No coloring:** all boxes will use the default color (below)
- **Color coding:** boxes will use the current color coding for each person as applied by the user
- **By Gender:** boxes will be colored based on a person's gender
- **By Lineage:** boxes will be colored based on the lineages of the starting person
- **X-Chromosome:** boxes will be colored based on the X-chromosome relative to the starting person
- **Y-Chromosome:** boxes will be colored based on the Y-chromosome relative to the starting person

Depending on which color scheme you select above, RootsMagic will offer settings for the various box values. For example, if you choose to color by gender, RootsMagic will let you select the colors for Male, Female, and Unknown boxes.

For boxes that wouldn't be colored for a particular color scheme, you can also enter default colors for those boxes.

RootsMagic also provides a "Fading" option, which can be: no fading, fade each successive generation, or fade by lineage.

## Descendant Charts

A descendant chart is a box chart of a person and their descendants (children, grandchildren, great grandchildren, etc.). The chart will also include spouses of descendants so that you can visualize which descendant marriage each child comes from.

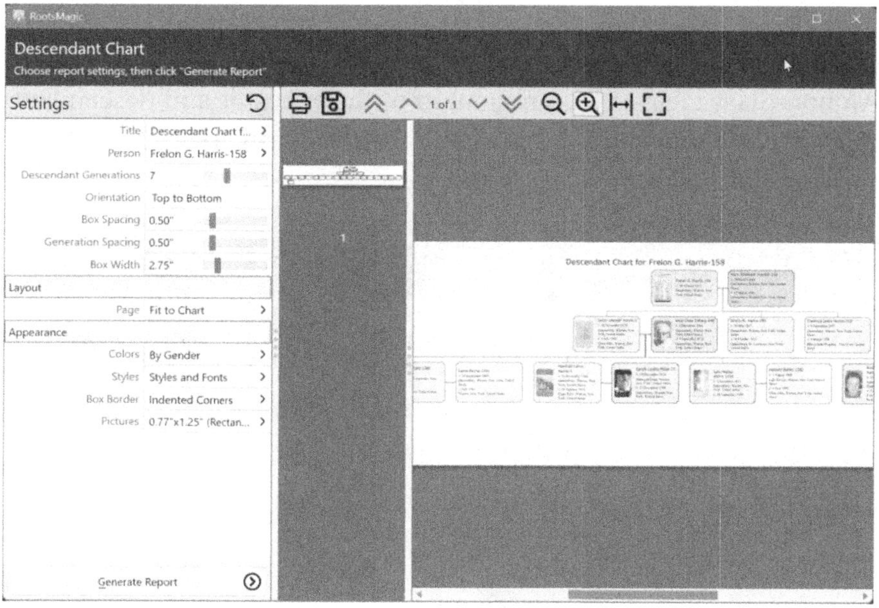


The two main settings you need to select are Person (the start person), and Descendant Generations (the number of generations to print).

*Orientation* lets you choose the direction of flow for the chart. You can choose from:

- *Left to right* lets the chart flow from the start person from left to right
- *Right to left* lets the chart flow from the start person from right to left
- *Top to bottom* lets the chart flow from the start person from top to bottom (this is the direction shown in the image)
- *Bottom to top* lets the chart flow from the start person from bottom to top

The next 3 options let you select how to size and space the boxes in the ancestor chart. These options are exactly the same as those described in the section "Ancestor charts".

Descendant charts also support the same Chart Layout and Chart Appearance settings as the "Ancestor Charts".

## HOURGLASS CHARTS

An hourglass chart is a combination of the ancestor and descendant charts. It includes both the ancestors of the start person, as well as the descendants of the start person.

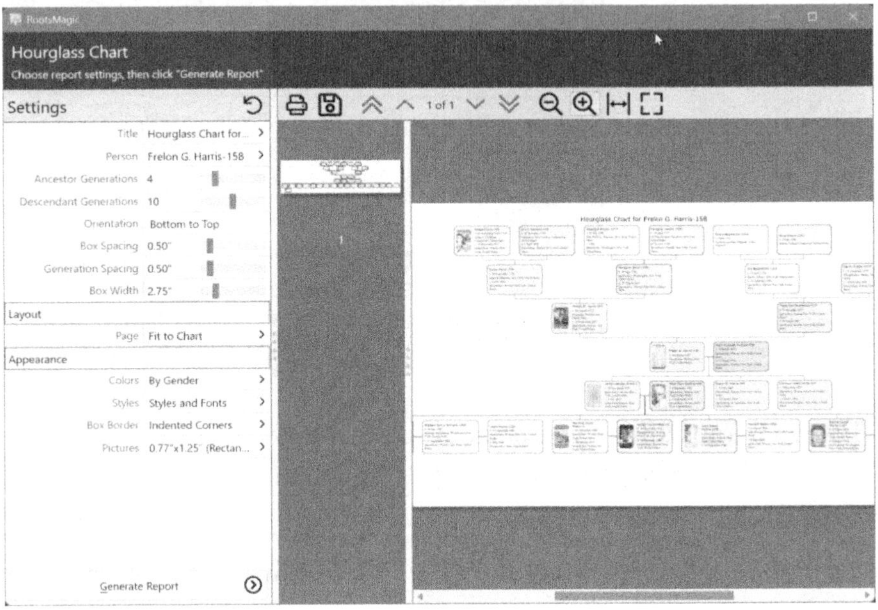


Once again, the main settings you need to select are Person (the start person) and both Ancestor Generations and Descendant Generations.

*Orientation* lets you choose the direction of flow from descendants to ancestors for the chart. You can choose from:

- *Left to right* lets the chart flow from left to right
- *Right to left* lets the chart flow from right to left
- *Top to bottom* lets the chart flow from top to bottom
- *Bottom to top* lets the chart flow from bottom to top (this is the direction shown in the image)

The next 3 options let you select how to size and space the boxes in the ancestor chart. These options are exactly the same as those described in the section "Ancestor charts".

Hourglass charts also support the same Chart Layout and Chart Appearance settings as the "Ancestor Charts".

## FAN CHARTS

A fan chart is a circular chart of a person and their ancestors. The start person is at the center of the fan chart, and each ring radiating outward is the next generation of ancestors. Each ring has double the number of segments as the previous one to hold the father and mother of each person in the previous ring.

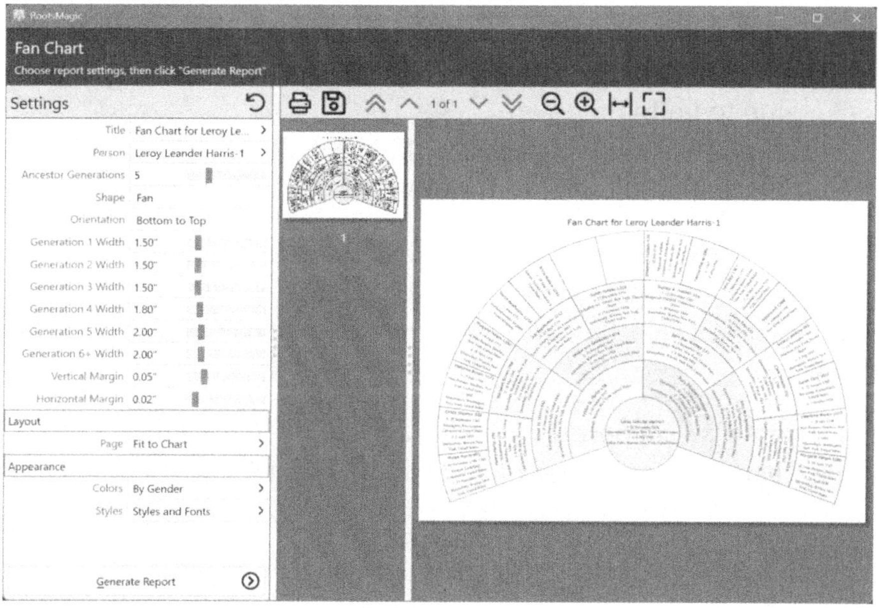


The main settings you will need to select for the fan chart are Person (the start person), the Ancestor Generations, and the shape.

Shape will make a big difference in the overall look of your fan chart, and can also make a difference in how much information can be shown at higher generations.

- *Full circle* generates a completely round fan chart

- *1/4 circle* generates a fan chart that is only one fourth of a full circle
- *1/3 circle* generates a fan chart that is only one third of a full circle
- *1/2 circle* generates a fan chart that is half a circle
- *Fan* generate a chart that is a bit over half a circle and resembles an actual fan (it is shown in the image above)

*Orientation* lets you choose the direction of flow for the chart. You can choose from:

- *Left to right* lets the chart flow from the start person from left to right
- *Right to left* lets the chart flow from the start person from right to left
- *Top to bottom* lets the chart flow from the start person from top to bottom
- *Bottom to top* lets the chart flow from the start person from bottom to top (this is the direction shown in the image)

The next 6 settings let you choose how wide each ring (generation) in the fan chart should be, while vertical margin and horizontal margin let you select the margins between the chart and edges of the page.

Fan charts also support the same Chart Layout and a subset of the same Chart Appearance settings as the “Ancestor Charts”.

# Custom Reports

If you want to get a list of information from RootsMagic in a particular format, but it isn't available in the program, then the custom report creator is the place to go.

The Custom Report creator is probably one of the most powerful features of RootsMagic. You can create your own customized lists that include almost any information about anyone in your database, sorted in any order and laid out in any position.

## Let's Create One

The easiest way to learn about custom reports is just to create one. Let's say you want a list of people in your database along with their birth date and place. When it is finished, you want it to look something like this:

| Name | Birth Date | Birth Place |
|---|---|---|
| Doe, John | 3 Sep 1906 | Albuquerque, New Mexico |
| Doe, Mary | 10 May 1943 | Provo, Utah |
| Jones, David | 8 Aug 1920 | Phoenix, Arizona |
| Smith, William | 4 Feb 1872 | Columbia, Missouri |
| Thomas, Bill | 12 Jul 1889 | Pittsburgh, Pennsylvania |

To design such a report, you will need to tell RootsMagic that for each person, you want to print from left to right the name, then the birth date, and finally the birth place. You will also need to tell RootsMagic to print the words "Name", "Birth Date", and "Birth Place" in the header at the top of each column. Let's create this report now.

*To create a custom report*, select "All reports and charts" from the Publish page, then select Custom Reports. RootsMagic will bring up the report viewer for custom reports.

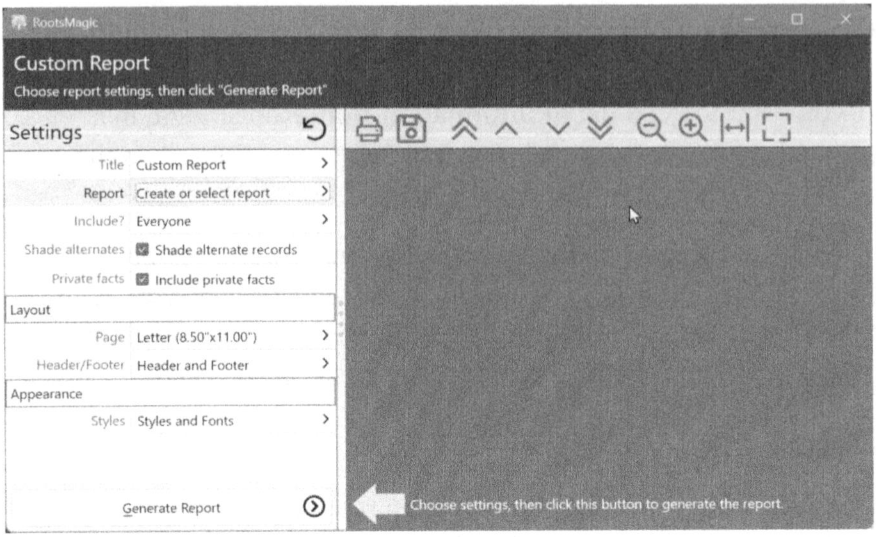


The two main aspects of creating a custom report are designing the report layout, and selecting the people to print in the report. To access your custom reports click the Report button in the settings.

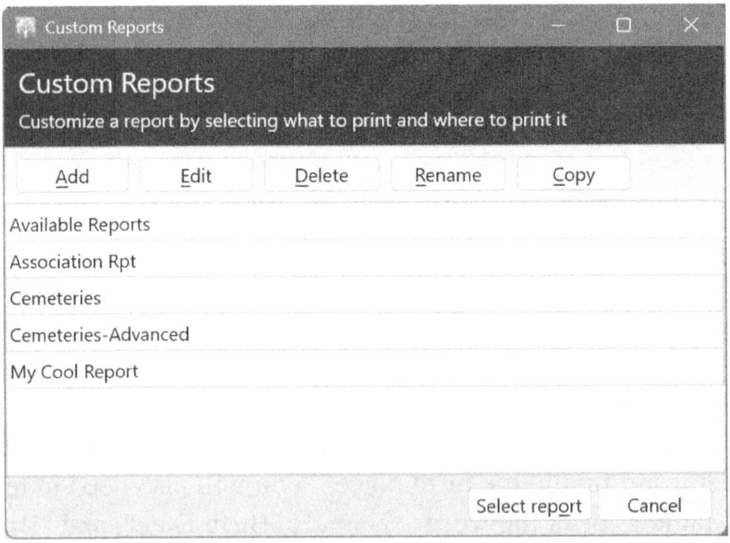


## Designing a Custom Report

To start creating our custom report, click the Add button on the custom report list. RootsMagic will display the screen where we will design our report. On this screen, we will tell RootsMagic what information we want to print for each person, and where to print it on the page.

### The Designer Screen

The designer screen is kind of like a spreadsheet. It has "cells" laid out in rows and columns, and your job is to tell RootsMagic what you want printed in each of those cells.

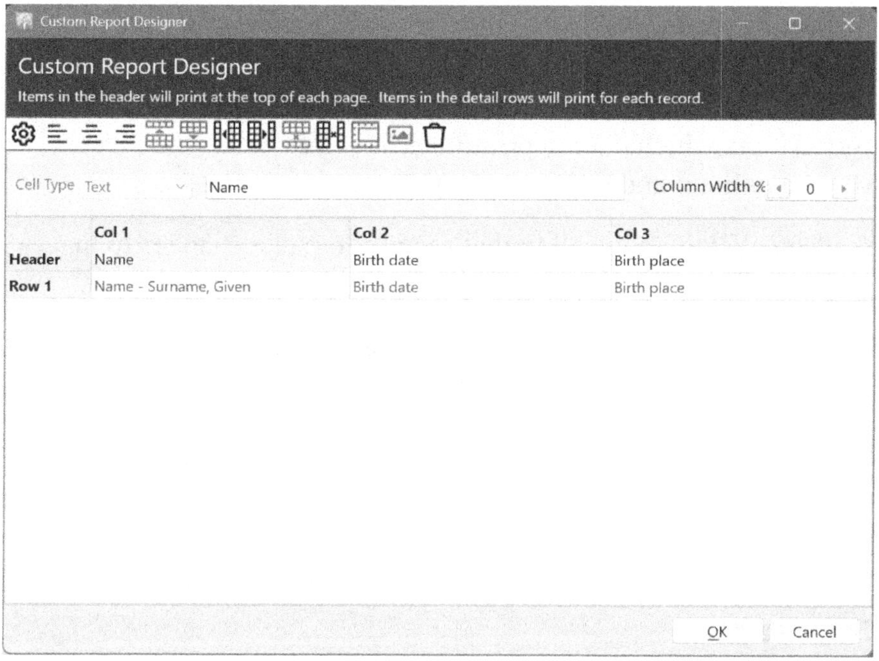


There are several sections that make up the Custom Report Designer.

At the top is the toolbar, where you can select various commands to build the custom report. You can hover over any button to see what it will do (options, align text, insert rows and columns, delete rows and columns, merge or unmerge selected cells, or clear the current selection.

Under the toolbar is the cell definition bar. This is where you can set the options for the highlighted "cell" in the custom report.

Below all of that are the rows and columns that will make up your custom report.

The top row is the "header", and that is where you enter the text you want printed at the top of each column on each page. The remaining rows are the "details", and that is where you will tell RootsMagic which data to print in each cell (a cell is the place where a column and row intersect).

You can click on any cell in that section to make changes to that cell, and you can use the arrow keys to move from cell to cell.

When you first start the custom report designer, it will show the header row, and one data row. It will also show 2 columns.

In our case, we want 3 columns (one each for the name, birth date, and birth place). We can click on one of the cells in column 2, and then click the Insert column right button on the toolbar.

## The Header

The Header is where you will enter text that you want to print at the top of each page.

To add text to the header, highlight the first cell in the header row, then select the entry field in the cell definition bar and begin typing the word Name. Now just repeat this action in the other two header cells to add Birth Date and Birth Place.

*To edit text once it is on the screen*, click on the cell, then edit the text in the cell definition bar above.

*To delete some text*, click on the cell, then delete the text in the cell definition bar above.

## The Details

The Details section is all the rows under the Header row, and is where you enter the information that you want to print for each person. Anything you put in these other rows will be printed once for every person that you include in the custom report.

In our case, we want to print the name, birth date, and birth place for every person, so we need to tell RootsMagic to print those three items for each person. We do this by telling RootsMagic which data to print in each cell.

*To tell RootsMagic what data to print in a cell*, click your mouse on the cell, then select the field type from the cell definition bar.

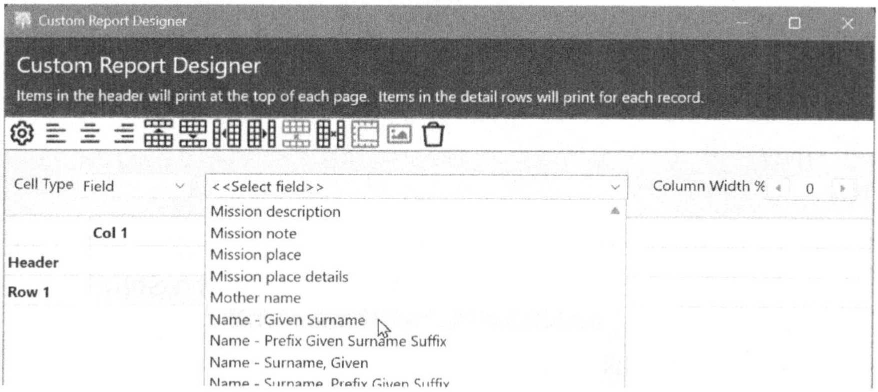


Since the person's name is the first item we want to print, select Name - Surname, Given from the list. The cell will now contain that field name. Now just repeat this action to add fields for Birth date and Birth place in the other two cells in Row 1.

*To delete a field*, click on the cell and change the field back to <<Select field>>.

## Custom Report Options

RootsMagic offers a number of options that apply to your custom report. Click the Options button to bring up the following screen. When you have selected the options you want, click the OK button to return to the Custom Report Designer screen.

*Report Title* is where you type the title you want to appear at the top of your custom report. For example, you might enter Birth List for the report we are creating now.

*Sort by* is where you tell RootsMagic how you want your report sorted. Select the sort order from the drop list. We can just pick "Surname" for this list, since we want the list to be sorted alphabetically by last name. If we later wanted to sort the list by birth date or birth place, we can change the sort order here.

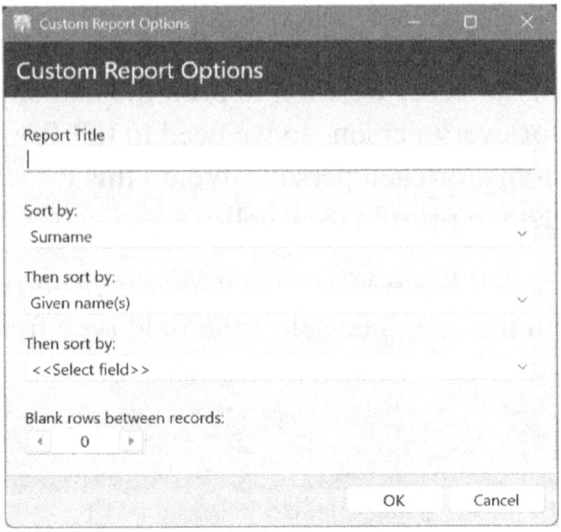


*Then sort by* fields let you further sort the list. For example, if you set the 2nd sort field to “Birth date”, then all the “John Smiths” who were grouped together by the “Surname” sort, will be sorted amongst themselves by birth date.

*Blank rows between records* lets you tell RootsMagic how to space individuals in your custom report. If you use the default value of 0, RootsMagic will print each person's information on one line after another. If you change this value to 1, RootsMagic will put 1 blank line between each person that it prints.

*To save your custom report once it is designed*, click the OK button on the Custom Report Designer. RootsMagic will ask you for a name for your report. RootsMagic will then display the name of the report you designed in the custom reports list. Once you have designed a custom report, you can reuse the same report over and over without having to redesign it.

## MODIFYING A CUSTOM REPORT

If you ever need to make changes to a custom report, highlight the report in the custom reports list, then click the Edit button. RootsMagic will load the selected report and open it in the Custom Report Designer where you can modify any of the report design. When you are satisfied with the changes, click the OK button to save the modified report.

If you just want to change the name of the report (instead of changing the way it looks), you can highlight the name of the report in the list and click the Rename button.

If you no longer need a custom report, just highlight it in the list and click the Delete button.

> ☺ **Tip**
>
> If you want to create a new report that is very similar to an existing report, highlight the existing report and click the Copy button. You can then modify that copy.

## PRINTING A CUSTOM REPORT

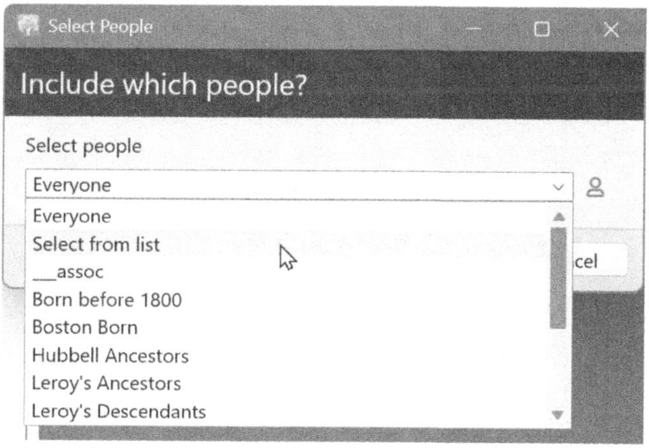


When you are ready to print a custom report that you have designed, select the report from the custom reports list, choose who you want to print the report for, then click "Generate Report". You can select the people to include by clicking the "Include?" button on the Report Viewer.

### Printing a Report of Every Person

If you select Everyone from the “include” list, RootsMagic will generate the custom report using everyone in your file.

### Printing People in a Named Group

If you have created any groups, those groups will be listed for you to select from.

### Selecting People to Print in Your Report

If you choose Select from list RootsMagic will ask you to select the individuals you want to include in the report. The RootsMagic Explorer (described on page 218) will help you select the people to include in your custom report.

# Publishing Your Family History

If you have ever tried to print several different narrative reports or charts, and then tried to combine them into a single book, you know what a pain it is trying to get everything working together.

The RootsMagic Publisher allows you to combine multiple reports into a single document (or book). This document can include narrative books (like the modified register), pedigree charts, family group sheets, and several other common printouts. The document can also include cover and title pages, a table of contents, other introductory pages, a shared index and source bibliography covering all the sections in the document.

## Creating a New Book

To create a book, select "New Book" from the Publish page.

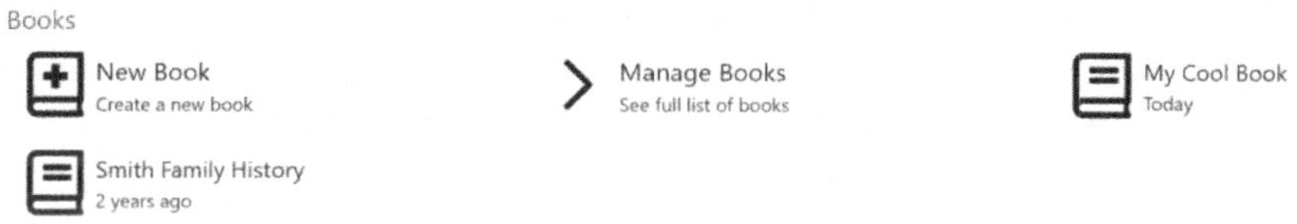


RootsMagic will ask you for some basic information for your book (title, author, and publisher), and will let you select any special chapters you will want to include (like title page, table of contents, etc.). Don't worry if you can't decide; you can always add or remove any chapter later.

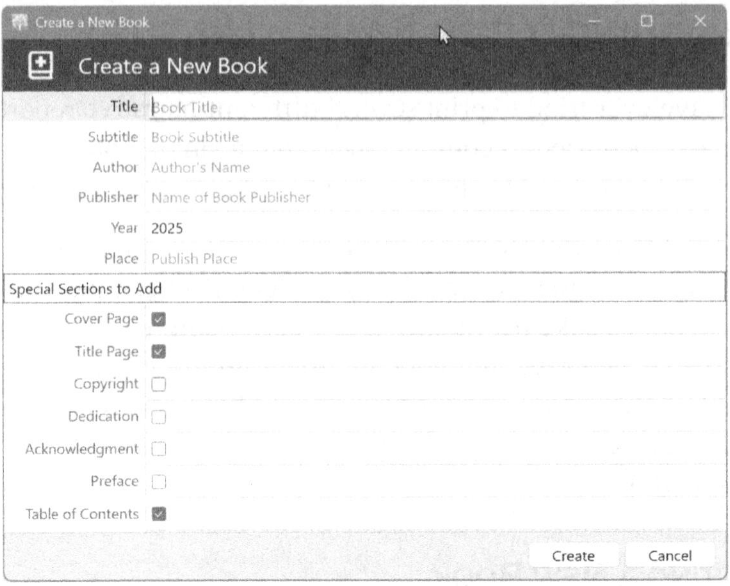


When you are satisfied with your settings, click Create to create the "book template" and open it in the Publisher.

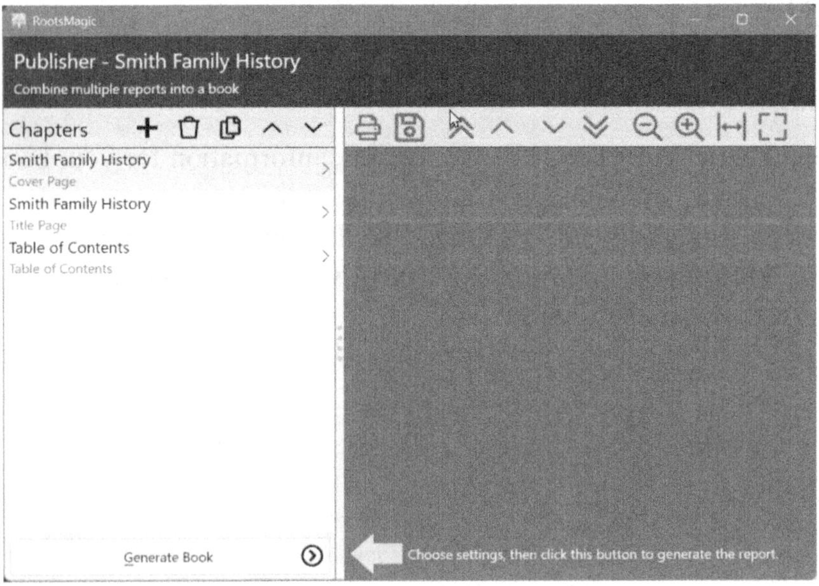


The Publisher looks very similar to the Print Preview screen described in "Printing Reports", except with a list of book chapters on the left side of the screen.

## Adding a New Chapter

*To add a new chapter to your book*, click the Add button above the chapter list to open the "Add Chapters" list.

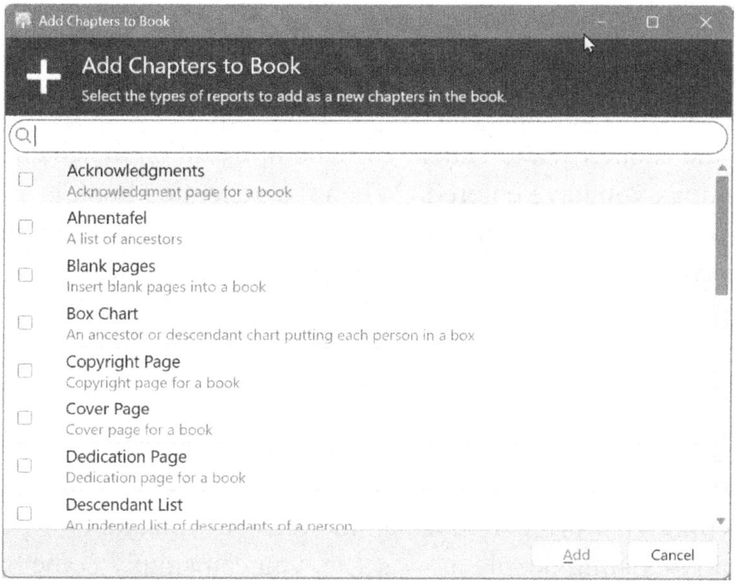


The "Add Chapters" list lets you add multiple chapters at once, so place a checkmark in front of each chapter type you want to add then click the "Add" button. The "Add" button will be disabled until you select at least one chapter type. The new chapters will be added to the end of the list but you can rearrange them later.

## Editing a Chapter

*To edit the settings of a chapter*, simply click that chapter in the list and RootsMagic will slide in the settings for that chapter. For special chapters (like title page, etc.) there will be some basic options to select from. For report chapters (like pedigree chart, family group sheet, etc.) the settings will be exactly the same as the settings for printing that report by itself (as described in the chapter "Printing Reports").

## Removing a Chapter

*To remove a chapter* highlight the chapter and click the Delete (trash can) button. RootsMagic will ask you to verify that you want to delete the chapter.

### Rearranging Chapters

If your chapters are not in the order you want, select a chapter in the list and use the up and down arrows to move the chapter into the desired order.

### Generating the Book

At any time in Publisher you can click the "Generate Book" button below the chapter list to generate the book based on the chapters and settings you have entered. When the generated book is displayed, you can use any of the usual Print Preview commands (print, save, zoom, etc.) described in the chapter "Printing Reports".

## Using an Existing Book

When you create a new book template, RootsMagic will store that template so you can access it at any time. This is especially useful for keeping your printed books up to date. As you add new people, or modify existing people in your file, you can simply come back to your book template and re-generate the book and it will automatically include the new information you have entered in your file.

You can access the book templates you have created by selecting "Manage Books" from the Publish page. RootsMagic will slide in a list of all the books you've created for this file.

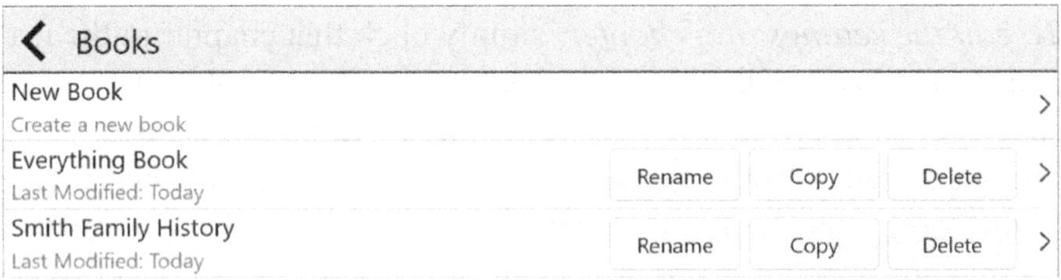


*To edit or generate a book*, select the book from the list and RootsMagic will open the book template in Publisher. You can then edit or generate the book in exactly the same way as when you originally created it.

*You can also rename, delete, or make a copy of a book* using the buttons to the right of each book's name in the list.

> **Note**
>
> When you create a book template, it is stored in the current database since the chapters you add are specific to people in the current database. For example, you can add a pedigree chart for John Doe, or a narrative book for Mary Smith.

## Layout, Sources and Indexes in Books

When publishing a book, you can adjust the layout of the book, as well as include sources and indexes for any chapters that support them. Simply edit the report settings for a chapter that includes layout, sources, and indexes. Changes to any report in the book will affect the entire book.

# Creating a Shareable Drive

RootsMagic makes it easy to create a copy of your database on a flash drive to share with others. The flash drive you create and share will automatically display an introduction page with a title, photo, introduction, and contact information. The introduction page will also have a button which will present your database in a read-only version of RootsMagic. To create a shareable drive, select "Create a shareable drive" from the Publish page. The first screen of the wizard will be informational. You can just click Next to continue.

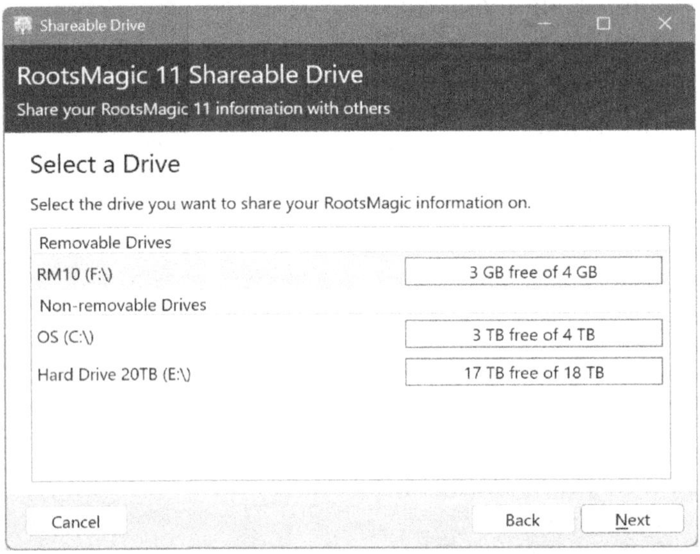


The next screen will let you select which drive to save the shareable drive to. Although the list will include fixed drives, RootsMagic will warn you that you probably don't want to do that. Select the removeable drive you want, then click "Next" and RootsMagic will bring up a form to enter information for the shareable drive.

Enter the title, photograph, and introduction for your intro page. If you don't want to choose a photograph, RootsMagic will use a default image. You can also enter your contact information; name, address, phone number, email address, and website.

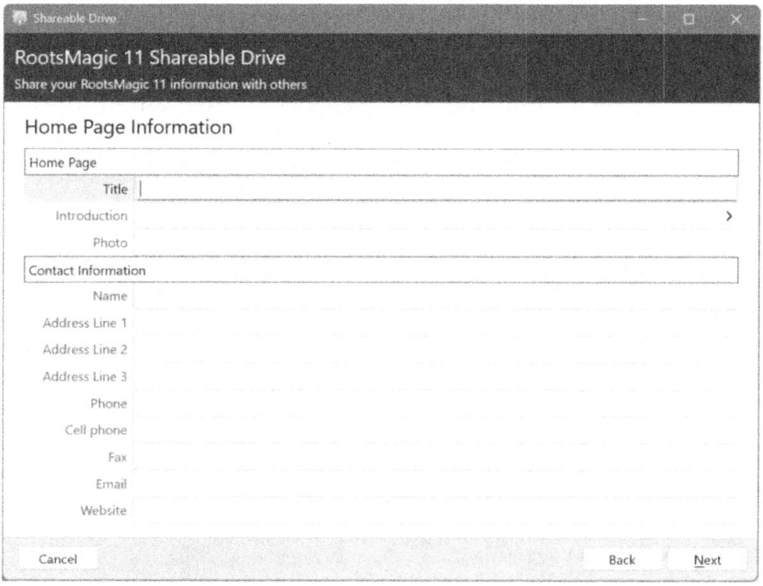


When you are ready to create your Shareable drive, click the "Next" button.

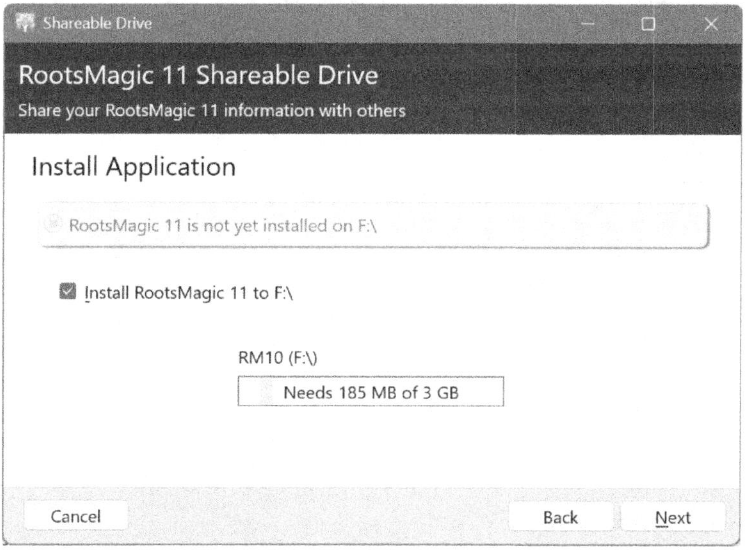


RootsMagic will verify that you want to copy the files to the selected drive, and clicking Next will organize the files and copy them to the selected drive.

You can then give the flash drive to family or friends. When they insert the flash drive, they will see a file to "Launch" the program. This will bring up an introduction screen like this, where they can run the read only version of RootsMagic, read the introduction you created, or display your contact information.

# PUTTING YOUR FAMILY ON THE WEB

With the explosive growth of the internet it is becoming easier to make contact with family members and other researchers. RootsMagic makes it easy to publish your family trees on my.RootsMagic.com, a free service for RootsMagic users. Your online trees can include: notes, sources, photographs, a name index, and contact information. RootsMagic also includes the ability to create basic html websites which you can upload to your own server.

## MYROOTSMAGIC

The heart of RootsMagic's online presence is your MyRootsMagic account. To begin working with MyRootsMagic, select "MyRootsMagic" from the Publish page. RootsMagic will display the MyRootsMagic screen, where you can create or sign into your account.

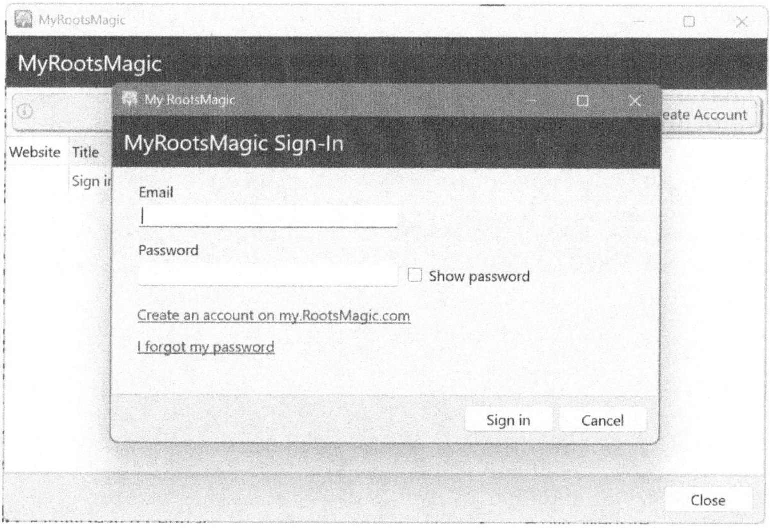


Click the "Sign In or Create Account" button and RootsMagic will display the above login screen. The first time you will want to click the "Create an account on my.RootsMagic.com" link, enter your email and desired password. After that just log in using the same email and password.

Once you have logged in you will see a list of any trees you have published. Of course the first time it will be empty, except for a line that says CLICK TO PUBLISH A NEW WEBSITE. Yes, all caps… because it wants you to see it.

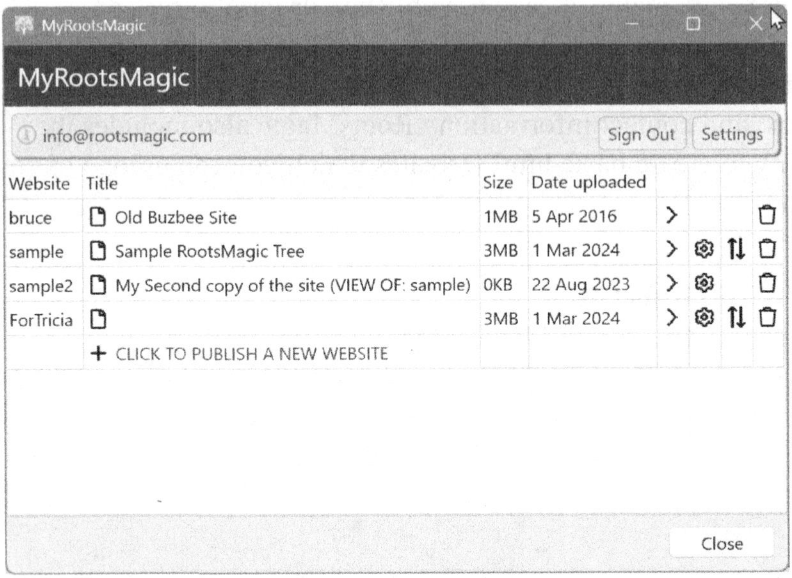


If you do as it demands and click it, RootsMagic will step you through publishing your tree online.

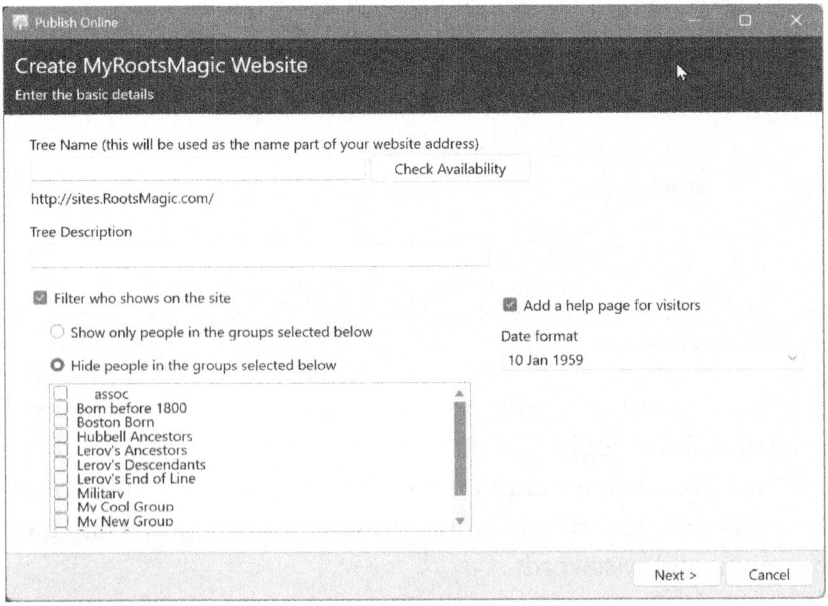

The tree name will be the most important decision you make. The name you choose will become part of the URL (website address) where your tree will be located. The tree name is case sensitive, so make sure you enter it exactly how you want visitors to type it. So if you enter "Smith" as the tree name, your website address will be:

http://sites.rootsmagic.com/Smith

There are a number of options to select from as you publish your tree: a description, date format, whether you want a help file (which RootsMagic provides), and whether to show all or only some of the people on your tree. Filtering people lets you choose to hide or only show people in selected groups.

The next page of the wizard is settings for designing the home page for your tree. You can enter a title, introduction, select a picture, and enter contact information.

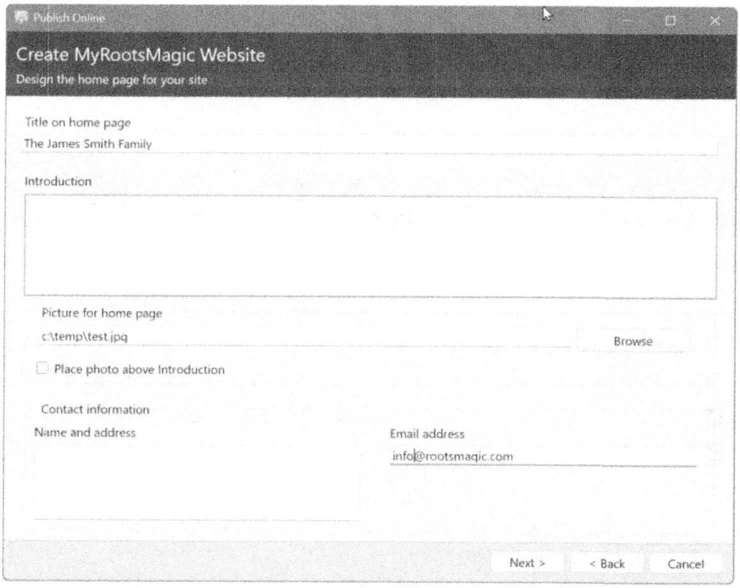


And the final page lets you select the information you want to include: notes, sources, pictures, even a GEDCOM file. You can also choose to "privatize" living people in your file (highly recommended). You can even create links to other sites to include with your tree.

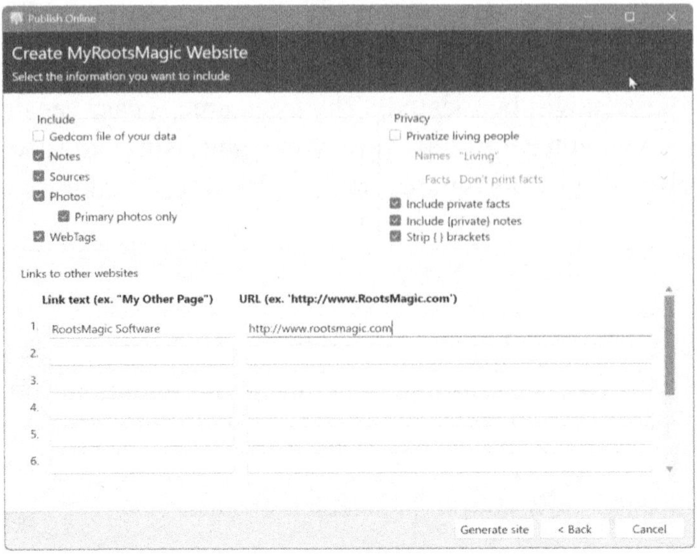


But don't worry if you can't decide exactly what settings to use. You can always go back in and change the settings for your online tree without having to republish it again. You can generate your new site now by clicking the "Generate site" button.

*Now let's get back to that original MyRootsMagic screen.*

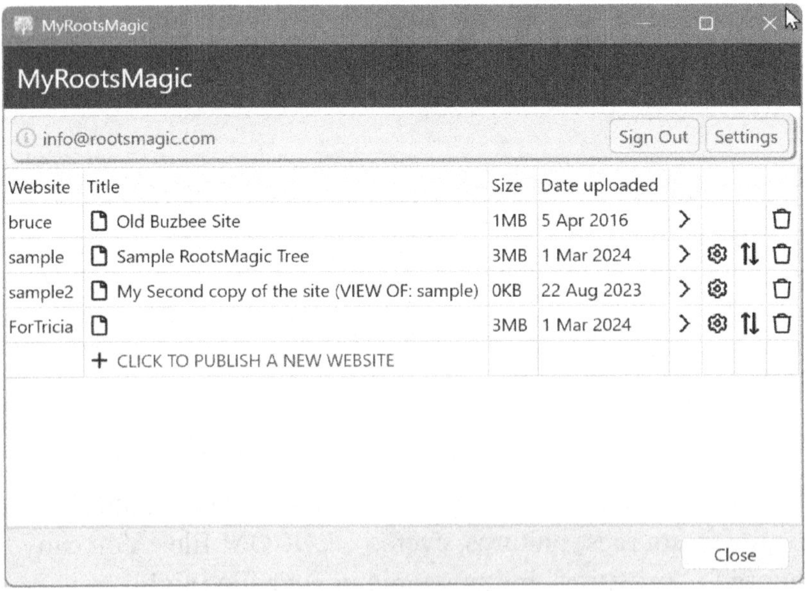

After you have published one or more trees, you will see your trees listed like above. In addition to the name, title, size, and upload date for each tree, there are 4 buttons to the right of each tree which let you visit, edit settings, republish, or delete your tree.

› Opens a web browser and displays the tree.

⚙ Opens a browser so that you can view or edit the settings for the tree. In addition to the settings you selected when you originally published the tree, you can also do things like password protect your website so that it is only visible to people you share the password with.

⇅ Re-uploads the current database to MyRootsMagic. All the settings for your tree remain unchanged, but you can go into the online settings to modify them. You only need to do this if you have added or changed information in your database that you want reflected in your online tree.

🗑 Deletes the tree from MyRootsMagic. You will be asked to confirm that you really want to do this.

*The Settings button* (which will only appear when you are logged into your MyRootsMagic account), lets you modify your account settings. You can log into your online admin panel, which is similar to the MyRootsMagic screen above, but lets you view and edit your tree settings directly from a web browser. You can also change your email address or password, or delete your MyRootsMagic account altogether.

## Creating HTML Files To Put on Your Own Server

Although your MyRootsMagic account makes it easy to publish your tree online, some people would rather create website files to put on their own server. If this describes you, RootsMagic lets you create basic html website files.

When you select Create HTML Website from the Publish page, RootsMagic will bring up wizard to step you through creating the html pages.

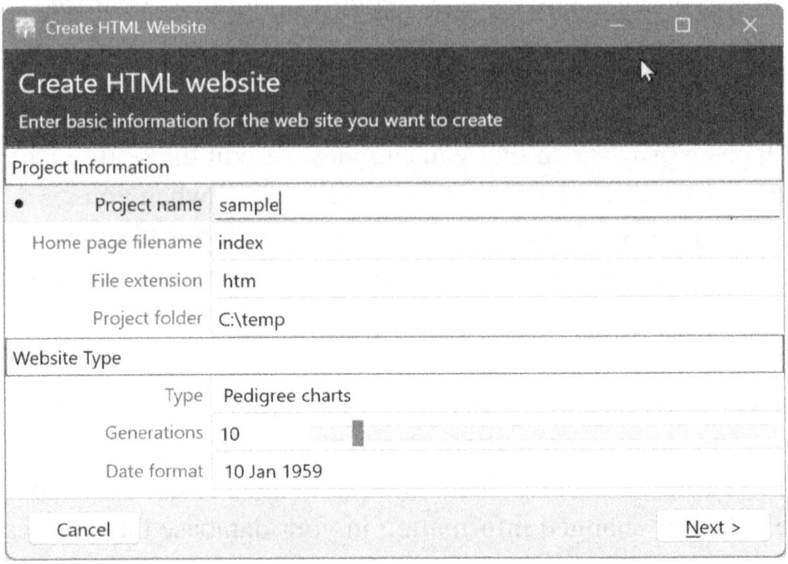


The first page asks you for basic information for your site.

- *Project name* is the name of your "project". RootsMagic will use this name to create a subdirectory in your project folder to hold all the project files.
- *Home page filename* is the name for the starting file for the website (usually either index or default).
- *File extension* is the extension for your files (either .htm or .html)
- *Project folder* lets you select where you want RootsMagic to create the project folder for your site.
- *Type* lets you select the type of website: Family group sheets, pedigree charts, pedigree charts w/ group sheets, ancestor book, descendant book, or alphabetical book.
- *Date format* lets you choose what format you want dates to be displayed on the website.

When you have finished filling in the first page, click the Next button to continue designing the home page of your site.

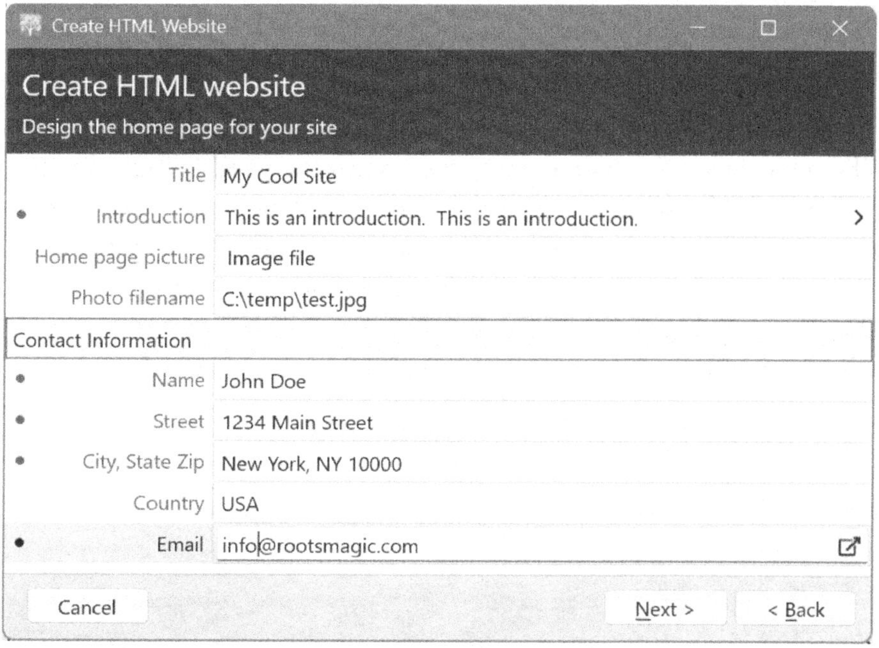


- *Title* lets you specify the text that is displayed at the top of your home page.
- *Introduction* is a brief paragraph or two where you can tell visitors about your family, research, surnames, or any other information. This provides an opportunity for you to enter a few lines explaining your purpose for creating the website, or a few details about the starting person for this website. For example, you might write something like "This site contains the descendants of Jeremiah Johnson. Jeremiah was one of the original settlers of Johnson County back in 1823".
- *Home page picture* lets you choose whether to include a photo on the home page, and whether it should be the picture of the starting person or one you select from your hard drive. If you choose the latter, you can select the file from the next field "Photo filename".
- *Contact information* allows you to enter a physical address and email address where visitors to your site can contact you. RootsMagic will place these addresses on your home page, and will even turn your email address into a link that visitors can click on to send you email.

When you are happy with your choices, click the Next button to continue. You can also click the "Back" button to move back to the previous screen in case you need to change something there.

The next screen lets you change the appearance and layout of your website. You can choose the position of the "navigation bar" that RootsMagic adds for your site (including "None" if you don't want a navigation bar). RootsMagic also lets you enter your own HTML for the header and footer. This is an advanced feature which helps you when trying to create a very customized site.

The final options allow you to pick the colors for your site: the main screen background and text, the navigation bar background and text, and the color of links (including a hover color).

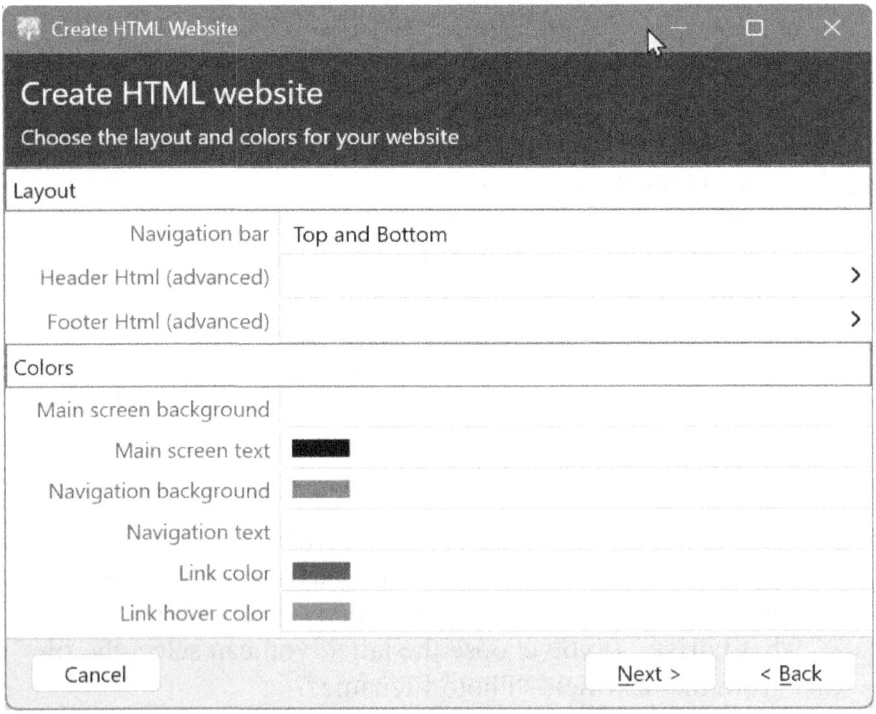


Click Next when ready and you are now able to select the information you want to include on your site.

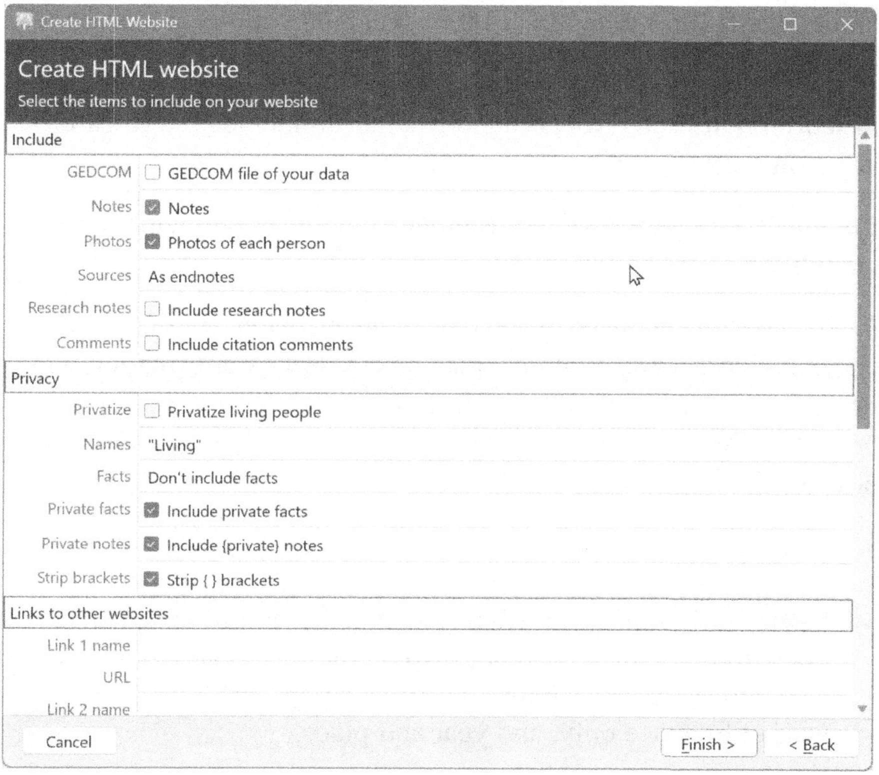


*GEDCOM file of your data* lets you tell RootsMagic to create a GEDCOM file of the people in your database. If you check this box, a GEDCOM file will be created and a link will be created on your site where a person can click and download the GEDCOM file.

> ☺ **Tip**
>
> You may not want to include a GEDCOM file of your data, since a visitor with common ancestors may just download the GEDCOM and never contact you. You may want to put a note in the Introduction of your website that says something like "If you find any information that we have in common, please send me an email and I will be happy to send you a GEDCOM file with my data".

*Notes* will include any notes you have entered for people.

*Photos* tells RootsMagic whether to include photos for people on your site.

*Sources* tells RootsMagic whether to include your sources on the site, and in what format.

*Research notes* tells RootsMagic whether to include the research notes on each citation.

*Comments* tells RootsMagic whether to include comments for each citation.

*Privacy options* lets you "privatize" your website. If you don't check the "privatize living people" box, people's information will be included whether they are living or not. If you do check this box, RootsMagic will use the two drop lists to determine exactly how to do the filtering.

- **Names:** Lets you choose whether to display the full name of living people, or whether to display the word "Living".
- **Facts:** Lets you select whether to display the full date and place for each fact, or to not display the fact at all. You can also choose from several other filtering options, like date only, year only, place only, and year and place.

*Include private facts* lets you choose whether RootsMagic should include any facts (birth, marriage, death, etc.) that you have marked as "private".

*Include private notes* and *Strip brackets* let you choose whether RootsMagic should include any private notes you have entered. Private notes are described in more detail on page 138.

*Links to other websites* lets you include up to 10 website links on your home page. Just enter the URL and the text you want to display for the link.

> **☺ Tip**
>
> You can choose to have RootsMagic ignore selected fact types when generating your website. Select **Lists > Fact type list** from the Person page menu to bring up a list of all fact types. Then double click on any fact type you want to disable, and uncheck the **"Publish online / create HTML"** checkbox for that fact. Repeat this for each fact you want to disable.

When you are ready to generate your website, click the **"Finish"** button and RootsMagic will create the files for the site and then display the following screen.

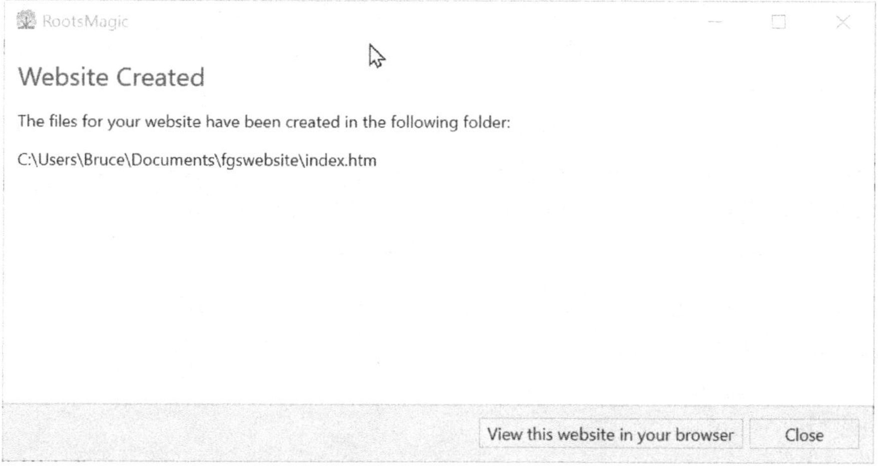


*View this website in browser* will bring up the website you just generated. This preview is just looking at the HTML files on your hard drive. They are not actually on the Internet until you upload them.

# FAMILYSEARCH FAMILY TREE

FamilySearch is the largest genealogy organization in the world. Millions of people use FamilySearch records, resources, and services to learn more about their family history. For over 100 years, FamilySearch has been actively gathering, preserving, and sharing genealogical records worldwide. Patrons may freely access their resources and service online or through thousands of FamilySearch Centers in numerous countries, including the renowned FamilySearch Library in Salt Lake City, Utah.

One of their many projects is the FamilySearch Family Tree. It is an online system that allows users to search for ancestors, contribute new persons and information, and retrieve missing information from a single, central database.

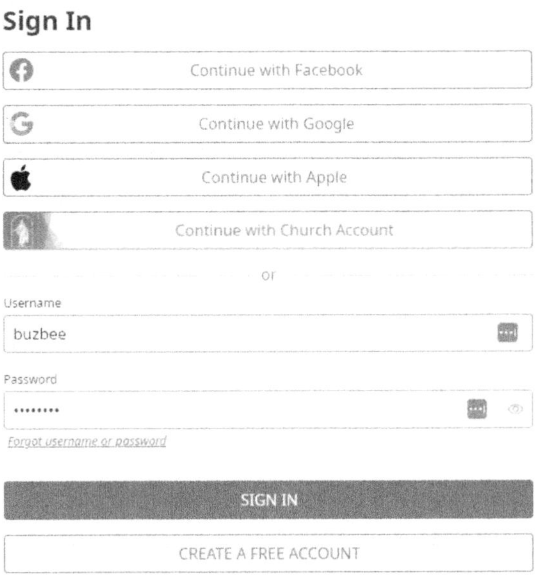


To start, select FamilySearch from the Publish page or click the FamilySearch button at the bottom of the side menu. FamilySearch will open in a separate browser window and ask you to log in (if you haven't already). RootsMagic will display this notice while you complete the FamilySearch login, and will automatically close it once you have signed in.

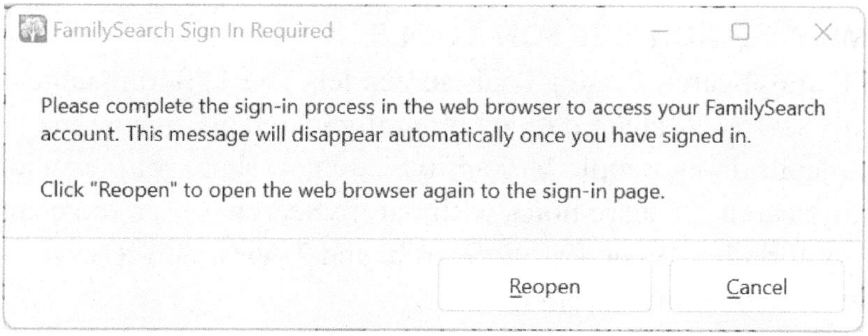


## ACTIVATING FAMILYSEARCH FEATURES

The FamilySearch features are not enabled by default and must be activated by the user. To enable the FamilySearch features, select the General settings from the Settings page and check "Enable FamilySearch support".

Once FamilySearch support is enabled, you will see an icon with the FamilySearch logo next to each person's name on the pedigree and family views on the People page. It will also be visible in the Info box in the Person page side panel.

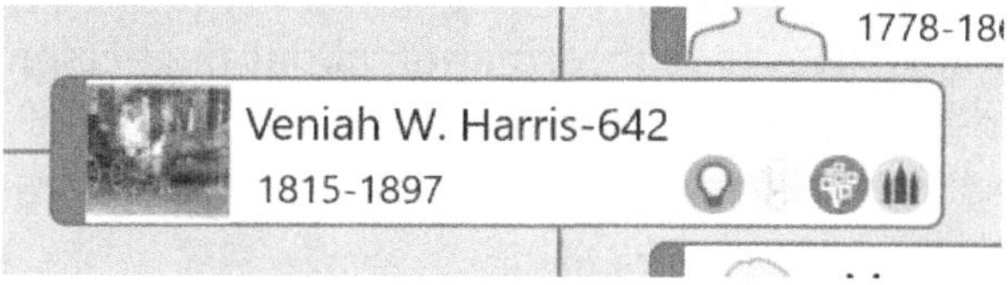


When the icon is blank it means your RootsMagic person hasn't been matched to FamilySearch yet. Clicking the icon and selecting “FamilySearch” will tell RootsMagic to see if it can find any matches on FamilySearch.

A blue icon means that the person has been matched up with a corresponding person on FamilySearch. Clicking the icon and selecting “FamilySearch” will tell RootsMagic to display your person side by side with the matching FamilySearch person, and let you copy data back and forth between RootsMagic and FamilySearch.

## FAMILYSEARCH PERSON TOOLS

The FamilySearch Person Tools screen lets you 1) find matches on FamilySearch, 2) share data with FamilySearch, 3) engage in discussions about people on FamilySearch, 4) share sources with FamilySearch, 5) share notes with FamilySearch, 6) see the change history for a person on FamilySearch, and 7) view and reserve ordinances on FamilySearch.

### Find Matches on FamilySearch

In order to work with FamilySearch, people in your RootsMagic file need to be matched with records on FamilySearch.

Why would you want to match people in your file to someone on FamilySearch? Here are a few reasons:

1. Monitor the person on FamilySearch for changes
2. Update the person on FamilySearch with information from your copy of the person
3. Retrieve information about the person on FamilySearch and add it to your own
4. If you are LDS, reserve and complete ordinances on behalf of the person

If FamilySearch support is enabled, you will see an icon next to each person's name on the pedigree, family, and Info box views on the Person page. If you see a blank icon next to a person's name, it means that the person is not matched to FamilySearch. Clicking on the icon and selecting FamilySearch will bring up the FamilySearch Matches screen:

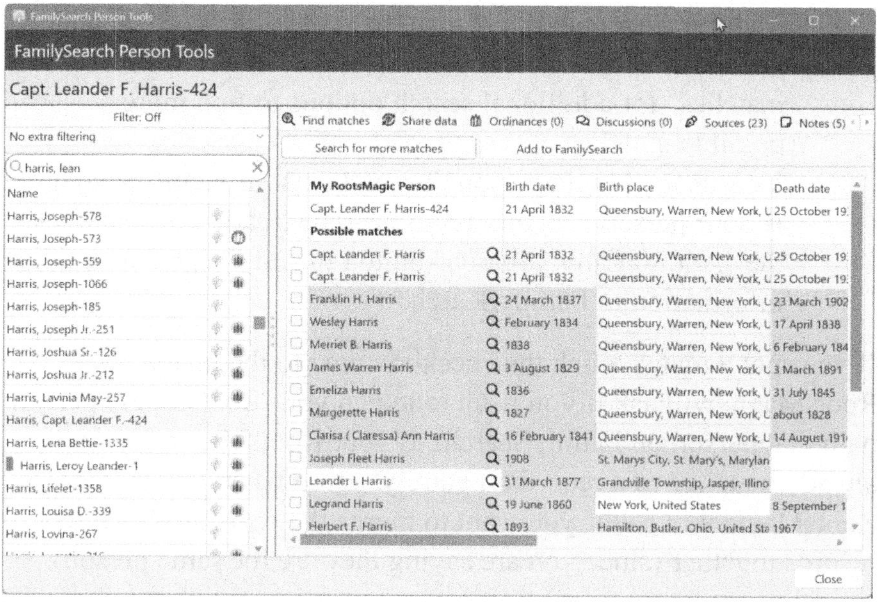


Your person in RootsMagic will appear at the top of the list. Next, the FamilySearch person that you are currently matched to, if any, will appear. And lastly, possible matches to your person that are found on FamilySearch.

There are columns for name, birth date, birth place, death date, death place, father, mother, and spouse. Colors are used to visually describe how well the information matches your own. The colors make it easy to spot good and poor matches without having to actually read the text of the records.

Green indicates an identical or near-identical match.

Yellow indicates a close match.

Red indicates a poor match.

To view more information about any of the matches, click on the information icon next to the name (a magnifying glass).

If no matches were found, there are three possibilities:

1. The person you are searching for is living. FamilySearch will not return matches for living persons.

2. There is not enough information about your RootsMagic person to find a match. You can click "Search for more matches" for additional search options to find more possible matches.
3. Your RootsMagic person does not exist in FamilySearch. If your person isn't on FamilySearch already you can click the "Add to FamilySearch" button to add the person and his information to FamilySearch.

If you spot a match, click the checkbox next to the match and RootsMagic will ask if you want to match your RootsMagic person with that person on FamilySearch. If your RootsMagic person is already matched to a record on FamilySearch when you do that, RootsMagic will ask if you want to merge the two FamilySearch records together (since you are saying they are the same person).

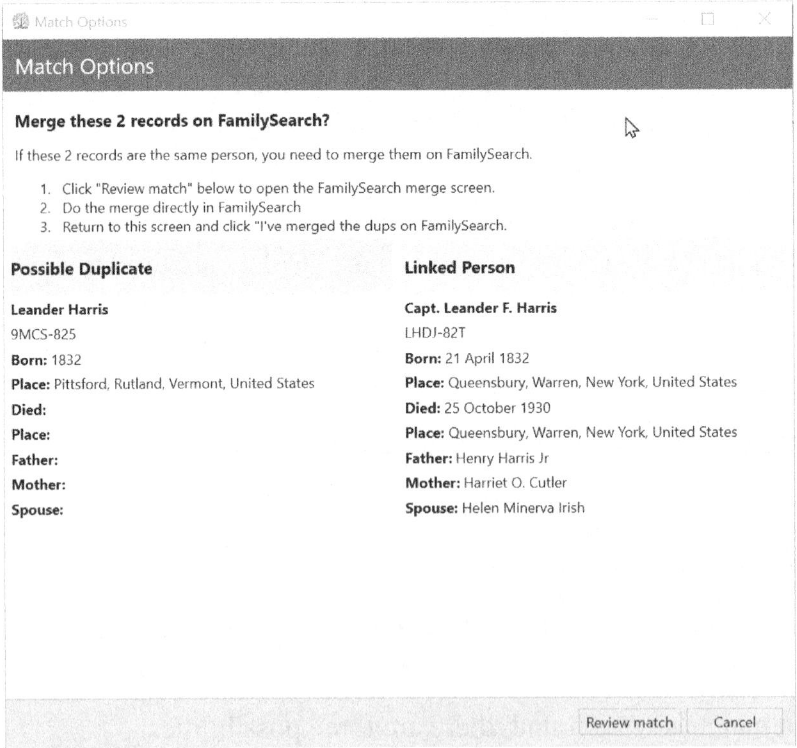


You can choose to review the match and then do the merge on the FamilySearch site.

RootsMagic will then search for any additional matches. When you are finished searching for matches, press Close to return to the main screen. If you matched your RootsMagic person to a FamilySearch person, the icon next to the person's name will now be blue.

*If you are unable to find a match* for your RootsMagic person in FamilySearch, press the "Search for more matches" button on the Find Matches page for additional search options. You will see this screen:

You may search by names and events or by the FamilySearch ID. RootsMagic will enter whatever information it knows about the person into the search fields. You can make your own changes or adjustments to the search, then click Search. Any records matching the search criteria will appear in the list of matches.

## Sharing Data with FamilySearch

Once a RootsMagic person has been matched to FamilySearch, you may wish to compare the two and exchange information between RootsMagic and FamilySearch. You can just click on the blue FamilySearch icon next to the person's name.

The FamilySearch Person Tools screen will come up with the "Share data" tab selected.

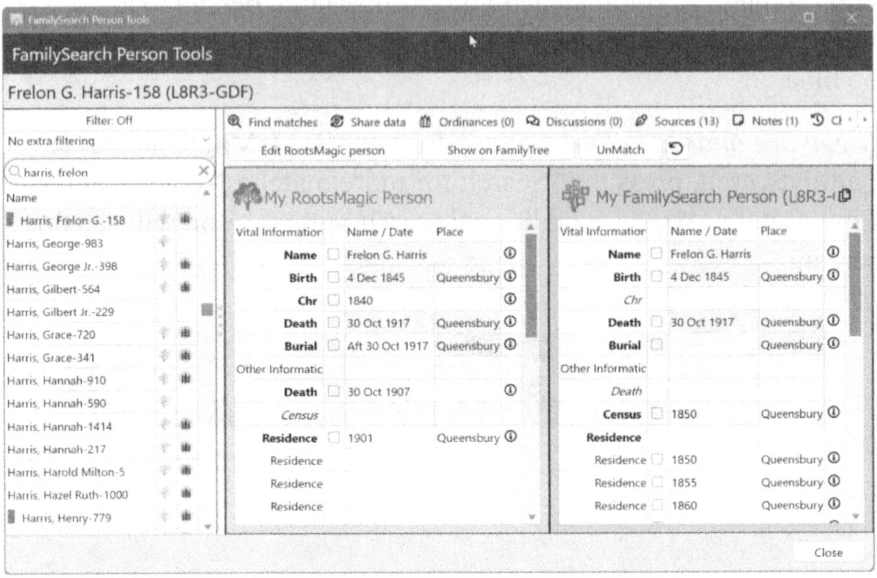


Your RootsMagic person will appear on the left, and the matching FamilySearch will appear on the right. RootsMagic will line up matching names, facts, events, and relationships between the two records. As mentioned before, color coding is used to visually describe how well the information matches your own. The colors make it easy to spot good and poor matches without having to actually read the text of the records.

Green indicates an identical or near-identical match.

Yellow indicates a close match.

To view more information about any of the facts, click on the information icon (the letter "i" in a circle) to the right of the fact.

You can copy a fact by clicking on the checkbox next to the fact. RootsMagic will pop up a menu of options available for that fact. You can copy facts or people from RootsMagic to FamilySearch, or from FamilySearch into your RootsMagic file. Just select the desired action and click OK.

## Discussions

Discussions are a feature of FamilySearch that allow you to collaborate with others to discuss what information is correct or incorrect for a person. RootsMagic has full support for discussions by clicking the "Discussions" tab on the FamilySearch Person Tools.

RootsMagic will display a list of all the discussions for a person on the left. Just click a discussion and RootsMagic will display the discussion and any comments about that discussion.

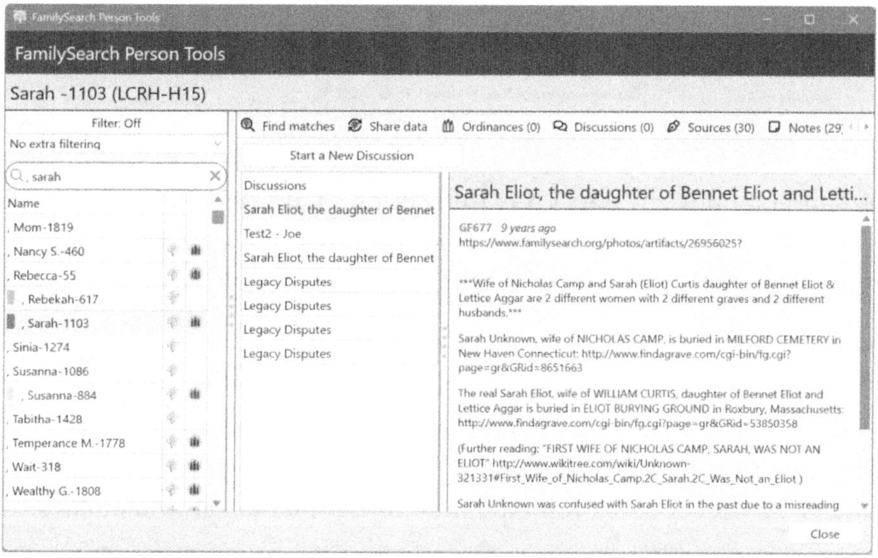


Keep in mind that not every person in FamilySearch can have discussions (living individuals for example).

## Sources

The sources tab lets you view the sources for your RootsMagic person and FamilySearch person side by side. You can click the information button for any source (the circle with an "i") to see the full source, including any links to the actual image. You can click the checkbox in front of a source to copy that source to the other person. When copying a source you can choose which fact to attach it to on the other side.

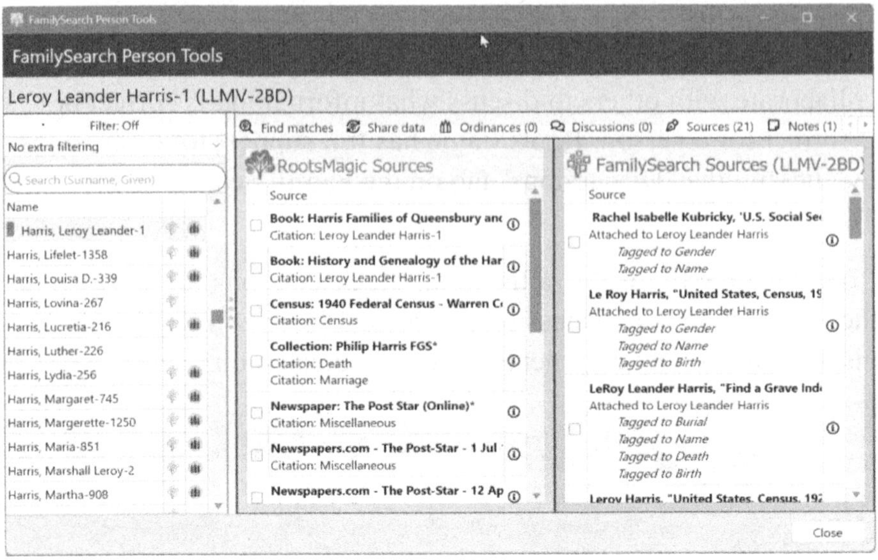


When you click the checkbox in front of a FamilySearch source you can also detach the source from the FamilySearch person, or tag the source to one of the events in FamilySearch.

## Notes

The notes tab lets you view the notes for both your RootsMagic and FamilySearch person. You can click the information button for any note (the circle with an "i") to see the full note. You can click any checkbox to copy the note from one person to the other.

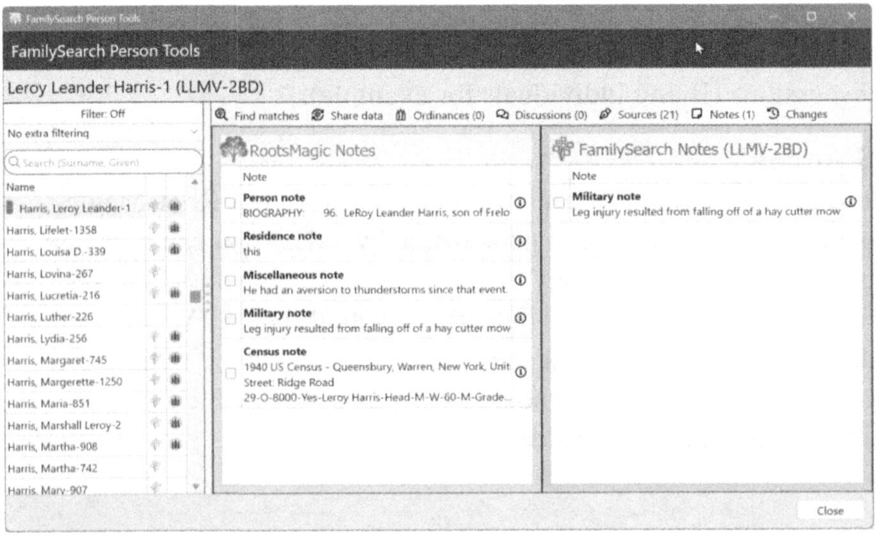

*When you click a note checkbox on the FamilySearch side*, you can also just edit the note on the FamilySearch side directly, or delete the note from FamilySearch.

*When you click a note checkbox on the RootsMagic side*, you can copy the note to FamilySearch either as a note, or convert it to a source on FamilySearch.

In either case, you can actually edit the note before copying it to the other person. The edit changes you make only affect the destination note. The original note remains unchanged.

## Change History

The Changes tab lets you see all of the changes which have been made to the person on FamilySearch. This includes changes to data, attaching or detaching of sources, and more. You can see the specific change, the date of the change, who made the change, and their reason.

Some changes may have a “Restore” link, which you can click on to restore the previous version of that person.

### Working with Multiple People

While RootsMagic makes it easy to work with individuals in FamilySearch with the FamilySearch Person Tools, it also allows you to work with groups of people just as easily.

*The people list* shows all persons in your RootsMagic database. Next to each name is the temple status icon (if LDS support is turned on) and the FamilySearch link icon. When you click on a name in the list RootsMagic will fill the "Find matches", "Share data", "Discussions", and other pages on the right with that person's data.

You may limit this list to smaller groups by using the two filters at the top of the list.

*The first filter* lets you select the ancestors of a person, or any group of people using groups.

*The second filter* provides special filtering based on FamilySearch settings. This filter is in addition to the first filter (both filters work together). You may choose from:

- No extra filtering
- People matched to FamilySearch
- People not matched to FamilySearch
- People changed on FamilySearch
- People ready for temple work
- People with temple work complete
- People not ready for temple work
- People with reserved ordinances

## FamilySearch Central

FamilySearch Central is a feature which brings together all of RootsMagic's powerful FamilySearch tools into one convenient screen. To open FamilySearch Central select FamilySearch Central from the Publish page or click the FamilySearch button at the bottom of the side menu.

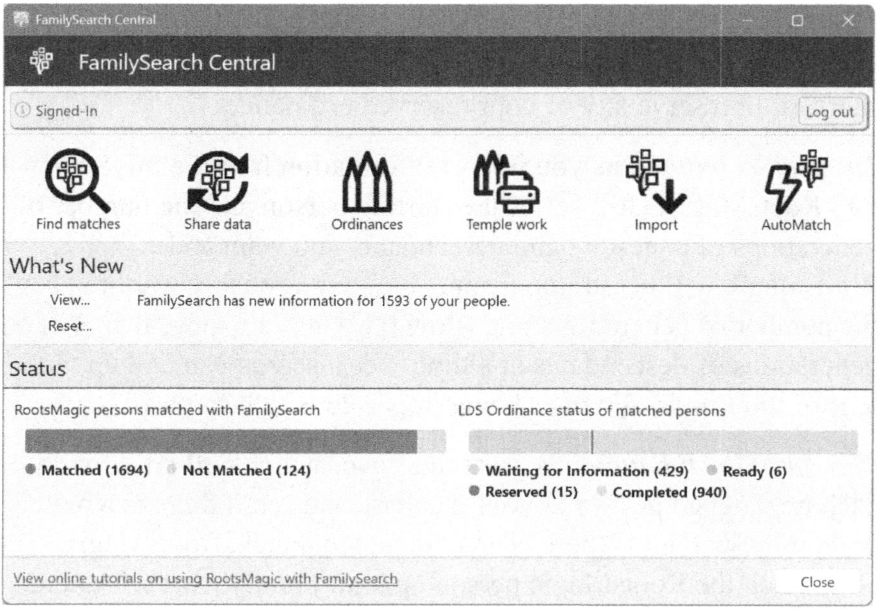


FamilySearch Central is divided up into three sections – toolbar buttons, "What's New", and "Status". Each section has clickable text which will take you to the screen to view the suggested information.

*The "What's New" section* shows the how many of the matched persons have been updated on FamilySearch since the last time you viewed that person.

*The "Status" section* displays the number of people matched and not matched with FamilySearch. It will also include the LDS ordinance status of matched persons if LDS support is turned on.

FamilySearch Central also includes buttons at the top of the screen – "Find matches", "Share data", "Ordinances", "Temple Work", "Import", and "Automatch". If you do not have LDS support turned on, the "Ordinances" and "Temple Work" buttons won't be visible. You can turn LDS support on the Latter-day Saint view of the Settings page.

The *Find matches*, *Share data* and *Ordinances* buttons simply open up the FamilySearch Person Tools with the appropriate tab selected.

*The Temple Work button* will open your browser and direct you to your FamilySearch Reservations screen where you can view, print, share, or unreserve any of your reserved ordinances.

*The Import button* lets you import information from FamilySearch into RootsMagic. Just select the starting person and the number of generations of ancestors and descendants you want and RootsMagic will begin importing. You will probably want to keep the number of generations fairly low (probably no more than 4 or 5 generations of descendants at a time) because you can end up with tens of thousands of names being imported which can take forever.

*The AutoMatch button* is a great timesaver which will go through each unmatched person in your database and see if there is a match on FamilySearch. If there is an undeniable match, RootsMagic will match the RootsMagic person up with FamilySearch. Again, for a large database this can take a very long time, but is still much faster than manually matching one person at a time.

## LDS Ordinances

One goal of the LDS genealogist is to submit names for temple ordinances. For members of The Church of Jesus Christ of Latter-day Saints, FamilySearch is the system through which temple ordinances are checked and reserved.

### Ordinance Status

When LDS Support is enabled, you have the option to display the LDS ordinance status next to each name in the pedigree and family views (similar to the FamilySearch icon).

By clicking on the temple status icon and selecting "Ordinances", RootsMagic brings up the FamilySearch Person Tools with the "Ordinances" tab selected. RootsMagic will display the "unofficial" ordinance information you have in RootsMagic alongside the "official" ordinance status on FamilySearch.

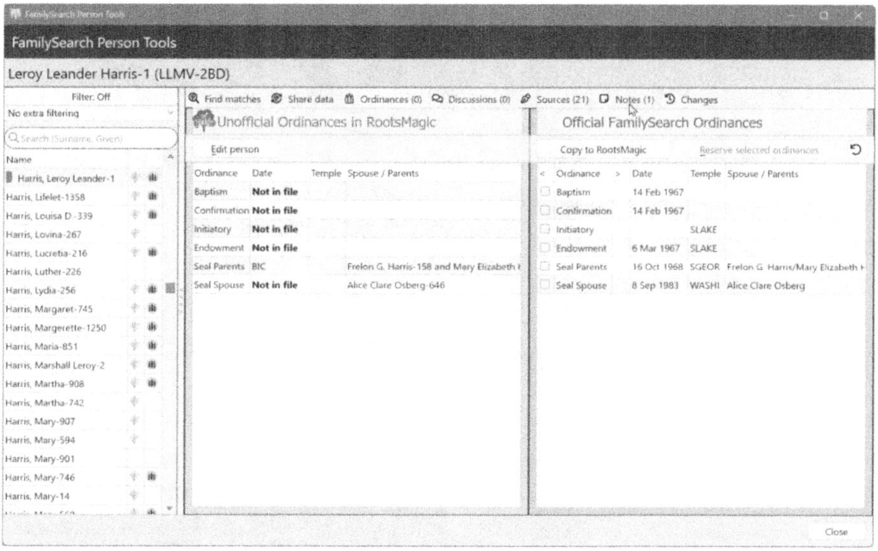

When viewing the official ordinance status, you may mark the checkbox for any FamilySearch ordinance and reserve that ordinance or copy it over to your RootsMagic person.

## Reserving Ordinances

When viewing the "official" ordinance status for a person, you can reserve any ordinances which FamilySearch says is Ready.

RootsMagic will display a list of the person's ordinances with a checkbox next to any available ordinances. Mark the ordinances you want to reserve and click "Reserve Selected Ordinances".

RootsMagic will display a confirmation screen where you can choose whether you want to do the ordinance work yourself, or submit it to the temple file. You will also need to agree to certain policies before you will be allowed to reserve the ordinances for the person.

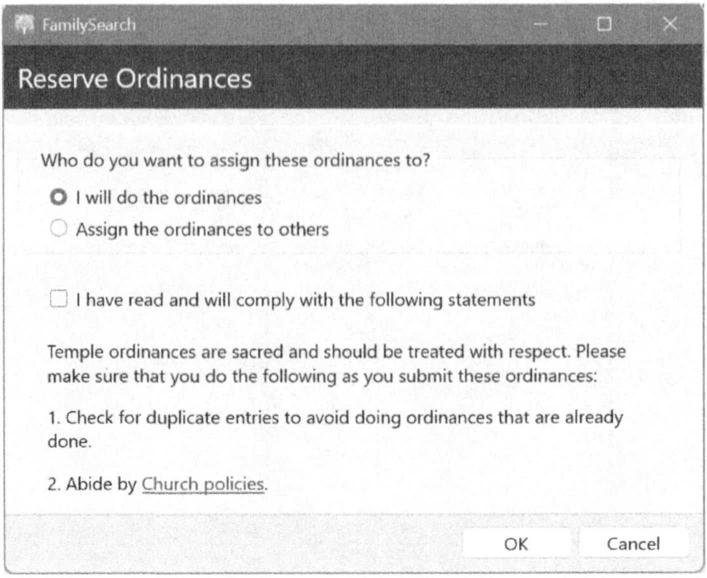


If you want to see a list of all the people in your database who have ordinances which can be reserved, open the FamilySearch Central screen and click the link that tells you how many people in your database are ready for temple ordinances.

When you click on the link to see people who are ready to have temple ordinances reserved, RootsMagic will display a list of those people. When you highlight one of those people RootsMagic will display the person's ordinances with a checkbox next to any available ordinances. Mark the ordinances you want to reserve and click "Reserve Selected Ordinances".

RootsMagic will display a confirmation screen where you can choose whether you want to do the ordinance work yourself, or submit it to the temple file. You will also need to agree to certain policies before you will be allowed to reserve the ordinances for the person.

## Preparing Names for the Temple

Once you have reserved names for temple work you can begin preparing those names for temple work. On the FamilySearch Central screen you can click the "Temple Work" button to open your browser and direct you to your FamilySearch Reservations screen where you can view, print, share, or unreserve any of your reserved ordinances.

# ANCESTRY TREESHARE

Ancestry is the largest genealogy company in the world. They not only have billions of historical records to search, but they also let you create family trees which can receive hints from these historical records. RootsMagic lets you link a local RootsMagic database with an online Ancestry tree using a feature called TreeShare. This lets you not only see your RootsMagic data side by side with Ancestry, but also lets your local file receive hints from the Ancestry historical records for that tree.

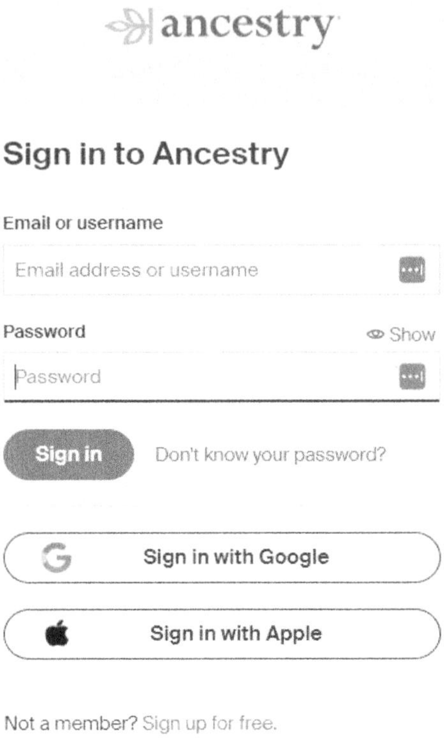


To start, select Ancestry TreeShare from the Publish page or click the Ancestry button at the bottom of the side menu. Ancestry will open in a separate browser window and ask you to log in (if you haven't already). RootsMagic will display this notice while you complete the Ancestry login, and will automatically close it once you have signed in.

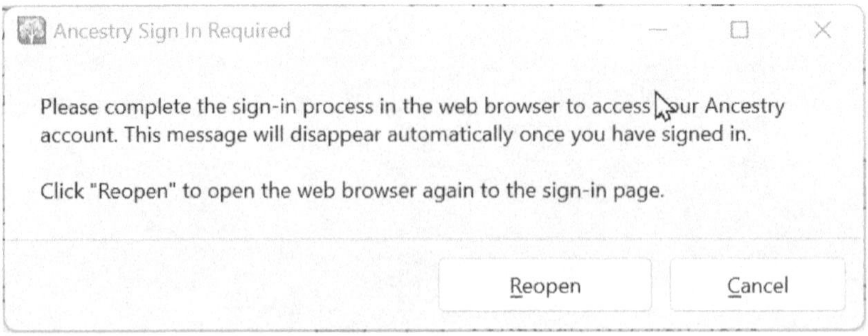

The first time you log into TreeShare, RootsMagic will give you two options: upload your RootsMagic file to a new Ancestry tree, or download an Ancestry tree into a new RootsMagic file.

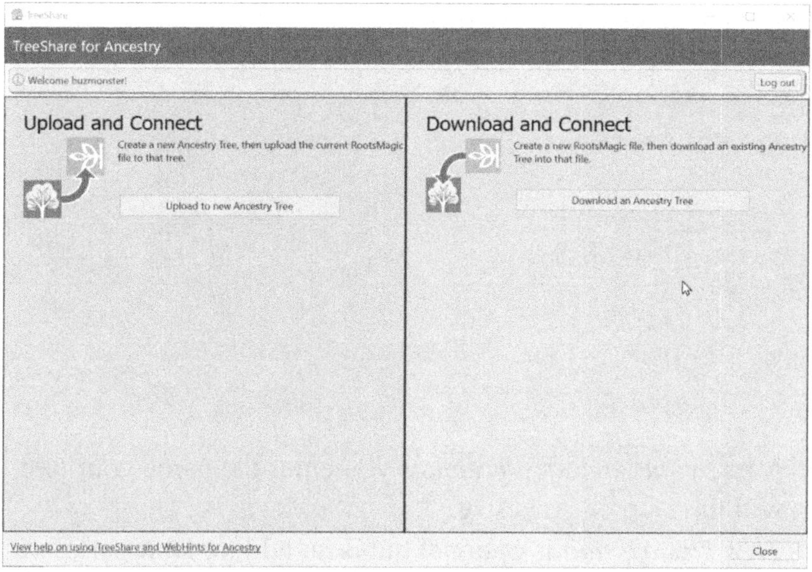


You must choose one or the other options to connect RootsMagic to Ancestry. It isn't possible to connect an existing RootsMagic file to an existing Ancestry tree.

## Uploading a RootsMagic File to Ancestry

If you choose to upload your RootsMagic file to a new Ancestry tree, RootsMagic will display a list of options. Just select which options you want and then click "Create Ancestry Tree and Upload RootsMagic File".

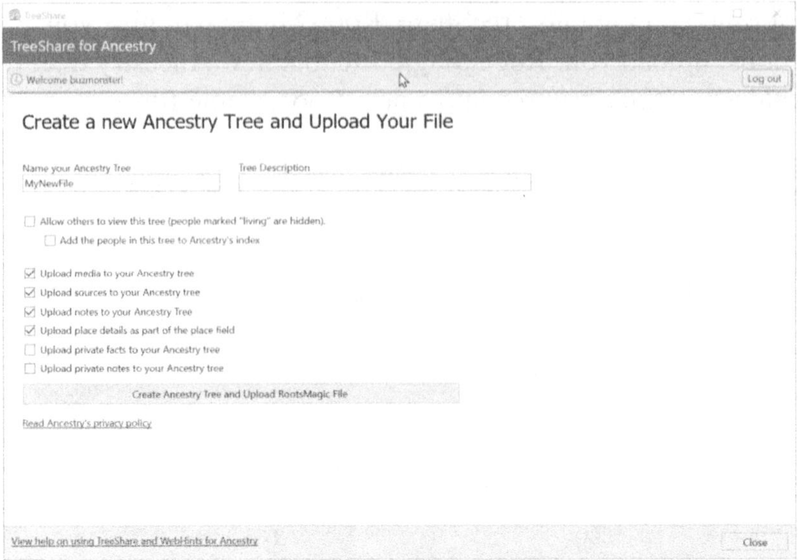


- *Name your Ancestry Tree* lets you enter the name your tree will have up on Ancestry.
- *Tree Description* is optional but is an additional description of your tree on Ancestry.
- *Allow others to view this tree* tells Ancestry whether to make your new tree publicly viewable.
- *Add the people in this tree to Ancestry's index* tells Ancestry whether to add each person in the new tree to its search index
- The next several options tell RootsMagic whether to upload any pictures, sources, notes, place details, or private facts or notes to your new Ancestry tree.

RootsMagic will upload your information in several stages, and can take quite some time if your RootsMagic file is really large or you have a lot of media to upload. When the upload is complete, RootsMagic will display the TreeShare view which lets you see your RootsMagic and Ancestry people side by side.

## Downloading an Ancestry Tree to RootsMagic

If you choose to download an existing Ancestry tree into a new RootsMagic file, RootsMagic will display a list of all your trees on Ancestry, including others trees that have been shared with you.

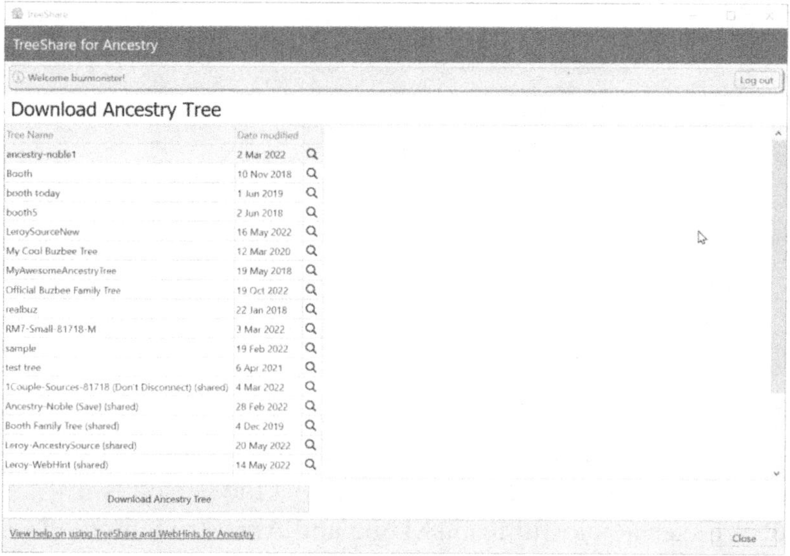


Simply select the tree you want to download, and click "Download Ancestry Tree". RootsMagic will download your information in several stages, and like the upload can take a while if your Ancestry tree is large or has a large amount of media. When the download is complete, RootsMagic will display the TreeShare view which lets you see your RootsMagic and Ancestry people side by side.

## The TreeShare View

Once you have connected RootsMagic and Ancestry by either uploading or downloading, RootsMagic can display the TreeShare screen which lets you see your RootsMagic and Ancestry people side by side.

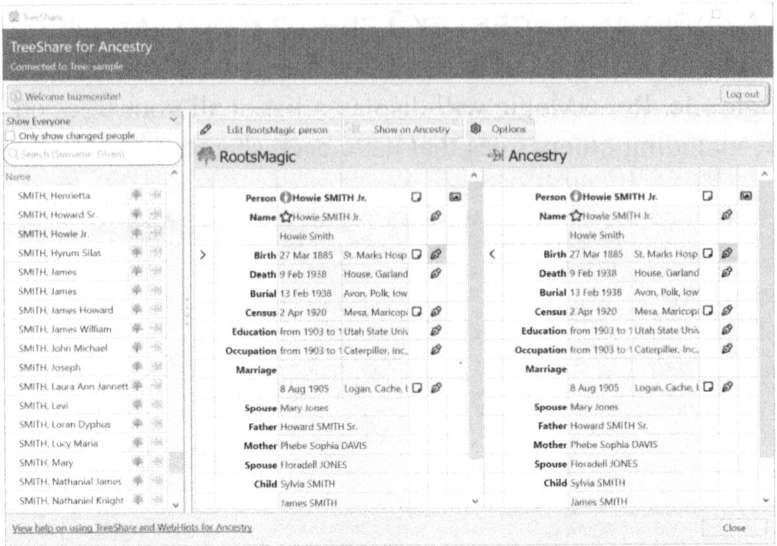

## People List

The left side of the TreeShare screen is a list of everyone in either your RootsMagic file or your Ancestry tree. If the person is in both, you will see a colorful RootsMagic and Ancestry icon to the right of the person's name. If they are only in one or the other (but not both), one of the icons will be blank (the one they are not in).

If there is a difference in the information between RootsMagic and Ancestry for a person, the icons will be a darker color than usual. If you only want to see those people who have differences, mark the checkbox "Only show changed people" above the people list.

There is a search box above the list where you can type in a name to search for specific people. Type it in the format last, first. You can also filter the list by clicking the drop list above that and selecting a group.

## Comparison View

The right side of the screen is a comparison view of the person who is highlighted in the list. The left side of the comparison view is the person in your RootsMagic file, while the right side is the person in your Ancestry tree. Their names, events, and family members will be lined up to make it easy to spot any missing information on either side. It will also be color coded to show you any discrepancies in the information.

If there are any differences, RootsMagic will display an arrow to the left of that piece of information. You can click that arrow to see options on how you can resolve the difference. Not all options will always be shown depending on the information itself.

- *Add as new* lets you add the piece of information (name, event, etc.) as a new item to the other side.
- *Update existing* is when there is a piece of similar information on the other side that you want to update.
- *Delete* lets you delete the information.

If you choose to update an existing fact on either RootsMagic or Ancestry, RootsMagic will let you select which pieces of information you want to update. If there are multiple copies of the information, the drop list at the top will let you select which one to update.

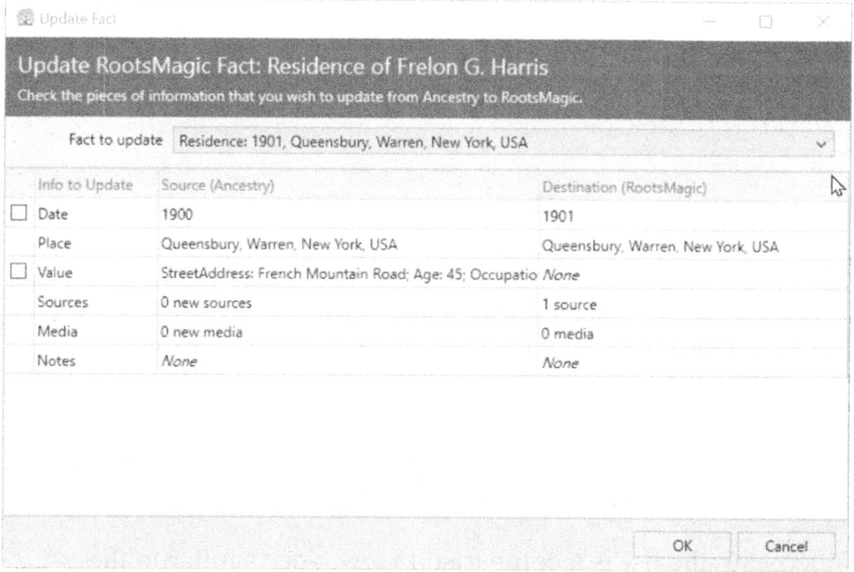


## ANCESTRY WEBHINTS

After you have connected RootsMagic and Ancestry via TreeShare, you will start seeing Ancestry WebHints showing up for people in your RootsMagic file. If you don't see them right away, log onto the Ancestry site and navigate around the tree to have it begin populating them. The hints you see in RootsMagic will be the hints on the Ancestry tree itself. That's why it is necessary to connect your RootsMagic file to Ancestry before you can see hints.

When you click on WebHints and select the Ancestry hints as described in the chapter "People Page", RootsMagic will display the following WebHints screen to let you accept the hint and any additional data the hint provides for the person.

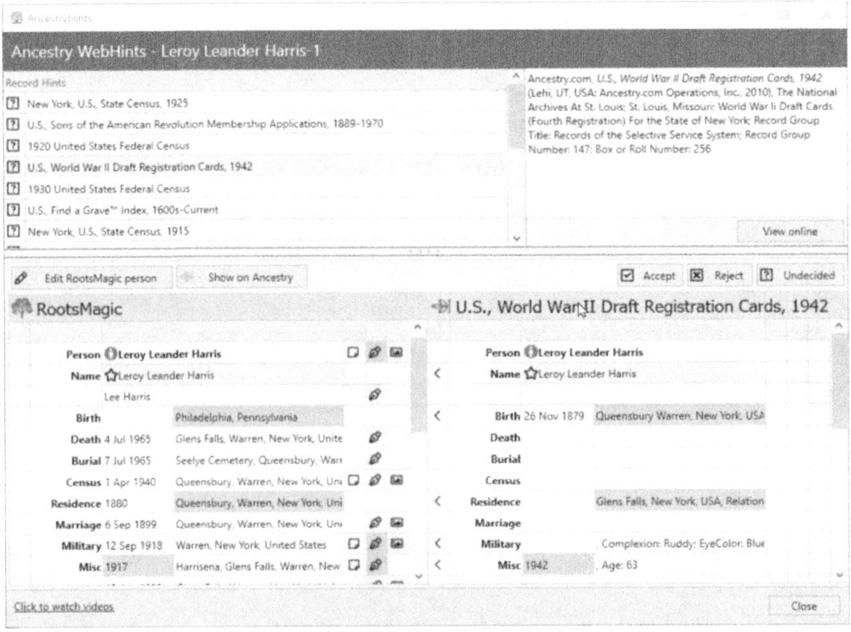


The upper left corner will be a list of available hints for the person. As you select a hint in the list, RootsMagic will display details about the hint to the right of the list. The "View online" button will take you to Ancestry to see the actual record.

Underneath the list is a comparison view, very similar to the comparison view in the TreeShare screen in the previous section. The difference is that instead of showing a matching person from Ancestry on the right, RootsMagic will show information that is available in the currently highlighted hint, along with the arrows to transfer information from the hint into RootsMagic.

As you select the information to transfer from the hint RootsMagic will display the information on the RootsMagic side in blue, but doesn't actually do the transfer yet. Instead, RootsMagic will show two buttons under the comparison view labeled "Accept changes" and "Cancel changes". Make whatever changes you want via the arrows, and then click "Accept changes" to make all the changes at once. If you change your mind you can just click "Cancel changes".

When you accept the changes, RootsMagic will add the new information (dates, places, etc.) to the person in RootsMagic, and will add the hint itself (including any image) as a source for that information.

RootsMagic also lets you mark the hint on Ancestry as accepted, rejected, or undecided. While these don't have any real effect in RootsMagic itself, it does affect how the hint is used on the Ancestry site.

# TOOLS

RootsMagic provides a large number of tools that make managing your data easier. Some of these tools are on the page for the type of data they work with (for example tools to work with people will be found on the People page). RootsMagic also gathers many of the tools (including some that aren't on other pages) into an easy-to-use Tools page.

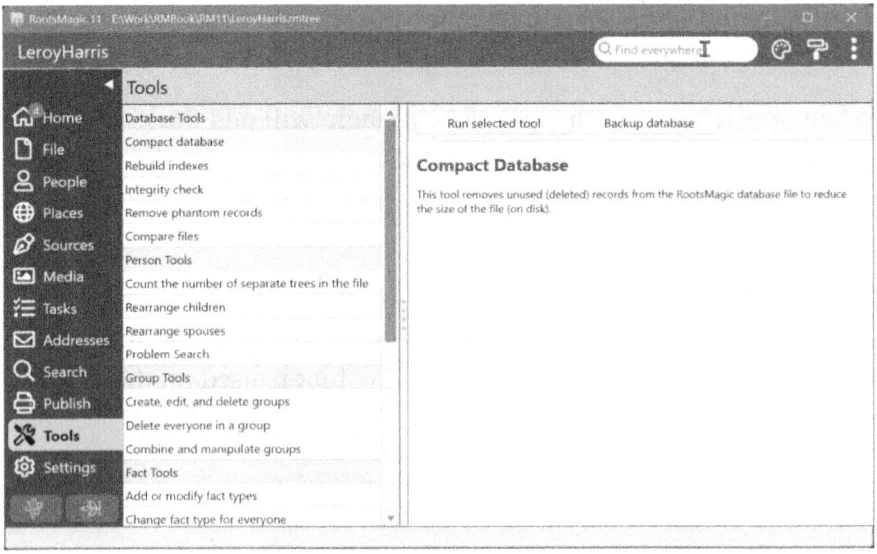


The left side of the Tools page is a list of tools ordered by category. As you select a tool on the list, RootsMagic displays information about that tool on the right side of the page.

## DATABASE TOOLS

The database tools include 4 simple tools for cleaning up and testing the integrity of your database.

**Compact database:** removes unused records in the database. This can reduce the size of your .rmtree file.

**Rebuild indexes:** rebuilds the underlying indexes in the database. These are the low level links between the basic records in the file.

**Integrity check:** tests the integrity of the underlying database structure. It looks for problems like database corruption, invalid indexes, etc.

**Remove phantom records:** cleans up phantom records, which include things like blank children in families, etc.

## COMPARING TWO ROOTSMAGIC FILES

There may come a time when you discover you have two different copies of the same RootsMagic database, but you don't know what the differences between the two are.

Compare Files lets you compare the current file with another RootsMagic file. RootsMagic will ask you to select the file you want to compare with the current file, and will analyze the two files and display a list of the people in each side by side. You'll need to be patient if your files are large as it can take a while to compare everyone in each file with everyone in the other file.

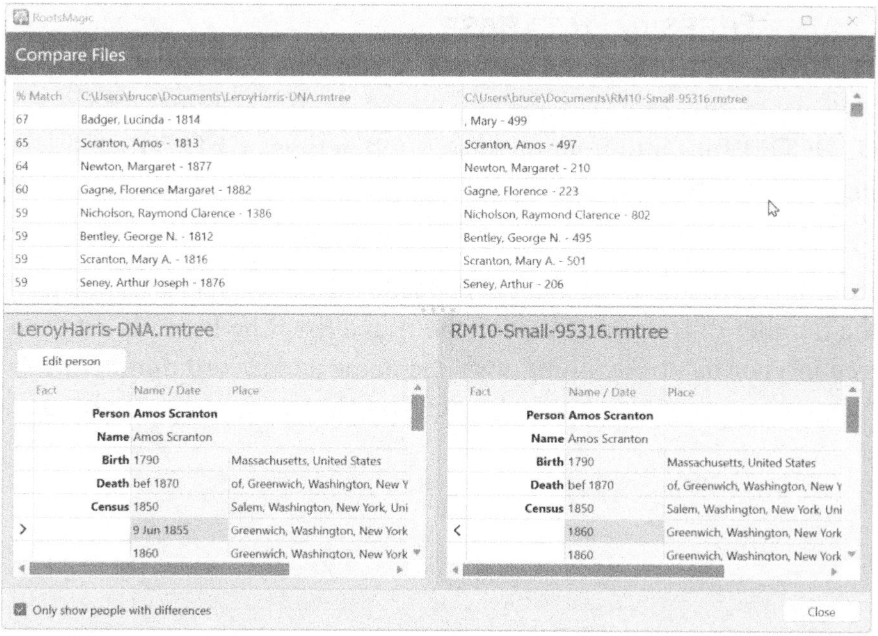


The list will display possible matches side by side, as well as show the percentage match between the two people. You can click on the header of any of the 3 columns to sort the list by that column.

When you highlight a matching pair, RootsMagic will display the two people side by side below the list. The information for the two people is color coded: green means that piece of information is in both files, yellow means it "kind of" matches, and red means it is different in each file.

From this side by side display you can edit the primary person, copy or replace a name or event from one file to the other, or copy notes, sources, or media from one file to another.

RootsMagic will also display people who are in one file but not the other. In this case there will be a "Copy person" button which will let you copy that person into the other file.

By default, RootsMagic will only display matches which have some difference. You can unmark the checkbox at the bottom of the screen and RootsMagic will display everyone in both files, even those that are a 100% match between the two files.

## Count Trees In Database

The "Count trees" command simply counts the number of trees in your database. This is especially useful if you have imported GEDCOM files into your database. Often those GEDCOM files may contain multiple unlinked trees that you are unaware of.

*To generate a list of the trees in your database*, select Count trees from the tools menu on the People view. RootsMagic will count the number of trees and display them in a list. The list will list each tree in your database, along with the name and record number of one person in each tree to help you find the tree in your database.

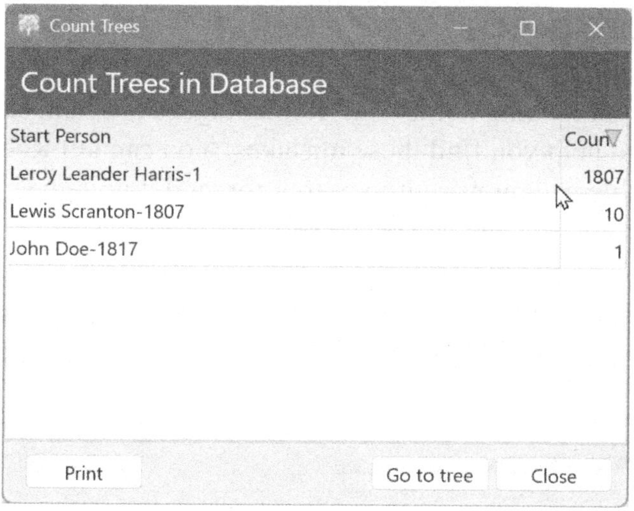


You can bring a tree up on the main screen by highlighting the tree in the list and clicking the "Go to tree" button.

## REARRANGING CHILDREN AND SPOUSES

On the People page edit menu RootsMagic provides functions to rearrange the children in a single family, or the spouses for a single person.

The "Rearrange children" and "Rearrange spouse" tools on the Tools page take these features to the next level and rearrange the children or spouses for the entire database.

*Rearrange children* will rearrange the children in every family in your file by birth date. Children without a birth date will sort to the top of the list of children in the family. You can still use the individual child rearrange to put them in the proper place afterwards.

*Rearrange spouses* will rearrange the spouses for every person in your file by their marriage date. Spouses without a marriage date will sort to the top of the list of spouses for the person. You can still use the individual spouse rearrange to put them in the proper place afterwards.

## PROBLEM SEARCH

When entering information into any program there is the possibility of making a mistake. RootsMagic's problem search is designed to help you find these mistakes. You can tell RootsMagic which problems you want it to search for, and it will generate a list of any person who has one of the selected problems.

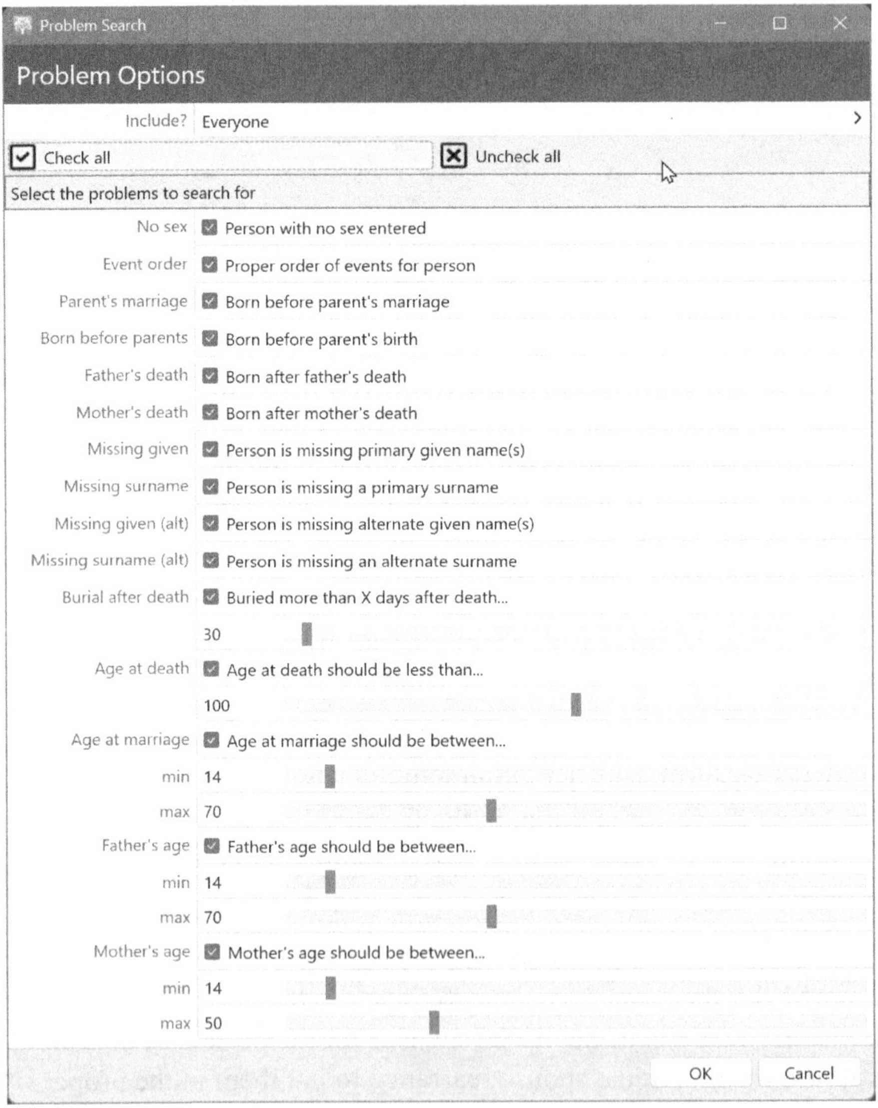

*Include?* lets you select which people to include in the search. By default RootsMagic will run the problem search on the entire file, but you can choose a group or select people from a list.

*No sex* will find individuals who have "Unknown" entered for their sex.

*Event order* will catch problems like a person getting married before their birth or after their death.

*Parent's marriage* will list individuals whose birth date falls before their parent's marriage date.

*Birth before parents* will list individuals whose birth date is earlier than their mother's or father's birth date.

*Father's death* will list individuals whose birth date is after their father's death date.

*Mother's death* will list individuals whose birth date is after their mother's death date.

*Missing given* will list individuals who have no given name entered.

*Missing surname* will list individuals who have no surname entered.

*Burial after death* will list individuals who were buried more than the number of days you enter after death.

*Age at death* will list individuals whose age at death is greater than the value you enter.

*Age at marriage* will list individuals whose age at marriage is outside the range you enter.

*Father's age* will list individuals whose father's age was outside the range you enter when the person was born.

*Mother's age* will list individuals whose mother's age was outside the range you enter when the person was born.

Once you click OK, RootsMagic will display a list of potential problems which looks like this.

RootsMagic lets you edit the person by highlighting the problem and clicking Edit person.

If a problem in the list isn't really a problem (for example if Aunt Mary really was 102 years old), you can highlight the non-problem and click the Not a problem button. RootsMagic will remove the item from the list and will not display it as a problem the next time you run the problem search. If you ever want to see what "problems" RootsMagic is ignoring, you can select "Not a problem list" from the tools menu on the People page. You can remove items from that list so that the problem search will detect them once again.

Sometimes you may not be able to (or have time to) fix a problem right away, so you can highlight the problem and click the "Add to task list" to add the problem to the task list.

If you want to print the problem list, simply click the "Print" button on the dialog.

> ☺ **Tip**
>
> Sometimes a single problem can trigger a bunch of error messages. For example, if you have a mother's death date entered 100 years too early, every one of her children will trigger the "Born after mother's death" error. If you have too many problems to work through at once, consider filtering by asking for less problem categories.

## Group Tools

RootsMagic lets you select a group of people in your database and give each of those groups a name.

For example, you can select everyone born in California and call that group "Born in California". You can then select that group by name to use in reports, exporting, etc.

### Create, Edit, and Delete groups

To view a list where you can add, edit, or delete groups, select the "Groups" tab on the side panel on the right side of the main RootsMagic screen, then click the edit (pencil) button in the groups header. This feature is described in detail on page 100.

### Delete Everyone in a Group

If you've ever needed to remove multiple people from your file at once, this is the tool for you. But it comes with a warning… you can't "undelete" people so make sure you have a backup first.

This feature lets you select a group that you have created, and will remove every person in that group from your database. By only deleting people in a created group, it allows you to look over the group carefully to make sure there aren't people in the group you didn't intend to remove.

### Combine and Manipulate Groups

There may be times when you need (or want) to combine two different groups together. This tool lets you do exactly that in a number of different ways. It is actually a fairly safe tool, as it combines two groups, but puts the results in a new third group without modifying the original groups.

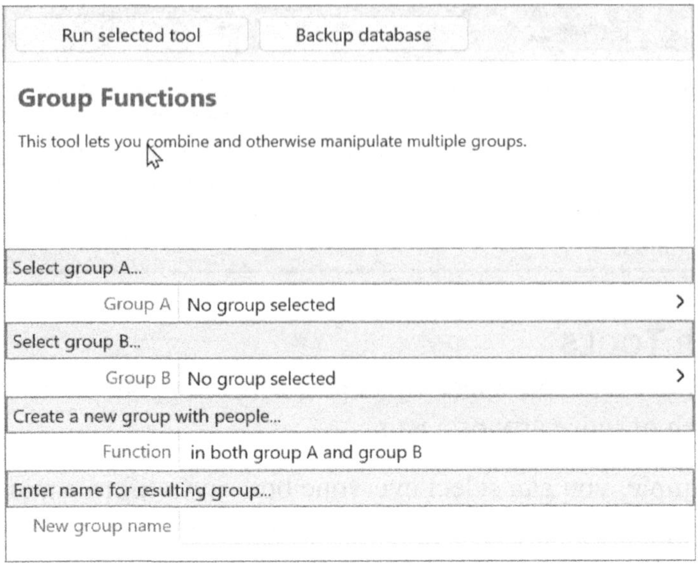


Select the two groups you want to combine, and enter a name for the new group you want to create. Finally, choose how you want the two groups to be combined.

- **In both group A and group B:** will only include people who are in both groups.
- **In group A but NOT group B:** will only include people who are in the first group but not the second. If a person is in both groups (or only in B) they will not be included.
- **In either group A or group B:** will include everyone in both groups.
- **In group A or B but not both:** will include everyone who is in only one of the two groups. Anyone in both groups will not be included.

## Fact Tools

Fact tools let you manipulate fact types, as well as facts in people's lives.

## Add or Modify Fact Types

This tool lets you create, edit, and delete fact types, and is found under the Tools menu on the People page. It is described in The Fact Type List (page 130).

## Change Fact Type for Everyone

The Change Fact Type tool is a special command which can change the type of a fact for everyone with that fact type. This can be useful for example if you wanted to change every instance of a baptism fact to a christening fact.

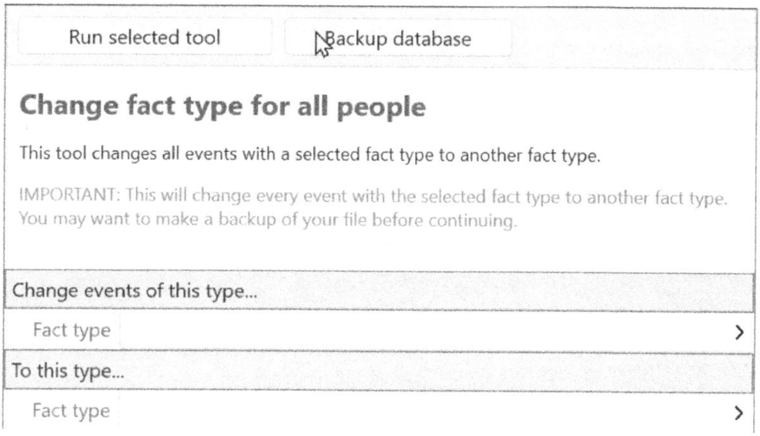


Select the fact type you want to change, and also the fact type you want to change it to. Keep in mind that this is not reversible, so you will want to make a backup of your database first just in case.

## Remove a Fact Type from Everyone

This tool will remove a particular type of fact from everyone in your file. This can be useful for example if you imported data and found that every record had a reference number fact that you didn't want. You could simply select the reference number fact and RootsMagic would remove that fact from everyone in your file. You will want to make a backup of your file first, since you can't "undelete" the facts.

## Add a Fact to Everyone in a Group

This tool lets you add a fact to everyone in a group. This is different from sharing a fact in that every person will have their own copy of the fact.

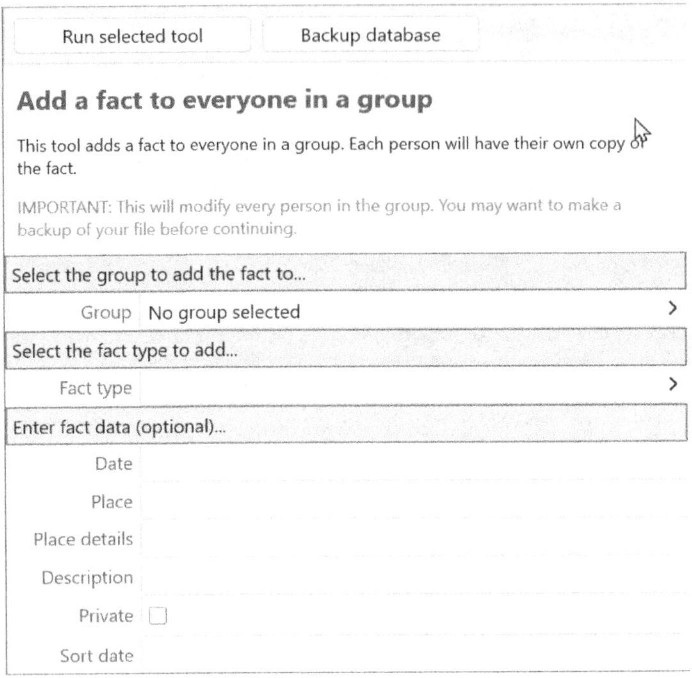


The only two requirements are to 1) select the group of people you want to add the fact to, and 2) select the type of fact (birth, census, residence, etc.) you want to add to each person. If you want to pre-populate the fact with some data that would be the same for every person, you can optionally provide that information as well.

## Place Tools

The 3 place tools are the same as those tools on the Places page. These tools are described in the chapter on Places.

- **CountyCheck:** described on page 153.
- **Gazetteer:** described on page 152.
- **Geocoding:** described on page 148.

## MEDIA TOOLS

When you add media items to RootsMagic, the media items are not stored inside the database file. RootsMagic stores a "link" to the media item (the path and filename). If you move media items to another folder, RootsMagic will no longer be able to find them and the "link" will show up as broken.

*Fix broken links* will search your hard drive for any broken links and attempt to fix them.

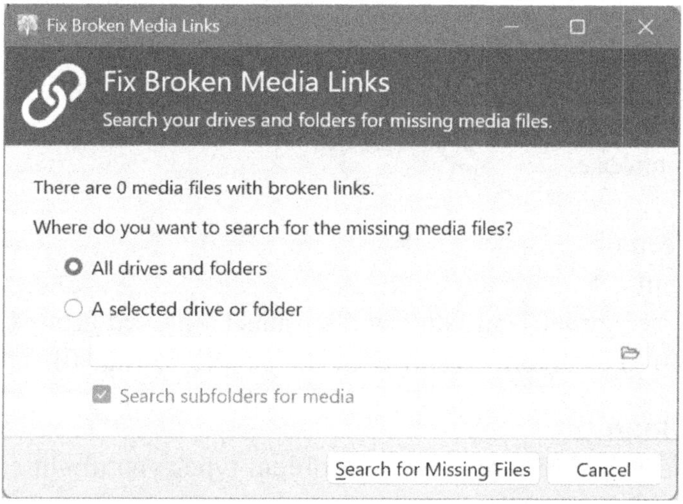


You can choose whether RootsMagic searches all your drives, or you can narrow it down to a single drive or folder. The second option is useful when you know where you moved the media items to. You can also choose to have it search any subfolders in case you organized your media in that way.

## CLEANING UP NAMES AND PLACES

As your database gets larger, you will find that the names and places you have entered will sometimes get a little messy. RootsMagic provides a tool called DataClean which will make cleaning up these names and places much easier.

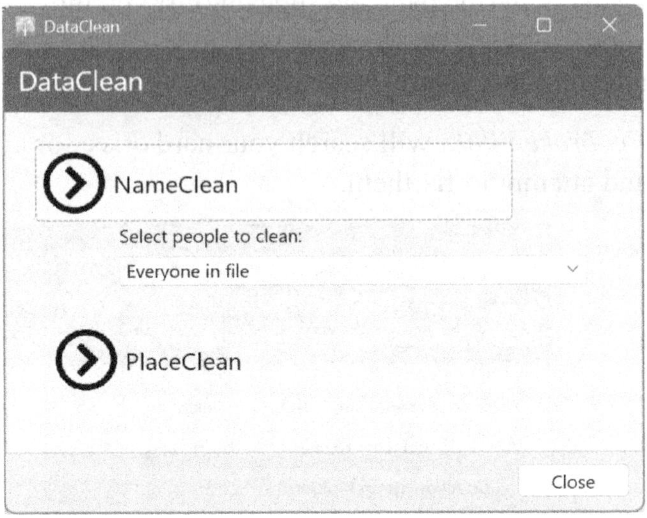


You can choose either NameClean or PlaceClean. If you choose NameClean you can also select a named group (see page 100) to clean only a subset of the people in your file.

### NameClean

NameClean will display a list of problem types you might encounter for names in your database.

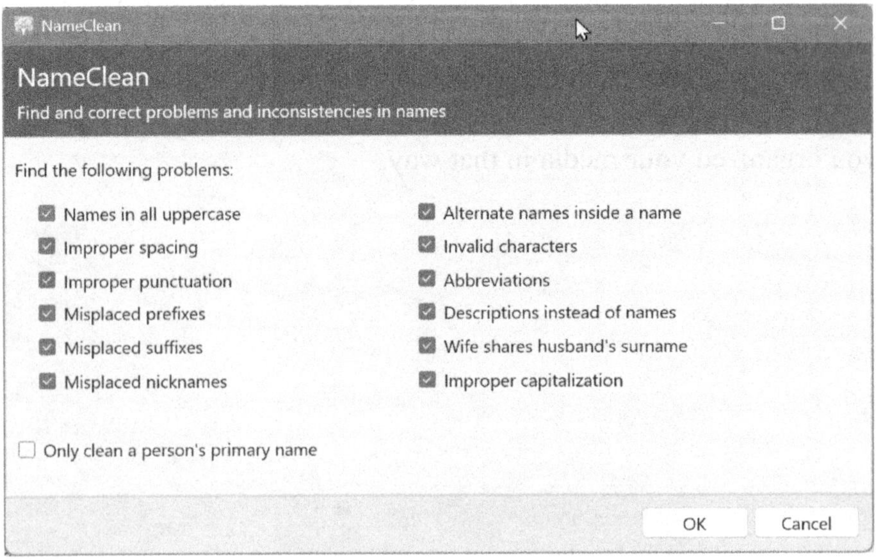

Just mark the checkbox next to whichever name problems you would like RootsMagic to find for you. RootsMagic will then scan your database and display a list of any names with one or more of the problems you searched for.

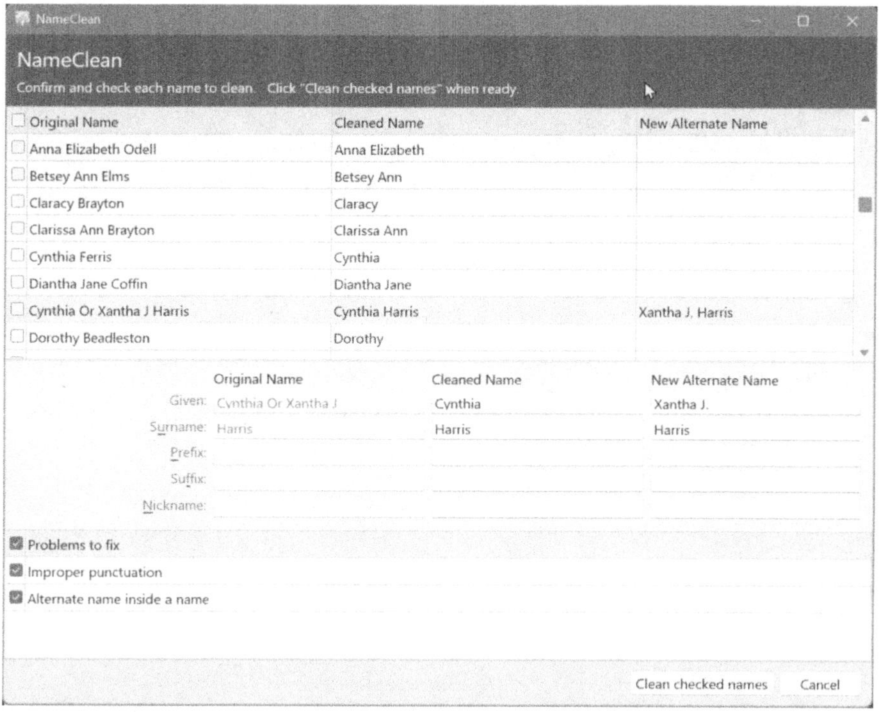


When you highlight a name in the list, you will see below it RootsMagic's recommendation. To accept that recommendation you can mark the checkbox in front of the name in the list. If you want to only accept part of the recommendation, mark the name in the list, but unmark checkboxes in the "Problems to Fix" section that you don't want RootsMagic to fix. And finally, if you want to make changes yourself, you can edit the "Cleaned Name" fields to have RootsMagic make changes your way.

When you have marked any of the names you want cleaned, click the "Clean Checked Names" button and RootsMagic will apply the changes to the names in your database.

### PlaceClean

As with NameClean, the PlaceClean will display a list of problem types for you to select from. But in addition you can also add or remove countries to places, or replace brackets with your own set of characters.

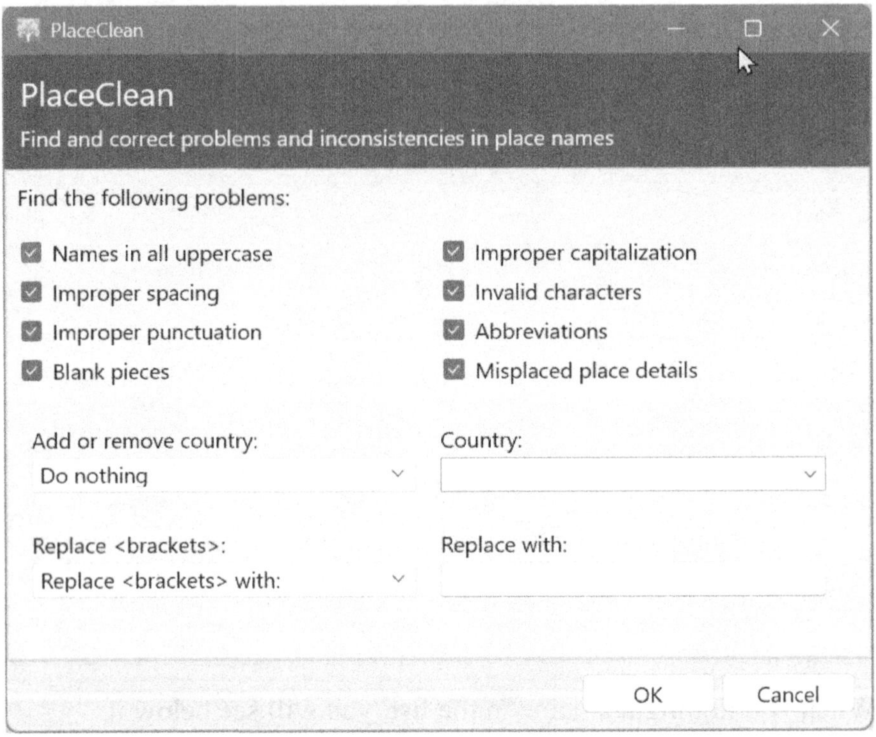


PlaceClean works almost exactly the same way as NameClean. You can mark the places you want cleaned, and you can either accept all the changes to the place, or just some of the changes, or you can hand enter your own changes.

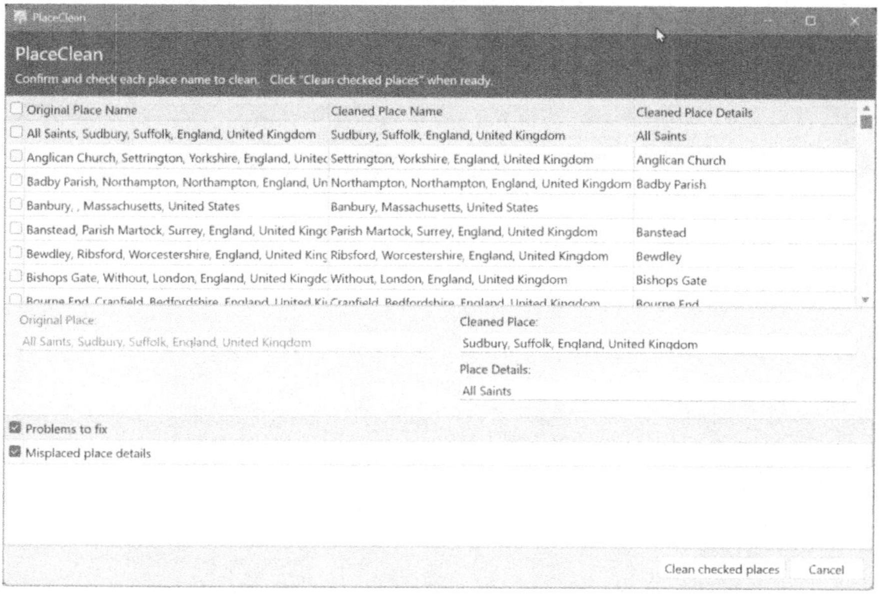


## Enhanced Properties List

Although the Home page provides a properties list for the current database, it is limited to simply the number of people, families, events, etc. in the current file.

The enhanced properties list on the Tools page provides a much deeper look into your database. Simply select and run the tool, and RootsMagic will generate and display the list.

Rather than just the number of people, the enhanced list will also break that down by male, female, and unknown. Other record types will similarly be broken down into greater detail… records that are unused, records with problems, and more.

| | |
|---|---|
| **Events w/ no sources:** | 2153 |
| **Associations:** | 10 |
| **Associations missing a person:** | 0 |
| **Places:** | 1077 |
| **Unused places:** | 30 (view) |
| **Place details:** | 88 |
| **Temples:** | 218 |
| **Places not geocoded:** | 153 (view) |
| **Sources:** | 178 |
| **Citations:** | 1351 |
| **Citation Links:** | 6746 |
| **Sources w/ no citations:** | 24 (view) |
| **Citations w/o a source:** | 0 |
| **Unused citations:** | 11 (view) |
| **Repositories:** | 33 |
| **Unused repositories:** | 1 (view) |
| **Addresses:** | 3 |

Some line items will also have a "(view)" link that you can click on to see that line item in more detail.

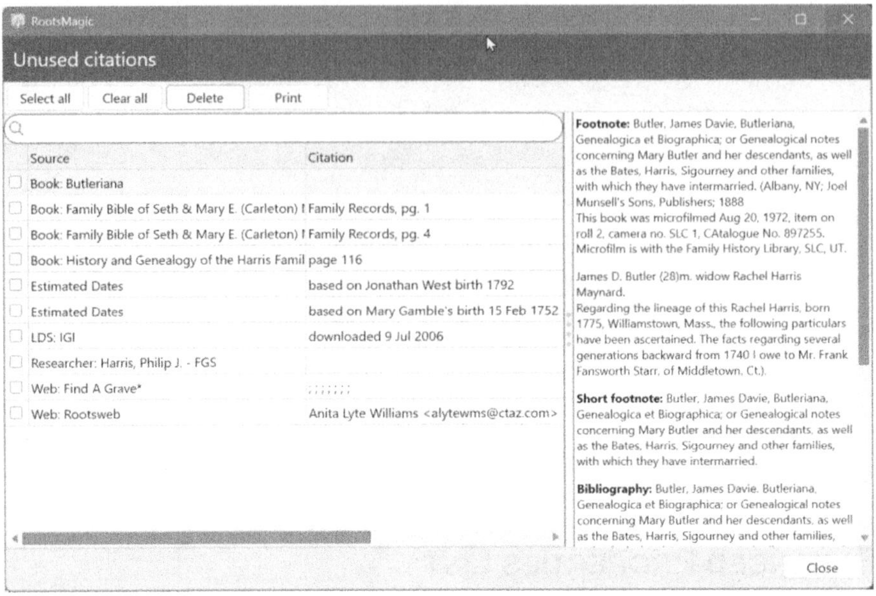


When viewing a list from the Enhanced Properties list, you can view more details about each item, and can print the list by clicking the printer button in the upper right corner.

A number of the lists (notably "unused" item lists), will also let you select any or all items in the list and delete them with the trash can button in the upper right.

# SETTINGS PAGE - ROOTSMAGIC OPTIONS

RootsMagic offers a number of options that you can use to personalize the way the program and your databases operate. Click on "Settings" on the side menu, then choose which category of options you want to change by clicking on the icons above the settings pages.

## PROGRAM SETTINGS

Program settings are those options that affect the program as a whole and are not specific to any one database.

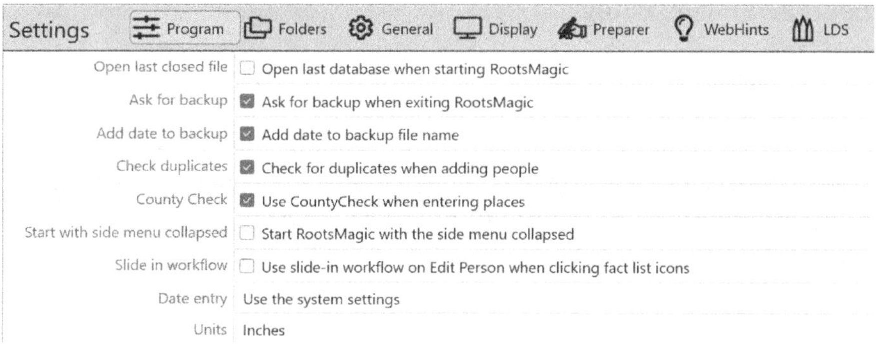


*Open last closed file* tells RootsMagic whether to automatically open up the database that was open the last time you used the program.

*Ask for backup* specifies whether RootsMagic will ask you if you want to make a backup when you exit the program.

*Add date to backup* lets you choose whether the current date will be added to the file name when you create a backup. This helps prevent you from overwriting the previous backup with each new one.

*Check duplicates* determines whether RootsMagic checks each time you add a new person to see if you may have already added them.

*CountyCheck* tells RootsMagic to check whether a place existed at the time of the event.

*Start with side menu collapsed* tells RootsMagic whether the side menu should be expanded or collapsed when you start the program.

*Slide in workflow* tells RootsMagic whether to slide in working lists when you select citations, media, or tasks from the Edit Person screen.

*Date entry* determines whether RootsMagic interprets dates entered like 1/2/1997 as January 2, 1997 (US) or February 1, 1997 (pretty much everywhere else).

*Units* tells RootsMagic whether to use inches or centimeters in report and other settings.

## Folder Settings

The Folders option allows you to enter default folders where RootsMagic will look for certain types of files. You can just type in the full folder name, or click the button with the folder at the right of each field to bring up a dialog to select the folder (you need to click the field before the button appears).

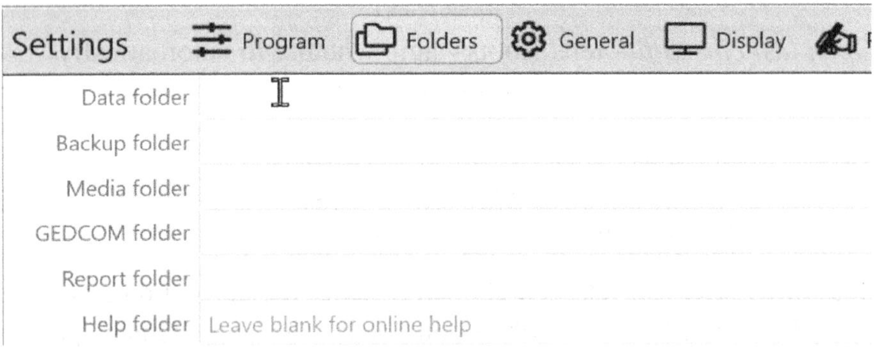


If the folder is blank, or you enter an invalid folder, RootsMagic will use the regular default folder.

In the case of the Help folder, leaving it blank will cause RootsMagic to use the online help (which is continually updated and requires internet access). You can download a copy of the help files from our website and unzip them into a folder on your hard drive. That is when you would want to enter the Help folder.

## General Settings

The "General" settings lets you choose options for the currently selected database, including formats and how you want RootsMagic to treat the database when it is opened.

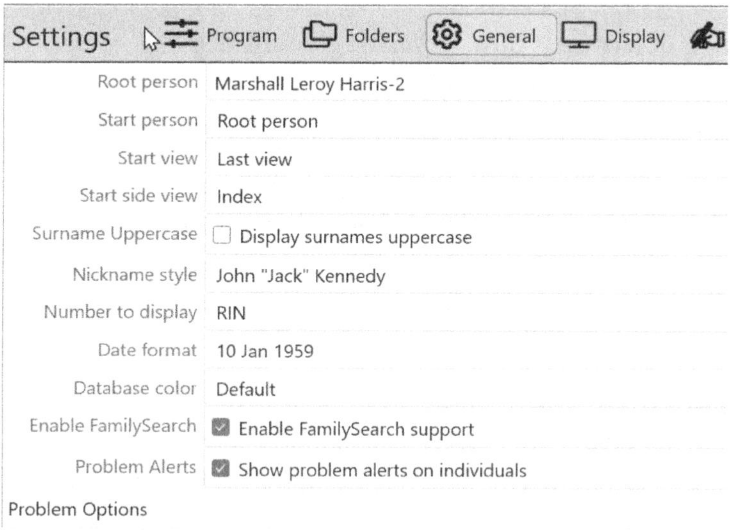


*Root person* lets you select the "root" person. The root person is the person that RootsMagic uses as the starting person on the main screen when you open a database. When you click "Root person", RootsMagic will display the search screen, where you can select the new root person. *If you ever get lost in your database*, you can click the "Home" button (looks like a house) on the People page to bring the root person back to the main screen.

*Start person* lets you choose whether to start with the root person when opening the database, or whether to start with the person who was highlighted the last time you used the database.

*Start view* lets you specify whether RootsMagic will start up in the Pedigree, Family, Descendants, People list, Couple list, or Association view. You can also just have RootsMagic open to the view from the last time you used the database.

*Start side view* lets you choose which of the side list tabs should open by default; index, family, history, bookmarks, or groups.

You can also have RootsMagic open to the tab from the last time you used the database.

*Surname Uppercase* tells RootsMagic whether you want it to display and print surnames (last names) in all uppercase.

*Nickname style* determines how RootsMagic will display nicknames that you enter for people. You can have nicknames displayed with either "quotes" or (parentheses) around them.

*Number to display* lets you choose which number to display after the person's name in the info view on the main screen. You can choose between the record number (RIN, which RootsMagic assigns), the reference number (REFN, which you can add as a fact), the FamilySearch ID (FSID), or no number.

*Date format* determines how RootsMagic will display dates you enter. You can actually enter dates in just about any format and RootsMagic will automatically convert them to the format you select here.

*Database color* lets you choose a color for your database. This color is displayed in the header bar at the top of the window. You can assign different colors to different files to provide a visual difference between different files.

*Enable FamilySearch* lets you choose whether support for interfacing with FamilySearch should be enabled.

*Problem Alerts* enables or disables the little red symbols which appear on the main views next to people who have a potential problem. The Problem options button lets you choose which problems RootsMagic should look for before displaying an alert.

## Display Settings

The Display settings let you change the font scaling, colors, and other display options in the program.

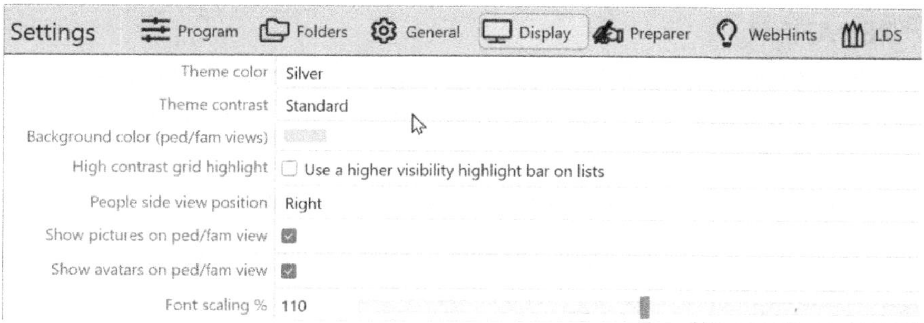


*Theme color* lets you select the color scheme used for the overall look of the RootsMagic window.

*Theme contrast* lets you choose how much contrast there is between text and background in the theme. You can choose from Standard, High, and Max.

*Background color (ped/fam views)* lets you select the background color for the pedigree and family views.

*High contrast grid highlight* tells RootsMagic whether to use a higher contrast between text and background color for the list highlighter.

*People side view position* tells RootsMagic whether to display the People page side panel on the left or right.

*Search criteria position* tells RootsMagic whether to display the criteria panel on the Search page on the left or right.

*Show pictures on ped/fam view* tells RootsMagic whether to display a person's primary picture on the Pedigree and Family view of the People page.

*Show avatars on ped/fam view* tells RootsMagic whether to display the blue, pink, or gray avatars on the Pedigree and Family view when no picture is available.

*Font scaling* lets you choose the magnification for fonts (70% - 150%) on RootsMagic screens. You will need to close and restart RootsMagic for the font scaling to take affect on all screens.

## PREPARER

The "Preparer" item in the options dialog allows you to enter the preparer (or submitter) name and address. This is the name and address that RootsMagic will print at the bottom of printouts if requested. Each database can have a different preparer.

## WEBHINTS SETTINGS

The WebHints options let you choose whether to display record hints, and which record provider(s) you wish to see hints from. Each provider will have different options. You can experiment with the different options to determine which settings work best for you.

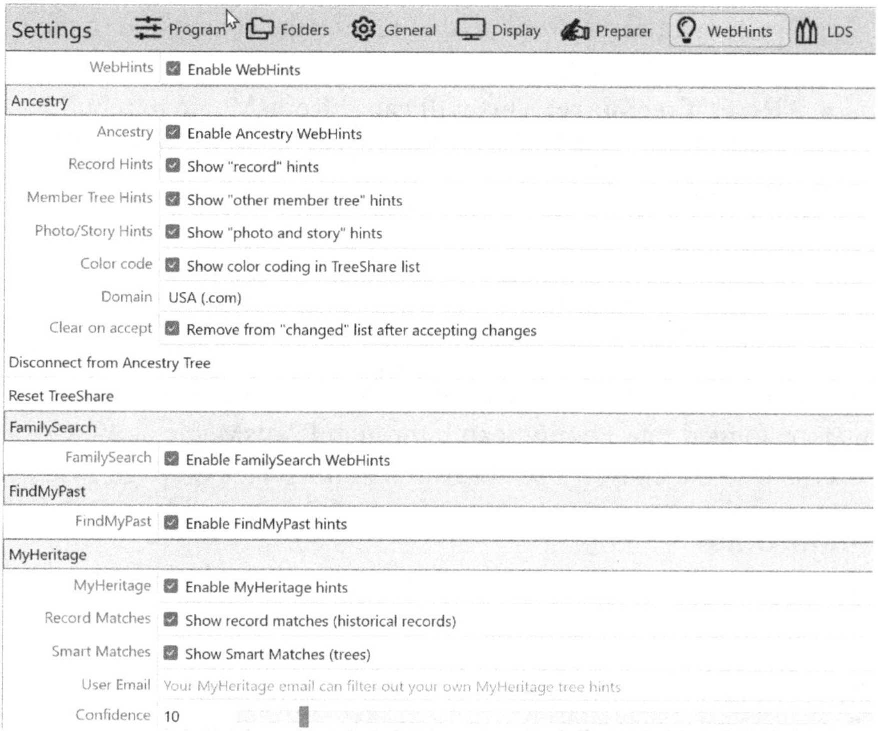


## Ancestry

Click the Ancestry checkbox to enable hints. Other options for Ancestry WebHints are:

- **Record Hints:** Show "record" hints
- **Member Tree Hints:** Show "other member tree" hints
- **Photo/Story Hints:** Show "photo and story" hints
- **Color code:** Show color coding in the TreeShare list
- **Domain:** Select the domain RootsMagic uses when clicking "Show on Ancestry"
- **Clear on accept:** Automatically remove the person from the "Changed" list in TreeShare after accepting the changes
- **Disconnect from Ancestry Tree:** Disconnects the current RootsMagic file from the Ancestry Tree. IMPORTANT NOTE: This cannot be undone. If you want to reconnect RootsMagic to Ancestry you will need to either 1) upload your RootsMagic file to a new Ancestry Tree, 2) download your Ancestry Tree into a NEW RootsMagic file, or 3)

restore an earlier backup that retains the connection to the Ancestry Tree.

- **Reset TreeShare:** This will cause RootsMagic to rebuild the links to your Ancestry Tree. With a large Ancestry Tree this can take a long time.

### FamilySearch

Click the FamilySearch checkbox to enable hints. There are no additional options for FamilySearch.

**Important Note:** In order to see hints from FamilySearch, you must be logged into FamilySearch through RootsMagic as described in the chapter FamilySearch Family Tree on page 314.

### FindMyPast

Click the FindMyPast checkbox to enable hints. There are no additional options for FindMyPast.

### MyHeritage

Click the MyHeritage checkbox to enable hints. Other options for MyHeritage WebHints are:

- **Record matches:** Show record matches (historical records)
- **Smart matches:** Show Smart Matches (trees)
- **User email:** Your MyHeritage email. This can help filter out your own MyHeritage tree hints
- **Confidence:** How high of a confidence do you want for matches

## Latter-day Saints Settings

The Latter-day Saint settings section has two checkbox options: 1) turn Latter-day Saint options on or off, and 2) whether to check for duplication when reserving ordinances.

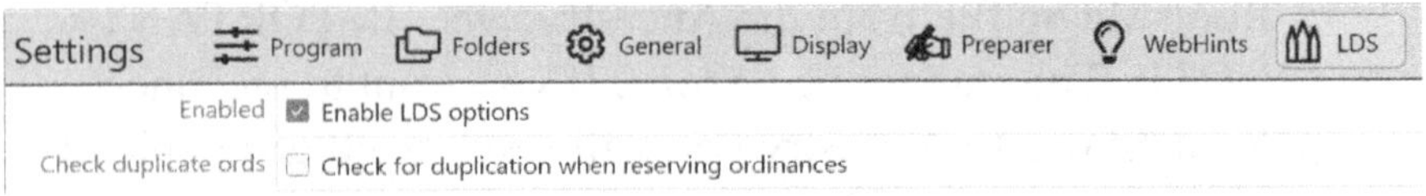

# APPENDIX

## BUILT-IN FACT TYPES

| Fact Type | Description |
|---|---|
| Adoption | Pertaining to creation of a child-parent relationship that does not exist biologically. |
| Alternate name | Another name by which a person is known. |
| Ancestral file number | A unique permanent record file number of an individual record stored in Ancestral File. |
| Annulment | Declaring a marriage void from the beginning (never existed). |
| Association | A non-family relationship between two people. |
| Baptism | The event of baptism (not LDS), performed in infancy or later. |
| Bar Mitzvah | The ceremonial event held when a Jewish boy reaches age 13. |
| Bas Mitzvah | The ceremonial event held when a Jewish girl reaches age 13, also known as "Bat Mitzvah." |
| Birth | The event of entering into life. |
| Blessing | A religious event of bestowing divine care or intercession. Sometimes given in connection with a naming ceremony. |
| Burial | The event of the proper disposing of the mortal remains of a deceased person. |
| Caste | A name assigned to a particular group that this person was associated with, such as a particular racial group, religious group, or a group with an inherited status. |
| Census | The event of the periodic count of the population for a designated locality, such as a national or state Census. |

| | |
|---|---|
| Census (family) | The event of the periodic count of the population for a designated locality, such as a national or state Census, attached to a couple. |
| Christen | The religious event (not LDS) of baptizing and/or naming a child. |
| Christen (adult) | The religious event (not LDS) of baptizing and/or naming an adult person. |
| Confirmation | The religious event (not LDS) of conferring the gift of the Holy Ghost and, among Protestants, full church membership. |
| Cremation | Disposal of the remains of a person's body by fire. |
| Death | The event when mortal life terminates. |
| Degree | A degree earned by a person (see also Graduation). |
| Description | The physical characteristics of a person, place, or thing. |
| Divorce | An event of dissolving a marriage through civil action. |
| Divorce filed | An event of filing for a divorce by a spouse. |
| DNA Test | Results of a DNA test |
| Education | Indicator of a level of education attained. |
| Election | An event where a person is elected to some office. |
| Emigration | An event of leaving one's homeland with the intent of residing elsewhere. |
| Engagement | An event of recording or announcing an agreement between two people to become married. |
| Excommunication | An event where a person is expelled from the communion of a church and deprived of its rights, privileges, and advantages. |

| | |
|---|---|
| First Communion | A religious rite, the first act of sharing in the Lord's supper as part of church worship. |
| Graduation | An event of awarding educational diplomas or degrees to individuals. |
| Illness | The state or condition of being sick. |
| Immigration | An event of entering into a new locality with the intent of residing there. |
| LDS Baptism | The event of baptism performed at age eight or later by priesthood authority of the LDS Church. |
| LDS Confirmation | The religious event by which a person receives membership in the LDS Church. |
| LDS Endowment | A religious event where an endowment ordinance for an individual was performed by priesthood authority in an LDS temple. |
| LDS Initiatory | A religious event where an initiatory ordinance for an individual was performed by priesthood authority in an LDS temple. |
| LDS Sealing to Parent | A religious event pertaining to the sealing of a child to his or her parents in an LDS temple ceremony. |
| LDS Sealing to spouse | A religious event pertaining to the sealing of a husband and wife in an LDS temple ceremony. |
| Living | The state of being alive at a particular time. |
| Marriage | A legal, common-law, or customary event of creating a family unit of a man and a woman as husband and wife. |
| Marriage Bann | An event of an official public notice given that two people intend to marry. |
| Marriage contract | An event of recording a formal agreement of marriage, including the prenuptial agreement in which marriage partners reach agreement |

| | |
|---|---|
| | about the property rights of one or both, securing property to their children. |
| Marriage license | An event of obtaining a legal license to marry. |
| Marriage settlement | An event of creating an agreement between two people contemplating marriage, at which time they agree to release or modify property rights that would otherwise arise from the marriage. |
| Military | The state of being in the military service, whether during peacetime or war. |
| Miscellaneous | An event which is so general that it doesn't fit in any category. |
| Mission | The state of being sent to an area to spread religion or carry on educational or charitable activities. |
| Namesake | An individual who a person is named after. |
| Nationality | The national heritage of an individual. |
| Naturalization | The event of obtaining citizenship. |
| Occupation | The type of work or profession of an individual. |
| Ordination | A religious event of receiving authority to act in religious matters. |
| Probate | An event of judicial determination of the validity of a will. May indicate several related court activities over several dates. |
| Property | Pertaining to possessions such as real estate or other property of interest. |
| Reference No | A description or number used to identify an item for filing, storage, or other reference purposes. |
| Religion | A religious denomination to which a person is affiliated or for which a record applies. |

| | |
|---|---|
| Residence | The act of dwelling at an address for a period of time. |
| Residence (family) | The act of dwelling at an address for a period of time, attached to a couple. |
| Retirement | An event of exiting an occupational relationship with an employer after a qualifying time period. |
| Separation | An event where the conjugal cohabitation of a husband and wife ceases. |
| Soc Sec No | A number assigned by the United States Social Security Administration. Used for tax identification purposes. |
| Stillborn | The event where an infant is dead at birth. |
| Title (Nobility) | A formal designation used by an individual in connection with positions of royalty or other social status, such as Grand Duke. |
| Will | A legal document treated as an event, by which a person disposes of his or her estate, to take effect after death. The event date is the date the will was signed while the person was alive. |

## Keyboard Shortcut Keys

There are shortcut keys on many RootsMagic screens. Here are a few shortcut keys you can use in RootsMagic.

| Main | |
|---|---|
| Shift+Ctrl+A | Add record (place, source, citation, task, media, address, association, etc.) |
| Shift+Ctrl+D | Delete highlighted record (place, source, citation, task, media, address, etc.) |
| Ctrl+P | Print a report |

| | |
|---|---|
| <Enter> | Edit the highlighted person |
| <Del> | Delete the highlighted person |
| Ctrl+F | Person list view |
| Shift+Ctrl+F | Couple list view |
| Shift+Ctrl+I | Add a new individual |
| Shift+Ctrl+S | Add a spouse to the highlighted person |
| Shift+Ctrl+P | Add parents to the highlighted person |
| Shift+Ctrl+C | Add children to the highlighted person |
| Shift+Ctrl+E | Edit record (person, place, source, citation, task, media, address, etc.) |
| Ctrl+1 ... Ctrl+n | Tabs on each page |
| Ctrl+S | Basic search |
| Ctrl+H | Go to home person |
| Shift+Ctrl+H | Move highlighted person to primary position (not in family view) |
| Shift+Ctrl+<Left> | Move back to previous person in history list |
| Shift+Ctrl+<Right> | Move to next person in history list |
| Shift+Ctrl+U | Reset program settings or clear registration |
| Ctrl+W | Create a website |
| <F1> | Open help screens |
| <F2> | Command palette |
| <F5> | Switch between databases |
| Ctrl+Cmd+F | Enter / exit fullscreen mode (Mac) |

| **Text Field** | |
|---|---|
| Ctrl+X | Cut text to clipboard |

| | |
|---|---|
| Ctrl+C | Copy text to clipboard |
| Ctrl+V | Paste text from clipboard |
| Ctrl+A | Select all text in field |
| Shift+End | Select to end |
| Shift+Home | Select to beginning |

| Note Editor | |
|---|---|
| Ctrl+X | Cut highlighted text to clipboard |
| Ctrl+C | Copy highlighted text to clipboard |
| Ctrl+V | Paste clipboard text at cursor position |
| Ctrl+Shift+V | Paste as plain text |
| Ctrl+Z | Undo last edit |
| Ctrl+B | Turn on BOLD |
| Ctrl+I | Turn on ITALICS |
| Ctrl+U | Turn on UNDERLINE |
| Ctrl+F | Find text in the note |
| F3 | Find next |
| Ctrl+T | Character map |
| Ctrl+Left | Move left one word at a time |
| Ctrl+Right | Move right one word at a time |

## Template Language Reference

Sentence templates allow you to tell RootsMagic how to write a sentence for a given fact or source citation. You simply write a sentence with "fields" and “switches” to show where things like names, dates, and places fit. Square brackets [ ] indicate the name of a field to be displayed, while angle brackets < > indicate a switch, or conditional statement, that will determine what, if any, data is displayed.

There are two types of templates: Fact Sentence Templates and Source Templates. Fact Sentence Templates are used when a particular fact is written in a narrative report or website. Source Templates are used when a source citation is written in a report or a website. While each type of template has its own unique features, they both share the same basic usage and rules.

## Fields

Fields are pieces of a template that are replaced with meaningful text at the time the sentence is written. They are written using square brackets with the name of the field inside. Field names are not case sensitive, so for example, [Date], [date], [daTe], [DATE] are all equivalent field names. Throughout this topic, most have the first letter Capitalized so they stand out, especially when several words are used together like PlaceDetails.

Fields in a fact sentence template may look like this:

```
[Person] was born< [Date]>< [PlaceDetails]>< [Place]>.
```

In this example, when RootsMagic encounters a person's birth when writing a narrative report, it takes this template and replaces [Person] with the person's name, [Date] with the date of the birth, [PlaceDetails] with the details (hospital or address) within the place where the birth occurred, and [Place] with the place (city, county, state, country) of birth.

Fields in a source template for the full (first) footnote may look like:

```
[Author], <i>[Title]</i> ([PubPlace]: [Publisher], [PubDate]).
```

while the fields in a source template for the bibliography might look like:

```
[Author:Reverse]. <i>[Title]</i>. [PubPlace]: [Publisher],
[PubDate:Year].
```

In this example, when RootsMagic encounters a book source, it replaces the source fields [Author] with the author of the book, [Title] with the title of the book, [PubPlace] with the place of publication, [Publisher] with the name of the publisher, and [PubDate] with the date of publications (usually a year).

RootsMagic also allows modifers which change the look or content of the fields. Notice the **<i>** and **</i>** formatting codes which tell RootsMagic to format the text in italics font, **:Reverse** tells RootsMagic to show the surname first, and **:year** tells RootsMagic to show only the year part of the date.

## Fact Sentence Fields

Fact sentence templates are created using a combination of pre-defined fields referring to a person or persons, pre-defined fields referring to fact details, as well as plain text and punctuation.

Formatting codes can be used in Fact sentence templates, if desired, but are more commonly used in the Notes field to emphasize a portion of the note text. The field names and field options in templates are not case sensitive – they can be all lower case, all upper case, or first letter of each word capitalized, etc. First letter capitalization is used here, particularly where multiple words are involved, to make it easier for people to read.

The pre-defined fields for use in fact sentence templates are:

| Field | Field Type | Description |
|---|---|---|
| **Fields referring to a person or persons:** | | |
| [Person] | 1 person | The principal person of the event |
| [Spouse] | 1 person | The spouse of the principal person |
| [Couple] | 1 or 2 people | Both the principal person and spouse, if entered |
| [Husband] | 1 person | The husband in the principal person's marriage |
| [Wife] | 1 person | The wife in the principal person's marriage |
| [ThisPerson] | 1 person | The main witness that the witness sentence is about. Witness fact sentences only. |
| [OtherPersons] | 1 or more person | All witnesses to the event, regardless of role. In witness fact sentences, this excludes the main witness. |
| [Role] | 1 or more person | All witnesses to the event with the specified role. The name of the role is typed in square brackets, e.g. [Witness], [Doctor], [Minister] |
| [Field(#)] | 1 person | In the case of fields that refer to more than one person, you can refer to a specific person by number by writing the number in parentheses after the field name. For example, to get the 3rd bridesmaid, type [Bridesmaid(3)]. |
| [Field 1,Field 2,...] | 1 or more person | Any number of person fields may be combined into a single group by |

| | | |
|---|---|---|
| | | writing all the field names within square brackets, separated by commas. For example, to get all the groomsmen and bridesmaids, type [Groomsman,Bridesmaid]. |
| **Fields referring to fact details:** | | |
| [Date] | Date | The date of the event |
| [Place] | Place | The place where the event happened |
| [PlaceDetails] | Place | Details about the place where the event happened (for example, the name of the church or cemetery, or the street address) |
| [Desc] | Description | The description of the fact |

## Source Fields

Source fields are not predefined by RootsMagic, but are defined for each source template. To use those fields in a template, type its name in square brackets into the respective template (full footnote, short footnote or bibliography). A source template is made up of source fields, plain text and punctuation, as well as formatting codes when required.

## Field Options

You can set options for every field that control both what is written and how it is written. You type the options within the field's square brackets. You can add as many options as necessary to a field, each option separated by a colon, but no extra spaces. For example:

[Person:Given:Surname]

[PublishDate:Year]

[Place:Reverse:Proper]

Most of these options can be used both in sentence templates and in source templates.

| Option | Field Types | Description |
|---|---|---|
| Capitalization Options | | |
| :NoCaps | Any | Default. Makes no changes in capitalization. |
| :Upper | Any | Changes to upper case, e.g. "JOHN DOE" |
| :Lower | Any | Changes to lower case, e.g. "john doe" |
| :Caps | Any | Capitalizes the first letter and makes no changes to subsequent letters, e.g. "John doe" |
| :Proper | Any | Forces "proper" capitalization, e.g. "John Doe" |
| Abbreviation Options | | |
| :NoAbbrev | Source Template | Default. Look for a "\|\|" and process the information that precedes it, e.g. Post Office Box 1010\|\|PO Box 1010 = Post Office Box 1010 |
| :Abbrev | Source Template | Look for a "\|\|" and process the information that follows it, e.g. Post Office Box 1010\|\|PO Box 1010 = PO Box 1010 |

| Option | Field Types | Description |
|---|---|---|
| **Name Part Options (May include one or more)** | | |
| :Full | Name & Witness names | Dr. John Robert "Johnny" Doe Jr. |
| :Reverse | Name & Witness names | Doe, Dr. John Robert "Johnny" Jr. (reverses first name in a group only) |
| :Given | Name & Witness names | John Robert |
| :First | Name & Witness names | John |
| :Surname | Name & Witness names | Doe |
| :Prefix | Name | Dr. |
| :Suffix | Name | Jr. |
| :Nickname | Name | Johnny |
| :Casual | Name & Witness names | Nickname, if known, otherwise first name |
| **Age Options** | | |
| :Plain | Age | No prefix. |
| :At | Age | "at the age of Age". Default for fact/role sentence ages |
| :Commas | Age | ", age Age," |
| **Fact Place Options** | | |

| Option | Field Types | Description |
| --- | --- | --- |
| :Original | Place in Fact/Role Sentences | Original version of place (default), e.g. “Brownsville, Utah Territory” |
| :Short | Place in Fact/Role Sentences | Abbreviated version of place, e.g. “Ogden, Utah” |
| **Place Options** | | |
| :Full | Place or Place Details in source template or fact/role sentence | Ames, Story, Iowa, United States |
| :Reverse | Place or Place Details in source template or fact/role sentence | United States. Iowa. Story. Ames |
| :ReverseComma | Place or Place Details in source template or fact/role sentence | United States, Iowa, Story, Ames |
| :First | Place or Place Details in source template or fact/role sentence | Ames |
| :Last | Place or Place Details in source template or fact/role sentence | United States |
| **Place & Description Prefix Options** | | |

| Option | Field Types | Description |
|---|---|---|
| :Plain | Place, Place Details, or Description | No prefix. Default for source templates and description fields |
| :In | Place, Place Details, or Description | "In Text". Default for fact/role sentence places |
| :At | Place, Place Details, or Description | "At Text". Default for fact/role sentence place details |
| :A | Place, Place Details, or Description | "A Text" or "An Other text" |
| **Date Options** | | |
| :Plain | Date | Full date, e.g. "6 Apr 1830", no "in" or "on" prefix. (Default for source templates) |
| :InOn | Date | "on 6 Apr 1830" or "in Apr 1830". (Default for fact/role sentences.) |
| :Year | Date | Year only, e.g. "1830" |
| :DayOfWeek | Date | Show the day of week with the date, e.g. "Tuesday 6 Apr 1830" |
| :NoDayOfWeek | Date | Removes the day of week from the date (default) |

| Option | Field Types | Description |
|---|---|---|
| :Commas | Date | Adds commas to the date, e.g. "6 Apr, 1830" or "Tuesday, 6 Apr, 1830" |
| :NoCommas | Date | Removes commas from the date (default) |
| **Person Options** | | |
| :Name | Fact Sentence People | Default. The names of the people in roles |
| :Poss | Fact Sentence People | Possessive form of names, e.g. John's. To get the full name possessive, i.e. "John Doe's", you would enter [Person:Full:Poss] |
| :HeShe | Fact Sentence People | He/She/They |
| :HisHer | Fact Sentence People | His/Her/Their |
| :HimHer | Fact Sentence People | Him/Her/Them |
| :Age | Fact Sentence People | Age of person at time of event |
| :Role | Fact Sentence People | Role of witness |
| :Count | Fact Sentence People | # of people in the group, i.e. [role1,role2,role3:count], e.g. [child:count] or [son,daughter:count] |

| Option | Field Types | Description |
|---|---|---|
| Person Name Cycling Options | | |
| :Cycle | Fact Sentence People | Prints the full name first and then cycles between He/She and the casual name in subsequent uses. Default for “Person” and “Couple” in regular fact sentences and default for “ThisPerson” in witness fact sentences. |
| :NoCycle | Fact Sentence People | Print the name as specified without cycling |

## Formatting Codes

Formatting codes allow you to tell RootsMagic how you want the font to look in the report. Formatting codes are contained inside of a left angle bracket "<" and right angle bracket ">". They are used in pairs - the first tells RootsMagic to turn on the formatting, and the second, with a "/" after the left angle bracket (</ >) to turn off the formatting. For example:

<i>[Title]</i>

The <i> and </i> formatting codes tell RootsMagic to display the title in italics font.

| Code | Used in | Description |
|---|---|---|
| Formatting Codes | | |
| <i> ... </i> | Fact sentence and Source templates, fields, and notes | Displays the text in italics |

| | | |
|---|---|---|
| <b> ... </b> | Fact sentence and Source templates, fields, and notes | Displays the text in bold |
| <u> ... </u> | Fact sentence and Source templates, fields, and notes | Displays the text in underline |
| <sup> ... </sup> | Fact sentence and Source templates, fields, and notes | Displays the text in superscript |
| <sub> ... </sub> | Fact sentence and Source templates, fields, and notes | Displays the text in subscript |

Formatting codes can be nested within other formatting codes or switches, but cannot be included within the square brackets indicating a field.

### Switches

A switch allows you to write different information, depending on the information that is available. Switches are contained inside of a less-than and greater-than sign (< >). Inside of the switch are any number of pieces, separated by a "|". For example:

<First Piece|Second Piece|Third Piece|Fourth Piece>

You can set the kind of switch by using a special character after the first less-than sign. There are five special switch characters, ? for the Value switch, % for the Gender switch, @ for the Living switch, # for the Plural switch, and ! for the Private switch. For example:

<%actor|actress>

In a switch that depends on information about a person or a group of people, such as value switches, gender switches, living switches, and plural switches, you can specify which person or group of people the switch applies to by writing the field names of the people either immediately after the special character (living, plural) or enclosed in square brackets ([value], [gender]) and then followed by the special character again.

<#Doctors#doctor|doctors>

Two of the switches, Gender (%) and Living (@), will refer directly to the focus subject if a field name is not entered. For example:

<@He is living|He is not living>.

The Private switch (!) is used in source templates to privatize things such as a street address data that you want to record, but not make public. The trigger that activates the Private switch is a checkbox in the Sources, Options tab in the Report Settings dialog.

### *Simple Switches*

A simple switch requires no special character and can have any number of pieces.

<First Piece|Second Piece|Third Piece|Fourth Piece>

RootsMagic will look at each piece, beginning with the first. If the piece has a field with a value, or has no fields, it is written and all the remaining pieces are skipped. For example, lets look at the basic birth sentence with conditional brackets added:

[Person] was born< [Date]>< [PlaceDetails]>< [Place]>.

The angle brackets < > indicate that if there is no value entered, neither the field nor the space before it will be shown. This applies to the [date], [placedetails] and [place] fields.

In the following source templates examples:

<privately held by [LastKnownOwner], >

would only write something if "[LastKnownOwner]" has a value, or in this example:

<[Format], |digital image,>

would write “database and digital images,” if that's what you entered into the [Format] field, or it would write "digital image,” if you didn’t enter anything into the [Format] field.

### *Value Switches*

A value switch is similar to a simple switch except that it allows you to check for a value without actually writing that value. It is indicated by a “?”.

<?[Expression]| Show this if True.>

<?[Expression]| Show this if True. | Show this if False.>

<?[Expression]|| Show this if False.>

For example:

<?[Nurse]|He had a nurse.>

<?[Nurse]|He had a nurse.|He didn't have a nurse.>

<?[Nurse]||He didn't have a nurse.>

would check to see if the role of [Nurse] had a value. If it did, it would write “He had a nurse.” If it did not have a value, it would write “He didn't have a nurse.”

Note that what comes after the “?” is different from the gender and living switches. The gender and living switches need the role of a person or group of people followed by their special character. The value switch takes any expression including fields in brackets and other switches.

### *Gender Switches*

A gender switch checks the gender of a person or group of people and writes the appropriate text. It is indicated by a “%”. It is of the form:

<% Males & Unknowns > or

<% Males & Unknowns | Females > or

<% Males | Females |Unknowns > or

<% Male | Female | Unknown | Multiples > or

<% Male | Female | Unknown | Male & Mixed Multiples | Female Multiples > or

<% Male | Female | Unknown | Male Multiples | Female Multiples | Mixed Multiples >

or it can take the form to process a list of one or more roles

<%roles%| Male | Female | Unknown | Male Multiples | Female Multiples | Mixed Multiples >

In this first example, the switch looks at the default [person]:

<%He was an actor.|She was an actress.>

In this second example, the switch looks at the role name [child]:

<%Child%[child] was a son.|[child] was a daughter.|[child] was a child.|[child] were sons.|[child] were daughters.|[child] were children.>

In the first example, the "person" is the focus person to which the sentence applies. In the second example, [child] refers to a role assigned to someone in a shared event. The role [child] could be assigned to one or more people.

Roles which are added as "Just type name of witness" menu, or "This person is NOT in the file" in Edit Share Event, do not have a gender, and may affect results of this switch.

### *Living Switches*

A living switch checks if a person or group of people is living and writes the appropriate text. It is indicated by a “@”. It is of the form:

<@ Living > or

<@ Living | Not Living >

<@roles@ Show this if all Living | Show this if one or more Not Living>

For example:

<@He has brown hair.|He had brown hair.> (This assumes that his hair never turned gray.)

<@Doctors,Nurses@They are doctors and nurses.|They were doctors and nurses.>

### *Plural Switches*

A plural switch looks at the number of people in a group and writes the appropriate text. It is indicated by a "#". It is of the form:

<#roles# Single > or

<#roles# Single | Plural > or

<#roles# Single | Plural | None >

For example:

<#Doctors#His doctor was|His doctors were> [Doctor].

They had <#Children#a child|<Children:count> children|no children>.

There <#Heir1,Heir2#was one heir|was more than one heir|were no heirs>.

### *Private Switches*

A private switch is used for fact sentence templates and source templates. For sources, this allows you to write different text depending on whether you have or have not checked the "Hide private data in the endnotes, footnotes, and bibliography" option in the Sources, Options tab, telling RootsMagic whether to display the private or the not private information for this switch. It is of the form:

<! Private | Not Private >

For example:

<!<[Address]>|(The address is private.)>.

If the checkbox is checked, "(The address is private.)" would print. If the checkbox was unchecked, the address data that was entered in the [Address] field would print, if one was entered, otherwise nothing would print.

## Escape Characters

If you ever want to write an actual <, >, /, [, or ] in your sentence, you must precede it by a "/". This tells RootsMagic to print the following character and to not treat it as a switch or a field. For example:

[Person] /[This is in brackets/]. would print:

John Doe [This is in brackets].

and [person] is a /[person/] would print

John Doe is a [person].

thus allowing the keyword "person" to be enclosed within square brackets without being interpreted as a field.

Tip: To include a field value within square brackets, such as [John Doe], you can enclose the field within a switch with the square brackets outside the switch, i.e. [<[person]>].

## Switches Within Switches

RootsMagic allows you to put switches within other switches, also known as nesting. This allows you to create very powerful and flexible sentence templates.

# INDEX

## D



## E



## F

### G



### H



### I



### J



### K



### L

## Q



## R



## S